MTS Programming
with Visual Basic®

Scot Hillier

SAMS

201 West 103rd St., Indianapolis, Indiana, 46290 USA

MTS PROGRAMMING WITH VISUAL BASIC®

Copyright © 1999 by Sams Publishing

International Standard Book Number: 0-672-7231425-8

Library of Congress Catalog Card Number: 98-86702

Printed in the United States of America

First Printing: April 1999

01   00   99   4   3   2

Trademarks

Warning and Disclaimer

EXECUTIVE EDITOR
Chris Denny

ACQUISITIONS EDITOR
Sharon Cox

DEVELOPMENT EDITOR
Anthony Amico

MANAGING EDITOR
Jodi Jensen

SENIOR EDITOR
Susan Ross Moore

COPY EDITOR
Margaret Berson

INDEXER
Bruce Clingaman

PROOFREADER
Eddie Lushbaugh

TECHNICAL EDITOR
Donna Matthews

SOFTWARE DEVELOPMENT SPECIALIST
Michael Hunter

TEAM COORDINATOR
Carol Ackerman

INTERIOR DESIGN
Anne Jones

COVER DESIGN
Anne Jones

LAYOUT TECHNICIANS
Brian Borders
Susan Geiselman
Mark Walchle

CONTENTS AT A GLANCE

TABLE OF CONTENTS

ABOUT THE AUTHOR

Scot Hillier is the Vice President of Technical Services of New Technology Solutions Incorporated. With offices in New Haven, CT, and Boston, MA, NTSI provides training and consulting services in Visual Basic, Visual InterDev, MTS, and related technologies. Scot has written several books, including the *Visual Basic 6.0 Certification Exam Guide* (McGraw-Hill) and *Inside Visual Basic Scripting Edition* (Microsoft Press). In addition to writing, Scot is a regular speaker at industry conferences such as VBITS and Developer Days. He is also a Microsoft Regional Director and runs the Connecticut New Technology Forum. Scot can be reached at `scoth@vb-bootcamp.com`.

DEDICATION

To Honor and those who cherish it.

ACKNOWLEDGMENTS

No one can create software alone. I am fortunate to be surrounded by many talented people who support and enhance my efforts to create distributed applications. In writing this book, I leaned on many of my colleagues. I would first like to thank Dan Mezick for providing the opportunity to write this book. He was instrumental in securing the deal that resulted in this work as well as focusing company resources to support it. Other members of the New Tech family assisted by working exercises and providing commentary as well as acting as a sounding board for ideas. Thanks to all of you.

The staff at Macmillan Publishing also deserves recognition. I want to thank Sharon Cox for bringing this project into Macmillan and Tony Amico for acting as the point for editing and generally keeping the project moving. Many thanks as well to Donna Matthews who had the unenviable task of working through all of the code and exercises in the book. Thanks also to Michael Hunter for creating the CD-ROM. Thanks also go to Susan Moore and Margaret Berson, editors on this book.

Finally, I could not accomplish anything without the loving support of my family. Thanks and love to you, Nancy, for everything. Ashley and Matt, you are both special and dear to me.

Thanks again, one and all.

TELL US WHAT YOU THINK!

As the reader of this book, *you* are our most important critic and commentator. We value your opinion and want to know what we're doing right, what we could do better, what areas you'd like to see us publish in, and any other words of wisdom you're willing to pass our way.

As the Executive Editor for the Visual Basic Programming team at Sams Publishing, I welcome your comments. You can fax, email, or write me directly to let me know what you did or didn't like about this book—as well as what we can do to make our books stronger.

Please note that I cannot help you with technical problems related to the topic of this book, and that due to the high volume of mail I receive, I might not be able to reply to every message.

When you write, please be sure to include this book's title and author as well as your name and phone or fax number. I will carefully review your comments and share them with the author and editors who worked on the book.

Fax: 317-817-7070

Email: vb@mcp.com

Mail: Chris Denny
          Executive Editor
          Visual Basic Programming
          Sams Publishing
          201 West 103rd Street
          Indianapolis, IN 46290 USA

INTRODUCTION

If you have been in the Visual Basic community for any time at all, you have undoubtedly heard the term "black-belt programming." This term encompasses a set of knowledge that revolves around the inner workings of Visual Basic, COM, and Windows. In this domain, you find discussions of the Windows API, V-tables, DLL addresses, and spawning your own threads. This book has little or none of that.

Instead, I like to think of this book as "blue-collar programming." To me, blue-collar programming focuses on the architecture, components, and tasks necessary to complete a distributed application. To that end, you will find that this book is dedicated to teaching you how to successfully create a distributed application. Other books will explain *why* COM components work, but this book will tell you *what* COM components you must build. The book represents a framework and a methodology for success.

I have no doubt that a few readers will disagree, perhaps strongly, with some of the architectural recommendations presented here. This is good. Inside the VB community, we need to begin a robust discussion dedicated to distributed application architecture. This book offers a no-nonsense approach that will lead you to success.

Good luck.

Scot Hillier
New Technology Solutions Incorporated

WHO SHOULD READ THIS BOOK

Any developer working on large-scale systems that are implemented across multiple platforms would benefit from the principles taught here. Even if you are a project manager who is contemplating such systems you should study the concepts here.

CAN THIS BOOK REALLY TEACH YOU MTS PROGRAMMING WITH VISUAL BASIC?

Yes, because this book leads you through the construction of actual working examples. As you sit down and master each chapter, you will be building a substantial foundation of knowledge and working projects. Many of your own applications can be constructed simply by modifying the projects that you have already created.

Additionally, the book provides numerous tips, notes, and cautions to speed your grasp of some of the different aspects of the technology. Following along and creating the examples should make every page interactive and exciting.

CONVENTIONS USED IN THIS BOOK

At the beginning of each chapter, the prerequisites for working through the chapter and the skills that you will learn are listed. New concepts and terms are explained. You can work through Quick Checks, or mini-exercises. A longer, more formal exercise at the end of most chapters takes you step by step through the procedures you need to learn. Then to wrap up you will develop a complete ATM system that will bring all of the concepts covered earlier into one real-world banking application.

This book also uses several common conventions to help teach the programming topics. Here is a summary of the typographical conventions:

- Commands and computer output appear in special `monospaced` computer font.
- Words you type appear in a **bold** font.
- If a task requires you to choose from a menu, this book separates menu commands with a comma. Therefore, this book uses **File, Save As** to indicate that you should open the **File** menu and choose the **Save As** command.
- When learning a programming language, you often must learn the syntax or format of a command. Lines similar to the following will be displayed to help you learn a new Visual Basic language command:

```
For CounterVar = StartVal To EndVal [Step IncrementVal]
    Block of one or more Visual Basic statements
Next CounterVar
```

The monospaced text designates code (programming language information) that you'll enter into a program. The regular monospaced text, such as `For` and `Next`, represents keywords you must type exactly. *`Italicized monospace`* characters indicate placeholders that you must replace with your own program's values. Bracketed information, such as [`Step IncrementVal`], indicates optional code that you can type if your program requires it.

In addition to typographical conventions, the following special elements are used to set off various pieces of information and to make them easily recognizable:

NOTE

Special notes augment the material you are reading in each chapter. They clarify concepts and procedures.

TIP

You'll find numerous tips that offer shortcuts and solutions to common problems.

CAUTION

Caution sections warn you about pitfalls. Reading them will save you time and trouble.

THE DATA SERVICES LAYER

PART

I

IN THIS PART

TIERED ARCHITECTURE AND THE MICROSOFT TRANSACTION SERVER

PREREQUISITES

This book assumes that readers have a strong Visual Basic background. Readers must have complete familiarity with all aspects of Visual Basic including ActiveX component creation. This allows a specific focus on architecture and techniques for building distributed applications. Readers who are unfamiliar with these concepts should spend time mastering these concepts before beginning.

Skills Learned

Mastering the Microsoft Transaction Server is a critical part of achieving certification as a Microsoft Certified Solution Developer (MCSD). Where applicable, we have identified the skills required by the certification exam and the chapter where they are covered. Skills are identified by the appropriate exam number (for example, 70-100) and a sequential item number. See the book introduction for more information about certification skills.

- 70-100(1): Given a business scenario, identify which solution type is appropriate. Solution types are single-tier, two-tier, and n-tier. Scenarios include multi-user with single data source, and multi-user with multiple data sources.
- 70-100(5): Given a conceptual design, apply the principles of modular design to derive the components and services of the logical design.
- 70-175(1): Given a conceptual design, apply the principles of modular design to derive the components and services of the logical design.
- 70-175(6): Install MTS.
- MTS(1): Use Visual Modeler to create code from an existing model.
- MTS(2): Use the Reverse Engineering Wizard to create a model from existing code.

Application design is a sorely neglected area in most software development efforts. Most programmers would agree that failure to design stems from schedule pressure and the ease with which graphical tools such as Visual Basic allow you to create software. As applications grow in size and complexity, however, design becomes critical. Issues of performance, scalability, and maintainability rise to the top. A good architectural design provides acceptable performance even as the application scales in size. The components used to create the application must also be easy to maintain, upgrade, and reuse.

SERVICES AND PARTITIONING

In any application, regardless of size, we can identify functions that perform definite roles in the retrieval and update of data. For example, all database applications obviously need a database and software functions that read and write to the database. The database and its associated software functions fill the role of *Data Services*.

When data is retrieved, it must be manipulated. This might require operations such as applying a discount to a purchase order or modifying an insurance policy based on claims activity. This type of manipulation implements what are called the *business rules* of the application. The business rules and associated software functions comprise the *Business Services*.

After the business rules are applied to the data, it must be displayed to the user. The application can allow both display and editing of data by a user. The data display and associated software functions comprise the *User Services*.

Although many developers have heard the terms for Data, Business, and User services before, it is important to recognize that they are not associated with a particular architecture. Rather, they exist in every database application. The difference is the level of separation between the services. In a single-user application, separation between the services might be imperceptible, but as applications increase in complexity, this separation becomes critical. The separation between services is known as *partitioning*.

TIERED APPLICATION ARCHITECTURE

For quite some time now, programmers have been receiving the message from Microsoft that they should be creating n-tier applications for use on the enterprise. The problem, however, is that most developers have not taken the message to heart. Developing n-tier applications is a great subject of conversation at development conferences, but very few programmers are actually involved in a serious effort to develop these applications. In fact, our experience is that fully half of all Visual Basic developers are still creating two-tier applications against Microsoft Access.

Adding to the confusion is the use of the term *n-tier* application. This term is used quite a bit in technical white papers, and it leads you to believe that applications can have any number of tiers beyond the standard of three. This contributes to a general mystification of tiered architecture and confusion about how to correctly develop it. Therefore, we begin by explaining each of these architectures as well as the advantages and disadvantages of each.

Two-Tier Architecture

Two-tier architecture is the most common and well understood approach to database applications. In this model, the display of data is tightly bound to the storage of the data in the database. In most of these applications, the user interface is merely a reflection of the underlying data structure. Developers often take a recordset directly from the database and display it in a grid where it looks exactly the same as it would if they open the table directly in the database. Users interact directly with the data for add, edit, update, and delete functionality. Business rules that perform functions on the data are either built directly into the user interface or reside in the database through such mechanisms as triggers. Figure 1.1 shows a simple representation of two-tier architecture.

FIGURE 1.1

A diagram of two-tier architecture.

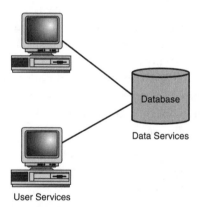

Database

Data Services

User Services

In a two-tier application, data access is most often performed through the use of cursors. Database cursors enable an application to maintain an open connection to the database while users scroll and manipulate the data. In most two-tiered applications, the database connection is established when the application is started, and it is maintained open until the application is closed. When cursors are combined with a constantly available database connection, applications can handle concurrency issues through the use of record locking. Record locking prevents two users from simultaneously making changes to the same database record.

Another hallmark of two-tiered applications is the use of SQL statements directly created in the application code or calls to stored procedures directly from the application code. In this design, the front end requires an intimate knowledge of the database structure and available stored procedures. If the database structure is changed or the stored procedure is altered, it might require a recompile of the application in response. This type of architecture is most limiting when combined with the use of data binding elements such as a data control and bound data grid.

Two-tiered applications are generally simpler to design and build than multi-tier applications. However, the simplicity does not come without a price. The tight binding between the database and the user interface almost always results in an unsatisfying design. Developers are often content to display database information in grids and lists without much fanfare or care for the end-user experience. This mentality reaches its pinnacle when developers dump thousands of records into a data-bound grid and declare their job complete simply because the data is now visible. The user is then left to fend for himself as he wades through thousands of records searching for the data he really needs.

Beyond issues of user interface, two-tier design also limits the capability of an application to scale. *Scalability* is the measure of the capability to add concurrent users to an application. Because two-tier applications generally open a database connection at the beginning of the session and keep it open until the session ends, scalability is immediately limited. The actual number depends on a number of factors; however, it should be immediately obvious that you cannot simply open a connection for every new user and scale an application endlessly. At some point, you will simply run out of connections. In fact, the biggest mistake made by programmers is designing an application to maintain an open database connection. As this book progresses, we will discuss strategies to use database connections in more efficient ways.

Another significant disadvantage of two-tier applications is that they are difficult to maintain. As we have pointed out, tight binding between the application and the database means that changes to either tier can have a disastrous effect on the other tier. This means that new versions of a product quite often require a complete rewrite of the application. In fact, our experience is that most companies have little or no reuse plan in effect—they rewrite for every new version. Does this sound familiar?

None of this is to say that two-tier applications should never be built. In fact, two-tier applications are currently receiving a bum wrap. Most of this negative press is because of the need to drive developers to three-tier architecture as a means to conquer the enterprise for Microsoft products. However, if you want to take advantage of the faster development cycles with two tiers while minimizing the disadvantages, see the accompanying sidebar for some ideas.

The single most important architectural decision you can make to improve two-tier applications is to abandon the use of cursors. For most applications, the use of cursors is a net negative. Sure, cursors make it easier to program database applications. After all, they manage concurrency as well as provide features such as scrolling, and they reflect changes to the underlying database structure. But improved application performance demands that you only connect to the database when it is absolutely necessary to read or write data.

One way to connect only when necessary is to use a disconnected recordset. Disconnected recordsets are supported as a feature of the ActiveX Data Objects 2.0 (ADO). Using these types of recordsets, you can connect to a data source, run a query, bring back records, and then break the connection between the recordset and the connection. After a recordset is disconnected, it can be viewed locally and edited. When all the edits to the recordset are made, you can reconnect the recordset to the data source and commit the changes as a batch. Using this strategy, you can add many times more users to an application because each client only connects to the database long enough to read or write data. This process is known as *optimistic batch updating*. Figure 1.2 shows a representation of optimistic batch updating.

FIGURE 1.2
Optimistic batch updating improves scalability.

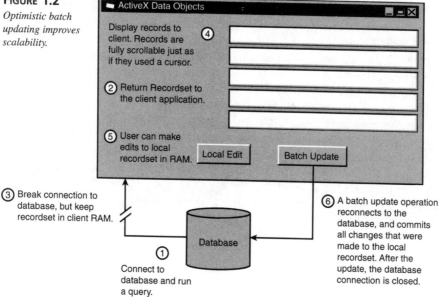

> **TIP**
>
> After running a command on the database connection and creating the record-set, it can be disconnected by simply setting the current connection property to Nothing. When the recordset is disconnected, the associated database connection might be closed. Even though the connection is closed, the records are still available in the memory of the client machine. The records might be viewed and edited freely by the client. When the edits are complete, a new connection might be opened and the recordset reconnected to the database. After the recordset is connected, the edited records are sent back to the database to be committed.
>
> As soon as developers are introduced to the concept of batch updating, they immediately have concerns. The obvious concern is the loss of pessimistic record locking to handle the concurrency issues. Although it is true that your records are unprotected from changes by another user, ADO provides a way for you to resolve any issues that might arise because of concurrency. When two people try to update the same record in a batch optimistic application, it results in a *collision*.
>
> A good batch solution should always check for collisions after an update occurs. In ADO, you can check for collisions by filtering the disconnected recordset. The Filter property allows you to filter a recordset according to some parameter. For batch updates, you filter by *conflicting records*. Any records that collided during update appear in this filter.
>
> Optimistic batch updating is an excellent solution for many types of two-tier applications. However, there are certain types of applications that do not make good candidates for this architecture. Any type of database application that has a high demand for a relatively few number of records does not work well with batches. Another poor candidate is any application that requires real-time data. You would certainly hate to be a stockbroker relying on a batch update program for stock quotes! In the end, however, many business applications do make good candidates for optimistic batch updating. If you are going to stick with two tiers, this is a good architecture. In fact, these concepts are not limited to two-tier application architectures. The principles described here are also used later to help partition applications with multiple tiers.

The following list details the essential features of a two-tier application:

- Database Cursors
- Direct manipulation of database
- Limited scalability
- Limited Reuse

Three-Tier Architecture

Three-tier architecture represents an improvement over the disadvantages of two-tier architecture. In this architecture, the database is separated from the user interface by an intermediate layer known as the Business Services layer. The purpose of the Business Services layer is to eliminate the tight binding between the user interface (called the User Services layer) and the database (called the Data Services layer). Separating the User Services from the Data Services results in immediate advantages. Because the intermediate layer can process the data before it is displayed, developers have the opportunity to massage the data into a form that is much easier for the user to work with. Instead of simply presenting data in a grid, it can be presented in much more meaningful formats. The Business Services layer makes this massaging easier to create and maintain. This separation of layers in an application results in improved partitioning over two-tier applications.

The partitioning of service layers also removes the intimate relationship between SQL statements, stored procedures, and the front-end code. This means that the front end can be changed easier without affecting the database and the database can be altered without a recompile of the user interface. The Business Services layer also provides a segregated home for the business rules that work on the data. In this way, the business rules might be changed without affecting the data or the user interface. This is superior to the use of database triggers that reside directly in the Data Services layer.

The separate Business Services layer also offers an opportunity to construct an application that shares components in the middle tier. This means that all clients using the application can take advantage of the functionality provided by the Business Services. This is a significant advantage in maintenance because changes to the shared central tier immediately affects all clients on the system. This type of design virtually eliminates the need to constantly revise software on many client machines. It also encourages the reuse of components by fostering a "building block" approach for applications. These components can participate in one or more applications simultaneously, making it easier to build and maintain new applications. Figure 1.3 shows a simple representation of three-tier architecture.

FIGURE 1.3

A diagram of three-tier architecture

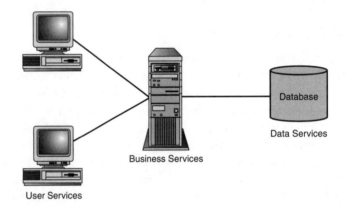

Creating a three-tier application is, of course, significantly more complicated than a two-tier application. Right away you have to deal with designing and creating distributed components that run remotely. Additionally, the machines that make up the Business Services are shared among many users, so the proper management of the shared resources is critical to the success of the application. This complexity is the single biggest disadvantage of n-tier applications and the main reason that so few of them are built.

N-Tier Architecture

An n-tier application adds to the partitioning of a system by creating separation within a layer. A typical separation layer might be created within the User Services, for example, to partition the data display from the state of the application. This can be done through the use of a separate ActiveX component in the User Services layer. This type of separation makes it easy to change just the way in which data is displayed. This separation, for example, makes it simple to drive a web page from the same logic that drives a VB form. Figure 1.4 shows an example of separation within one of the three main tiers.

FIGURE 1.4
N-Tier applica-
tions separate the
main tiers into
additional layers.

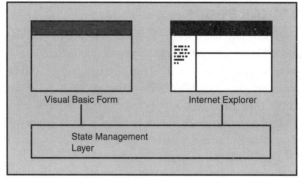

User Services Tier

N-tier architecture represents an improvement over the standard three-tier model and encourages developers to using components at all levels of the application. Partitioning service layers can be done in any layer and should be encouraged. In the business layer, partitioning into multiple components can help performance, scalability, and maintainability. Imagine, for example, that you create an application that has just one class in the business layer. This single class would be designed to have all the functionality for the entire application. For the sake of argument, assume the class has 100 methods in it. If your application has 100 users, what is the probability that all 100 users will be seeking services from the one class in the business layer simultaneously? The answer is obviously 100 percent. Now imagine that we take our one monolithic class and break it into 100 different classes. Furthermore, imagine that we take those 100 separate classes and place them on 100 separate machines. Now what is the probability that any two users will actually be competing for middle-tier resources? The answer is fairly low. Of course, these scenarios represent the ridiculous extreme in component design, however, you can see how increasing the numbers of components within a tier can lead to better scalability and maintainability.

VISUAL BASIC TIERED APPLICATIONS

Visual Basic is built from the ground up to support the development of tiered applications even without external support from a product such as the Microsoft Transaction Server (MTS). Visual Basic provides a specific project type—known as the ActiveX EXE—designed to be distributed on the enterprise. Client applications—often built as Standard EXE projects—can make remote calls to ActiveX EXE components using the Distributed Component Object Model (DCOM). DCOM is a subsystem of Windows NT that is available to all distributed applications running on a network.

DCOM Configurations

Because DCOM is built into the operating system, using it is as simple as using any COM object. DCOM relies on system registry entries to dictate remote creations and security management. Most of the settings can be made using a utility known as the DCOM Configuration Utility (DCOMCNFG). Typing DCOMCNFG.EXE into the command line in Windows NT runs the utility. When started, DCOMCNFG allows you to set the machine where a remote component can be found as well as specify the Windows NT users who have permission to launch and access the services of the component. Figure 1.5 shows the DCOMCNFG utility.

FIGURE 1.5

This is the DCOMCNFG utility.

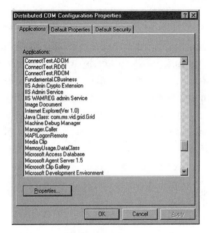

RemoteServerName

One of the most important Registry entries set by DCOMCNFG is the RemoteServerName setting. RemoteServerName specifies the name of another machine on the enterprise where the desired object can be found. When a client requests services from an ActiveX component, it uses the local Registry information to locate and instantiate the object. In the case of DCOM, when the client accesses the Registry, instead of finding information about the object locally, it is directed to another machine via the RemoteServerName setting. After the machine is identified, DCOM takes over to make a remote procedure call to the appropriate machine where the object is instantiated and services provided to the calling client. In all cases, DCOM requires entries in the client system registry before a connection can be made with a remote component. Typically, the setup program makes these entries during client installation.

QUICK CHECK 1.1

DCOM CONFIGURATION

1. This example uses the DCOM Configuration utility from Windows NT 4.0 Server. From the command line in Windows, run DCOMCNFG.

2. When DCOMCNFG first starts, you will see a list of applications. This is a list of components that supports remote calls from clients through the DCOM subsystem.

3. Click the **Default Properties** tab. This tab contains information about how remote clients access components on this machine by default. The default authentication level determines how calling clients are authenticated when they call a component on this machine. Windows NT is a secure system, so clients cannot receive services from a distributed component without proper security credentials. You can authenticate clients at many different levels, including each time they call for service.

4. The default impersonation level determines what services can be provided for the client by the component on this machine. For example, a client might call and request a remote component to start another process. If the remote component is impersonating the client, the new process is started with the clientís security context.

5. Click the **Default Security** tab. This tab is used to set the access and launch permission for components. In this tab, you can create Access Control Lists (ACL) used by DCOM to determine if a client has permission to launch or access a component on this machine. Clients that do not have permission, receive an Access Denied runtime error.

Instancing

Although Visual Basic ActiveX EXE projects and the DCOM system can work together to create tiered applications, these types of projects have some significant limitations when it comes to properly managing the shared resources of the Business Services layer. Specifically, many clients will use the functionality of a distributed ActiveX EXE component so it must properly manage the use of resources to handle the clients without affecting the performance of the overall system. ActiveX EXE components manage resources through the use of the `Instancing` property. The Instancing property is available to a class module in Visual Basic when that class is a member of an ActiveX EXE or ActiveX DLL project. The property determines how a component responds when clients request service from the component at runtime.

Although several settings are available for the `Instancing` property, only two are of interest when creating tiered applications: Multi-Use and Single-Use. If you construct an ActiveX EXE and designate the class modules within as Multi-Use, a single running copy of the ActiveX EXE handles all client requests. The number of available threads limits the number of clients that can successfully use the component simultaneously. Visual Basic allows you to specify the number of available threads for an ActiveX EXE component using the project properties dialog. Figure 1.6 shows the project properties dialog.

FIGURE 1.6

ActiveX EXE projects can use a thread pool.

For an ActiveX EXE project, you might specify to create a new thread for each new object or to use a thread pool. At first glance, it might seem that requesting a new thread for each object leads to the best performance. In fact, many developers are under the mistaken impression that multithreading is a panacea for scalability. The truth, however, is much bleaker. A microprocessor is capable of running only one active thread at a time. This is the very nature of a microprocessor—it can only perform one instruction at a time. Demanding that a new thread be created for each object that calls quickly buries the microprocessor in requests and destroys system performance. Therefore, you should specify a thread pool when you use an ActiveX EXE. The size of the pool should be at least three times the number of processors on your machine. For a standard single-processor computer, the pool size should be at least three threads. Therefore, an ActiveX EXE designated as Multi-Use with a pool of three threads can process three requests simultaneously. Figure 1.7 shows a diagram that represents the relationship between components and instances in a Multi-Use component.

Three threads certainly seem like a small pool for an application designed for hundreds of simultaneous users. As an option, you could specify the distributed ActiveX component to be Single-Use. Single-Use components create a new instance of the ActiveX EXE for each client request. Because clients get their own dedicated copy of the component, no one has to wait. However, at the microprocessor level, all the new processes must now be managed and executed. This is hardly an ideal situation for scaling an application. Figure 1.8 shows a diagram that represents the relationship between components and instances in a Single-Use component.

FIGURE 1.7
One component has many instances in a Multi-Use ActiveX EXE component.

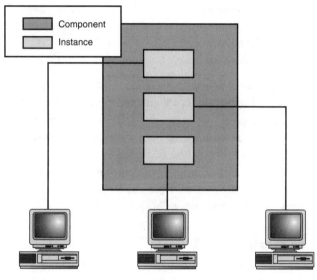

FIGURE 1.8
Single-Use ActiveX EXE

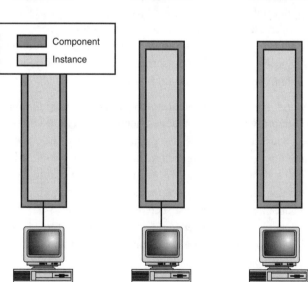

THE MICROSOFT TRANSACTION SERVER

After examining the features of ActiveX EXE applications, you might be left feeling that the scalability of these solutions is in question. In order to build true enterprise solutions that can support hundreds of users, we need more help in managing the vital resources of the middle tier. This is the very reason that MTS was created. Instead of creating software aimed at managing resources, you can focus solely on the business requirements. In this section, we introduce some of the key features that make MTS a valuable part of any tiered application. This book covers all these features in detail in subsequent chapters.

MTS simplifies the process of creating scalable applications by providing many of the services necessary to distribute an application on the enterprise. Although we have had the ability to build distributed applications in the past, creating them has required a lot of additional work on the part of the programmer. Some of the most demanding work has centered on the process of sharing and managing system resources. In particular, if you intend to centralize business functionality on machines located on the network, you must be concerned with managing available threads, object instances, and data source connections. Fortunately, this is exactly where MTS shines.

Thread Management

Windows NT is a pre-emptive, multitasking operating system capable of running multiple threads in multiple processes. In Windows, a process is essentially an instance of an application. Multitasking is the ability to execute multiple processes simultaneously—or nearly simultaneously. The truth is that Windows manages to run more than one process at a time by shuttling the microprocessor time between concurrent processes, giving the impression of simultaneous execution.

Within a process, many threads might be executing. A thread is simply an execution point within the process. Some languages, such as Visual C++ or Java, are said to be multithreaded because they might have more than one execution point operating simultaneously within a process. Other languages, such as Visual Basic 4.0, might have only one execution point operating at a time. These languages are said to be single threaded. Visual Basic 6 does support apartment threading. This support, however, is primarily intended to enable host applications, such as MTS, to use Visual Basic components as opposed to allowing a programmer to directly spawn new threads within the VB application. Threading support can have a significant impact on how MTS is able to support scaling a business object.

MTS manages threads for all the objects running under its control. MTS not only manages the threads, but also provides a pool of threads for use by COM components. This concept of pooling is vital to sharing all resources—not just threads. Pooling is the process of sharing a limited number of resources amongst a large number of clients. When resources are pooled, clients use a resource and then return it to the MTS pool so it might be recycled. Each resource managed by MTS uses the concept to minimize the requirements to service many clients. In this way, the total number of items in the pool is actually a fraction of the total number of clients serviced.

MTS supports two types of threading models: Single and Apartment. Single-threaded components are the simplest to understand, but the least scalable. All calls to the component must use one thread to request services from the component. Because all calls are pushed through a single thread, clients are forced to wait in a queue for services. This scenario can cause serious problems for clients attempting to share resources. In fact, clients can easily establish a situation where they place mutually exclusive locks on key resources and freeze the system. This situation is known as a *deadlock*. In single thread-ed objects, a deadlock occurs when two or more clients attempt to place locks on resources that are in high demand.

Preventing deadlocks is accomplished by using a multithreaded model known as Apartment threading. Apartment threading enables a COM component to handle more than one thread at a time. Apartment threading is a special case of multithreaded components that separates the data and objects used by one thread from that of another.

Visual Basic ActiveX components designed to run under MTS control should be ActiveX DLLs that support Apartment threading. Designating the components as ActiveX DLLs enables them to run in the process space of MTS, while designating them as apartment-threaded allows them to support multithreading. When creating COM components for MTS using Visual Basic, you choose to create apartment-threaded objects using the pro-ject property dialog. Figure 1.9 shows the project properties dialog.

FIGURE 1.9

ActiveX DLL com-ponents support Apartment Threading.

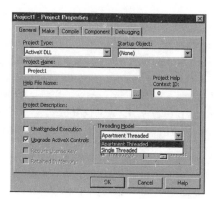

Object Instance Management

Threads are only one of the vital resources that must be managed if the Business Services layer is to support many users. Certainly, the use of memory must also be effectively managed. The primary use of memory within the Business Services layer is to create instances of business objects. These instances must be created for each client calling for services. In many large systems, these instances are pooled to minimize the overhead necessary to create new instances. This is an excellent strategy that furthers scalability.

The most important point to remember about object instance pooling is that MTS does not support it. However, Microsoft has promised to support object instance pooling in a future release of MTS. Understanding how MTS will eventually implement this type of resource management can help you prepare to migrate your objects to newer versions of MTS. The key for programmers using MTS now is that the same techniques that will eventually enable object pooling in the future also ensure proper resource management today.

Although MTS does not actually pool object instances, we still want to write our applications as if this were true. Under the apartment-threading model, MTS has the capability to use multiple threads inside of a single COM object. Each of these threads can be thought of as an object instance for the purpose of creating your enterprise architecture. The key to remember here is that MTS cannot reuse an object (or apartment) until the client specifically notifies MTS that it is safe to do so. Under MTS, COM components stay in memory as long as a thread is currently accessing them. When all threads have finished running, the COM object can be unloaded from memory for more efficient resource management.

State Management

For quite some time now, developers have been inundated with the call for object-oriented design and programming. We have been told to leave the world of reusable functions and enter the world of objects. This means that we are supposed to think of our environment in terms of nouns. We think about customer objects, product objects, and supplier objects. These objects contain data members, or properties, that describe the object. We have the Name property, the Address property, the Age property, and so on. So it is now natural for a developer to think of a business application that uses customer objects and keeps some data in the Name property.

The essential problem with this model is that it does not scale well. If you maintain the name and address of a customer in a business object on the server, that object cannot be given to another client because the new client will overwrite the original name and address. Therefore in order to reuse an object, all the data must be cleared. The immediate impact of this design on MTS applications is that, generally speaking, MTS objects should not maintain state for any length of time. Maintaining state in an object prevents reuse. Instead, the state of an application is typically moved from the Business Services layer to the User Services area. We alluded to this design earlier when we discussed n-tier applications.

Resource Dispensers

MTS applications are all about effectively managing resources to provide scalability. In addition to thread and object management, MTS provides further resource management through Resource Dispensers. Resource Dispensers are pooled resources, such as database connections, that can be shared among clients. The ODBC Resource Dispenser specifically provides pooling for connections to ODBC data sources, while the OLEDB Resource Dispenser pools connections to OLEDB data stores.

The way that the database Resource Dispensers work is simple. Every time a client requests a connection to a database resource, MTS looks in the connection pool for an unused connection. If none exists, a new connection is made and given to the client. Each time a client finishes using the connection, the client will release the connection. The client thinks the connection is closed, but MTS maintains the connection in a live state and returns it to the pool. When a new client calls, the connection might be reused without waiting. The end result is that the connection pool rises to a number necessary to support the total number of concurrent connections to the database. This number is a small fraction of the total system users, which allows your application to scale gracefully.

Transaction Management

Along with resource management, MTS is also designed to support transactional applications. Transactions allow you to group together the work of several objects as a single unit of work. Similar to any transaction, the work of many separate methods calls is made to succeed or fail as a batch. MTS provides complete commit and rollback capability for the objects under its control.

Security Management

Previously, we saw how DCOM could be used to create secure applications that limit a user's ability to launch or call an object. DCOM is useful for establishing security; however, the DCOMCNFG interface is considerably more difficult to use than the security features provided in MTS. MTS abstracts the DCOM system into a graphical interface that allows you to easily associate Windows NT users with permissions. Using this system, you can restrict access to a component down to the interface level.

ESTABLISHING A TEST ENVIRONMENT

This book is intended to teach you how to design and build distributed systems with MTS. Throughout the book you will find many exercises to help you learn the skills necessary to build tiered applications. The exercises assume a certain configuration. For simplicity, the applications are all designed to run on a single machine. After you build on a single machine, you will distribute various components to complete the application. Building on a single machine and then distributing allows you to focus on creating the software and ignore network connectivity issues. Therefore, you should have a computer available with the following software installed.

Windows NT 4.0 Server, Service Pack 4.0

When installing Windows NT server, we expect that your server is either a primary domain controller (PDC) or a standalone server. In either case, you should be designated as the administrator for the machine. This book also assumes basic competence in administrator tasks such as establishing user accounts and setting permissions. Service Pack 4.0 is required to perform many debugging tasks within MTS.

CAUTION
The distributed applications created in this book are heavily reliant on the TCP/IP protocol. Be sure to install and configure TCP/IP when you setup Windows NT 4.0 Server.

SQL Server 7.0

Many of the database exercises in this book use SQL Server 7.0. In many cases, the book makes use of the pubs database that ships with SQL Server. You must also be designated as the administrator for SQL Server, although it is perfectly acceptable to leave unchanged the default system administrator designation of sa with no password. Generally, we assume that SQL Server security is separate and not integrated with Windows NT security (that is, Standard Security). When this book makes use of custom SQL Server databases, you will generally find batch SQL files that you can run to set up the databases. Therefore, you should be familiar with essential SQL Server administrator tasks such as creating accounts and establishing permissions for database objects. For users of SQL Server 6.5, alternative instructions are provided with the exercises for backward compatibility.

Internet Information Server 4.0

Internet Information Server (IIS) 4.0 is used to create applications that have both a client/server interface and an intranet interface. You need to have some rudimentary understanding of IIS to get the most out of the book; however, we do not assume an expert level of knowledge.

CAUTION
When installing IIS from a Windows NT 4.0 disk, be careful to note the version that is installed. Some older Windows NT 4.0 installations might still use IIS version 2.0. Make certain that you have IIS version 4.0 installed for use with this book.

Microsoft Transaction Server 2.0

MTS is perhaps one of the easiest applications you will ever install. The simplest way to install MTS is in conjunction with other software either through the Windows NT Option Pack or through Windows NT Server Enterprise Edition. You will find the Windows NT Option Pack as a member of the Visual Studio 98, Enterprise Edition.

MTS is capable of running on Windows 98, Windows NT Workstation, and Windows NT Server. Although support for various operating systems adds to flexibility, if you are developing MTS applications for serious enterprise use, you should always use Windows NT Server. Windows NT Server will always be the final production server for MTS support and we have found that development and deployment is simplified if you simply build your application there from the start. Windows NT Workstation is a suitable substitute for development if you just cannot gain access to a server; however, do not deploy applications using Windows NT Workstation because MTS is limited to ten user connections in this configuration.

Visual Studio 98 Enterprise Edition

Visual Studio 98 Enterprise Edition contains all the software necessary to code the exercises in this book. They are all created in Visual Basic 6.0; however, several other applications are required to support the projects. In particular, this book relies heavily on the Microsoft Visual Modeler to set up the initial architecture for projects. Many of the projects in this book are too complex to be built from scratch, so the Visual Modeler provides a starting point for analyzing the architecture and generating code. If you are unfamiliar with the Visual Modeler, you will want to work the exercise at the end of this chapter, which provides an overview of the tool.

> **CAUTION**
>
> There are significant differences between the Enterprise Edition and the Professional Edition of Visual Studio. To successfully work the exercises in this book, you must install the Enterprise Edition.

Microsoft Message Queue

The Microsoft Message Queue (MSMQ) enables MTS applications to engage in asynchronous communication. It is an ideal product for applications that require a high degree of reliability or must accept data transaction requests even when the database is unavailable. This book covers MSMQ in a single chapter. In order to work the exercise in the chapter, you must install MSMQ.

EXERCISE 1.1: USING VISUAL MODELER

This book uses the Microsoft Visual Modeler extensively in the projects to help you understand and build applications. In this exercise, you will use Visual Basic and the Microsoft Visual Modeler to create an application that retrieves information about resources available on a network machine.

Building the New Model

Step 1

Using the Windows Explorer, create a new directory named MTS/MODELER.

Step 2

Start a new Standard EXE project in Visual Basic. Because this project uses the Visual Modeler, you must set up Visual Basic to use round-trip engineering by enabling the Visual Modeler add-ins. Open the Add-In Manager by selecting Add-Ins, Add-In Manager from the menu. In the Add-In manager, activate the Visual Modeler Add-In and Visual Modeler Menus Add-In. Visual Modeler expects these add-ins to be present whenever Visual Basic is running. Therefore, check the Load on Startup option for each of these add-ins. Press **OK** to close the Add-In Manager. Figure 1.10 shows the Add-In Manager dialog.

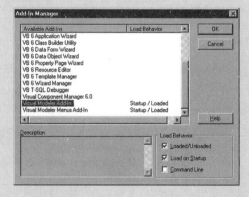

FIGURE 1.10

Enable the Visual Modeler Add-Ins to load on startup.

Step 3

Open the project properties dialog by selecting Project, Project1 Properties from the menu. In the project properties dialog, change the name of the project to FrontEnd. Push the **OK** button to close and save the changes.

Step 4

Select **Form1** in the Project Explorer. Using the properties window, change the name of Form1 to `frmClient`.

Step 5

Add a new ActiveX DLL project to Visual Basic by selecting File, Add Project from the menu. This component is the business object we will use to retrieve information about a host computer. Open the project properties dialog for the ActiveX DLL project. Change the name of the project to `MemoryUsage`. While the dialog is open, be sure that the threading model is set to apartment threading.

Step 6

Select **Class1** in the Project Explorer. Change the name of the class to `DataClass`.

Step 7

Save your project into the directory you created earlier.

Step 8

Visual Modeler works in conjunction with Visual Basic to build models from code and code from models. This process is called *round-trip engineering*. We will use this process to create a new model from this project. Select The `FrontEnd` project in the Project Explorer. Create a new model for this project by selecting **Add-Ins, Visual Modeler, Reverse Engineering Wizard**.

Step 9

The Visual Modeler add-in presents you with the model selection dialog. Push the **New** button to build a new model. This starts Visual Modeler. Figure 1.11 shows the model selection dialog.

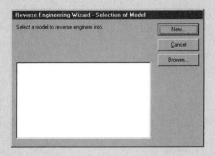

FIGURE 1.11

Select to create a new model.

Step 10

The first step of the Reverse Engineering Wizard is an introduction screen. Push **Next** to move to the next step.

Step 11

The second step of the wizard asks you to select which components to reverse engineer. The wizard works with only one project at a time, so it only displays the form from the FrontEnd project and not the class from the ActiveX DLL. Accept the default settings here and push the **Next** button. Figure 1.12 shows the second step in the wizard.

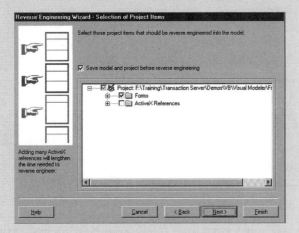

FIGURE 1.12

Accept the default settings to reverse engineer the FrontEnd project.

Step 12

The third step of the wizard asks you to assign the form to one of the three tiers in the model. Carefully drag frmClient to the User Services folder and drop it. The Visual Modeler displays the form as a member of the User Services layer. Push the **Next** button. Figure 1.13 shows the third step of the wizard.

Step 13

The wizard now displays a summary of the conversion work. Read the summary and then press **Finish** to build the model. When the wizard is finished, press **Close** and you will see a component labeled frmClient in the User Services layer.

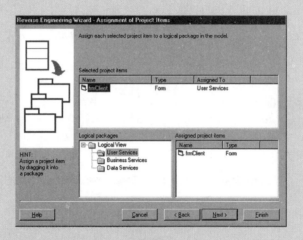

FIGURE **1.13**

Assign the form to the User Services layer.

Step 14

Immediately save the model to the directory you created earlier by selecting File, Save from the menu. Name the file MODELER.MDL.

Step 15

Minimize Visual Modeler and return to Visual Basic. Now select the MemoryUsage project from the Project Explorer. Reverse engineer this project by selecting **Add-Ins, Visual Modeler, Reverse Engineering Wizard** from the menu. When the model selection dialog opens, select to reverse engineer into the MODELER.MDL model you built for the FrontEnd project. Figure 1.14 shows the model selection dialog.

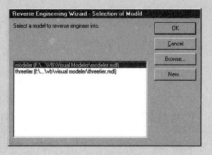

FIGURE **1.14**

Select to add to the existing model.

Step 16

This time, work your way through the wizard, but make the `DataClass` object part of the Business Services layer. When you have both the form and the class in the model, save the model.

Step 17

Using Visual Modeler, we can create properties, methods, and associations for objects in the model. First, we'll create an association between the form and the class. On the Visual Modeler toolbar, carefully locate the Unidirectional Association button. This button allows you to specify that the form will contain an instance of the class. Figure 1.15 shows the button to select.

FIGURE 1.15
Select the Unidirectional Association.

Step 18

Click the **Unidirectional Association** button and drag an association from the form to the class. When the line appears showing the association, double click the line to open the **Association Specification** dialog.

Step 19

The **Association Specification** dialog allows you to establish how code is generated from the relationship. In the **General** tab, you can name the roles that each component fulfills. In the dialog, role A is the class and role B is the form. Name the role for A as `objData`. Name the role for B as `objFrontEnd`. Figure 1.16 shows the **General** tab.

Step 20

Click the **Visual Basic A** tab. This tab designates how property procedures should be created for the component in role A. When you first create the relationship, properties are not automatically created. However, we can change these characteristics. Push the **Edit Set...** button to edit the property procedure characteristics. This opens the **Options** dialog. Figure 1.17 shows the **Visual Basic A** tab.

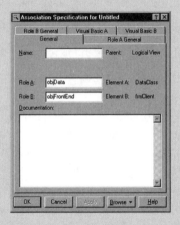

FIGURE 1.16

Name the roles for the object and form.

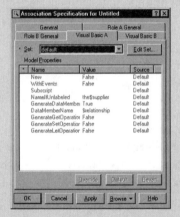

FIGURE 1.17

Use the Edit Set button to affect code generation for the relationship.

Step 21

In the Options dialog, you can create new sets of property procedure attributes. Push the **Clone** button to define a new set of property procedure characteristics. You will be prompted to name the new set. When prompted, name the new set Child. Press the **OK** button. Figure 1.18 shows the options dialog.

FIGURE 1.18

Use the Clone button to create a new set of relationship attributes.

Step 22

The Child set now is a clone of the default set. In the characteristics list, change the following characteristics. Figure 1.19 shows the completed set of new attributes.

TABLE 1.1 CHILD CHARACTERISTICS

Characteristic	Value
New	True
Generate Get	True
Generate Set	True

Step 23

Changing the characteristics for code generation causes an instance of the class module to be automatically created and a set of property procedures generated. After you have changed the characteristics for the Child set, press **OK** to exit the editing dialog.

Step 24

Now that you have created a new set of characteristics, choose the Child set for the object in role A. Press **OK** again to exit the specification dialog.

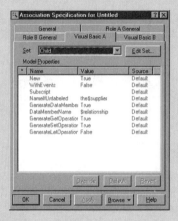

FIGURE 1.19

Change the relationship attributes after cloning.

Step 25

Right click on the `DataClass` object in Visual Modeler and select **Open Specification...**
from the menu. This opens the specification dialog where you can add new properties
and methods. Click the **Methods** tab. Figure 1.20 shows the specification dialog.

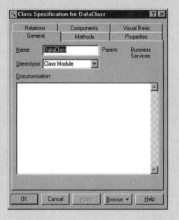

FIGURE 1.20

The specification dialog allows you to create new methods for a component.

Step 26

In the Methods tab of the specification dialog, right click and select **Insert** from the pop-up menu. This adds a new method template called NewMethod. Change the name of this method to Process by typing directly into the list where the new method appears. Set the return type of the method to **Long** using the drop-down list in the dialog. Click **OK** to close the specification dialog. Figure 1.21 shows the completed method definition.

FIGURE 1.21

Close the specification dialog when the method is defined.

Step 27

Save the model.

Coding the Application

Now that you have added an association and a method, you are ready to generate code.

Step 28

Select to generate code for both the form and the class by selecting Edit, Select **All** from the menu. Then start the code generation by selecting **Tools, Generate Code** from the menu. This starts the Code Generation Wizard. Figure 1.22 shows the items selected in the Visual Modeler.

Step 29

The first step of the wizard is just an introduction screen. Press **Next** to continue.

FIGURE 1.22
Select the classes to generate code.

Step 30

In the second step of the wizard, you are asked to select the classes you want to generate code for. Notice in this dialog that you cannot generate code directly for forms. Visual Modeler only generates new classes. To use Visual modeler with a form, the form must already exist in a project. Press **Next**.

Step 31

In the third step of the wizard, you can preview the code generated by the wizard. This lets you modify the definitions of properties and methods before generating the code. Press **Next**.

Step 32

The fourth step of the wizard allows you to specify general coding options such as error handling and debugging code. Clear all these check boxes with the exception of Save Model And Project Before Generating Code. Press **Next**. Figure 1.23 shows the fourth step of the wizard.

Step 33

The fifth screen is a summary of work to be done by the wizard. Review this screen and then press **Finish** to generate your code.

Step 34

When the wizard is finished, close it and save your model.

Step 35

Close Visual Modeler and return to Visual Basic. When you return to VB, you will see that Visual Modeler has added the Process method as well as some comments that contain information about the model. Youíll also notice that the Project Explorer now contains an entry for the model in the Related Documents folder.

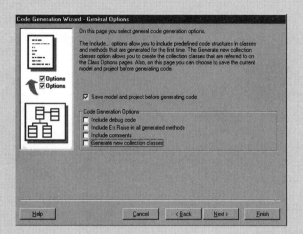

FIGURE 1.23
Clear the special coding options before generating code.

Step 36

Although Visual Modeler generates the members for a class, it does not implement the class. You must still write the code yourself. In this exercise, you will use the `GlobalMemoryStatus` API call to return information about resource usage on a target machine. In the [General][Declarations] section of DataClass, add the code in Listing 1.1 to declare the API call and associated structure. You might want to use the Visual Basic API Viewer to retrieve the definition for the API call and structure.

LISTING 1.1 CODE TO DECLARE MEMORY STATUS API CALL

```
Private Declare Sub GlobalMemoryStatus Lib "kernel32" _
(lpBuffer As MEMORYSTATUS)

'Structure for data
Private Type MEMORYSTATUS
        dwLength As Long
        dwMemoryLoad As Long
        dwTotalPhys As Long
        dwAvailPhys As Long
        dwTotalPageFile As Long
        dwAvailPageFile As Long
        dwTotalVirtual As Long
        dwAvailVirtual As Long
End Type
```

Step 37

The `Process` method makes the API call and returns information about memory usage. The `GlobalMemoryStatus` API can return a lot of different information, but in this exercise, we will return an indicator of the percentage of memory in use. Add the code in Listing 1.2 to the `Process` method to retrieve the information and pass it to the calling client.

LISTING 1.2   CODE TO BE ADDED TO THE *Process* METHOD

```
On Error GoTo ProcessErr

    'Variables
    Dim objMemory As MEMORYSTATUS

    'Get System Data
    objMemory.dwLength = Len(objMemory)
    GlobalMemoryStatus objMemory
    Process = objMemory.dwMemoryLoad

Exit Function

ProcessErr:
App.StartLogging "", vbLogAuto
    App.LogEvent Err.Description, vbLogEventTypeError
```

Creating the Front End

Step 38

The front end for this application uses a form to display the available resources for any machine that has the MemoryUsage component installed. Open `frmClient` in Visual Basic. Figure 1.24 shows how the form is constructed. It uses a single TextBox and a ProgessBar control. If it is not in your toolbox, you must insert the ProgressBar control by selecting Microsoft Windows Common Controls 6.0 from the components dialog. Use the Item list below to set the design-time properties for the controls on the form. Figure 1.25 shows the user interface you must build.

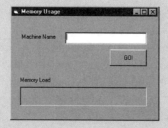

FIGURE 1.24
This is the front end for the exercise.

TABLE 1.2   `frmClient` ITEM LIST

Item	Control	Property	Value
Item 1	Form	Caption	Memory Usage
Item 2	Label	Name	lblMachine
		Caption	Machine Name
Item 3	TextBox	Name	txtMachine
		Text	<empty.
Item 4	CommandButton	Name	cmdGO
		Caption	GO!
Item 5	Label	Name	lblLoad
		Caption	Memory Load
Item 6	ProgressBar	Name	pbrLoad

Step 39

This form wants to be able to call the MemoryUsage component on any machine, so we will use late binding to create it. Therefore, add the following code to the [General][Declarations] section.

```
Private objBusiness As Object
```

Step 40

All the action takes place when the button is clicked. In this event, we create an instance based on the name typed into the TextBox and call the object to get a percentage of the memory in use on that machine. The value is then presented in the progress bar. Add the following code to cmdGO_Click to call the business object.

```
Set objBusiness = CreateObject("MemoryUsage.DataClass", txtMachine.Text)
pbrLoad.Value = objBusiness.Process
```

Step 41

Try running the front end and calling your local computer to see the percentage of memory in use. When you first run this application, you will likely notice that it often returns a value of zero. This is true if you have very little activity on your system. The memory load changes, however, if you analyze the system while performing an intense operation such as a query.

Components such as this one can be used to analyze the system resources available on a machine prior to attempting to create a distributed instance. This assists in using all network resources effectively in a process known as *load balancing*. If this component were to be distributed to several machines, we would need to ensure that it has the required permissions to run and is properly packaged in MTS. We investigate security and distribution issues in detail later in the book.

ADMINISTERING MTS

PREREQUISITES

This is the only chapter dedicated to administrative tasks with MTS. It represents foundational knowledge, but is not technically taxing. Before beginning this chapter, however, you should be familiar with fundamental COM principles as well as Windows NT security features such as users and groups.

Skills Learned

- 70-175(5): Configure a server computer to run Microsoft Transaction Server (MTS).
- 70-176 (7): Set up security on a system package.
- 70-175(22): Import existing packages.
- 70-175(23): Assign names to packages.
- 70-175(24): Assign security to packages.
- 70-175(25): Add components to an MTS package.
- 70-175(26): Set transactional properties of components.
- 70-175(27): Set security properties of components.
- 70-175(28): Use role-based security to limit use of an MTS package to specific users.
- 70-175(29): Create roles.
- 70-175(30): Assign roles to components or component interfaces.
- 70-175(31): Add users to roles.

In the previous chapter, you saw how ActiveX EXE components can be used with DCOM to create distributed applications with Visual Basic. You also learned about several limitations and concerns when developing multi-user applications with these methodologies. MTS improves the performance of maintenance of distributed applications by acting as a container for components. In the end, MTS is essentially an abstraction that provides an improved graphical interface to the functionality of DCOM while adding other essential features such as resource pooling. In this chapter, we will prepare to build distributed applications with MTS by examining the setup and administration features. Many of the features are covered in more detail later in the book and are presented here to provide a framework for later discussion.

ADMINISTERING WITH MTS EXPLORER

Managing all the components maintained by MTS is a relatively simple chore. The primary interface used to manage MTS is the MTS Explorer. The MTS Explorer runs inside of the Microsoft Management Console (MMC). The MMC is a centralized place where you can perform many administrative tasks in Windows NT. Administrative services are installed under MMC using a system of *snap-ins* that enable third parties to develop custom administrative tools and have them run in a common, familiar framework. Figure 2.1 shows the MTS Explorer.

FIGURE 2.1

The MTS Explorer is used to manage the installation.

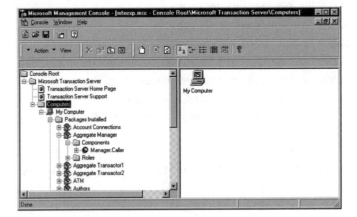

MTS Explorer Appearance and Operation

The MTS Explorer divides COM components into a hierarchical structure with a tree view in the left pane and a list view in the right. The structure is exactly the same as the Windows File Explorer. In the MTS Explorer, the first level in the hierarchy is the

Computers folder. Using the Computers folder, you can examine the objects contained on any computer in the enterprise that is running a copy of MTS. We'll discuss remote component administration in the Remote Administration section later in this chapter.

MTS also shows the local computer in the Explorer as My Computer. You can change attributes associated with the local computer through a property dialog. To access the properties of the local computer, right-click the **My Computer** icon in the MTS Explorer and select **Properties...** from the pop-up menu. Figure 2.2 shows the properties dialog.

FIGURE 2.2

Properties for the computer are set using this dialog.

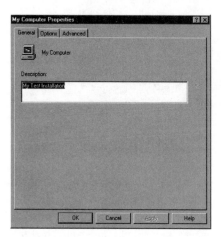

My Computer Properties

The property dialog for My Computer contains three tabs: General, Options, and Advanced. The *General* tab simply allows you to provide a description for the local computer. The Options tab allows you to specify information about transaction duration and replication. Using the Transaction Timeout entry, you can specify the amount of time that a transaction can be active before MTS automatically terminates it. This value is normally 60 seconds; however, you can specify any time you want. You can also disable the function by entering a value of zero for the timeout.

The *Options* tab also allows you to configure replication features if you are running MTS with the Microsoft Cluster Server (MSCS). MSCS is a technology that enables multiple computers to behave as a single node on a network. If you want to run MTS with MSCS, MTS must be installed on each computer in the cluster only after MSCS is installed and configured. When using MSCS, a Replication Share name is used to specify a shared location on the master computer of the cluster. This share is used to replicate information from MTS to other computers in the cluster. The Remote Server Name entry is used to designate what machine clients should use to access components replicated from this machine. If you do not place an entry here, client setups that you build from MTS will target the installation where the setup was built. We discuss application setup and component distribution in chapter 10. Figure 2.3 shows the Options tab.

FIGURE 2.3

The Options tab configures replication attributes.

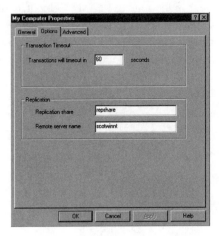

The *Advanced* tab allows you to specify information about how to view information and log activities. MTS manages transactional work across components using a service known as the Microsoft Distributed Transaction Coordinator (MSDTC). This book covers transactions in chapter 6; however, you should understand that the MSDTC is the primary service responsible for ensuring that transactions initiated within MTS are properly managed. In the View section of the Advanced tab, you can specify how often information about transactions is updated and traced. The Log section allows you to specify the location and size of the MTS log file. Figure 2.4 shows the Advanced tab.

FIGURE 2.4

Use the Advanced tab for MSDTC and log settings.

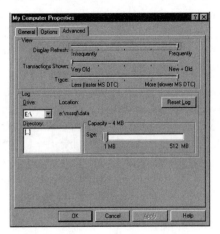

MTS Explorer Menus

Along with the properties for My Computer, you can control many aspects of MTS through the menus associated with My Computer. If you select the **My Computer** and click the **Action** menu, you will see several actions available from **My Computer**. You can start and stop the MSDTC directly from this menu. Whenever your components are involved in transactional work, the MSDTC should be running. You can also shut down all server processes from this menu. Shutting down all server processes causes MTS to unload every component in every package. This is most useful when you want to update a component. You cannot replace components while they are in memory, so you must shut down the process to upgrade. After you upgrade a component, you will want to read in any new data from the registry. The My Computer menu allows you to refresh all components, which updates MTS with the latest registry settings for all components. A normal upgrade usually requires shutting down the process, replacing the component, and refreshing all components.

Underneath the My Computer icon, you will find entries for the Transaction List, Transaction Statistics, and Trace Messages. These windows allow you to view information about MTS transactions. You can see the status of transactions using the Transaction List. The Trace Messages window provides information about MSDTC activities, and the Transaction Statistics window shows aggregate information about successful and failed transactions.

MTS Packages

Of course, the true purpose of the MTS Explorer is to allow you to easily administer objects on the local computer. You might add, delete, and edit components directly from the MMC. Components that you want to place under MTS control are grouped on a computer inside of MTS Packages. A *package* is simply a collection of COM objects that are running under a shared context. This means that components in the same package have permission to access each other. Components in the same package can also participate in transactions together.

Before you can install a component in MTS, you must create a package. To create a package, select the computer you want from the **Computer** folder. Expand the selected computer to reveal the Packages Installed folder. Click the **Packages** folder and select **Action, New, Package** from the menu. MTS presents the Package Wizard to facilitate creating a new package. Figure 2.5 shows the Package Wizard.

2

ADMINISTERING
MTS

FIGURE 2.5

Use the Package Wizard to create new packages.

When creating a package, you can choose to create a new package or import an existing package. MTS has built-in capabilities that allow you to export and import packages from one instance of MTS to another. MTS also contains special client installation utilities. Most often, you will create a new package, and when you do, MTS asks you to provide a package name. You might name the package virtually anything. MTS does not track packages by name, but rather it uses a global unique identifier (GUID) to identify every package you create. The GUIDs are maintained in the Registry and components are associated with packages using these numbers. Figure 2.6 shows a name in the Package Wizard.

FIGURE 2.6

Package names can be almost anything you want.

Adding Components to a Package

After a package is created, you might add components to it. In order to add components to a package, click the package in the MTS Explorer. When the package expands, it lists a Components folder that contains all the installed components. Adding a new component is a matter of clicking on the Components folder and selecting **Action, New, Component** from the menu. When you select **To Add A New Component**, MTS presents the Component Wizard. The Component Wizard allows you to add new components that are not yet registered on the machine, or it simply takes registered components and places them under MTS control. Figure 2.7 shows the Component Wizard.

FIGURE 2.7

Use the Component Wizard to put components in a package.

2

ADMINISTERING MTS

Adding Remote Components

If you want to add components that are not on the local machine, you must have the DLL file available. MTS prompts you for the file to install. If, however, the component is already registered on the machine, MTS presents you with a list of components to choose from. Components in the system registry do not necessarily run inside MTS. You must specifically import them to gain the benefits of resource pooling that MTS provides. From the wizard, it is a simple matter of selecting the desired component from the list. Figure 2.8 shows the list generated by the Component Wizard.

When you first place components in packages, you might believe that installing new or already registered components are similar operations. Actually, they are different. Both options will, of course, add a component to a package. However, installing components that are already registered does not give MTS any information about the interfaces supported by a component. If you want MTS to list all the interfaces your components support, they must be installed as new components. When you develop MTS applications on a single machine, Visual Basic registers your components when they are compiled, so you might be tempted to add your components from the registry list. We recommend, however, that you always choose to Install New Component(s) from the Component Wizard because this always adds information about component interfaces. Don't worry about choosing this option if your component is already registered, MTS can treat a component as new even if it already has a registry entry.

FIGURE 2.8

The Component Wizard builds a list of registered components.

QUICK CHECK 2.1

EXAMINING COMPONENT INTERFACES

1. Start the MTS Explorer.

2. Expand the tree view in the MTS Explorer and locate My Computer.

3. Expand My Computer and locate the Packages Installed folder.

4. Expand the Packages Installed folder and locate the Utilities package. This package is installed with MTS and contains a special interface used to start transactions.

5. Expand the Utilities package and locate the Components folder.

6. Expand the Components folder and locate the `TxCTx.TransactionContext` object.

7. Expand the `TxCTx.TransactionContext` object and locate the Interfaces folder. This folder contains the interface used by this object to start transactions.

8. Expand the Interfaces folder and locate the ITransactionContext interface.

9. Expand the ITransactionContext interface and locate the Methods folder.

10. Expand the Methods folder. Now examine the methods in the folder. Many of these should look familiar because they are fundamental COM methods. MTS allows you to view the interfaces and member methods as well as set security features down to the interface level.

After a component is installed in MTS, it can be called just as any other distributed or local component. Applications that live on the local machine can instantiate the object directly. Remote clients can simply use DCOM support to get the component services. In any case, MTS kicks in to provide the resource management necessary to scale the component and provide functionality to many users. The big advantage of using MTS is that you never have to use the DCOMCNFG utility again, and you don't worry about writing software to properly manage shared resources.

Administering Package Properties

After packages and components are installed, you can administer them by working with the package and component property dialogs. The property dialogs are accessible by selecting any package or component and choosing Action, Properties... from the menu. The property dialogs provide control over the various features of packages and components. Beginning with the package properties, you will find five tabs available: General, Security, Advanced, Identity, and Activation.

The General Tab

The first tab, marked General, shows the package name and description. You can also see the GUID used by MTS to track the package and distinguish it from all other packages. Figure 2.9 shows the General tab.

FIGURE 2.9

The General tab contains the package GUID.

2

ADMINISTERING MTS

The Security Tab

The second tab, marked Security, is used to manage the security options for the selected package. MTS uses two forms of security: programmatic and declarative. Programmatic security is used to create a custom set of security interfaces to your components. Declarative security is used to establish predefined Roles that a component can use to determine the privileges authorized for a user. Security is enabled by checking the box marked Enable Authorization Checking. You can also set the level of security checking with the Authentication Level list. Figure 2.10 shows the Security tab.

FIGURE 2.10

The Security tab configures package security.

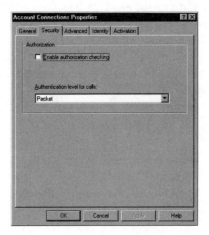

Although you can use programmatic security in your components, the preferred method is declarative security through role definition. Roles are predefined identities that the MTS administrator creates. When created, the administrator can assign NT domain users to the roles and the MTS components can verify client requests against the role membership. Defining a new role is done directly in the MTS Explorer. Underneath the Packages folder you will find a Roles folder. To define a new role, simply click on the **Roles** folder and select **Action, New, Role** from the menu. The role dialog appears. Figure 2.11 shows the role dialog.

FIGURE 2.11

The Role dialog is used to create new roles for a package.

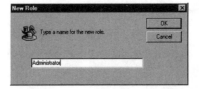

In the Role dialog, you can define any role name you want. Names are completely arbitrary and are simply used as a way to group users with similar permissions. When defined, you will find the role is the MTS Explorer, where you can assign domain users. Simply click on the **Users** folder under the **Roles** folder and select **Action, New, User** from the menu. MTS presents a list of domain users that you can assign to the role. When assigned, any object in the package can check the role of a calling client and validate his request. Programming security is covered in detail in chapter 7. Figure 2.12 shows how to assign users to a role.

FIGURE 2.12

Assign Windows NT users and groups to roles.

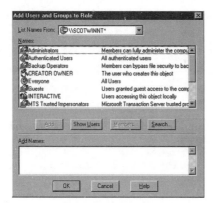

QUICK CHECK 2.2

ROLES AND USERS

1. Start the MTS Explorer.

2. Expand the tree view in the MTS Explorer and locate My Computer.

3. Expand My Computer and locate the Packages Installed folder.

4. Click the **Packages Installed** folder and select **Action, New, Package** from the menu. This starts the Package Wizard.

5. Using the Package Wizard, select to create an empty package. Define a new package named **My Package**. Set the identity to **Interactive User** and press **Finish**.

6. Expand the **My Package** package and locate the **Roles** folder. This is the folder where you can define new roles for a package.

continues

continued

> 7. Click on the **Roles** folder. When it is highlighted, select **Action, New, Role** from the menu. The new role dialog appears.
>
> 8. Add a new role named **My New Role** to the package. Press the **OK** button.
>
> 9. Expand the Roles folder and locate the new role you added.
>
> 10. Expand the role My New Role and locate the Users folder.
>
> 11. Click the **Users** folder and select **Action, New, User** from the menu. MTS responds by searching the current domain for Windows NT user IDs that you can add to the role. If you are not connected to the network, use the names of users on your local machine. Select a user and add it to the new role.
>
> 12. Even when a user is associated with a role, MTS has not fully enabled security. This is done in the properties dialog for the package. Select the **My Package** package and choose **Action, Properties...** from the menu.
>
> 13. In the Security tab, select **Enable Authorization Checking**. This turns security on for the current package. Press **OK**.
>
> 14. When you are finished, delete the package by clicking My Package and selecting Action, Delete from the menu.

Administrator System package

When first installed, MTS does not have administrative security enabled. This means that anyone who is an administrator on the host machine can also administer MTS. In order to restrict administrator capabilities to authorized users, MTS has a special package called the System package. The System package is used to give Windows NT domain users permission to access and modify the properties of packages and components.

If you want to have full administrator abilities, you should place your Windows NT user ID in the System package under the Administrator role for each computer running MTS. When your user ID is under the Administrator role, use the properties dialog for the System package to enable authorization checking. Enabling authorization checking for the System package causes MTS to restrict administration privileges to only those users in the Administrator role. Therefore, you must never enable authorization checking on the System package until you have added at least one user to the Administrator role. Otherwise, you might never be able to get back in to the MTS Explorer.

QUICK CHECK 2.3

SETTING ADMINISTRATIVE SECURITY

1. Start the MTS Explorer.

2. Expand the tree view in the MTS Explorer and locate My Computer.

3. Expand My Computer and locate the Packages Installed folder.

4. Expand the Packages Installed folder and locate the System package. This package is installed with MTS and contains the role definition for administrators.

5. Expand the System package and locate the Roles folder.

6. Expand the Roles folder and locate the Administrator role.

7. Expand the Administrator role and locate the Users folder.

8. Adding a user to the Administrator role gives that user administrator privileges in MTS. Add a user by clicking the Users folder and selecting Action, New, User from the menu. This opens a user dialog for the current domain. If you are not connected to a network, select users from your local machine. Add yourself to the Administrator role.

9. When you have added yourself to the Administrator role, you can turn on security for the System package. Click on the System package and then select Action, Properties... from the menu. This opens the package properties dialog.

10. Select the Security tab. In this tab, check the box to enable authorization checking. When you turn on security for the System package, MTS warns you to be sure you have added a user to the Administrator role before enabling security.

11. After you enable security, MTS limits access to the MTS Explorer functions to administrators only.

CAUTION

Enabling security without first putting a user in the Administrator role prevents access to the MTS Explorer by all users and render your installation useless.

The Advanced Tab

The third tab on the Packages Properties dialog, marked Advanced, is used to manage when an object is unloaded from memory. This is the only real tuning tool available in MTS. You can specify that a package be held in memory indefinitely or unloaded from memory after a certain period of time. Keeping packages in memory improves performance, but uses more resources. This tab also contains to boxes that allow you to prevent this object from being deleted or modified. Figure 2.13 shows the Advanced tab.

FIGURE 2.13

Use the Advanced tab to specify the life of a package.

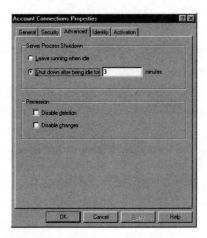

The Identity Tab

The fourth tab, marked Identity, is used to specify the security context under which the component runs. Using this option, you have the ability to run the component under the context of the calling client or under a separate context reserved just for MTS. When you select to run the component under the Interactive User you specify that the component should be given the permissions associated with the calling client. This is advantageous because it ensures that no client can access resources they are not specifically authorized by Windows NT to access. If you choose This User, however, you can assign a specific user ID to MTS and use declarative security to determine which functions a component runs. This is advantageous because it greatly simplifies the security issues that the administrator has to handle. It also allows for highly effective database connection pooling designs that we will discuss in chapter 4. Figure 2.14 shows the Identity tab.

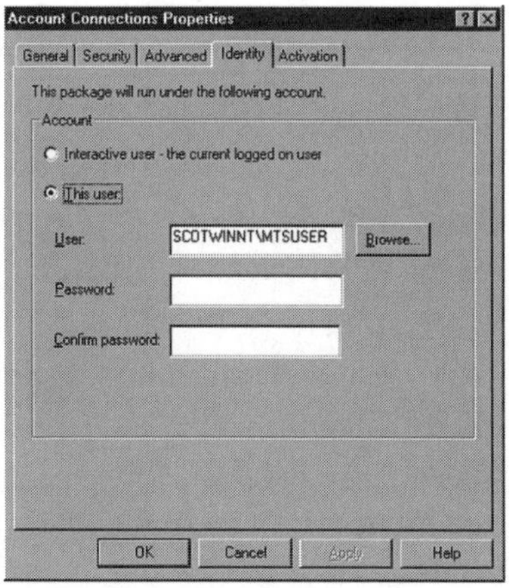

FIGURE 2.14

Use the Identity tab to set the security context for a package.

Account Connections Properties

General | Security | Advanced | Identity | Activation |

This package will run under the following account.

Account

◯ Interactive user - the current logged on user

◉ This user:

User: `SCOTWINNT\MTSUSER` [Browse...]

Password:

Confirm password:

[OK] [Cancel] [Apply] [Help]

QUICK CHECK 2.4

SETTING PACKAGE IDENTITY

1. Using the Start button in Windows NT, locate the Administrative Tools program group.

2. From the Administrative Tools, start the User Manager for Domains.

3. The User Manager is used to manage Windows NT accounts and passwords. In the User Manager, create a new account by selecting User, New User... from the menu. This opens the New User dialog.

4. Add a new user named MTSUSER and set the password as mtspassword. *Note that case is important on the password!* This is a special account we often use to run packages under if we want them to have more privileges than a calling client might have. You can add privileges to this account as necessary to let the components in your package access Windows NT services. If you are not a domain administrator, you can still add this account to your local machine by selecting User, Select **Domain...** from the User Manager and choosing your local machine.

5. Close the User Manager after you have added the new account.

6. Start the MTS Explorer.

7. Expand the tree view in the MTS Explorer and locate My Computer.

8. Expand My Computer and locate the Packages Installed folder.

continues

continued

> 9. Click the **Packages Installed** folder and select **Action, New, Package** from the menu. This starts the Package Wizard.
>
> 10. When the Package Wizard starts, select to create a new package.
>
> 11. In the second step of the Package Wizard, name the new package My Package. Press **Next**.
>
> 12. In the third step of the Package Wizard, select to run the package under **This User**. Use the **Browse** button.
>
> 13. Locate the MTSUSER account you created earlier. Enter the password for this account and close the package properties. The package now runs under the security context of this account regardless of who calls it. Press **Finish**.

The Activation Tab

The last tab, marked Activation determines whether the component is created to run inside the memory space of MTS or in the memory space of the calling client. To run your package in MTS, select the option **In a Dedicated Server Process** and to run in the client's process, select **In the Creator's Process**. Packages running in MTS are called *Server* packages, while packages running inside clients are called *Library* packages.

If you choose to run your component in the memory space of a calling client, you will gain performance because calls to the client will be faster, but you will suffer from several restrictions. First of all, in order to run in the client's memory, the client must be on the same machine as the component. Secondly, components that run in the client's memory are not isolated from the client so a component crash means a client crash. Finally, when components run outside MTS, they cannot implement declarative security. All things considered, it is generally best to run all your components inside the memory space of MTS. Figure 2.15 shows the Activation tab.

Package Component Properties

Similar to a package, any individual component also has a Property dialog. The Component Property dialog is accessible by clicking a component and selecting Action, Properties... from the menu. The Component Property dialog has three tabs on it. The first tab, marked General, shows the ProgID of the component and has a place for you to enter a description. The tab also lists the DLL that contains the component and the CLSID of the component itself. The package to which the component belongs is also listed. Figure 2.16 shows the General tab.

FIGURE 2.15

Use the Activation tab to isolate a package.

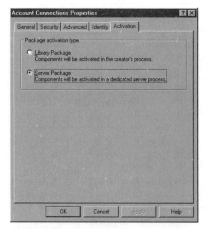

FIGURE 2.16

The General tab displays essential component information.

The second tab, marked Transaction, is used to specify how this component participates in a transaction. One of the major features of MTS, as the name implies, is the initiation, committal, and monitoring of transactions. These transactions can be made up of functions performed by various components in MTS. Chapter 6 describes in detail how to program MTS components for transaction processing. Figure 2.17 shows the Transaction tab.

The final tab, marked Security, is used to enable authorization checking for this component. Similar to the package options, you can use declarative or programmatic security with an individual component. MTS lets you establish security checking all the way down to the interface level for a component. This is why you always want interface information present in MTS for your components. Figure 2.18 shows the Security tab.

FIGURE 2.17

Use the Transasaction tab to define transactional component behavior.

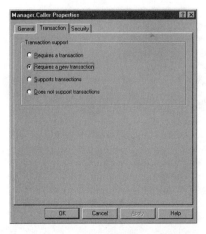

FIGURE 2.18

Use the Security tab to enable security checking.

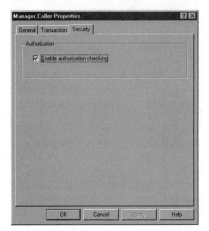

Management With The Action Menu

Besides the property dialogs, you can manage packages and components from the Action menu. If you select a package within MTS, you can shut down the process associated with that package from the Action menu. This is similar to shutting down processes at the My Computer level, except that this only shuts down a single package. You can also move a component from one package to another by selecting the component and choosing Move from the Action menu. This prompts you for the name of a destination package within the same installation of MTS. MTS also allows you to view the components in various ways by using the View menu.

QUICK CHECK 2.5

COMPONENT VIEWS

1. Start the MTS Explorer.

2. Expand the tree view in the MTS Explorer and locate My Computer.

3. Expand My Computer and locate the Packages Installed folder.

4. Expand the Packages Installed folder and locate the Utilities package.

5. Expand the Utilities package and locate the Components folder.

6. Expand the Components folder and locate the `TxCTx.TransactionContext` object.

7. With the `TxCTx.TransactionContext` object visible, click the **Components** folder in the Utilities package. When you have a folder selected, you can change how the information in the folder is presented using the View menu.

8. Select **View**, **Property View** from the menu. Examine the types of information shown in this view. You will see many of the properties that you worked with in the Property dialog.

9. Select **View**, **Status View** from the menu. This view shows the status of the objects. Currently the information will be blank because the components are not actively participating in an application. Later when we build applications, you can use this view to see how the objects are working.

REMOTE ADMINISTRATION

Using the MTS Explorer, you can view and manage packages installed on other computers that are also running MTS. New computers can be added to your explorer by clicking the Computers folder and selecting **Action, New, Computer** from the menu. When you select **To Add A New Computer**, MTS prompts you for the name of the computer. If you do not know the name, MTS allows you to browse the domain and select the computer to add. When added, the computer appears in the Computers folder and you can examine the packages installed.

When you have contact with a remote MTS installation, you can export components from one installation to another. Exporting components is done through the Remote Components folder. To export a component, click the **Remote Components** folder for the computer where you want to establish a new package. Then select **Action, New, Remote Component** from the menu in your MTS Explorer. MTS displays the Remote

Components dialog. In this dialog, you can select the computer that contains the package you want to export. After you select the computer, you can select the package and finally the components. Press the **OK** button to export the selected components to the desired computer. MTS installs remote components in a special directory. If you install MTS in the default directory, the remote components are placed in C:\Program Files\MTS\Remote.

When exporting remote components, watch out for a few issues. First of all, ensure that you have Administrator permission on all the MTS installations where you want to export packages. Next, be sure that the components you want to export are contained in a shared directory that can be accessed by the machine receiving the export. MTS installations use sharing to receive export information. Finally, be sure that you have permission to access the shared directory as specified by the NTFS file permissions.

If you do not have permission to export directly using the Remote Components folder, MTS allows you to export manually. Manual exports are accomplished by right-clicking a package and selecting Export from the pop-up menu. When you export a package directly, MTS creates a special file with a PAK extension. You can save this file and then use it to create a new package on another installation of MTS.

EXERCISE 2.1: A SIMPLE MTS APPLICATION

This exercise uses the fundamental administrative skills required in MTS. You will create a package and install components in the package. After you have a component under MTS control, you will build a simple front end to call the component.

Step 1

Using the File Explorer, create a new directory called MTS/EXERCISE2.1.

Step 2

Start a new ActiveX DLL project in Visual Basic. We will discuss the exact nature of the relationship between ActiveX components and MTS in the next chapter, "Designing Components for MTS," but for now just recognize that MTS uses ActiveX DLL components as opposed to ActiveX EXE components.

Step 3

Open the project properties dialog by selecting Project, Project1 Properties... from the Visual Basic menu. In this dialog, change the name of the project to SimpleObject. While the dialog is open, ensure that the threading model for you component is set to Apartment Threaded. All MTS components should use apartment threading to allow MTS to handle the thread pooling for the component. Push **OK** to close the Project properties.

Step 4

Select **Class1** in the Project Explorer. Change the name of the class to `Simple`.

Step 5

Open the code window for class `Simple`. In the code window, add a new method to the class by selecting Tools, Add Procedure from the menu. Add a new method named `Process`. Make this method a Public Function. When you have added the new method, modify the function signature to return a String data type. The completed function signature follows:

```
Public Function Process() As String
End Function
```

Step 6

The `Process` method is a trivial routine designed just to allow you to work with packages and components. As such, add the following code to the Process function to return a message to the calling client.

```
Process = "I got your call!"
```

Step 7

Compile your ActiveX DLL by selecting File, Make Simpleobject.Dll from the menu. When you have completed the compile, save your work in the directory you created earlier and exit Visual Basic.

Step 8

Open the MTS Explorer. Locate My Computer and expand the tree view until you see the Packages Installed folder. Click the **Packages Installed** folder. Then choose **Action, New, Package** from the menu. This starts the Package Wizard.

Step 9

In the first step of the Package Wizard, choose to create an empty package. Figure 2.19 shows the first step of the wizard.

FIGURE **2.19**
Create a new package.

Step 10

In the second step of the Package Wizard, name the new package Simple. Click **Next**. Figure 2.20 shows the second step of the wizard.

Step 11

In the third step of the Package Wizard, set the package identity as Interactive User. Press **Finish** to create the package. Figure 2.21 shows the third step of the wizard.

FIGURE 2.20

Name the package Simple.

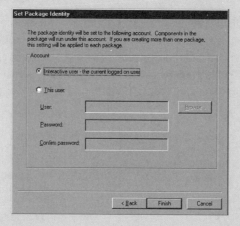

FIGURE 2.21

Run the package under Interactive User.

Step 12

When the package is created, locate it in the MTS Explorer. Expand the tree view until you find the Components folder. Click the **Components** folder and select **Action, New, Component** from the menu. This starts the Component Wizard.

Step 13

In the first step of the Component Wizard, select to **Install New Component(s)**. Figure 2.22 shows the first step of the wizard.

FIGURE 2.22
Select to install new components.

Step 14

In the second step of the Component Wizard, push the **Add Files** button. Use the file
dialog to search for and locate the file SIMPLEOBJECT.DLL that you created earlier.
When you select this file, the object inside the DLL will be listed in the Add
Components dialog. Click **Finish** to add the component to your package. You are now
ready to call the component from Visual Basic. Figure 2.23 shows the components located by the wizard.

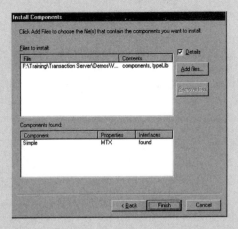

FIGURE 2.23
Add the components from the ActiveX DLL.

Step 15

Return to Visual Basic and start a new Standard EXE project. This project will be a front end to the component in MTS.

Step 16

Open the references dialog for the new project by selecting Project, References from the menu. In the references dialog, set a reference to SimpleObject. Close the references dialog.

Step 17

As a simple example of calling an MTS component, we will just create an instance of the SimpleObject component. Double-click **Form1** in the Project Explorer. Add a **CommandButton** to **Form1** from the toolbox. Change the caption on this button to **Process**.

Step 18

Open the code window for Form1. In the Command1_Click event, add the following code to create an instance of the SimpleObject component and call the Process method.

```
'Create Business Object
Dim objSimple As SimpleObject.Simple
Set objSimple = New SimpleObject.Simple

'Call Business Object
MsgBox (objSimple.Process)
```

Step 19

Save your work, but DO NOT run the project yet. The very first time a component starts in MTS, the component must be loaded into memory. Therefore, the first call to a package can have a noticeable delay. Start your Standard EXE project. When you are ready to time the response, press the button to call the component.

Step 20

When you get a response from MTS, leave the MsgBox visible and examine the Simple object in the MTS Explorer. You should see the component ball spinning, which indicates it is active. If you close the MsgBox by pressing OK, the animation stops.

Step 21

Now press the button again. You should see an immediate response from the component because it is already loaded into memory. This is typical behavior for MTS.

Step 22

Now return to the MTS Explorer and click on the **Simple** package. With the package selected, choose **Action, Shut Down**. This unloads the package from memory. Now press the **Process** button on Form1 again. How long does it take for the component to respond? Did you expect this?

DESIGNING COMPONENTS FOR MTS

PREREQUISITES

Before beginning this chapter, you should have a firm understanding of the fundamentals of MTS, including administrative tasks. You should be able to create packages and install components easily without detailed instructions. You should also be familiar with the process of creating ActiveX DLL components in Visual Basic.

Skills Learned

- 70-100(9): Design the properties, methods, and events of components.
- 70-175(10): Create a Visual Basic client application that uses a COM component.
- 70-175(12): Create call-back procedures to enable asynchronous processing between COM components and Visual Basic client applications.
- 70-175(14): Implement error handling for the user interface in distributed applications.
- 70-175(17): Design and create components that will be used with MTS.
- 70-175(19): Choose the appropriate threading model for a COM component.
- 70-175(32): Compile a project with class modules into a COM component.
- MTS(4): Use the ObjectControl interface to receive Activate and Deactivate information.
- MTS(5): Use the Shared Property Manager to persist application state.
- MTS(6): Pass a Safe reference from an MTS component to a client.

Scaling applications with MTS is all about properly managing resources in the common Business Services layer. This means using database connections, threads, and memory only when necessary and only for the minimum amount of time required to perform a function. Although philosophically the idea is relatively straightforward, designing and creating components that successfully meet these criteria requires significant changes in implementation.

Taking advantage of the resource management features of MTS is more than simply placing a component in a package. Consider the scenario where a component is installed in an MTS package and a client application wants to access the component. In order to create an instance of the component, the client will, of course, have to declare a variable. For the sake of argument, assume the variable is declared in the [General][Declarations] section of a standard module in the client. The application is written to create an instance of the desired component in Sub Main as soon as the program starts. By design, the instance is then maintained by the client until the application terminates. Now imagine that a user starts the application, uses it for a while, and then goes to lunch. Because the instance variable is maintained with application-level scope, the component in MTS will not shut down. This means that valuable memory is used by the Business Services layer to maintain an instance that is not in active use. Now imagine that hundreds of users log in to the application and also go to lunch. Complete disaster.

Allowing clients to create and maintain instances in the shared Business Services layer destroys scalability because the resources in the middle tier are limited. Instead, an application should create an instance, make a method call, and then destroy the instance. Objects in the middle tier must live for the minimum amount of time necessary to perform a function.

Your response to this situation might be to declare the variable with less scope. Perhaps we can declare a locally scoped variable only in the procedures where the application needs access to the distributed component. This is certainly a better idea, but not the best. Local variables cause the component in MTS to be created and destroyed many times, which does not give MTS a chance to effectively manage memory. The essential problem in the design of the application is that the client is controlling the management of resources in the middle tier through variable scope. The best solution to instance management is to enable MTS to automatically manage instances.

UNDERSTANDING THE `ObjectContext`

In order to gain control over the life and state of an object, MTS supports a special object known as the `ObjectContext`. The `ObjectContext` is created by MTS when a component is loaded into memory. The `ObjectContext` "observes" a component and provides information to MTS about when the business object can be reused. Until now, we've used MTS without knowing that the `ObjectContext` existed, but once we know it's there, we can communicate with it and affect how MTS handles our ActiveX components.

The `ObjectContext` is created to contain state information about the particular component under the care of MTS. This is not to be confused with state information contained within the component itself. For example, an MTS component might contain state for an application through internal variables, whereas the `ObjectContext` contains state about the MTS component. This state information includes the security context under which the component is running, the transaction context in which the component is participating, and the time that another client can reuse the component. Without the `ObjectContext`, MTS would be unable to provide any meaningful resource management features to the components under its control. Figure 3.1 shows a conceptual diagram of the `ObjectContext` and how it relates to an MTS component.

FIGURE 3.1

The `ObjectContext` *contains state information about a component.*

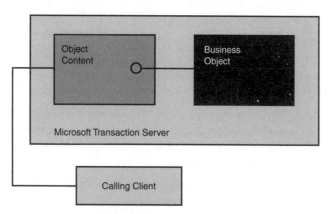

Clients call business objects in MTS. They maintain a constant reference to the ObjectContext which helps MTS create instances of the business object on demand.

Communicating with the `ObjectContext`

In order to communicate with the `ObjectContext`, we must first set a reference to the Transaction Server API. As with all object model references in Visual Basic, we set it with the References dialog. The reference should be set from within the ActiveX DLL project that will become your business object. In the References dialog, select **Microsoft Transaction Server Type Library**. After the reference is set, you can easily access the functionality of the `ObjectContext`. Figure 3.2 shows the references dialog in Visual Basic.

FIGURE 3.2

Set a reference to the Microsoft Transaction Server Type Library.

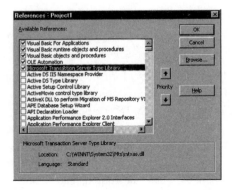

Retrieving a reference to the ObjectContext is done with the Transaction Server API call GetObjectContext(). The GetObjectContext() function returns a reference that is similar to any object reference held and managed in Visual Basic. Therefore, you should simply declare a variable as the appropriate type and fill it with the ObjectContext reference. The following code shows how to retrieve the ObjectContext for any business object.

```
Dim objContext As MTxAS.ObjectContext
Set objContext = GetObjectContext()
```

Retrieving the ObjectContext is always done inside the component associated with MTS. No other part of the application has any use for the ObjectContext. A component that has a reference to its ObjectContext should never attempt to pass that reference to another object because one component cannot make use of the ObjectContext for another component. This is true even if the second business object is running in MTS. The ObjectContext returned by GetObjectContext() only applies to the business object that called the function. Additionally, components should destroy the object variable carrying the ObjectContext when they have finished using it. This destruction might be an explicit release achieved by setting the variable to the VB keyword Nothing or an implicit release occurring as the result of a variable losing scope.

Generally, an MTS component retrieves a reference to its ObjectContext and releases that reference within a single method call. Therefore each method of the business object repeats the same simple code at the beginning and ending of the function. The following code shows a typical template for a component method.

```
Public Function MyFunction() As Boolean

On Error GoTo MyFunctionErr

    'Get Object Context
    Dim objContext As MTxAs.ObjectContext
```

```
    Set objContext = GetObjectContext()


    'Place Code Body Here!


    'Tell Object MTS we are done
     objContext.SetComplete

MyFunctionExit:
    Exit Function

MyFunctionErr:
    'Tell MTS we failed
     objContext.SetAbort

    Debug.Print Err.Description
    App.StartLogging App.Path & "\error.log", vbLogToFile
    App.LogEvent Err.Description, vbLogEventTypeError
    Resume MyFunctionExit

End Function
```

Because the `ObjectContext` code is redundant and must exist in every method, we have included a special add-in on the CD-ROM you can use to replace the standard Visual Basic procedure dialog box with one that includes the ability to add MTS code to a function. We find this utility useful in creating all kinds of standard method structures including error handling and property procedures. Although none of the exercises in the book assume you have the enhanced procedure dialog, you might want to install it to save work. Figure 3.3 shows the enhanced procedure dialog.

FIGURE 3.3

The Enhanced Procedure Dialog writes template MTS code for you.

Controlling Reuse

The primary reason for referencing the `ObjectContext` is to enable MTS to reuse the resources occupied by the current object instance. Using the `ObjectContext`, a business object can notify MTS that the current object instance is ready for reuse. This notification drastically improves resource management and enables MTS to effectively reuse memory resources. The process of reusing memory resources through the `ObjectContext` is known as Just In Time (JIT) Activation and As Soon As Possible (ASAP) Deactivation. Implementing JIT Activation and ASAP Deactivation is accomplished through the `SetComplete` and `SetAbort` methods of the `ObjectContext`.

The `SetComplete` method of the `ObjectContext` explicitly notifies MTS that the state of the business object is such that it can be freely reused. MTS can then reuse the resources dedicated to the current instance. If the object causes an error, the `SetAbort` method tells MTS that the business object can be reused, but whatever work was performed by the business object has failed. Both `SetComplete` and `SetAbort` enable MTS to reuse the currently occupied resources, but `SetAbort` is specifically used by MTS to rollback any transactions that this object was supporting. Transactions are covered in detail in chapter 6, but for now recognize that both these methods simply enable JIT/ASAP resource management.

Although calling the `SetComplete` method ensures that the memory resources of the middle tier are properly managed, you might be wondering what happens to the client application if it is still holding an object variable reference to the now defunct object. What happens when the client uses the same instance variable to call the business object again? The answer is simple. MTS creates a new instance of the desired object and provides it to the calling client. Although the new instance is completely different from the original instance, the client is unaware of any differences and happily accepts services from the new instance.

TIP

Key Principle: When creating clients that work with MTS components, you should declare variables at higher levels of scope rather than constantly creating instances and then setting them to Nothing in the client code. Let the `ObjectContext` manage the life of the business object for you. This principle goes by the phrase "Create Instances Early, Release Them Late".

All this is made possible through the work of the `ObjectContext`. This is because at the time a client holds a reference to an object running under MTS, it actually communicates with the `ObjectContext` and not directly with the business object. The `ObjectContext` is capable of providing the appearance of a persistent business object to the calling client, while MTS recycles the objects behind the scenes. All this is done to ensure that clients cannot create instances in the middle tier and then simply hold them forever. Scalability is determined by the proper management of middle tier resources.

Because the calling client is not capable of holding an instance of a business object indefinitely, it stands to reason that the client cannot rely on the values of any variables within the component to be persistent across calls. The actual instance provided by MTS to a client might well be different each time the client calls a method. This is why you hear developers discussing stateless objects in MTS. Without object instance persistence, storing state in the object is futile.

TIP

Key Principle: Because MTS objects must constantly be recycled, they should not store application state.

Because state should not be kept in the business objects, we must move the stateful information out of the business object and into another tier. This is typically accomplished by returning stateful information from the Business Services layer to the User Services layer. This information might be transferred in any format as long as the business object and client object agrees on the packaging of the information. This might be as simple as returning a string from a function or as complex as returning a recordset. The type of data is much less important than the technique. In chapters 4 and 5, we discuss in detail ways to transfer stateful information between tiers. For now, simply recognize that if you cannot store state in the Business Services layer, it must be stored somewhere else. Figure 3.4 shows a conceptual diagram illustrating this point.

The notion of moving state away from the Business Services layer is not new. Many mainframe programmers yawn with boredom during this discussion because they have lived and died by these rules for a long time. However, those of us without a wealth of big iron experience do have a model we can draw on to understand scalability—the Internet. The Internet is the ultimate scalable application. After all, it has millions of users. The Internet, just as MTS, is also a stateless environment. You might not realize this, but every contact between the browser and the server is a single stateless transaction. Therefore, if an Internet application wants to store the state of an application, the

Internet application must move it from the server to the client. This is done through the use of *cookies*. Cookies are little bits of stateful information written by the Web server onto the browser computer. If you cannot remember state in one layer, move it to another.

FIGURE 3.4

Application state must be moved out of the Business Services layer.

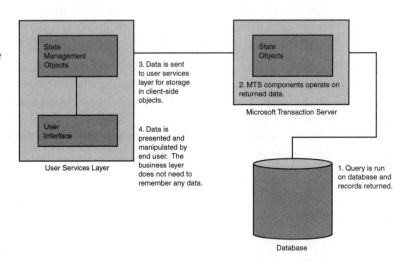

Internet application must move it from the server to the client. This is done through the use of *cookies*.

TIP

Key Principle: If you create a method in a component intended for use under MTS, be sure to pass all arguments By Value using the ByVal keyword. Because ByVal arguments are passed as a copy of the original data, they are much more efficient in distributed applications.

QUICK CHECK 3.1:

INVESTIGATING OBJECT STATE

1. Using the CD-ROM for the book, locate the directory TEMPLATES\QUICK CHECK3.1. This directory contains a partially completed project you can use to investigate state management in MTS.

2. On your hard drive, create a new directory with the Windows Explorer named MTS\QUICK CHECK3.1. Copy the contents from the CD-ROM directory into the new directory you just created.

3. Because the CD-ROM creates read-only copies of the project files, select all the files you copied, right-click them and select **Properties** from the pop-up menu. In the properties dialog, uncheck the **Read-Only** flag. Close the dialog.

4. Start Visual Basic. Open the project group named QUICK CHECK3.1.VBG. This project should have an ActiveX DLL project named Stateful and a Standard EXE project named FrontEnd.

5. Select the **Stateful** project in the Project Explorer. Using the references dialog, set a reference to the Microsoft Transaction Server Type Library.

6. In the **Stateful** project, locate the class module named Customer. Open the code window for the Customer class. In this class, you will see that it has one property defined using a set of property procedures. This property is the Name property and it is implemented using private data members and property procedures. The difference, however, is that the property procedures make calls to the ObjectContext after every read and write to notify MTS that the instance can be recycled. Also note that the property is initialized to a value of "EMPTY" by the class. The code in Listing 3.1 shows the Property Let procedure from class Customer.

LISTING 3.1 NAME Property Let PROCEDURE.

```
Public Property Let Name(strName As String)

On Error GoTo NameErr

    'Get Object Context
    Dim objContext As MTxAS.ObjectContext
    Set objContext = GetObjectContext()

    'Return value
     m_Name = strName

    'Tell MTS we are done
     objContext.SetComplete

NameExit:
    Exit Property

NameErr:
    'Tell MTS we failed
     objContext.SetAbort

    Debug.Print Err.Description
    App.StartLogging App.Path & "\error.log", vbLogToFile
```

continues

continued

```
        App.LogEvent Err.Description, vbLogEventTypeError
        Resume NameExit

End Property
```

7. Now locate the FrontEnd project in the Project Explorer. This project has a single form in it named frmClient. Figure 3.5 shows the user interface for the form.

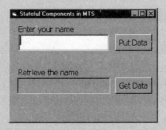

Figure 3.5

This form allows you to read and write the Name *property.*

8. With the FrontEnd project selected, use the references dialog to set a reference to the Stateful project.

9. In this form, you will add some code to read and write to the Name property of the Customer class. Double click the **Put Data** button to open the code window. Under the cmdPut_Click event, add the following code to write the data from the TextBox into the Name property.

    m_Customer.Name = txtName.Text

10. Now locate the click event for the CommandButton cmdGet. This button reads the data back from the Customer class and displays it in a Label control. Add the following code to the cmdGet_Click event to read the Name property and display the data.

    lblName.Caption = m_Customer.Name

11. After you have added the new code, save your project. Now compile both projects by selecting File, Make Project Group from the menu. After the projects are compiled, exit Visual Basic.

12. Before you can run the project, you must place it under MTS control. Open the MTS Explorer and create a new package named Stateful using the package wizard. Run the package as the Interactive User.

13. Using the Component Wizard, install the `Customer` class in the new package.

14. After the component is installed in MTS, run the compiled FrontEnd project. Type your name into the TextBox and set it into the `Customer` class. Now try to read the property. What is the result?

When first explained, all this creating and destroying can seem a little confusing. After all, we can't really see the resource recycling. MTS, however, offers a way for you to gain notification in your business object when it is created by a client or destroyed through the `SetComplete` and `SetAbort` methods. This additional control comes in the form of a special interface known as the ObjectControl interface. The ObjectControl interface has three methods: `CanBePooled`, `Activate`, and `Deactivate`.

CanBePooled Method

The `CanBePooled` method is used to notify MTS if your object is capable of true object instance pooling. If your object returns True when MTS calls this method, MTS uses object instance pooling to manage your business object. If you remember, however, earlier in this book we stated emphatically that MTS did not support object instance pooling. Instead, MTS simply creates and destroys instances with each client call. So what good is the `CanBePooled` method? The answer is that Microsoft has provided `CanBePooled` for forward compatibility. Microsoft has promised true object instance pooling at a future date. Objects that implement the `CanBePooled` method will easily take advantage of pooling without rewriting when MTS supports it. For now, `CanBePooled` is optional and returning True from the method won't do anything.

Even though returning True from the `CanBePooled` method currently has no effect on your components, you should be careful about adding this method thoughtlessly to your classes. The reason that MTS does not currently support object pooling is because the Apartment threading model is ill-suited to handle the concurrency issues raised by pooling. In order to successfully pool, an object must support free threading. Free threading removes the restrictions placed on threads that run under Apartment threading that keep threads from colliding.

WARNING

Visual Basic components do not support free threading, so when pooling is implemented, legacy components that have this interface might run into problems if they return True.

3

DESIGNING COMPONENTS FOR MTS

Activate and Deactivate Methods

The `Activate` and `Deactivate` methods are more useful and interesting than the `CanBePooled` method. `Activate` and `Deactivate` are called by MTS whenever an object is taken out of or returned to the object pool. The `Activate` method is called whenever an object is removed from the object pool and assigned to a client. `Deactivate` occurs when the object is returned to the pool. Once again, however, because MTS does not really support pooling, these methods currently fire when an object is created or destroyed. This means that `Activate` and `Deactivate` are essentially identical to `Initialize` and `Terminate`. After MTS implements true pooling, however, the `Initialize` and `Terminate` events no longer fires for each client call as they do now. Objects only `Initialize` the first time their package starts them and `Terminate` only when the complete package is shut down. Under those circumstances, the `Activate` and `Deactivate` methods become critical substitutes for `Initialize` and `Terminate`.

Using these methods, you can perform special work when your object is activated or deactivated as well as track the life of the object. Activation and deactivation are tracked on a per client basis. Therefore, the `Activate` and `Deactivate` events always fire in pairs for a given client. Activation occurs when a method call is made and `Deactivate` occurs when `SetComplete` or `SetAbort` is called.

QUICK CHECK 3.2:

THE OBJECTCONTROL INTERFACE

1. Using the CD-ROM for the book, locate the directory TEMPLATES\QUICK CHECK3.2. This directory contains a partially completed project you can use to investigate the ObjectControl interface.

2. On your hard drive, create a new directory with the Windows Explorer named MTS\QUICK CHECK3.2. Copy the contents from the CD-ROM directory into the new directory you just created.

3. Because the CD-ROM creates read-only copies of the project files, select all the files you copied, right-click them and select **Properties** from the pop-up menu. In the properties dialog, uncheck the **Read-Only** flag. Close the dialog.

4. Start Visual Basic and open the project group QUICK CHECK3.2.VBG. In the Project Explorer, you should see two projects. One is an ActiveX DLL project named Pool and the other is a Standard EXE named FrontPool.

5. Select the **Pool** project in the Project Explorer. Using the references dialog, set a reference to the **Microsoft Transaction Server Type Library**.

6. Select the **FrontPool** project in the Project Explorer. Using the references dialog, set a reference to the **Pool** project.

7. In the **FrontPool** project, locate the form. Open the code window for the form and note how we have declared a variable in the [General][Declarations] section. This means that the scope of the variable is the life of the form. At first glance it appears that the form keeps the instance alive indefinitely. The truth is, however, that the `ObjectContext` manages the life of the business object for us.

8. In the **Pool** project, locate the class module named `Test`. Open the code window for class `Test`. The code window should be empty with the exception of an `Option Explicit` statement.

9. Class `Test` implements the `ObjectControl` interface to receive `Activate` and `Deactivate` notifications from MTS. In the [General][Declarations] section of class `Test`, add the following code to use the `ObjectControl` interface:

   Implements MTxAS.ObjectControl

10. In order to implement the `ObjectControl` interface, you must select `ObjectControl` from the object box in the code window. When you do, the procedure box displays the three methods `Activate`, `CanBePooled`, and `Deactivate`. Add these three methods to class `Test`. Figure 3.6 shows the code window and methods.

FIGURE 3.6

Add the three methods from the `ObjectControl` interface to class `Test`.

continues

continued

11. The `CanBePooled` method simply returns a Boolean value indicating if the object supports pooling. Because Visual Basic components do not support free threading, we will simply return False from this method. However, the return value currently has no effect on the way in which MTS handles your components. Add the following code to the `CanBePooled` method to return False.

```
ObjectControl_CanBePooled = False
```

12. When the `Activate` and `Deactivate` methods are called, we simply use the logging capability of the `App` object to write the event out to a log file. In this way, we can keep track of the life of an instance. Add code to both the `Activate` and `Deactivate` methods to write to a log file. Listing 3.2 shows the completed methods after you add the code.

LISTING 3.2   CODE FOR `Activate` AND `Deactivate` METHODS.

```
Private Sub ObjectControl_Activate()
    App.StartLogging App.Path & "\pool.log", vbLogToFile
    App.LogEvent "MTS Test Object Activated!"
End Sub

Private Sub ObjectControl_Deactivate()
    App.StartLogging App.Path & "\pool.log", vbLogToFile
    App.LogEvent "MTS Test Object Deactivated!"
End Sub
```

13. The purpose of this exercise is to show how the `ObjectContext` effects the life cycle of an instance. In order to do this, we will add a method to the class that does not call the `ObjectContext`. This prevents MTS from recycling the object. Add the code in Listing 3.3 to class `Test` to create a method call that prevents recycling.

LISTING 3.3   CODE FOR A `KeepAlive` METHOD

```
Public Function KeepAlive() As String

    'This function does not
    'release the business object
    KeepAlive = "Help! I can't recycle!"

End Function
```

14. When creating methods that allow recycling, you must get an instance of your `ObjectContext` and call the `SetComplete` method when the current

function ends. Add the code in Listing 3.4 to class Test to provide a method call that allows recycling.

LISTING 3.4   CODE FOR THE Recycle METHOD

```
Public Function Recycle() As String

    'This function uses JIT/ASAP
    'Resource Management

    Dim objContext As MTxAS.ObjectContext
    Set objContext = GetObjectContext()

    objContext.SetComplete

    Recycle = "I'm Recycling! Check the log file!"

End Function
```

15. After you have coded the application, compile the project by selecting File, Make Project Group from the menu. When the project compiles successfully, exit Visual Basic.

16. Before you can run the project, you must place it under MTS control. Open the MTS Explorer and create a new package named Pool using the package wizard. Run the package as the Interactive User.

17. Using the component wizard, install the Test class in the new package.

18. After you have set up the package and component, run the FrontPool executable. This form allows you to call either the KeepAlive or Recycle methods in class Test. Figure 3.7 shows the form.

FIGURE 3.7

Use this form to call the MTS component.

continues

3

DESIGNING
COMPONENTS FOR
MTS

continued

> 19. Start by calling the `KeepAlive` method. When you make this call, you will notice the characteristic delay that occurs when MTS first starts a package. When the package starts, however, you will receive a return value. At this point, locate and open the log file POOL.LOG. This file contains a single entry indicating that the `Activate` method has fired, but the `Deactivate` method has not. This means that the object is still alive and using resources. *This is bad!*
>
> 20. Now use the front end to call the `Recycle` method. When you receive a return value, open the POOL.LOG file again. This time you'll see that both the `Activate` and `Deactivate` methods fired. This means that the object instance existed for the minimum amount of time necessary to process your request. This is good!

MANAGING SHARED PROPERTIES

Although we have gone to great lengths to explain the pitfalls of stateful components in a distributed application, sometimes you simply require the ability to retain state in the middle tier. For these times, MTS provides a facility for maintaining state across the entire application known as the *Shared Property Manager (SPM)*.

The Shared Property Manager is a separate facility of MTS for use with stateful information in the business layer. The SPM allows you to create property groups that can subsequently contain individual property data. Using this hierarchical scheme, developers can store and share state information within components in the same package. The SPM creates a sort of global variable that can easily be accessed by all clients using a specific package. The SPM consists of three objects in a hierarchy: the `SharedPropertyGroupManager`, the `SharedPropertyGroup`, and the `SharedProperty` object. Figure 3.8 shows the SPM object model.

Before you can use the SPM in a project, you must set a reference to the object model. The SPM model is independent of the standard MTS type library. You will find this reference listed as Shared Property Manager Type Library. When set, you can begin to code to the model using the following objects.

FIGURE 3.8
The Shared Property Manager can be used to maintain application state.

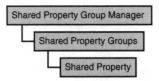

SharedPropertyGroupManager

The `SharedPropertyGroupManager` is the topmost object in the hierarchy and is considered a resource dispenser. Just as the resource dispensers for ODBC and OLEDB, the `SharedPropertyGroupManager` allows resources to be shared among many clients. In this case, the clients share data.

MTS applications cannot use global variables in modules because the `ObjectContext` prevents the proper synchronization of clients and variables. The `SharedPropertyGroupManager` properly manages concurrency issues allowing for locking data when it is being changed by a client. In order to properly handle these concurrency issues, components that want to share data must be placed within the same package. Never make a call from one package to another and attempt to share state.

SharedPropertyGroup

The `SharedPropertyGroup` is created through the use of the `CreatePropertyGroup` method of the `SharedPropertyGroupManager` object. This object is used to define a group of shared data. It does not represent the actual shared data, but rather a logical grouping of related data.

SharedProperty

The `SharedProperty` object actually contains the shared data. It is returned from the `CreateProperty` method of the `SharedPropertyGroup` object. When this object is created, you can use it to read and write data shared by objects in the same package.

Because no calling client knows for sure whether or not another client has already created this property, each call to the `SharedProperty` is treated as if it were the first call. In this way, the `CreateProperty` method of the `SharedPropertyGroup` is always executed. The second argument of the `CreateProperty` method is a Boolean that is True if the `SharedProperty` already exists. Components use this returned value to determine if the value of the `SharedProperty` should be initialized or updated.

QUICK CHECK 3.3:

THE SHARED PROPERTY MANAGER

1. Using the CD-ROM for the book, locate the directory TEMPLATES\QUICK CHECK3.3. This directory contains a partially completed project you can use to investigate shared properties in MTS.

2. On your hard drive, create a new directory with the Windows Explorer named MTS\QUICK CHECK3.3. Copy the contents from the CD-ROM directory into the new directory you just created.

3. Because the CD-ROM creates read-only copies of the project files, select all the files you copied, right-click them and select **Properties** from the pop-up menu. In the properties dialog, uncheck the **Read-Only** flag. Close the dialog.

4. Start Visual Basic and open the project group file QUICK CHECK3.3.VBG. In the Project Explorer, you should see a Standard EXE project named FrontEnd and an ActiveX DLL named SharedProperty. This project builds a shared property that allows you to count the number of users that have used an application.

5. Select the **SharedProperty** project in the Project Explorer. Open the references dialog and set a reference to the **Shared Property Manager Type Library** and **Microsoft Transaction Server Type Library**.

6. Select the **FrontEnd** project in the Project Explorer. Using the references dialog, set a reference to the SharedProperty project.

7. In the Project Explorer, locate the class Count in the SharedProperty project. This object has a method named GetUserNumber that counts the number of users who access it . Listing 3.5 shows the function definition as it exists when you open the project.

LISTING 3.5 CODE FOR THE GetUserNumber METHOD

```
Public Function GetUserNumber() As String

On Error GoTo GetUserNumberErr

    'Variables
    Dim blnExists As Boolean

    'Get the Object Context
    Dim objContext As MTxAS.ObjectContext
    Set objContext = GetObjectContext()

    '***StartAdding Code Here!***
```

```
      'Get the Name of this computer
      Dim lngResult As Long
Dim strComputerName As String * 255
      strComputerName = String(255, vbNull)

      lngResult = GetComputerName(strComputerName, 255)

      'Return Value
      GetUserNumber = "You are client no. " _
      & objProperty.Value & " on " & strComputerName

      'Tell MTS we are done
      objContext.SetComplete

GetUserNumberExit:
      Exit Function

GetUserNumberErr:
      objContext.SetAbort
      GetUserNumber = Err.Description
      Resume GetUserNumberExit

End Function
```

8. Within this function, you will add the code to create a shared property. Add your code into the method at the point where the comment designates. This code creates a shared property. Start by adding the following code to create a `SharedPropertyGroupManager`.

```
Dim objManager As MTxSpm.SharedPropertyGroupManager
Set objManager = New MTxSpm.SharedPropertyGroupManager
```

9. When the `SharedPropertyGroupManager` is created, you can create a `SharedPropertyGroup`. This is done by calling the `CreatePropertyGroup` method. In this method, you can specify arguments that determine the nature of the locking. You can also specify when the shared property values are destroyed. Add the following code to lock the property whenever it is accessed and destroy the values when the package is shut down.

```
Dim objGroup As MTxSpm.SharedPropertyGroup
Set objGroup = objManager.CreatePropertyGroup _
("Users", LockSetGet, Process, blnExists)
```

continues

continued

10. When the property group exists, you can use it to create the property. The `SharedProperty` object is always created as if it were the very first time. The `CreateProperty` method returns a True value to the second argument if the property already exists. In this way, no client has to worry about whether or not another client has already created the property. Add the following code to create the new property and set its value.

```
Dim objProperty As MTxSpm.SharedProperty
Set objProperty = _
    objGroup.CreateProperty("Number", blnExists)

'Set Property
If Not blnExists Then objProperty.Value = 0
objProperty.Value = objProperty.Value + 1
```

11. When you have coded the application, compile the project by selecting File, Make Project Group from the menu. When the project compiles successfully, exit Visual Basic.

12. Before you can run the project, you must place it under MTS control. Open the MTS Explorer and create a new package named Share using the package wizard. Run the package as the Interactive User.

13. Using the component wizard, install the `Count` class in the new package.

14. When you have set up the package and component, run the FrontEnd executable. When you do, you will see it respond that you are User #1. Run a second instance of the form and see what happens. Now try closing both of the open instances and running the EXE again. What happens?.

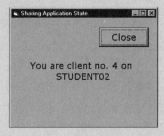

FIGURE 3.9

Use this form to call the SPM component.

OBTAINING SAFE REFERENCES

Because of the involvement with the `ObjectContext`, business objects can get into trouble when they attempt to pass references to themselves to another object. This need typically arises during callback situations in which one object registers itself with another. In these cases, MTS components should never directly pass a reference using the `Me` keyword. Instead, they must use the `SafeRef` function. This function provides a reference to the current instance that can be used by another component.

Callbacks are a beneficial way for objects to receive notification when key events occur in a distributed system. However, we have noted many developers having tremendous difficulty implementing callback schemes across a network. The biggest issues concern security. If a component needs to callback, it must do so under a valid security context.

Because a callback also amounts to a DCOM call, the roles of client and server are reversed. Therefore, a client that wants to receive a callback must be running on a DCOM server. This is usually not true with the typical windows client machine. All in all, callbacks are not trivial. At this point, they are probably not worth the trouble if they can be avoided.

UNDERSTANDING THREADS

MTS manages threads for all the objects running under its control. MTS not only manages the threads, but also provides a pool of threads for use by COM components. MTS handles thread pooling based on the type of threading supported by a COM component. Each COM component specifies the threading model it supports through a Registry entry named ThreadingModel. This entry can be seen directly from the MTS Explorer by shifting the explorer into Property View.

The threading model attribute seen in the MTS Explorer is read from the system registry where information about COM components under MTS control is maintained. You can find this information by examining the key

```
HKEY_LOCAL_MACHINE\
  Software\
    Microsoft\
      Transaction Server\
        Components\
          {clsid}\
            ThreadingModel
```

Visual Basic ActiveX components designed to run under MTS control should be ActiveX DLLs that support Apartment threading. Designating the components as ActiveX DLLs enables them to run in the process space of MTS while designating them as Apartment threaded enables them to support multi-threading. When creating COM components for MTS using Visual Basic, you must choose to create Apartment-threaded objects using the project property dialog.

TIP

Key Principle: Always designate your ActiveX DLL components as supporting apartment threading when you intend to place them under MTS.

EXERCISE 3.1: BUILDING MTS COMPONENTS

This exercise uses the principles taught in this chapter to create a common error-logging component for a distributed application. Client applications can use this component as a centralized log for all errors.

Step 1

Using the CD-ROM for the book, locate the directory TEMPLATES\EXERCISE3.1. This directory contains a partially completed project to start off this exercise.

Step 2

On your hard drive, create a new directory with the Windows Explorer named MTS\EXERCISE3.1. Copy the contents from the CD-ROM directory into the new directory you just created.

Step 3

Because the CD-ROM creates read-only copies of the project files, select all the files you copied, right-click them and select **Properties** from the pop-up menu. In the properties dialog, uncheck the **Read-Only** flag. Close the dialog.

> **WARNING**
>
> Visual Modeler will not work correctly unless the Visual Modeler Add-Ins are set to load at startup. Use the Add-In Manager to set this attribute.

Viewing the Model

A model is useful for understanding the overall structure of the application.

Step 4

Start Visual Basic and open the project group file EXERCISE3.1.VBG. In the Project Explorer, you should see two ActiveX DLL projects and one Standard EXE project. This project also has a model associated with it. To see the model, click a class module in one of the ActiveX DLL projects and select **Add-Ins, Visual Modeler, Browse Class Diagram** from the VB menu. This starts Visual Modeler. Figure 3.10 shows the model for this project.

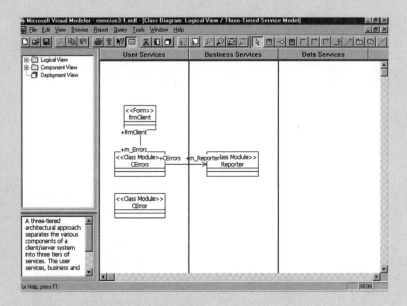

FIGURE 3.10
This model represents the architecture of the project.

Step 5

The model shows that this application uses a form as a front end and that two classes—
CErrors and CError—are contained in the User Services layer. In this design, any runtime errors generated by the User Services layer results in the creation of a CError
object. The CErrors collection contains all the CError objects until the client instructs
the collection to dump its data. When the collection dumps its data, the information from
all the CError objects in the collection are sent as a batch to the Reporter object. The
Reporter object then writes the information as a batch to a central log file.

Step 6

The project is largely complete, with the exception of the functionality that dumps the
error information. To complete this project, you will have to add a method to both the
Reporter class and the CErrors class.

Step 7

Double-click the Reporter class in the Visual Modeler to open the Class Specification
dialog. The specification dialog is used to manage the features of the class. Click the
Methods tab to see the methods defined for this class. Figure 3.11 shows the **Methods**
tab for the Reporter class.

FIGURE 3.11
Use the Specification dialog to manage features of the class.

Step 8

In the Methods tab, add a new method by right-clicking and selecting Insert from the pop-up menu. Name the new method LogItems and set its Return type as Boolean. This method is called by an instance of CErrors and passes the collected error information from the client.

TIP

You have to click in the **Return Type** column to activate a ListBox before you can select a Return type.

Step 9

While the specification dialog is still open, you can define an argument for the LogItems method. Arguments are defined by double-clicking the method entry in the list. Double-click the LogItems method to reveal the Method Specification dialog. Click the **Argument** tab. Figure 3.12 shows the **Argument** tab.

Figure 3.12

Use the Argument tab to add arguments to a method.

Step 10

In the argument tab, add an argument by right-clicking and selecting Insert from the menu. Name the new argument arrErrors and set its type as Variant. Close the Method Specification dialog by clicking the OK button. Then close the Class Specification dialog by clicking the OK button.

Tip

The OK button becomes enabled only after the type list is closed.

Step 11

Double-click the CErrors class to open the Class Specification dialog. Click the **Methods** tab. In the **Methods** tab, define a new method by right-clicking and selecting **Insert** from the menu. Name the new method Dump and set its Return type as Boolean. Close the Class Specification dialog when you are finished. This method calls the Reporter class and passes the collected error information.

Step 12

Save the model.

Coding the Application

Now that you have added the two new method definitions, you can use the Visual Modeler to generate the code for the classes.

Step 13

Select the CErrors and Reporter classes by clicking on each class and holding down the **CTRL** Key. After choosing the classes, select **Tools, Generate Code** from the menu. This starts the Code Generation Wizard.

Step 14

Using the Next button, work your way through the Wizard accepting the defaults until you reach the General Options step. In this step, clear all the check boxes before generating the code. When the check boxes are clear, push the **Finish** button to generate code for the new methods in your classes. Figure 3.13 shows the General Options in the Code Generation Wizard.

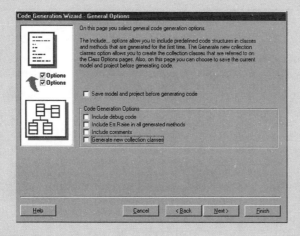

FIGURE 3.13
Clear all the General Options before generating code.

WARNING

You might receive messages from the Code Generation Wizard that it cannot locate a VBP file. Carefully note the name of the file and locate the file manually.

Step 15

When the code is generated, save the model and exit Visual Modeler. Return to Visual Basic and examine the CErrors and Reporter classes. You should now see a Dump method in CErrors and a LogItems method in class Reporter.

Step 16

Before adding code to the project, you must set the appropriate references. Using the following table, set the designated references for each project.

TABLE 3.1 PROJECT REFERENCES

Project	*Reference*
FrontEnd	ErrorEngine
ErrorEngine	ErrorLog
ErrorLog	Microsoft Transaction Server Type Library

Step 17

The LogItems method is used by the class Reporter to write all data out to a log file. This data is provided to the object in the form of a Variant array passed by the CErrors class. Add the code in Listing 3.6 to the LogItems method to write to the log file.

LISTING 3.6 CODE FOR THE LogItems METHOD

```
On Error GoTo LogItemErr

    LogItems = True

    'Get Object Context
    Dim objContext As MTxAS.ObjectContext
    Set objContext = GetObjectContext()

    'The errors are passed through
    'a Variant array
    Dim i As Integer
    For i = 0 To UBound(arrErrors)
        App.LogEvent _
            arrErrors(i, ntsNumber) & ": " & _
            arrErrors(i, ntsDescription), _
            arrErrors(i, ntsSeverity)
    Next

    'Tell MTS we are done
    objContext.SetComplete
```

```
LogItemExit:
    Exit Function

LogItemErr:
    'Tell MTS we failed!
     objContext.SetAbort

    LogItems = False

    App.LogEvent Err.Description, vbLogEventTypeError
    Resume LogItemExit
```

Step 17

The Dump method packages all the data in the CErrors collection into an array and passes the array to the Reporter object. Add the code in Listing 3.7 to the Dump method to complete the CErrors class.

LISTING 3.7 CODE FOR THE Dump METHOD

```
Dim objError As CError
Dim i As Integer

'Create a Variant array full of
'the error information
ReDim vErrors(Me.Count - 1, 3) As Variant
i = 0

'Fill the array
For Each objError In Me
    vErrors(i, ErrorLog.ntsSeverity) = _
        objError.Severity
    vErrors(i, ErrorLog.ntsNumber) = _
        objError.Number
    vErrors(i, ErrorLog.ntsDescription) = _
        objError.Description
    i = i + 1
Next

'Call the reporter
Dump = m_Reporter.LogItems(vErrors)
```

Building the Front End

Step 18

In the Project Explorer, locate the Standard EXE project named FrontEnd. From this project examine the frmClient form. This form accepts a numeric input corresponding to an error code and generates a runtime error. Figure 3.14 shows the form.

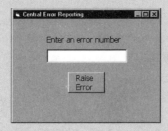

FIGURE 3.14
Use this form to generate runtime errors.

Step 19

Open the code window for frmClient. The form needs a variable to manage the collection of errors. In the [General][Declaration] section of frmClient, add the following variable declaration.

```
Private m_Errors As ErrorEngine.CErrors
```

Step 20

When the form loads, it creates an instance of the CErrors class to track all the runtime errors that occur on the front end. Add the following code to the Form_Load event to create the instance.

```
Set m_Errors = New ErrorEngine.CErrors
```

Step 21

When the form is unloaded, the collection is instructed to dump all accumulated error information to the central log. Add the following code to the Form_Unload event to dump the errors to the log.

```
If Not m_Errors.Dump Then
    MsgBox "Error During Dump!"
    Cancel = True
End If
```

Step 22

In this example, you can manually raise an error by entering an error number and pressing the Raise Error button. Add the code in Listing 3.8 to the cmdRaise_Click event to raise runtime errors in the form.

LISTING 3.8 CODE FOR THE cmdRaise_Click EVENT

```
On Error GoTo RaiseErr

    'Raise the error
    Err.Raise CLng(txtNumber.Text)
    Exit Sub

RaiseErr:
    'Add a new item to the collection
    MsgBox Err.Description, _
        vbOKOnly + vbExclamation, "Error Logging"
    m_Errors.Add vbLogEventTypeError, _
        Err.Number, Err.Description
    Exit Sub
```

Step 23

Compile the projects by selecting File, Make Project Group from the menu. When finished, save the project and exit Visual Basic.

Running the Project

Step 24

Open the MTS Explorer and create a new package using the package wizard. Name the package Error Logging and run it under the Interactive User. Add the Reporter class to the new package.

Step 25

When the Reporter class is in the package, run the compiled FrontEnd project. Try generating some runtime errors. Now unload the form. This dumpthe error information to the log. Locate the file called ERROR.LOG and open it in a text editor. You should see all the errors you generated with the form.

3

DESIGNING
COMPONENTS FOR
MTS

THE BUSINESS SERVICES LAYER

PART

II

IN THIS PART

ACCESSING DATA FROM MTS

PREREQUISITES

Before beginning this chapter, you should be familiar with data access techniques in Visual Basic. In particular, you should be familiar with the fundamental objects available in the ActiveX Data Objects (ADO) model. This chapter goes beyond the basics of ADO to discuss techniques appropriate for MTS applications.

Skills Learned

- 70-100(2): Identify which technologies are appropriate for implementation of a given business solution.
- 70-100(3): Choose a data storage architecture. Considerations include volume, number of transactions per time increment, number of connections or sessions, scope of business requirements, extensibility requirements, reporting requirements, number of users, and type of database.
- 70-100(8): Evaluate whether access to a database should be encapsulated in an object.
- 70-175(2): Assess the potential impact of the logical design on performance, maintainability, extensibility, scalability, availability, and security.
- 70-175(3): Design Visual Basic components to access data from a database in a multitier application.
- MTS(7): Describe data access methodologies appropriate for use with MTS components.
- MTS(8): Implement connection pooling in an MTS application.
- MTS(9): Implement collision resolution in an MTS application.

Every programmer will agree that data access is the backbone of all business applications. You would think that an area as important as data access would be mastered with great enthusiasm by developers, but our experience is that Visual Basic programmers shy away from the nasty details of data access. Understanding the intricate details of data access operations, performance tradeoffs, and design considerations is left to a few so-called "hard-core" programmers, whereas many developers are content to use bound data controls, grids, and dynamic cursors. In this chapter, we attack some long-standing data access practices that damage scalability and show you the correct way to interact with a database from an MTS application.

DATABASE CONNECTIONS AND RESOURCE DISPENSERS

As any programmer can attest, connecting to a database can be an expensive operation. Depending upon the database and the techniques used to connect, delays can be significant and run into many seconds. For this reason, many VB applications are written to connect to the database early in the application and retain a connection throughout the life of the application. Visual Basic developers believe they are improving performance by holding open database connections, but what they are actually doing is crippling scalability.

The problem with connecting early in an application and holding the connection open is that you have automatically limited the number of users the application can host. We can argue about the exact number, but clearly if you give a connection to each user, you will eventually run out of resources. Because scalability is directly related to the management of key shared resources, we have to develop a new technique for managing connections.

In the previous chapter, we described the correct management of shared memory resources through the use of the `ObjectContext`. This object allowed MTS to destroy an existing instance and recycle the resources for use by another client. Our approach to database connections will follow this exact strategy. Instead of connecting to the database and holding on, we will connect to the database only when necessary to perform an actual read or write with the database. This will make database connection resources available to more users.

When developers are first introduced to the notion of connecting only when necessary, they often counter with the argument that performance will suffer unacceptably. Without MTS you might have reason to be concerned; however, MTS provides a mechanism for improving connection performance in the form of a Resource Dispenser. In general, a resource dispenser allows a shared resource to be pooled and reused among many clients, and MTS provides two particular resource dispensers for use with database connections: the ODBC resource dispenser and the OLEDB resource dispenser.

The resource dispensers allow database connections made to ODBC and OLEDB databases to be reused and shared. This reuse of database connections eliminates any significant performance hit when making and breaking connections in an application. The resource dispensers work by taking database connections that are released by a client and pooling them so that subsequent clients do not have to open a new connection. Although the ODBC resource dispenser is available to VB developers, in this chapter, we focus on the use of the OLEDB resource dispenser with the ActiveX Data Objects (ADO) from Visual Basic.

Writing code to enable the OLEDB resource dispenser is not difficult, but requires a change in the way you think about data access. Instead of opening a connection at the beginning of an application, we will open the connection only when needed. In fact, we will write our components to open a database connection in each and every method where data access is required. In almost no case is a database connection maintained past a single method call. We open the connection at the beginning of the method, read or write to the database, and release the connection. This allows the OLEDB resource dispenser to pool the associated connection.

TIP

Key Principle: Open database connections for only the minimum amount of time necessary to read or write to the database. This principle is embodied in the phrase "get database connections late, release them early."

QUICK CHECK 4-1:

THE OLEDB RESOURCE DISPENSER

1. Using the CD-ROM for the book, locate the directory TEMPLATES\QUICK CHECK4-1. This directory contains a partially completed project you can use to investigate connection pooling in MTS.

2. On your hard drive, create a new directory with the Windows Explorer named MTS\QUICK CHECK4-1. Copy the contents from the CD-ROM directory into the new directory you just created.

3. Because the CD-ROM will create read-only copies of the project files, select all of the files you copied, right-click them, and select **Properties** from the pop-up menu. In the properties dialog, uncheck the read-only flag. Close the dialog.

continues

continued

4. Start Visual Basic. Open the project group named QUICK CHECK4-1.VBG. In the Project Explorer, you will find an ActiveX DLL project named Dispenser and a Standard EXE project named FrontEnd.

5. In the Dispenser project, locate the class named Pool. Open the code window for this class and you should see a single method named Connect. This method is used to establish a connection to the pubs database in SQL Server. It doesn't run any queries; it simply makes a connection.

6. Examine the code for the Connect method. In this code, you will see that the method immediately retrieves its ObjectContext. Just as with any well-written MTS component, SetComplete is called at the end of the method, and SetAbort is called if an error occurs within the method.

7. The heart of the method, however, is the connection code. Note that the connection variable is declared, a connection is made, and the variable is released—all within the same method. Also note that the connection object never specifically calls the Close method. Instead of calling the Close method, we simply set the connection object to Nothing. Listing 4.1 shows the portion of the code where the connection is managed.

LISTING 4.1 CODE SNIPPET FROM THE Connect METHOD

```
'Connect
    Set objConnection = New ADODB.Connection
    objConnection.Provider = "SQLOLEDB"
    objConnection.ConnectionString = _
    "Data Source=(local);UID=sa;PWD=;Database=pubs;"
    objConnection.Open

    'Tell MTS we succeeded
    objContext.SetComplete

ConnectExit:
    Set objConnection = Nothing     Exit Function
    Exit Function
```

CAUTION

The connection made by this project assumes that the SQL Server installation resides locally on the same machine as the component. It also uses the default system administrator credentials. If this is not your case, you may have to change the code.

8. The Dispenser project is called from the FrontEnd project. Locate the frmClient form in the FrontEnd project. This form is used to call the Connect method and make connections to SQL Server. Figure 4.1 shows the form.

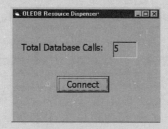

FIGURE 4.1

Use this form to make SQL Server connections

9. Compile the application by selecting File, Make Project Group from the menu. When the application is successfully compiled, save your work and exit Visual Basic.

10. Start the MTS Explorer. In the Explorer, create a new package using the Package wizard. Name the new package "Resource Dispenser." Run the package as the interactive user.

11. Using the Component wizard, place the Dispenser component into the package.

12. After the package is made and the component installed, you are ready to examine the pooling behavior of the OLEDB resource dispenser. To examine the pooling, you will need to start the SQL Server Profiler. This utility is an event collector that shows, among other things, when connections are made to SQL Server. You can find the SQL Server Profiler in the SQL Server program group. Figure 4.2 shows the profiler. (SQL Server 6.5 users should note that the SQL Performance Monitor can be used to show connections to SQL Server 6.5).

13. In the SQL Server Profiler, you will have to start a new trace to collect connection events by selecting File, New, Trace from the menu. In the New Trace dialog, name the trace "test." Click on the Capture to File box and name the file "test." After you set up the trace, the SQL Server Profiler immediately begins recording events.

14. Start the FrontEnd executable that you created. While you're monitoring the connection activity, click the Connect button. When the MTS package starts, you should see a new connection event listing the Windows/NT user name as well as the SQL Server login credentials for the new connection. Click the

continues

4

continued

> button again; this time you may see a second connection open. Click the button three or more times. Each time, your application will connect; however, the SQL Server Profiler will not show any new connection events. The pool remains steady, and subsequent connections are provided from the pool with minimal delay.
>
>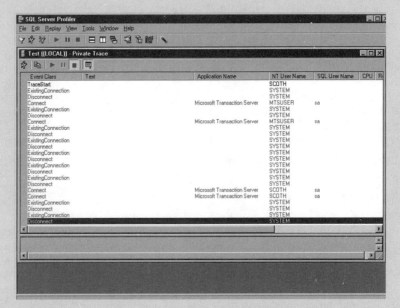
>
> FIGURE 4.2
> *Use the SQL Server Profiler to see connection events.*
>
> 15. After making several connections, sit back and watch the SQL Server Profiler. If you stop making connections to the database, you should see the number of connections in the pool begin to decrease after about a minute. Eventually, the pool will return to the original level that represents the connections being used by Windows/NT services.

Connection Pooling

Connection pooling offers the way for us to create scalable applications that efficiently share access to the database. However, pooled connections do not come without their own drawbacks. First of all, pooling database connections is always done on a per account basis. This means that database connections pooled by one SQL Server account cannot be used by another. Because a connection is opened using a certain set of security credentials, sharing across accounts would result in a glaring security hole. Additionally, because the connections are only pooled for about one minute, it is unlikely that a single user would get records, edit them, and write the changes back before the connections in the pool are released.

In order to use the OLEDB resource dispenser across multiple users, we must funnel all of the users through a single account. This one account then pools all of the connections for the application so that they can be used by any user. We normally establish a single account in SQL Server for all users that contains the limited number of permissions necessary to run the application logic. We typically set this account up under the user name "MTSUSER." Figure 4.3 shows the account in the Windows/NT account manager.

When the common account is established, we can force the components in MTS to run under this single account by setting the `Identity` of the package in the properties dialog. When the application is subsequently used by a large number of clients, they will ensure that the pool never reaches zero because someone will always be accessing the database. Figure 4.4 shows the Identity tab of a typical package we have set up to run under the MTSUSER account.

FIGURE 4.3

Set up a master account for packages to implement OLEDB connection pooling.

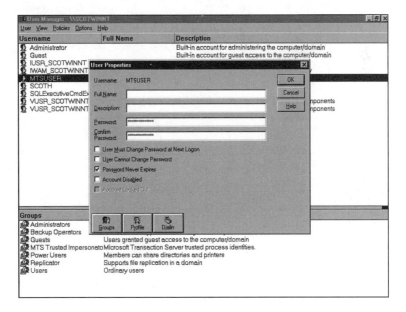

In addition to a single Windows/NT account, you may also have to specify a SQL Server account depending upon whether or not you are running SQL Server with standard or integrated security. We typically use standard SQL Server security and build a common data access account in SQL Server. The user name and password for this account are then used when building the connection string. You should set this account up with the

4

ACCESSING DATA
FROM MTS

minimum number of permissions necessary to accomplish the needs of the application. Many of the exercises in the book also require you to establish a Windows/NT account for MTS packages. You should create this account before completing this chapter.

FIGURE 4.4

Set the Identity of data access packages to a single master account.

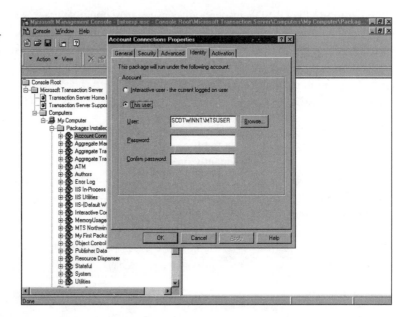

TIP

Key Principle: Create a Windows/NT account specifically for MTS components. This allows connections to be pooled under a single account. If you use standard security for SQL Server access, you should also establish a common account in SQL Server for data access.

When using a single account to access a database, you should not be concerned that the identity of the calling client is lost to the master identity. MTS gives you a way to retrieve the Windows/NT account of the user that is actually calling the data access component. This technique utilizes additional features of the `ObjectContext`. We discuss these and other security features in detail later in the book.

Along with concerns about accounts, connection pooling also raises issues with the nature of the connection itself. When creating any database connection, you must specify a number of features for that connection. These include things like the maximum number of rows returned and the initial catalog (also called the default database) for the connection. When a connection is pooled, these features are also pooled such that subsequent users of the pooled connection must live with the features of the connection as it was originally established.

All of this means that you must be careful when utilizing pooled connections in your components. You must establish consistent values for all of the properties of a connection. Do not, for example, set the maximum number of rows to 10 on a connection if another connection needs 50. MTS components should never alter the default database through SQL as in the statement "USE PUBS".

Returning Records Using Cursors

Database connection pooling fundamentally changes the way that you connect to a database, but it also affects the way in which you send records to a client. In the previous section, we showed that database connections are made and broken all within a single method call of an MTS component. This implies that the connection information is known only to the component running under MTS and not to the actual client wanting to view the data. This is a significant change because historically Visual Basic applications have contained intimate knowledge of the database directly in the user interface.

Developers have historically coded the database access directly into the front end so that they can use cursors to access the database. Cursors are not well understood by many developers, yet they have more impact on the overall performance of database applications than almost anything else. ADO provides four different types of cursors each with different features and performance implications.

adOpenDynamic

When you set the CursorType property of an ADO Recordset object to adOpenDynamic, you open records with a dynamic cursor. The dynamic cursor has the most features of any cursor in ADO. Using a dynamic cursor, you can scroll forward and backward through the recordset. You can also use bookmarks if they are supported by the OLEDB provider you are using. Dynamic cursors also reflect additions, deletions, and modifications made to the underlying database.

The problem with the dynamic cursor is that all of its functionality comes at a tremendous price. The dynamic cursor is the poorest performing cursor of all. Couple this type of cursor with pessimistic record locking, and you have a recipe for disaster. You should never use this cursor type in any application. You must especially not use it with MTS because the poor performance will destroy scalability.

adOpenKeyset

When you set the CursorType property of an ADO Recordset object to adOpenKeyset, you open records with a keyset cursor. The keyset cursor is similar to the dynamic cursor except that it does not reflect additions to the database in your cursor. It does, however, still reflect edits from other users. This type of cursor is less expensive than a dynamic cursor; however, it is still unusable for MTS applications.

adOpenStatic

When you set the CursorType property of an ADO Recordset object to adOpenStatic, you open records with a static cursor. A static cursor allows you to view and edit records, but it does not reflect any changes, additions, or deletions made by other users of the database. This cursor is a viable option for MTS applications. We can combine this type of cursor with the connection pooling strategy outlined earlier in the chapter to produce good results in MTS. We'll look at exactly how to use this cursor a little later in the chapter.

adOpenForwardOnly

When you set the CursorType property of an ADO Recordset object to adOpenForwardOnly, you open records with a cursor capable of only moving through the recordset in the forward direction. This is the default cursor type in ADO. When developers are first introduced to the forward-only cursor, they often wonder what good it is. After all, what do you do with a cursor that doesn't allow you to go backwards? How does the user scroll the data? The answer is that this cursor type is an excellent cursor for scalable applications because we can use it to rapidly retrieve data and store it in another location. We will examine how to use this cursor with MTS later in the chapter.

RETURNING RECORDS USING ADO

Most database applications that we see today rely heavily on cursors. In fact, many of them use the dreaded dynamic cursor. Developers like cursors because they make coding easy. The connection is simply held open while the user utilizes the dynamic cursor to navigate and edit records. In an MTS application, however, the client can have no knowledge of the database or the parameters required to connect to it. The connection lives in the shared MTS component, which is normally distributed on another machine. Because the client does not actually connect to the database, this immediately raises the question, "How do the records get back to the calling client?" The answer is that the records must be read by the MTS component, packaged, and sent back to the client as the return value of a function. Figure 4.5 shows a conceptual diagram of the relationship between an MTS component and a calling client.

FIGURE 4.5

Records are sent
to calling clients
as a return value
from an MTS
component.

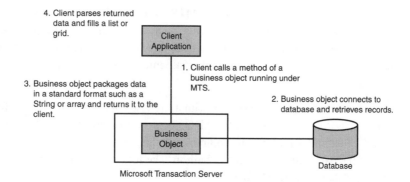

Sending data to a calling client as a return value can be accomplished in many ways. The fundamental requirement is that the calling client understand the format of the data being sent by the MTS component. In the simplest case, this data could be sent as a delimited string with no other special information. This may occur, for instance, when you want to populate a lookup list on a client. The data for the list is rapidly returned as a string and is used by the client to fill a list.

Because records are returned to calling clients without maintaining an open database connection, dynamic and keyset cursors are no longer attractive options. Instead of the heavy cursors, ADO offers you two excellent lightweight techniques for returning records at high speed from an MTS component. The techniques are known as the "fire-hose" cursor and the disconnected recordset.

Firehose Cursors

A firehose cursor is a rapid-delivery forward-only recordset. Don't let the name fool you—although it has the word "cursor" in its name, the firehose cursor is not really a cursor at all. It simply rapidly dumps data into a recordset object with very little over-head. Firehose cursors are high-speed, no frills recordsets. To create one, you must set the properties of the ADO `Recordset` appropriately before running the query. Firehose cursors require you to define a forward-only, server-side cursor with a cache size of 1. The following table shows the necessary settings to create a firehose cursor:

Property	*Value*
CursorLocation	adUseServer
CursorType	adOpenForwardOnly
LockType	adLockReadOnly
CacheSize	1

When you utilize a firehose cursor in MTS, you typically use it to rapidly fill a container with data. This container can be a String, an array, a user-defined type, or an object collection. It really doesn't matter what. The point is that you have rapidly transferred the data from the database and into another structure so that your database connection can be pooled.

One of the best ways to return data with a firehose cursor is to create a delimited string with the GetString method of the ADO Recordset object. This method allows you to specify a delimiter for both the columns and the rows. It then creates a string representation of the data with the delimiters built in. The following code shows how you might return a data string from a function:

```
Public Function Lookup() As String

    Dim objRecordset As ADODB.Recordset
    Set objRecordset = New ADODB.Recordset

    'Run Query
    objRecordset.ActiveConnection = _
    "Provider=SQLOLEDB;Data Source=(local);Database=pubs;UID=sa;PWD=;"
    objRecordset.CursorLocation = adUseServer
    objRecordset.CursorType = adOpenForwardOnly
    objRecordset.LockType = adLockReadOnly
    objRecordset.CacheSize = 1
    objRecordset.Source = _
    "SELECT pub_name FROM Publishers"

    objRecordset.Open

    'Pass string to client
    Lookup = objRecordset.GetString

End Function
```

Notice that in the preceding code, the recordset object is used without an associated connection object. ADO recordsets can open connections and run queries all alone if you set the Source property and ActiveConnection property before calling the Open method. When the recordset is open, GetString is used to return the delimited string. Because the recordset object is defined locally to the procedure, it is terminated at the end of the procedure. This function ensures that the database is opened for only the minimum amount of time necessary to get the data.

After you have retrieved the data, the client can receive it and use it to fill a list. The client needs to understand what delimiter was used to create the string so that it can be parsed. Our favorite way to do this is with the new Split function in Visual Basic. Split creates an array from a delimited string. If you assume the delimiter is a tab character, the following code would parse a delimited string and give you an array full of the entries:

```
Dim vData As Variant
vData = Split(ReturnedString,vbTab)
```

In addition to returning data in string format, many applications use Variant arrays to return data. Variant data types are capable of representing all kinds of data, including arrays. In this technique, you use the GetRows method of the ADO Recordset object and return data into a Variant. The GetRows method automatically converts a recordset into an array that can be transported from the MTS component to the business services layer. The following code shows how a set of data may be returned with this technique:

```
Public Function GetData() As Variant

    Dim objRecordset As ADODB.Recordset
    Set objRecordset = New ADODB.Recordset

    'Run Query
    objRecordset.ActiveConnection = _
    "Provider=SQLOLEDB;Data Source=(local);Database=pubs;UID=sa;PWD=;"
    objRecordset.CursorLocation = adUseServer
    objRecordset.CursorType = adOpenForwardOnly
    objRecordset.LockType = adLockReadOnly
    objRecordset.CacheSize = 1
    objRecordset.Source = _
    "SELECT * FROM Publishers"

    objRecordset.Open

    'Pass string to client
    GetData = objRecordset.GetRows

End Function
```

When the client receives the Variant return value, it already has the data inside formatted as an array. The array is a two-dimensional array representing columns and rows. You can determine the size of the data using the UBound function and read the data as you would any array.

QUICK CHECK 4-2:

FIREHOSE CURSORS

1. Using the CD-ROM for the book, locate the directory TEMPLATES\QUICK CHECK4-2. This directory contains a partially completed project you can use to investigate returning data in MTS.

2. On your hard drive, create a new directory with the Windows Explorer named MTS\QUICK CHECK4-2. Copy the contents from the CD-ROM directory into the new directory you just created.

3. Because the CD-ROM will create read-only copies of the project files, select all of the files you copied, right-click them, and select **Properties** from the pop-up menu. In the properties dialog, uncheck the read-only flag. Close the dialog.

4. Start Visual Basic. Open the project group named QUICK CHECK4-2.VBG. In the Project Explorer, you will find an ActiveX DLL project named Lookup and a Standard EXE project named FrontEnd.

5. In the Lookup project, locate the class "Publishers. This class is the component we intend to run under MTS. Open the code window for class Publisher.

6. In the code window for class Publisher, you will see a method named Query. This method connects to the pubs database in SQL Server and runs a query to return all of the publisher names. We want to use this data to fill a list in the FrontEnd project. Notice that the method returns a string. This is a delimited string generated by the GetString method of the ADO Recordset object. Add the code in Listing 4.2 to the Query method to run the query and return a delimited string.

CAUTION

The connection made by this project assumes that the SQL Server installation resides locally on the same machine as the component. It also uses the default system administrator credentials. If this is not your case, you may have to change the code.

LISTING 4.2   CODE TO BE ADDED TO THE Query METHOD

```
On Error GoTo QueryErr

    Dim objRecordset As New ADODB.Recordset
    Set objRecordset = New ADODB.Recordset

    'Get Records
    objRecordset.ActiveConnection = _
        "Provider=SQLOLEDB;Data
Source=(local);Database=Pubs;UID=sa;PWD=;"
objRecordset.CacheSize = 1
    objRecordset.CursorLocation = adUseServer
    objRecordset.CursorType = adOpenForwardOnly
    objRecordset.LockType = adLockReadOnly
    objRecordset.Source = _
    "SELECT pub_name FROM Publishers"
    objRecordset.Open

    'Return Data
    Query = objRecordset.GetString(, , , vbTab)

QueryExit:
    Exit Function

QueryErr:
    Query = Err.Description
    Resume QueryExit
```

7. In the Project Explorer, locate the FrontEnd project. This project uses the returned delimited string to fill a standard list box in the form frmClient. Figure 4.6 shows the form.

FIGURE 4.6
This form fills a list from the returned string.

continues

4

ACCESSING DATA
FROM MTS

continued

8. Open the code window for frmClient. In the code window, locate the `cmdFill_OnClick` event. This event fires when you click the button on frmClient. In this event, add the code in Listing 4.3 to fill the list from the returned string.

LISTING 4.3 CODE FOR THE `cmdFill_OnClick` EVENT

```
Dim strTemp As String
Dim intTemp As Integer
Dim varData As Variant

'Call Method
strTemp = objBusiness.Query

'Fill List
varData = Split(strTemp, vbTab)

For intTemp = 0 To UBound(varData) - 1
    lstPublishers.AddItem varData(intTemp)
Next
```

9. Save your project. In this exercise, we will not compile the project; however, you certainly can put the components under MTS control later if you want. All you should have to do is run the project inside Visual Basic, click the button, and the list should show a list of publishers.

Disconnected Recordset

An alternative to the firehose cursor is the disconnected recordset. The disconnected recordset is a set of records that are retrieved from the database into a standard ADO `Recordset` object, but after the query is run, the recordset object disassociates itself from the open connection. This creates a recordset that can be sent to a client as the return value of a function. The advantage of this type of object is that you can use all of the features of a recordset object without maintaining an open database connection. Just like the firehose cursor, the disconnected recordset is not a true cursor and has very little overhead. The following table shows the necessary settings to create a disconnected recordset:

Property	*Value*
CursorLocation	adUseClient
CursorType	adOpenStatic
LockType	adLockBatchOptimistic

After you have created the disconnected recordset and run a query, you must disassociate the database connection. This is accomplished by setting the `ActiveConnection` property of the recordset to `Nothing`. After you have dissociated the connection, you may freely pass the recordset as a return value from a function. Listing 4.4 shows how you might run a query in an MTS component and return a disconnected recordset.

LISTING 4.4   CODE SHOWING A QUERY IN AN MTS COMPONENT

```
Public Function Query () As ADODB.Recordset

    Set Query = Nothing

    'Variables
    Dim objRecordset As ADODB.Recordset
    Set objRecordset = New ADODB.Recordset

    'Run Query
    objRecordset.ActiveConnection = _
"Provider=SQLOLEDB;Data Source=(local);Database=pubs;UID=sa;PWD=;"
    objRecordset.CursorLocation = adUseClient
    objRecordset.CursorType = adOpenStatic
    objRecordset.LockType = adLockBatchOptimistic
    objRecordset.Source = _
    "SELECT * FROM Publishers

    'Get Data
    objRecordset.Open

    'Disconnect Recordset
    Set objRecordset.ActiveConnection = Nothing

    'Return the Records
    Set Query = objRecordset

End Function
```

After the disconnected recordset is received by the client, it behaves just like any other recordset. You can navigate the recordset with `MoveFirst`, `MoveLast`, `MoveNext`, and `MovePrevious`. You can edit the data and save the changes locally. You can even add and delete records. The changes are simply not permanent until you reconnect the recordset to the parent database and commit the changes.

4

ACCESSING DATA
FROM MTS

QUICK CHECK 4-3:

DISCONNECTED RECORDSETS

1. Using the CD-ROM for the book, locate the directory TEMPLATES\QUICK CHECK4-3. This directory contains a partially completed project you can use to investigate disconnected recordsets in MTS.

2. On your hard drive, create a new directory with the Windows Explorer named MTS\QUICK CHECK4-3. Copy the contents from the CD-ROM directory into the new directory you just created.

3. Because the CD-ROM will create read-only copies of the project files, select all of the files you copied, right-click them, and select **Properties** from the pop-up menu. In the properties dialog, uncheck the read-only flag. Close the dialog.

4. Start Visual Basic. Open the project group named QUICK CHECK4-2.VBG. In the Project Explorer, you will find an ActiveX DLL project named "Disconnect" and a Standard EXE project named FrontEnd.

5. Locate the class Titles in the Disconnect project. Open the code window for class Titles. In this class you will find a single method named Query. Notice that this method returns an ADO Recordset object directly. Add the code in Listing 4.5 to the Query method to create and return a disconnected recordset.

CAUTION

The connection made by this project assumes that the SQL Server installation resides locally on the same machine as the component. It also uses the default system administrator credentials. If this is not your case, you may have to change the code.

LISTING 4.5   CODE FOR THE Query METHOD

```
On Error GoTo QueryErr

    'Variable
    Dim objRecordset As ADODB.Recordset
    Set objRecordset = New ADODB.Recordset

    'Set key properties
    objRecordset.CursorLocation = adUseClient
    objRecordset.CursorType = adOpenStatic
    objRecordset.LockType = adLockBatchOptimistic
```

```
    objRecordset.ActiveConnection = _
    "Provider=SQLOLEDB;Data Source=(local);Database=Pubs;UID=sa;PWD=;"
    objRecordset.Source = _
"SELECT * FROM Titles"

    'Run query
    objRecordset.Open

    'Return records
    Set objRecordset.ActiveConnection = Nothing
    Set Query = objRecordset

QueryExit:
    Exit Function

QueryErr:
    Debug.Print Err.Description
    Resume QueryExit
```

6. Because the `Titles` class returns a recordset directly, you can use its data-binding features easily in a front end. In the Project Explorer, locate the FrontEnd project and open the frmClient form. This form takes the returned recordset and displays it in a databound grid. Figure 4.7 shows the form.

FIGURE 4.7

Disconnected recordsets can be displayed in databound controls.

7. The data is returned to the client when the GO! button is clicked. Add the following code to the `cmdGO_Click` event to retrieve the records:

   Set grdTitles.DataSource = objBusiness.Query

8. For this example, we will not build a package, although you can do that on your own later. Instead, simply save the project and run it in Visual Basic. When you click the GO! button, you should see the grid populated with records.

UPDATING RECORDS

Regardless of whether you decide to use a firehose cursor or a disconnected recordset, you will have still have to find a way to update the database to reflect changes made by the user. Perhaps you have already figured out that updating the database can be problematic because releasing the database connection means that the records are not locked. Therefore, another user can easily get the same records, edit them, and attempt to update the database at the same time you do. Solving this problem will require some work.

At this point, you need to stop and answer some questions about the application you are building. Although it is true that a possibility exists of overwriting changes made by other users, you have to decide what the probability is that two users will attempt to edit the same data at the same moment. The answer to this question affects how you deal with concurrency.

Imagine you are building an application that allows project managers to see and edit information about scheduling and milestones in ongoing projects. In this case, assume each project manager is in charge of a unique project and that no two managers make entries for the same schedule. In this case, it is clear that there is little or no possibility of one project manager interfering with another.

Contrast this application with an order fulfillment system used to process orders and send customer invoices. In this case, we have several people who are working on the system. Anyone on the system can update balances, print invoices, and update product inventory. In this case, we have a much higher possibility of problems. The amount of work you have to do to successfully implement this system is much higher than in the first example.

When you use firehose cursors, updates are normally performed by building SQL UPDATE, DELETE, or INSERT statements to directly manipulate the database. Users receive data in the form of a string, array, or collection. They edit the data in this format and then submit their changes. The changes are used to generate SQL statements that are fired directly against the database. Because there is no direct handling of concurrency, it can be easy to overwrite data.

Disconnected recordsets, on the other hand, are updated by reconnecting them to their original database. Reconnecting a recordset is simply a matter of establishing a new connection and setting the ActiveConnection property of the recordset. The database then attempts to imprint the changes onto the database. The changes made by the user are sent back to the database as a batch using the UpdateBatch method. The UpdateBatch method will fail if any of the attempted changes conflict with changes made by a previous user. The following code shows how an MTS component might receive a recordset as an argument and perform an update on the database:

```
Public Function Update _
    (ByVal objRecordset As ADODB.Recordset) As Boolean

    Update = True

On Error GoTo UpdateErr

    'Reconnect and attempt update
    objRecordset.MarshalOptions = adMarshalModifiedOnly
    objRecordset.ActiveConnection = _
    "Provider=SQLOLEDB;Data Source=(local);Database=pubs;UID=sa;PWD=;"
    objRecordset.UpdateBatch

Exit Function

UpdateErr:
    Update = False
    Exit Function

End Function
```

When you're using disconnected recordsets, it is important to understand how ADO goes about making an update. Disconnected recordsets determine what data to update by comparing current values in the database with the data that was originally retrieved from the database. This is possible because the disconnected recordset keeps a copy of the original data as well as the changes you make. That's right; it keeps two copies of the recordset for comparison. You can access the current value of a record by using the `Value` property. If you want to see the original value, you can access it through the `OriginalValue` property. The actual value in the database is read through the `UnderlyingValue` property. When a disconnected recordset is reconnected with the original database, it sends records that have been changed back to the database based on differences between the `Value` and the `OriginalValue` properties.

Although the `Value` and `OriginalValue` properties are sufficient to determine what records have changed, they are not enough to absolutely determine where the updates should be made. As an example of problems that arise when using disconnected recordsets, consider the following scenario. Imagine that you write a query to return the last names of all authors in the pubs database:

```
Select au_lname FROM Authors
```

Using a disconnected recordset, you can retrieve and display the list of names. Now suppose a user edits a name, changing, for example, the name "Green" to "Greene." The `Value` property of the recordset is now "Greene" and the `OriginalValue` property is "Green." Upon reconnecting to the database, we want to make our changes. The question, however, is how does the database know what record to update? With only "Green" and "Greene," it is impossible for the database to figure out where the data belongs.

There certainly isn't any guarantee that there is only one "Green" in the database—there might be hundreds of authors with that last name.

Now imagine that we write a slightly different query. This one will return not only the last name, but also the primary key. Now we have something to work with. Because the disconnected recordset contains the primary key, the database can easily figure out which record should be updated.

Whenever you write SQL statements or stored procedures for use with disconnected recordsets, be sure to return the primary keys for all tables involved in the query. This allows the data to be properly located during the update process. ADO looks for this primary key information in the WHERE clause of a SQL statement, therefore you must express the table joins in the WHERE clause as opposed to using the INNER JOIN syntax. The following SQL statement shows an example of a correctly written query:

```
SELECT * FROM Title, Authors WHERE Titles.au_id=Authors.au_id
```

Unfortunately, if you use the data tools that ship with Visual Basic to construct your SQL queries, they will be built with the INNER JOIN syntax. This is a problem for ADO because it specifically examines the WHERE clause for primary key information. The following code shows how the VB data tools might create the same query using the INNER JOIN clause:

```
SELECT * FROM Title INNER JOIN Authors ON Titles.au_id=Authors.au_id
```

The good news, however, is that if you used a stored procedure to generate the initial recordset, it does not matter which syntax you use. This is because the stored procedure is compiled and the WHERE clause is not available for examination anyway. Stored procedures are superior to creating SQL statements in code because the syntax is not important and the performance is better.

> **TIP**
>
> Wherever possible, use stored procedures in your MTS applications.

Handling Collisions

Before beginning to write any application logic to deal with update collisions, you must first determine what collisions are possible in your application and how much you care about them. Collisions occur in only a few well-defined cases. First, a collision may occur if you attempt to update a field in a record where someone else has already updated that record. In this case, the OriginalValue is not the same as the UnderlyingValue.

You may also get a collision if other fields in the record were updated. In this case, fields you have changed were not updated, but unrelated fields in the same record were. This can cause an update to fail.

Deleted records can cause several types of collisions. You may, for example, attempt to edit a field, but the underlying record was deleted. You may try to delete a record that has been modified by someone else. Finally, you may try to delete a record that was previously deleted.

All of these collisions are possible because scalable applications do not have the same concurrency controls as cursor applications. However, most of these collisions are not critical in a run-of-the-mill business application. In many cases, simply refreshing a client's data might be sufficient to overcome the problem. In any case, you must determine how critical these collisions are to your particular application.

You can control several aspects of collisions through the use of the Update Criteria property. The Update Criteria is not a property that you can access directly from a recordset object. Instead, it is a member of the Properties collection. The Update Criteria property must be set before you open the recordset but after you set the CursorLocation to adUseClient. The property is read-only after you run a query. You can set this value to one of four possibilities: adCriteriaKey, adCriteriaAllCols, adCriteriaUpdCols, and adCriteriaTimeStamp. The following code shows how to set the property:

```
Dim objRecordset As ADODB.Recordset
Set objRecordset = New ADODB.Recordset
objRecordset.CursorLocation = adUseClient
objRecordset.Properties("Update Criteria")=adCriteriaKey
```

The default value for Update Criteria is adCriteriaUpdCols. This setting determines conflicting updates based upon only the changed fields in your recordset. In this case, the UnderlyingValue is compared to the OriginalValue only for the fields you edited. If these values are different, the database assumes that a problem exists and fails the update.

The adCriteriaAllCols option causes all of the fields in the record to be examined for collisions and the update fails in the UnderlyingValue differs from the OriginalValue in any case. Setting Update Criteria to adCriteriaKey uses the primary keys found in your query to update the database regardless of whether someone else has made changes. Finally, you can use a timestamp field with the adCriteriaTimeStamp option.

In any case, a collision is generated when the update criteria is not met. A collision results in a trappable runtime error. Generally you will receive error -2147217864, which

4

ACCESSING DATA
FROM MTS

tells you that the targeted field could not be found for modification. This is usually because the OriginalValue property does not match the UnderlyingValue. Many times, this is not a big deal, so in the error handler, we might try to resynchronize with the underlying values and commit again. Resynchronizing is done by calling the Resync method. Using the Resync method, you can replace the OriginalValue property with the current UnderlyingValue. The Resync method allows you the option of resynchronizing just the current row, just the collided records, or the whole recordset. The following code resynchronizes the collided records and tries the update again:

```
objRecordset.Resync _
adAffectAllChapters, adResyncUnderlyingValues
objRecordset.UpdateBatch
```

If you attempt to resynchronize and the batch update fails, its usually because there are deleted records in the batch. This situation generates the runtime error -2147217887 "Errors Occurred." This is the generic cop-out message for updates and resyncs that fail for other reasons. When you receive this error, you can either completely refresh the data and start again, or you can try to manually resolve the collisions.

Manually resolving collisions is done by presenting the collided records to the user and asking for resolution. In order to see the collisions in a disconnected recordset, you must use the Filter property. The Filter property allows you to screen out records so that they are hidden within the recordset. They are not deleted, but they will now be available when you loop through the recordset. To Filter the disconnected recordset and show collisions, set the Filter property to adFilterConflictingRecords. After you have turned on the filter, you can loop through the records and display them.

One caution is appropriate here. If your update fails because you have attempted to inter-act with records that were deleted in the database, you will get an error -2147217885 when you try to examine the UnderlyingValue for the record. While you are looping through the collided records, be sure to trap this error. When you do, you can simply place an entry such as "DELETED" in the display to inform the user that the record is unavailable. In any case, when the collisions are resolved either through synchronization or manual updates, you should requery the database. This starts the client off with fresh data guaranteed to be good—for the moment anyway. Figure 4.8 shows a diagram outlin-ing the data access process with an MTS application utilizing disconnected recordsets.

FIGURE 4.8

Follow this process to successfully use disconnected recordsets.

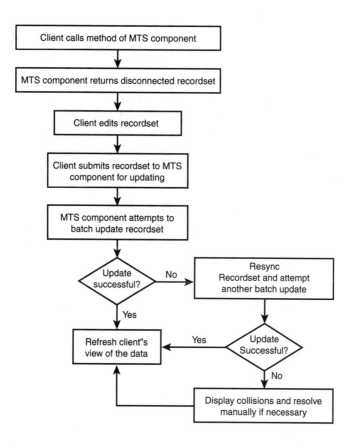

Before we leave the topic of collisions, let's step back and examine the importance of collisions. Although many programmers seem very concerned with collisions, in most business applications, they are relatively harmless. In fact, most applications can simply use the adCriteriaKey setting for the Update Criteria. This means that every change made by every user is simply written to the database without checking for many varieties of collisions. In this case you may have users overwriting each other's data with reckless abandon. So what? Does it really matter to your application if users write over each other? In most case, probably not. But if this is critical to your application, you will have to engage in more complex collision resolution.

SUMMARY

As you work your way through architectural decisions surrounding your MTS application, keep in mind that there are only two real choices for data access. The first choice is to use firehose cursors and the `GetString`/`GetRows` methods to read data and transfer it to the client. After data has been edited, it is sent back to the MTS components for update via direct SQL statements. This type of application has no built-in collision detection. If you care about collisions, you will have to write the detection code yourself.

The second viable technique is using the disconnected recordset to transport data between the tiers. This technique has the advantage of providing built-in collision detection and update capability. However, the collision resolution can be tricky as you `Resync` recordsets, examine record status, and retry updates. In either case, you will have to work harder than traditional applications that use cursors, but the payoff in scalability and performance will be worth the effort.

EXERCISE 4-1: DATA ACCESS WITH MTS

Accessing data in an MTS application requires significant changes in the way an application is built. In this exercise, you will investigate the use of firehose cursors and disconnected recordsets. Although this exercise does not complete the detailed architectural requirements to build successful MTS applications, it will teach you some of the fundamental principles upon which MTS applications are based.

Step 1

Using the CD-ROM for the book, locate the directory TEMPLATES\EXERCISE4-1. This directory contains a partially completed project to start off this exercise.

Step 2

On your hard drive, create a new directory with the Windows Explorer named MTS\EXERCISE4-1. Copy the contents from the CD-ROM directory into the new directory you just created.

Step 3

Because the CD-ROM will create read-only copies of the project files, select all of the files you copied, right-click them, and select **Properties** from the pop-up menu. In the properties dialog, uncheck the read-only flag. Close the dialog.

Step 4

Start Visual Basic and open the project group file EXERCISE4-1.VBG. In the Project Explorer, you should see one ActiveX DLL project named BusinessData and one Standard EXE project named FrontEnd.

Building the Business Object

The business component is a critical link between the display software and the database.

Step 5

Locate the class Books in the BusinessData project. This class performs all direct access with the database. It returns delimited strings or disconnected recordsets depending upon the method you call. Open the code window for this class.

Step 6

Locate the method Lookup in the code window. This method is used to return a delimited string for filling a list with the names of publishing companies from the pubs database. It uses a firehose cursor and the GetString method to generate the list. In the Lookup method, add the code in Listing 4.6 to create the return string.

4

ACCESSING DATA
FROM MTS

CAUTION

The connection string in this code assumes that you are using the default
system administrator login. If you are not, you will have to edit the code.

LISTING 4.6   CODE TO BE ADDED TO THE Lookup METHOD

```
On Error GoTo LookupErr

    'Variables
    Dim objRecordset As ADODB.Recordset
    Set objRecordset = New ADODB.Recordset

    'Run Query
    objRecordset.ActiveConnection = _
    "Provider=SQLOLEDB;Data Source=(local);Database=pubs;UID=sa;PWD=;"
    objRecordset.CursorLocation = adUseServer
    objRecordset.CursorType = adOpenForwardOnly
    objRecordset.LockType = adLockReadOnly
    objRecordset.CacheSize = 1
objRecordset.Source = _
    "SELECT pub_name,pub_id FROM Publishers"

    'Return data
    objRecordset.Open

    'Pass string to client
    Lookup = objRecordset.GetString(, , "¦", vbTab)
    Exit Function

LookupErr:
    'Error Logging
    Debug.Print Err.Description
    App.StartLogging "", vbLogAuto
    App.LogEvent Err.Description, vbLogEventTypeError
    Exit Function
```

Step 7

After the client builds a lookup list, the user can select a publisher from the list. This
value is used as a parameter for the Query method. The Query method returns a disconnected recordset object to the calling client with data about the books published by the
selected company. The Query method also allows you to pass in an enumerated value for
the Update Criteria. Because Update Criteria must be specified before the recordset
is opened, it is passed into the method. Add the code in Listing 4.7 to the Query method
to run the query and return a disconnected recordset.

The connection string in this code assumes that you are using the default system administrator login. If you are not, you will have to edit the code.

LISTING 4.7 CODE FOR THE Query METHOD

```
On Error GoTo QueryEr
    Set Query = Nothing

    'Variables
    Dim objRecordset As ADODB.Recordset
    Set objRecordset = New ADODB.Recordset

    'Run Query
    objRecordset.ActiveConnection = _
    "Provider=SQLOLEDB;Data Source=(local);Database=pubs;UID=sa;PWD=;"
    objRecordset.CursorLocation = adUseClient
    objRecordset.Properties("Update Criteria") = lngCriteria
    objRecordset.CursorType = adOpenStatic
    objRecordset.LockType = adLockBatchOptimistic
    objRecordset.Source = _
    "SELECT pub_id,title_id,title FROM Titles WHERE pub_id = '" _
& strPublisherID & "'"

    'Return data
    objRecordset.Open
    Set objRecordset.ActiveConnection = Nothing

    'Return the Records
    Set Query = objRecordset
    Exit Function

QueryErr:
    'Error Logging
    Debug.Print Err.Description
    App.StartLogging "", vbLogAuto
    App.LogEvent Err.Description, vbLogEventTypeError
    Exit Function
```

Step 8

After the client views and edits the records, they must be returned for updating. This is done through the Update method. The Update method reconnects to the database and attempts a batch update. If the update fails, the code can automatically call the Resync method and try the update again based on the check box on the Retry client form. If either the Resync method or the second UpdateBatch call fails, the code simply returns the recordset to the client for collision resolution. This is a key part of collision handling. You should examine the comments in the code carefully after you add the the code in Listing 4.8 to the Update method.

CAUTION

The connection string in this code assumes that you are using the default system administrator login. If you are not, you will have to edit the code.

LISTING 4.8   CODE FOR THE Update METHOD

```
On Error GoTo UpdateErr

    Set Update = objRecordset

    'Attempt an Update
    objRecordset.MarshalOptions = adMarshalModifiedOnly
    objRecordset.ActiveConnection = _
    "Provider=SQLOLEDB;Data Source=(local);Database=pubs;UID=sa;PWD=;"
    objRecordset.UpdateBatch

UpdateExit:
    'This exit routine is called if
    'the database cannot be updated.  The
    'recordset is not resyncronized.

    'Disconnect Recordset
    Set objRecordset.ActiveConnection = Nothing

    Exit Function

UpdateResync:
    'This exit routine is called if the
    'batch update attempt failed the first
    'time.  We will try to resync and run the
    'update again.  If it fails the second time,
    'then we use the normal exit routine and
    'the resync does not occur.

    'Resync the recordset
    objRecordset.Resync adAffectAllChapters, _
adResyncUnderlyingValues

    'Retry the commit
    objRecordset.UpdateBatch
```

```
'Disconnect Recordset
Set objRecordset.ActiveConnection = Nothing

Exit Function

UpdateErr:
    'Log the error
    Debug.Print Err.Number & ": " & Err.Description
    App.StartLogging "", vbLogAuto
    App.LogEvent Err.Number & ": " & _
    Err.Description, vbLogEventTypeError

    'Handle Errors
    'We try to resync if the error simply states that
    'the record was not found.  Resyncing may allow
    'the update to succeed.
    If Err.Number = ntsTargetFieldNotFound And blnRetry Then
        Resume UpdateResync
    Else
        Resume UpdateExit
    End If
```

Building the Client

This section builds the application front end. You will be modifying an existing form to call the business object.

Step 9

In the Project Explorer, locate the form `frmClient` in the `FrontEnd` project. This form is the primary user interface for the application. It contains a `ListBox` for the list of publishing companies and a grid for the title information. Figure 4.9 shows the form.

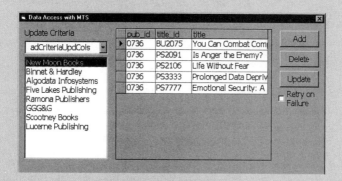

FIGURE 4.9

The primary user interface for the exercise.

Step 10

Open the code window for `frmClient`. When the form is first created, it must create an instance of the business object. Remember, clients declare business object variables at high levels of scope and allow MTS to manage the actual life cycle. This form already has a `Private` variable declared for the business object. Add the following code to the `Form_Initialize` event to create the instance:

```
Set objBusiness = New BusinessData.Books

'Set the default Update Criteria
cboCriteria.ListIndex = adCriteriaUpdCols
```

Step 11

After creating the business object, the list must be filled with publisher information. The list is filled by calling the `Lookup` method of the `Books` business object, which returns a delimited string. This string is then parsed and used to fill the list. Add the code in Listing 4.9 to the `Form_Load` event to create the list.

LISTING 4.9   CODE TO ADD TO THE `Form_Load` EVENT

```
'Variables
Dim strTemp As String
Dim intTemp As Integer
Dim intPipe As Integer
Dim varRows As Variant

'Call Method to get entries for ListBox
strTemp = objBusiness.Lookup

'Fill List from returned string
varRows = Split(strTemp, vbTab)

For intTemp = 0 To UBound(varRows) - 1
    strTemp = varRows(intTemp)
    intPipe = InStr(strTemp, "¦")
    lstPublishers.AddItem Left$(strTemp, intPipe - 1)
    lstPublishers.ItemData(lstPublishers.NewIndex) = _
    CLng(Right$(strTemp, Len(strTemp) - intPipe))
Next
```

Step 12

After the list is filled, the user can click on the list and retrieve all of the titles information for the selected publisher. The code window contains a custom procedure named `FillGrid`, which calls the `Query` method in the `Books` class. Add the code in Listing 4.10 to the `FillGrid` routine to run the query and display the results.

LISTING 4.10 CODE FOR THE FillGrid PROCEDURE

```
Set objRecordset = objBusiness.Query _
    (Format$(lstPublishers.ItemData(lstPublishers.ListIndex) _
    , "0000"), cboCriteria.ListIndex)
Set grdTitles.DataSource = objRecordset

'Enable buttons, if we have records
If objRecordset.RecordCount > 0 Then
    cmdAdd.Enabled = True
    cmdDelete.Enabled = True
    cmdUpdate.Enabled = True
Else
    cmdAdd.Enabled = False
    cmdDelete.Enabled = False
    cmdUpdate.Enabled = False
End If
```

Resolving Conflicts

This section shows how to handle collisions that result from multiple users.

Step 13

In this exercise, records may be edited directly in the grid. Updates are made to the database by calling the Update method. When the Update method is called, it returns a Boolean value indicating if the update failed due to conflicts that could not be resolved. If this happens, the conflicts are displayed in the form frmConflict. Figure 4.10 shows the form for displaying conflicts.

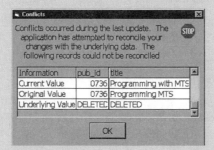

FIGURE 4.10

This form displays unresolved conflicts.

Step 14

Open the code window for frmConflict. This form contains a custom function for displaying the conflicts named ShowConflicts. This code sets the Filter property to uncover conflicts and display them in a grid. Because the conflicts may have been caused by a deleted record in the underlying data, we must provide error handling that checks for the special error -2147217885. This error will occur if you attempt to read the UnderlyingValue property of a row that was deleted. Add the code in Listing 4.11 to the ShowConflicts function to display unresolved conflicts.

LISTING 4.11   CODE TO ADD TO THE ShowConflicts FUNCTION

```
On Error GoTo ConflictsErr

    ShowConflicts = False

    'Variables
    Dim i As Integer
    Dim strStatus As String
    Dim strValue As String
    Dim strOriginalVal As String
    Dim strUnderVal As String
    Dim strFieldName As String

    'Set the filter to hide
    'all records except conflicts
    objRecordset.Filter = _
    FilterGroupEnum.adFilterConflictingRecords

'Initialize grid for display
    grdConflicts.Clear
    grdConflicts.Rows = 0
    grdConflicts.Cols = objRecordset.Fields.Count + 1

    'Fill Conflict Grid
    If objRecordset.RecordCount > 0 Then

        ShowConflicts = True

        Do While Not objRecordset.EOF

            'This grid displays the record status.
            'the current value, original value, and
            'underlying value so you can see exactly
            'why the update failed.

            strFieldName = "Information" & vbTab
            strValue = "Current Value" & vbTab
            strOriginalVal = "Original Value" & vbTab
```

```
                    strUnderVal = "Underlying Value" & vbTab
                    strStatus = "Record Status: " & _
                    GetRecordStatus(objRecordset.Status)

                    'Get property information for
                    'each field that conflicted
                    With objRecordset.Fields
                        For i = 0 To .Count - 1
                            strFieldName = strFieldName _
                                & .Item(i).Name & vbTab
                            strValue = strValue _
                                & .Item(i).Value & vbTab
                            strOriginalVal = strOriginalVal _
                                & .Item(i).OriginalValue & vbTab
                            strUnderVal = strUnderVal _
                                & .Item(i).UnderlyingValue & vbTab
                        Next
                    End With

                    'Show data in grid
                    grdConflicts.AddItem _
                        Left$(strFieldName, Len(strFieldName) - 1)
                    grdConflicts.AddItem strStatus
                    grdConflicts.AddItem _
                        Left$(strValue, Len(strValue) - 1)
                    grdConflicts.AddItem _
                        Left$(strOriginalVal, Len(strOriginalVal) - 1)
                    grdConflicts.AddItem _
                        Left$(strUnderVal, Len(strUnderVal) - 1)
                    grdConflicts.FixedRows = 1

objRecordset.MoveNext
        Loop
    Else
        Exit Function
    End If

    'Display Form
    Show vbModal
    Exit Function

ConflictsErr:

    'IMPORTANT!!
    'Referencing a row in a recordset
    'that is actually deleted, causes
    'a runtime error.  If any of the
    'conflicts occur because of deleted
    'data, we just indicate that and keep processing.
```

continues

LISTING 4.11 CONTINUED

```
If Err.Number = ConflictsEnum.ntsReferencedDeletedRow Then
    strUnderVal = strUnderVal & "DELETED" & vbTab
    Resume Next
End If

Exit Function
```

Running the Application

In this section, we run and test the application.

Step 15

After you have all of the code in place, compile the application by selecting File, Make Project Group from the menu. You do not have to put this project under MTS control because it is not coded to use the `ObjectContext`. If you decide later to use the `Books` class with MTS, you should add appropriate `ObjectContext` code in accordance with the principles discussed in Chapter 3.

Step 16

Locate the compiled FRONTEND.EXE file and run two copies of the executable. These two copies represent two different users of the application. Using the two running copies, try to create each of the different conflicts discussed in this chapter. This includes conflicting edits and attempted operations on deleted records. You should find that the project adequately handles the conflicts or informs you of conflicts that cannot be resolved.

PARTITIONING MTS APPLICATIONS

PREREQUISITES

Before beginning this chapter, you should be completely familiar with data access and the SQL language. You should have some familiarity with the use of stored procedures from SQL Server. You should also have a complete understanding of creating components for use in MTS including data access and the object context.

Skills Learned

- 70-100(6): Incorporate business rules into object design.
- 70-100(7): Access the potential impact of the logical design on performance, maintainability, extensibility, scalability, availability, and security.
- 70-175(15): Determine how to send error information from a COM component to a client computer.
- 70-175(16): Create a COM component that implements business rules or logic. Components include DLLs, ActiveX controls, and active documents.
- MTS(10): Encapsulate Data Access in the data services layer.
- MTS(11): Use interfaces to define the communication between components.
- MTS(12): Manage application state with collections and data binding.

Up to this point, our discussion of MTS applications has focused primarily on scalability through the management of middle-tier resources. To this end, we have investigated the management of threads, connections, and memory in the business layer. In this chapter, we examine maintainability, reliability, and performance through the use of partitioning among components in an MTS application. *Partitioning* refers to the construction of an MTS application as a series of small components that can easily be replaced or upgraded. Each of the components can be treated as a separate and distinct project where we can focus on the particular tasks performed. This approach makes it easier to build, maintain, and deploy distributed applications. We refer to small lightweight components as "fine" components and larger components with many functions as "coarse" components.

> **TIP**
>
> Key Principle: Many fine components are easier to create, deploy, and main-tain than few coarse components. Therefore, you should always build fine components.

All MTS applications begin as three-tier applications. We have already seen that three-tier applications consist of the data services, business services, and user services layers. Generally, we understand that the data services provide the means of access to the database. Business services provide the management of application logic, whereas user services displays data for the client. In previous chapters, we have investigated components in the business layer in detail. In this section, we investigate the relationships of the data services and user services to these components.

DATA SERVICES LAYER

The data services layer contains components that are responsible for reading and writing the database. In a typical MTS application, the database might be SQL Server with many stored procedures already part of the database. These stored procedures are considered to be part of the data services layer. Stored procedures have an intrinsic partitioning because the body of a stored procedure can be changed without affecting the code that calls it—provided, of course, that the number and types of arguments are not changed.

In an MTS application, we take the partitioning of the data services layer one step fur-ther. In particular, we normally use a class module to encapsulate each of the stored procedures in the database. Encapsulating a stored procedure in a class effectively separates it from the code that calls the procedure. This means that you can not only change the body of the stored procedure in the database, but you can also change the signature of the stored procedure because the class provides insulation through the signature of its methods. You can even go so far as to completely change the database, or even shift away from stored procedures for queries without affecting the rest of the application.

As an example, consider an application that needs to retrieve and display publisher information from the pubs database in SQL Server. Imagine that we write the SQL statement to return this information directly into the front-end code and call it from ADO. The following code shows an unacceptably tight link between the data access code and the SQL query statement:

```
Dim objRecordset As ADODB.Recordset
Set objRecordset = New ADODB.Recordset
objRecordset.ActiveConnection = _
"Provider=SQLOLEDB;Data Source=(local);Database=pubs;UID=sa;PWD=;"
objRecordset.Source = _
"SELECT pub_id,Pub_name FROM Publishers"
objRecordset.Open
```

The preceding code works fine until we decide to change the query. When this happens, we will have to recode, recompile, and retest the application. The solution to this problem lies in generating a stored procedure for the query. Because stored procedures are accessed by name, changes to the body of the procedure do not affect the calling code. This is the essence of partitioning—the ability to make changes within a component without affecting other components in the application. The following code calls a stored procedure named sp_GetPublishers:

```
Dim objRecordset As ADODB.Recordset
Set objRecordset = New ADODB.Recordset
objRecordset.ActiveConnection = _
"Provider=SQLOLEDB;Data Source=(local);Database=pubs;UID=sa;PWD=;"
objRecordset.Source = "EXECUTE sp_GetPublishers"
objRecordset.Open
```

Although stored procedures allow changes to the body of the query without recompiling the code, you cannot make any changes to the type and number of arguments without affecting the calling code. Changing the number or type of arguments alters the function "signature." The signature of a function is the combination of its name, number of arguments, and argument data types. If we want to partition an application to allow changes to the function signature, we must encapsulate the stored procedure within a class module. This class module can then be placed in an MTS component. In this case, we might

5

PARTITIONING
MTS
APPLICATIONS

create a method that accepts any number of arguments and calls the stored procedure in turn. The following code shows an example of a generic method that will accept any set of arguments:

```
Public Function Query _
    (Optional ByVal Args() As Variant)As ADODB.Recordset

    'Variables
    Dim objRecordset As ADODB.Recordset
    Set objRecordset = New ADODB.Recordset

    'Run Query
    objRecordset.ActiveConnection = _
    "Provider=SQLOLEDB;Data Source=(local);Database=pubs;UID=sa;PWD=;"
    objRecordset.CursorLocation = adUseClient
    objRecordset.Properties("Update Criteria") = lngCriteria
    objRecordset.CursorType = adOpenStatic
    objRecordset.LockType = adLockBatchOptimistic
    objRecordset.Source = _
    "EXECUTE sp_GetPublishers '" & Args(0) & "','" & Args(1) & "'"

    'Return data
    objRecordset.Open
    Set objRecordset.ActiveConnection = Nothing

    'Return the Records
    Set Query = objRecordset
    Exit Function

End Function
```

Notice how the Variant array index divorces the signature of the stored procedure from the signature of the method call. This sort of generic coding improves the partitioning of stored procedure calls from business logic. Of course, when you provide a Variant array as an argument, you have lost all of the type checking provided by Visual Basic. For this reason, you should always include assertions as the first line of code in the method call. An assertion is designed to detect when the passed arguments are outside the bounds of the expected values. The following code might be used with the preceding method to ensure that only two arguments are passed and that each argument has a value:

```
Debug.Assert UBound(Args) = 1
Debug.Assert Not(IsNull(Arg(0)))
Debug.Assert Not(IsNull(Arg(1)))
```

> **TIP**
>
> Key Principle: Always use assertions as the first part of any method call in a partitioned application. Visual Basic immediately breaks when an assertion is not true. Unfortunately, assertions do not do anything after an application is compiled; however, they can be valuable testing and debugging tools.

QUICK CHECK 5-1:

CREATING AND MANAGING STORED PROCEDURES

1. This exercise is designed to show you how to create and manage stored procedures in SQL Server using various tools and techniques. These skills are important because they are used in several other hands-on exercises in the book. This book cannot provide exhaustive coverage of stored procedures or Transact SQL, so if you need additional information, consult other sources.

2. You can create stored procedures easily from any of three different utilities. These include the SQL Enterprise Manager, the Microsoft Data Tools that ship with Visual Basic, and the Query Analyzer utility that ships with SQL Server. (In SQL Server 6.5, the Query Analyzer utility is called ISQL_w.) To start, open the SQL Enterprise Manager and locate the pubs database. (In SQL Server 6.5, the Enterprise Manager will look a little different, but you can still manage stored procedures from it.) Figure 5.1 shows the Enterprise Manager.

3. Locate the Databases folder and open it. In the folder, you will find the pubs database. Under the pubs database, locate the Stored Procedures folder. This is where all of the stored procedures are defined. Right-click this folder and select **New Stored Procedure** from the menu. This will open the New Stored Procedure dialog. In this dialog, you can create and edit stored procedures. Figure 5.2 shows this dialog.

4. In this dialog, create a new stored procedure by typing the code in Listing 5.1 into the dialog. Note that you should completely replace any code that is already in the dialog with this code.

continues

5

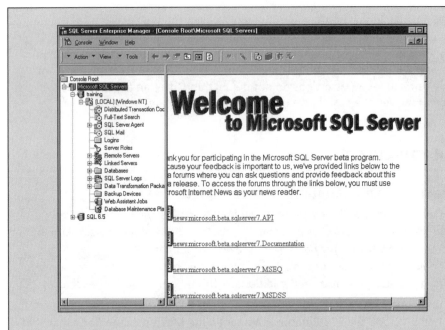

FIGURE 5.1

The SQL Enterprise Manager is used to manage databases and stored procedures.

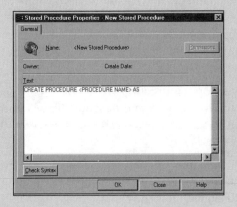

FIGURE 5.2

Use this dialog to create and edit stored procedures.

LISTING 5.1 STORED PROCEDURE BODY

```
Create Procedure sp_GetTitlesByAuthor
@LastName varchar(50)
As
SELECT titles.title, authors.au_lname, publishers.pub_name,
titleauthor.title_id,titles.pubdate FROM authors
INNER JOIN titleauthor ON authors.au_id = titleauthor.au_id
INNER JOIN titles ON titleauthor.title_id = titles.title_id
INNER JOIN publishers ON titles.pub_id = publishers.pub_id
WHERE au_lname = @LastName
    return (0)
```

5. After the code is written, save it by clicking the OK button in the dialog. Notice that this stored procedure requires a single input parameter, @LastName. This parameter is used in the WHERE clause of the procedure. This value is normally passed in from Visual Basic code as an ADO Parameter object.

6. One of the key concepts in managing stored procedures is being able to save them as scripts. You can save stored procedures from the database by right-clicking the database and choosing Tasks, Generate SQL Scripts from the pop-up menu. This opens the Generate SQL Scripts dialog. Figure 5.3 shows this dialog.

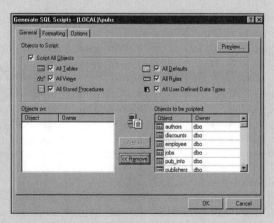

FIGURE 5.3

Use this dialog to generate scripts for database objects.

continues

5

PARTITIONING
MTS
APPLICATIONS

7. Save the stored procedure you just created by selecting it in the left-hand list and moving it to the right-hand list. When you have moved the stored procedure, click the OK button. You will be prompted to save the script file. Name the file MYPROCEDURE and save it to your desktop. The script will automatically be appended with the .SQL extension.

8. Close the SQL Enterprise Manager and start Visual Basic 6.0. You do not need a specific project open in Visual Basic to use the data tools, so simply open a new Standard EXE project. When the project is open, access the data tools by selecting View, Data View Window.

9. In the data tools, right-click the Data Links folder. Add a new data link to the pubs database. When you have established the link, you should see a Stored Procedures folder with the new stored procedure name listed. Double-click the stored procedure, and Visual Basic opens the procedure for editing. Figure 5.4 shows the stored procedure in the data tools.

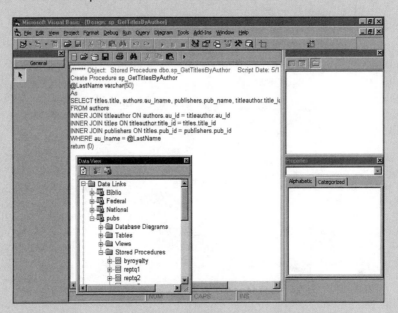

FIGURE 5.4
The Visual Basic data tools allow you to edit stored procedures.

10. In the Data View window, select the stored procedure and press the Delete key on your keyboard. This will delete the stored procedure you just created. You must have permission to delete stored procedures for this operation, so it's best to be logged in as the system administrator.

11. Close Visual Basic and open the Query Analyzer utility from the SQL Server program group. When this utility opens, log in to SQL Server and select the pubs database. Figure 5.5 shows the Query Analyzer utility logged into the pubs database.

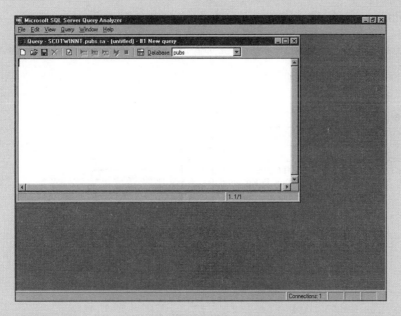

FIGURE 5.5
The Query Analyzer utility is a command-line interface to SQL Server.

12. Open the script you created earlier by selecting File, Open from the menu. Locate the file MYPROCEDURE.SQL on your desktop and open it. The script contains a batch set of SQL statements to build the stored procedure you created earlier. Be sure that you select the Pubs database in the Query Analyzer before continuing.

13. Run the batch by pushing the green Execute Query arrow button. This will rebuild the stored procedure in the pubs database. This is a great way to preserve work that you have done or move database objects from one database to another.

If you properly partition components, you can ensure that changes to one component do not affect other components. The degree to which you partition your application is part of the design process. You must decide for each part of the application how much partitioning is necessary. These decisions are a critical part of the design process and must be made before the application is coded. Your data services layer may be as simple as a single stored procedure or as complicated as a separate class encapsulating each stored procedure and multiple ActiveX DLLs containing those classes. Figure 5.6 shows a diagram of a typical data services layer.

TIP

Key Principle: Encapsulate stored procedures within class modules in the data services layer.

FIGURE 5.6

The data services layer may contain many classes and ActiveX DLLs.

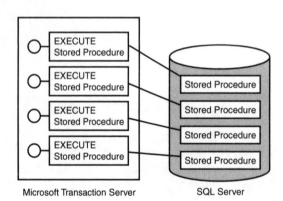

Data Services Layer

USER SERVICES LAYER

The user services layer serves many critical functions in the distributed MTS application. These functions include not only the display of data, but the maintenance of application state, control of the workflow process, and the transferring of data to and from the business services layer. These divisions allow partitioning to support maintenance in much the same way that many components in the data services layer facilitate maintenance.

The boundary between the user services layer and the business services layer is defined by the transfer of data from an MTS component to the client machine via a DCOM method call. This transmission of data across the network is defined between components dedicated to simply moving the data. This means we create a component in MTS to return data in a standardized package and a component in the user services layer to receive and unpack the data. These components perform no other function than to transfer data. We call the MTS component that transfers data the "stub" object. The component in the user services layer is termed the "proxy." These terms are borrowed from the Component Object Model (COM) specification, where similar objects are used to transfer data across a boundary.

When you create proxy and stub components for your MTS applications, standardizing the data transfer is critical to success. One of the key ways to standardize the data transfer is to use a standard package to move the data. Our preferred standard package is the disconnected recordset or Variant array. Data in this form can easily be moved from the data services, through business services, and finally transferred to the user services via the proxy object. Figure 5.7 shows the path a recordset might take from the database to the client.

FIGURE 5.7

Data moves from the database to the client as a standardized package returned from method calls.

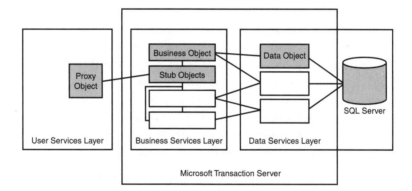

Defining Communication Standards

As you can see from our discussion, the process of building and maintaining distributed applications is made easier through standard techniques and data packages. Standardizing is accomplished when you use standard return values, standard arguments, and standard method names. Standardizing function signatures in this way creates a clear boundary between layers in the application and is at the heart of partitioning. Visual Basic provides a strong tool for guaranteeing the standardization of function signatures. This tool is known as polymorphism.

Standardizing Functionality with Polymorphism

In our opinion, polymorphism is the single best feature of Visual Basic and the most critical technology in the construction of MTS applications. Polymorphism is also the least understood of all Visual Basic features. In our experience, precious few developers understand the nature of polymorphism and even fewer understand how to use it to guarantee success in MTS applications.

Polymorphism can accurately be defined as two different classes with methods by the same name. As an example, consider two different components that reside in the data services layer. One component has a class named QueryAuthors and another component has a class named QueryPublishers. These classes are different because one class queries for information about authors, whereas the other queries for information about publishers. To get the data from these objects, however, a client always calls the GetData method. This can either be QueryAuthors.GetData or QueryPublishers.GetData. In this way, we have defined a standard method for retrieving data from the database named GetData. This method name is used regardless of the type of data you want. This is polymorphism: two objects of different type with a method by the same name.

When we build MTS applications, we want to standardize the methods in the components to the greatest extent possible. This helps developers know what to expect from a function as well as what arguments to pass. Before Visual Basic had polymorphism, we used to recommend that companies create a document that defined the standard function signatures that would be used by developers when they created various types of components like data access components. After the document was written, it could be used during code reviews to ensure that developers followed the corporate standards. These standards then ensured a high level of maintainability in the application.

The problem with documented corporate standards, however, is that they require enforcement through these code reviews. Someone has to look at the code, point out where the code deviates from the standards, and then rework the code. This requires quite a commitment on the part of a project team, and frankly, we see very few teams capable of getting off the "death march" long enough to perform adequate code reviews. Although code reviews are still an essential part of any project, Visual Basic makes the enforcement of standards considerably easier through the use of polymorphism. Using Visual Basic's polymorphism, we can define corporate standards in code and then have the compiler perform our "code review" at compile time.

Abstract Classes

Defining standard function signatures in Visual Basic is accomplished by creating "abstract classes." Abstract classes are class modules that contain the definitions of function signatures, but do not have any code within them. For example, assume we wanted to define a standard function signature for any class wanting to encapsulate a stored procedure. We might create a standard method such as `Query` and then dictate that this method will always accept a Variant array as an argument. The following code shows the standard signature:

```
Public Function Query _
    (Optional ByVal Args() As Variant)As ADODB.Recordset
End Function
```

If we want to use this signature as a standard, it should be placed in a class module in a separate ActiveX DLL. Additionally, we will not place any code at all in this function. That's right. This function is simply left blank in its own ActiveX DLL project. This allows us to standardize the function signature creating what is known as an "Interface". Interfaces are definitions of function signatures that can be used for standardization. Whenever you create an abstract class as an interface, you should prefix the name of the class with a capital "I". Thus, we could create a class named `IGetData` with the function `Query` defined inside.

After the interface is defined, it can be used to standardize any other class. This is accomplished by setting a reference in the project you want to standardize to the project that contains the interface definition. After the reference is set, a new class module can use the interface by declaring that the interface is "implemented" in the new class. This is done with the following code:

```
Implements IGetData
```

When a class declares that it implements a polymorphic interface, it is signing a contract with the Visual Basic compiler. This contract promises that the new class will contain every member of the interface within the new class. Thus, if the interface defines a method `Query` with a Variant array, the new class must in turn define the same method. Failing to define the new method will prevent Visual Basic from compiling the new class. In this way, the compiler acts as the standards enforcer for the project. It simply will not allow the new class to compile if the interface is not properly implemented.

Fortunately, Visual Basic helps us implement the required methods of an interface. If a class declares that it implements an interface, Visual Basic will place the name of the interface in the object box of the code window. When you select the object in the code window, Visual Basic lists all of the members of the interface in the procedure box of the code window. Figure 5.8 shows the code window when a class implements our `IGetData` interface.

FIGURE 5.8

Visual Basic lists implemented interfaces in the code window.

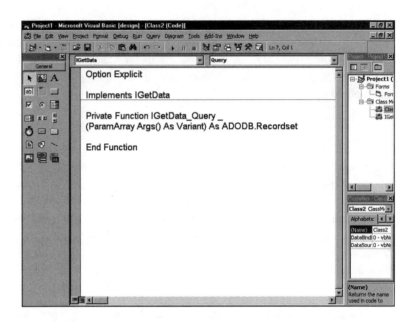

When you build a class that implements an interface, you must use the code window to add each of the members of the interface to your new class. Then you can write code in the new procedures to define what happens when the method is called. Notice that when Visual Basic adds an interface member to your class, it is defined as a private procedure. For example, the following code shows the implementation of the IGetData interface:

```
Private Function IGetData_Query _
    (Optional ByVal Args() As Variant) As ADODB.Recordset

End Function
```

The reason that the members of the interface are Private in the implementing class is that the Public part of the interface is maintained by the abstract class we built earlier. This is what standardizes the function signatures. The abstract class acts as the public gateway for each and every class that implements the interface. All you have to do is write the code for the functionality. This can be identical to the code that you would write if you did not implement any interfaces in the component. The following code shows a complete implementation for the Query method:

```
Private Function IGetData_Query _
    (Optional ByVal Args() As Variant) As ADODB.Recordset

    'Variables
    Dim objRecordset As ADODB.Recordset
    Set objRecordset = New ADODB.Recordset
```

```
'Run Query
objRecordset.ActiveConnection = _
"Provider=SQLOLEDB;Data Source=(local);Database=pubs;UID=sa;PWD=;"
objRecordset.CursorLocation = adUseClient
objRecordset.Properties("Update Criteria") = lngCriteria
objRecordset.CursorType = adOpenStatic
objRecordset.LockType = adLockBatchOptimistic
objRecordset.Source = _
"EXECUTE sp_GetPublishers '" & Args(0) & "','" & Args(1) & "'"

'Return data
objRecordset.Open
Set objRecordset.ActiveConnection = Nothing

'Return the Records
Set IGetData_Query = objRecordset
Exit Function

End Function
```

The preceding code calls the stored procedure sp_GetPublishers, but you can use the interface to call any stored procedure that accepts arguments and returns a disconnected recordset. This is exactly the standardization we are looking to create. This standardization reaches its fruition when we examine the client code necessary to call the Query method.

Encapsulating Stored Procedures

Clients who want to call the Query method through the standardized interface can do so by declaring a variable and creating a new instance. However, we do not write this code in the usual way. Instead, we declare an object variable as the interface, but create an instance of the desired object. For example, suppose the implementation code is in a class named QueryPublishers. The following code creates an instance of this object for use by a client:

```
Dim objDataObject As IGetData
Set objDataObject = New QueryPublishers
```

Notice how this code declares the variable not as the name of the desired object, but as the name of the interface. This is critical in defining the communication points between the two objects in the MTS application. Because the code in the client refers to the standard interface, you can easily modify the manner in which the interface is implemented in the QueryPublishers class without affecting the code in any other component that calls QueryPublishers. Additionally, the interface has served to standardize the members of all data access classes that encapsulate stored procedures. This makes development and maintenance considerably easier than it would be if each developer defined his own custom method calls for encapsulating stored procedures.

> **TIP**
>
> Key Principle: Use interfaces to define the communications points between components in an MTS application.

Because interfaces define the standards for components in an MTS application, they should be used widely throughout the entire application. Anywhere a component engages in standard behavior such as encapsulating stored procedures, returning disconnected recordsets, or maintaining application state, interfaces should be used to define the function signatures. This also means that the interfaces must be defined before the implementing classes are coded. In fact, the interfaces should be one of the first parts of an application that you create. Because interfaces are no more than function signatures without code, you can create them by simply agreeing among the key application architects on method names and argument types. Thus, it is appropriate to create the interfaces for an application shortly after the architects have modeled the application.

QUICK CHECK 5-2:

> ### USING INTERFACES WITH MTS APPLICATIONS
>
> 1. This exercise uses the stored procedure you created in Quick Check 5-1. Be sure you have completed that exercise prior to beginning this one.
>
> 2. Using the CD-ROM for the book, locate the directory TEMPLATES\QUICK CHECK5-2. This directory contains a partially completed project you can use to investigate interfaces with MTS.
>
> 3. On your hard drive, create a new directory with the Windows Explorer named MTS\QUICK CHECK5-2. Copy the contents from the CD-ROM directory into the new directory you just created.
>
> 4. Because the CD-ROM will create read-only copies of the project files, select all of the files you copied, right-click them, and select **Properties** from the pop-up menu. In the properties dialog, uncheck the read-only flag. Close the dialog.

CREATING THE INTERFACE

5. Start Visual Basic. Open the project group named `QUICK CHECK5-2.VBG`. With the project group open, add the projects DataInterfaces.vbp and DataServices.vbp, if they do not already appear in the group. In the Project Explorer, you should now see two ActiveX DLL projects and a Standard EXE project.

6. In the Project Explorer, locate the project named `DataInterfaces`. In this project, open the class module named `IGetData`. This class contains a single method definition to be used as an interface for objects that encapsulate stored procedures. The following code shows the interface definition:

```
Public Function Query(ParamArray Args() As Variant) As Variant

'The interface for encapsulated stored procedures

End Function
```

7. In the Project Explorer, locate the project named `DataServiceProcs`. This is a project that will encapsulate stored procedure functionality in the data services layer.

8. In order to use the interface defined in `IGetData`, you have to set a reference to the `DataInterfaces` project. With the `DataServiceProcs` project selected, open the references dialog and set a reference to the `DataInterfaces` project.

9. In the `DataServiceProcs` project, locate the class named `QueryTitles`. Open the code module for this class. In the [General][Declarations] section, add the following code to implement the `IGetData` interface:

```
Implements DataInterfaces.IGetData
```

10. In the object box, locate and select the `IGetData` interface. This will cause Visual Basic to automatically add the following code to the class module:

```
Private Function IGetData_Query _

    (ParamArray Args() As Variant) As Variant

End Function
```

11. The `Query` method of the `IGetData` interface is used to run a stored procedure and return the data as a `Variant` array. The `Variant` array is created by using the `GetRows` method on a firehose cursor. Add the code in Listing 5.2 to the `IGetData_Query` function to return the data.

continues

continued

LISTING 5.2   CODE TO ADD TO THE IGetData_Query FUNCTION

```
On Error GoTo GetDataErr

    'Get Object Context
    Dim objContext As MTxAS.ObjectContext
Set objContext = GetObjectContext

    'Run Stored Procedure
    Dim objRecordset As ADODB.Recordset
    Set objRecordset = New ADODB.Recordset

    objRecordset.Source = _
        "EXECUTE sp_GetTitlesByAuthor '" & Args(0) & "'"
    objRecordset.CursorLocation = adUseServer
    objRecordset.CursorType = adOpenForwardOnly
    objRecordset.LockType = adLockReadOnly
    objRecordset.CacheSize = 1
    objRecordset.ActiveConnection = _
    "Provider=SQLOLEDB;Data Source=(local);Database=pubs;UID=sa;PWD=;"
    objRecordset.Open

    'Return Records
    IGetData_Query = objRecordset.GetRows

    'Tell MTS we succeeded
    objContext.SetComplete

    Exit Function

GetDataErr:
    'Tell MTS we failed
    objContext.SetAbort

    IGetData_Query = Err.Description
    Exit Function
```

Creating the User Interface

12. In the Project Explorer, locate the FrontEnd project. In this project, the form frmClient is used to call the data object. Figure 5.9 shows the form.

Figure 5.9
This form is used to access the data component.

13. The FrontEnd project must be able to access the interface and the data component. Using the references dialog, set a reference to the `DataInterfaces` and `DataServiceProcs` projects.

14. Open the code window for frmClient. In the [General][Declarations] section, declare a variable for the data component. Notice how the following code is declared against the interface and not the class that implements the interface.

    ```
    Private objData As DataInterfaces.IgetData
    ```

15. When the form loads, we have to create an instance of the data component. Add the following code to the `Form_Load` event to create the instance. Notice how the code creates an instance of the data component even though the variable is declared against the interface.

    ```
    Set objData = New DataServiceProcs.QueryTitles
    ```

16. After the code is added, compile the projects by selecting File, Make Project Group from the menu.

17. After the projects are compiled, open the MTS Explorer and create a new package. Name the package "Data Interfaces," and add both the interface and the data component to the new package.

18. Run the application. Try typing in the name "Greene" and returning title information from the database.

HANDLING ERRORS IN BUSINESS OBJECTS

Standard communication interfaces are critical for correctly partitioning MTS applications; however, no matter how well the communication interfaces are defined, MTS components will still generate errors. When this happens, your components must be able to gracefully handle errors and report them to the client if necessary. Handling errors that occur in distributed components has never been simple, but when those components are also running under MTS, error handling takes on new dimensions.

The first aspect of error handling that you should consider relates to data access. When a component in the data services layer calls a stored procedure in SQL Server, many different kinds of errors are possible. In fact, SQL Server can send many different messages to your component. Some of these messages may be critical, whereas others may be simply informational. For this reason, every time a component performs data access, it should check for messages returned from SQL Server.

ADO offers a way to collect and examine the messages returned from SQL Server. This is accomplished with the ADO `Errors` collection. The ADO `Errors` collection is cleared automatically before each operation performed by ADO. You can examine this collection after each database operation to see if any messages have been left by SQL Server. Error messages take the form of `Error` objects in the collection. ADO creates an instance for each message returned. You can examine all of the entries in the collection and get specific information through the `Number` and `Description` properties. In most cases, when an error object is added to the collection, you will receive a runtime error in your code. However, you may not receive a runtime error if you are performing asynchronous data access with ADO events.

In addition to data access errors, you may receive other types of runtime errors. Normally in a distributed application, you have two options in handling runtime errors. The first option is to do nothing within the distributed component. Unhandled runtime errors are normally passed from the component to the calling client with no work on your part. The second option is to trap all runtime errors, attempt to resolve them, and pass an error code back to the client as a return value from a function.

Because of the nature of the `ObjectContext`, the first error-handling option is not available in an MTS application. Unhandled errors in MTS will result in the termination of the current process as opposed to raising an error in the calling client. Additionally, we want to trap errors in business objects anyway because it allows us to call the `SetAbort` method of the `ObjectContext`. This allows any transactional work done by the component to be rolled back. (We cover the details of transactions later in the book.) All of this means that you should always code an error handler into each method of an MTS component. This error handler should attempt to resolve the error, but if it can't, the error should be passed to the component in a controlled fashion as a return value from a function.

> **TIP**
>
> Key Principle: Report errors from MTS components to the client as return values from functions.

MAINTAINING APPLICATION STATE

After the proxy object receives the data from the business services layer, it must be converted to a format appropriate for display. This is accomplished by creating a custom collection. The recordset returned to the proxy is used to create objects that maintain the state of the application. These objects are stored in a collection that is used to populate the graphic user interface (GUI). In this way, the GUI designer does not need to know anything about the database or the recordset to create the display mechanisms.

Many developers ask us why it is necessary to insulate the recordset from the display through a collection. Why not simply show the disconnected recordset in databound controls? Although it is possible to show the disconnected recordset using simple databound controls, it allows direct access to the underlying data set without any control over what the user can edit. Encapsulating the recordset within an object allows you to place data validation code within your custom objects as well as build read-only properties that cannot be edited. Additionally, isolating the recordset from the GUI means that you can change the form of the passed data without impacting the display. For example, imagine that you changed the data received by the proxy from a recordset to a string. If you are using databound controls, the GUI will break. If you use a collection, the GUI will not have to be edited. Figure 5.10 shows the components that make up the user services layer.

> **TIP**
>
> Key Principle: Data returned from the business layer to the client should be separated from the GUI by a custom collection class.

Custom collections have a significant role in the MTS application because they form the partition between the disconnected recordset and the GUI. Because they are such an important part of the application, their design should be carefully considered. Chief among the design considerations for collections is that they be standardized. Just as in the case of defining communication points between layers, we use polymorphism to define the structure of all custom collections in MTS applications.

5

PARTITIONING MTS APPLICATIONS

FIGURE 5.10

The user services layer consists of a proxy, collections, and GUI.

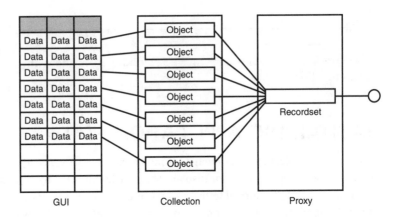

The collection classes we design take their structure from the standard `Collection` object found in Visual Basic. This object defines three methods and one property that have become the de facto standard for all collections. The standard methods for a collection include the `Add` method for adding new objects, the `Remove` method for taking objects out of the collection, and the `Item` method for accessing one particular object. The standard collection also describes a single property—`Count`—for determining how many items are in the collection. Therefore we define an interface named `ICollection` that defines the `Add`, `Remove`, `Item`, and `Count` members. The following code shows the definition of the `ICollection` interface:

```
Public Sub Add(ParamArray vArray())
    'The Add method takes a ParamArray
    'full of data for the new item to add
    'to the collection
End Sub

Public Sub Remove(vKey As Variant)
    'The Remove Method removes
    'an item from the collection
End Sub

Public Function Item _
    (vKey As Variant) As UserInterfaces.IItem
    'This returns an item from the collection
End Function

Public Property Get Count() As Long
    'Return number of items in collection
End Property
```

```
Public Property Get NewEnum() As IUnknown
    'Supports For...Each
End Property
```

The `ICollection` interface can be modified to meet the particular design needs of your organization, but the point is that the standard exists. The `ICollection` interface guarantees that every collection created for an MTS application has the same essential features. Notice that our definition even ensures support for the `For...Each` syntax through the `NewEnum` method.

The `ICollection` interface describes the structure of a collection, and it is responsible for containing items within. However, we cannot predict at the outset what objects we want in the collection. These objects may include authors, publishers, titles, or any other objects we create from data in the database. Because we do not know the nature of an object contained within the collection, we must define an interface for items that belong to a collection. We call this interface `IItem`. This interface is implemented by any object that wants to be a member of a collection and ensures that each object has a primary key. The following code shows the definition for the `IItem` interface:

```
Public Property Get Key() As Variant
End Property

Public Property Let Key(varKey As Variant)
End Property
```

Collection classes in MTS applications are created by the `Proxy` object when a disconnected recordset is returned from the business layer. After the collection is created, it can easily be used to display data in the GUI. Users of the application can then manipulate the GUI and edit the individual objects within the collection. When the user finishes editing the objects in the collection, the collection is then used to update the recordset. The recordset is subsequently sent back to the middle tier to attempt a batch update.

Simple Data Binding

When you utilize collections to encapsulate recordset objects, you can take advantage of Visual Basic's databinding features to make your coding simpler. Data binding allows you to tie the properties of an object in the collection directly to fields in the disconnected recordset. Visual Basic provides a built-in object named the `BindingCollection` to manage the binding of object properties to recordset fields. Using the `BindingCollection` object to map fields to properties is known as "simple binding."

To use the `BindingCollection`, you must first set a reference to the "Microsoft Data Binding Collection." After setting a reference, you can create an instance of the `BindingCollection` in the `Initialize` event. After you've created the instance, you have to set the `DataSource` property of the `BindingCollection` to the ADO recordset object you want to bind to your class. Then for each property in the class, you must use the `Add` method of the `BindingCollection` to bind the field to the property.

QUICK CHECK 5-3:

SIMPLE BINDING

1. Using the CD-ROM for the book, locate the directory TEMPLATES\QUICK CHECK5-3. This directory contains a partially completed project you can use to investigate simple binding with MTS.

2. On your hard drive, create a new directory with the Windows Explorer named MTS\QUICK CHECK5-3. Copy the contents from the CD-ROM directory into the new directory you just created.

3. Because the CD-ROM will create read-only copies of the project files, select all of the files you copied, right-click them, and select **Properties** from the pop-up menu. In the properties dialog, uncheck the read-only flag. Close the dialog.

4. Start Visual Basic. Open the project group named QUICK CHECK5-3.VBG. In the Project Explorer, you will find two ActiveX DLL projects and a Standard EXE project.

5. In the Project Explorer, locate the project named "SimpleBind." In the project, open the code window for the class named `Title`. This class will be simple-bound to a disconnected recordset.

6. This class already has several property procedures defined that represent data returned from the business services layer. There is also a blank procedure named `Populate`, which is called by the front end to retrieve the data and bind the properties. This procedure uses the `BindingCollection` object. Add the code in Listing 5.3 to the `Populate` method to retrieve data and bind the class properties.

LISTING 5.3   CODE TO ADD TO THE `Populate` METHOD

```
'Run the Query
Set objRecordset = objData.GetData(strAuthor)

'Bind Data
Set objBind.DataSource = objRecordset
objBind.Add Me, "TitleID", "title_id"
objBind.Add Me, "Title", "title"
objBind.Add Me, "Author", "au_lname"
    objBind.Add Me, "Publisher", "pub_name"
```

7. The Title class acts as a pseudocollection. The bound recordset is used as the collection of data, and the property procedures allow direct access to the fields in the current record.

8. Now examine the MoveNext and MovePrevious methods. These methods move the cursor in the recordset contained within the class. The properties are then automatically updated by the BindingCollection object.

Complex Data Binding

Simple data binding allows a way to map fields and properties in a one-to-one relationship. For maximum flexibility, however, you can encapsulate an entire recordset within a collection through "complex binding." Complex binding allows you to expose a recordset without hard-coding the names of properties in a containing object. Complex binding allows you to change the fields returned in a recordset without changing the collection code.

Complex binding is implemented by setting the DataBindingBehavior of a class module to vbComplexBound. This setting causes Visual Basic to add DataSource and DataMember properties to the class. The DataSource property is used to receive an entire recordset, whereas the DataMember property can be used to designate which values you want the class to expose. When you utilize this methodology, you typically expose data through a Properties collection in your class.

QUICK CHECK 5-4:

COMPLEX BINDING

1. Using the CD-ROM for the book, locate the directory TEMPLATES\QUICK CHECK5-4. This directory contains a partially completed project you can use to investigate complex binding with MTS.

2. On your hard drive, create a new directory with the Windows Explorer named MTS\QUICK CHECK5-4. Copy the contents from the CD-ROM directory into the new directory you just created.

3. Because the CD-ROM will create read-only copies of the project files, select all of the files you copied, right-click them, and select **Properties** from the pop-up menu. In the properties dialog, uncheck the read-only flag. Close the dialog.

continues

4. Start Visual Basic. Open the project group named QUICK CHECK5-4.VBG. In the Project Explorer, you will find two ActiveX DLL projects and a Standard EXE project.

5. In the Project Explorer, locate the project named "ComplexBind." In this project, open the class module named `Titles`. This is the class that will be complex-bound to a returned disconnected recordset.

6. Select the `Titles` class in the Project Explorer. In the Properties window, locate the `DataBindingBehavior` property. Set this property to `vbComplexBound`. When you set this property, Visual Basic will automatically add the `DataSource` and `DataMember` properties. Add the code in Listing 5.4 to these properties to create the following result.

LISTING 5.4 CODE FOR THE `DataSource` AND `DataMember` PROPERTIES

```
Public Property Get DataSource() As DataSource
    Set DataSource = objRecordset
End Property

Public Property Set DataSource(ByVal objDataSource As DataSource)
    Set objRecordset = objDataSource
End Property

Public Property Get DataMember() As DataMember
    DataMember = m_DataMember
End Property

Public Property Let DataMember(ByVal DataMember As DataMember)
    m_DataMember = DataMember
    End Property
```

7. Now examine the `Populate` method. This method uses the `DataMember` value as a parameter to pass to the business services layer. The business services layer then returns a recordset that is exposed through the `Properties` method. Examine the `Properties` method to see how the fields are exposed.

SUMMARY

Application partitioning is critical to successfully implementing MTS applications. Correct partitioning makes applications simpler to build and maintain. In the data services layer, applications are partitioned by creating separate classes for each stored procedure in the database. In the business layer, partitioning is accomplished by creating separate components for each business function and stubs to return data. In the user services layer, partitioning is accomplished by creating proxies that build collections. Recordsets are bound to collections through either complex or simple binding. The bound collections maintain state and workflow information. The collections are then used to drive the GUI.

Above all the layer partitioning reside the interfaces. Interfaces define the communications points between layers in the application and components within the same layer. You must always design the interfaces to the maximum extent possible before beginning to create the application. Polymorphism is the key to successfully completing applications in a timely manner.

EXERCISE 5-1: PARTITIONING APPLICATIONS

This exercise creates an application that uses many of the principles described in this chapter. You will be required to create stored procedures, classes, components, and a front end. Additionally, this application utilizes some simple conflict resolution.

Step 1

Using the CD-ROM for the book, locate the directory TEMPLATES\EXERCISE5-1. This directory contains a partially completed application that you will finish.

Step 2

On your hard drive, create a new directory with the Windows Explorer named MTS\EXERCISE5-1. Copy the contents from the CD-ROM directory into the new directory you just created.

Step 3

Because the CD-ROM will create read-only copies of the project files, select all of the files you copied, right-click them, and select **Properties** from the pop-up menu. In the properties dialog, uncheck the read-only flag. Close the dialog.

Step 4

In the SQL Server program group, start the Query Analyzer utility. Log in to SQL Server and select the pubs database. This application uses four stored procedures to read author data from the pubs database. These stored procedures are created by running a script. In the Query Analyzer utility, select File, Open from the menu and locate the EXERCISE5-1.SQL file, which can be found in MTS\EXERCISE5-1\DATA SERVICES. Open the script and run it in Query Analyzer to create the four stored procedures in the pubs database.

Step 5

Start Visual Basic. Open the project group named EXERCISE5-1.VBG. In the Project Explorer, you will see several different projects. These projects represent interfaces, MTS components, and the user services.

Step 6

This project has a model associated with it. You can use this model diagram to help understand the architecture of the application. To see the model, you must select a class module in one of the ActiveX DLL projects. For simplicity, locate the AuthorStub class in the BusinessStub project. With the class active, select Add-Ins, Visual Modeler, Browse Class Diagram. This will start the Visual Modeler. Figure 5.11 shows the diagram.

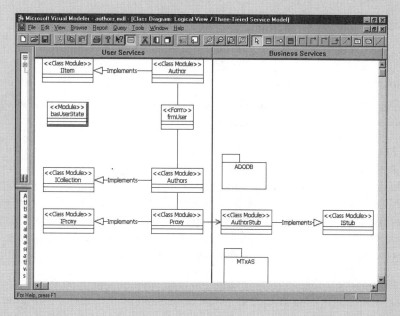

FIGURE 5.11
This diagram shows the application model.

Step 7

Examine the application model. Locate the component named `AuthorStub`. This is the only component that runs under MTS in this application. `AuthorStub` runs one of the four stored procedures based on an enumerated type. The `AuthorStub` then creates a disconnected recordset that is returned to the user services layer. The `AuthorStub` class implements an interface called `IStub`, which is an example of a standard you might use for all stub objects.

Step 8

The user services receives the disconnected recordset into the `Proxy` class. This class takes the disconnected recordset and generates a custom collection. The `Proxy` object implements the `IProxy` interface, which defines a standard for all objects that behave as proxies.

Step 9

In this application, we build a complete custom collection to manage the returned data. This is the most complex way to maintain state as we do not use any type of data binding in this layer. The collection contains instances of the `Author` class that represent information returned by the stored procedures. Both the collection `Authors` and the contained class `Author` implement interfaces that define their behavior.

Step 10

After you are satisfied that you understand the architecture of the exercise application, close the Visual Modeler and return to Visual Basic.

The Business Services Layer

In this section, you will create the Business services layer. This layer implements an interface to standardize communications.

Step 11

In the Project Explorer, locate the project named BusinessStub. This is the MTS component. In this project, locate and open the AuthorStub class. This class contains two simple methods for reading and writing data: Query and SubmitChanges. This component is more coarse than we would create for a complete application. In other words, this component contains code to directly access the database even though it is officially in the business services layer. Nonetheless, the principles are the same.

Step 12

The Query method is used to run a stored procedure and return a disconnected recordset. The selected stored procedure is based on an enumeration named QueryTypes located in the [General][Declarations] section. Add the code in Listing 5.5 to the Query method to run the selected stored procedure.

LISTING 5.5   CODE TO ADD TO THE Query METHOD

```
On Error GoTo QueryErr

    Dim objRecordset As ADODB.Recordset
    Dim strSource As String

    'Get Object Context
    Dim objContext As MTxAS.ObjectContext
    Set objContext = GetObjectContext

    'Select Query
    Select Case lngType
        Case AllAuthors
            strSource = _
            "EXECUTE sp_GetAllAuthors"
        Case AuthorsByName
            strSource = _
"EXECUTE sp_GetAuthorsByName '" & strParameter & "'"
        Case AuthorsByCity
            strSource = _
            "EXECUTE sp_GetAuthorsByCity '" & strParameter & "'"
        Case AuthorsByLetter
```

```
        strSource = _
            "EXECUTE sp_GetAuthorsByLetter '" & strParameter & "'"
    End Select

    'Run query
    Set objRecordset = New ADODB.Recordset
    objRecordset.CursorLocation = adUseClient
    objRecordset.Open strSource, _
        ntsConnect, adOpenStatic, adLockBatchOptimistic
    Set objRecordset.ActiveConnection = Nothing
    Set IStub_Query = objRecordset

    'Tell MTS we succeeded
    objContext.SetComplete

QueryExit:
    Exit Function

QueryErr:
    'Log the error
    App.StartLogging "", 0
    App.LogEvent Err.Description

    'Tell MTS we failed
    objContext.SetAbort

    Set IStub_Query = Nothing
    Resume QueryExit
```

Step 13

Updating the database is done by passing the disconnected recordset back to the business services layer. This begins by calling the Update method of the collection. The collection in turn calls the Business services layer where the SubmitChanges method attempts a batch update and returns a Boolean value indicating success or failure. Conflicts are not resolved. Instead, any failure results in a refresh of the data by the client. Add the code in Listing 5.6 to IStub_SubmitChanges in the AuthorStub class to update the database.

LISTING 5.6 CODE TO ADD TO THE Update METHOD

```
On Error GoTo ChangeErr
    IStub_SubmitChanges = True
Dim objConnection As ADODB.Connection

    'Get Object Context
    Dim objContext As MTxAS.ObjectContext
    Set objContext = GetObjectContext
```

continues

5

PARTITIONING
MTS
APPLICATIONS

LISTING 5.6   CONTINUED

```
    'Connect to database
    Set objConnection = New ADODB.Connection
    objConnection.CursorLocation = adUseClient
    objConnection.Open ntsConnect$

    'Submit Changes
    Set objRecordset.ActiveConnection = objConnection
    objRecordset.UpdateBatch

    'Tell MTS we succeeded
    objContext.SetComplete

ChangeExit:
    Exit Function

ChangeErr:
    'Log the error
    App.StartLogging "", 0
    App.LogEvent Err.Description

    'Tell MTS we failed
    objContext.SetAbort

    IStub_SubmitChanges = False
    Resume ChangeExit
```

The User Services Layer

In this section, you will cose the User Services layer. This layer also uses an interface to standardize the methods.

Step 14

The user services layer connects to the business services through the `Proxy` class. Locate the `Proxy` class in the `UserState` project. Open the code window for this class. This class contains functions that create items for the `Authors` collection or reads the collection and builds a recordset for update.

Step 15

The `Populate` function fills the `Authors` collection from a recordset passed in by the business services layer. The collection is populated by calling the `Add` method of the collection for each record in the recordset. Add the code in Listing 5.7 to the `Populate` function to build the collection.

LISTING 5.7   CODE FOR THE Populate FUNCTION

```
On Error GoTo PopulateErr

    IProxy_Populate = True

    'Run Query
    Set m_Recordset = _
        m_Business.Query(lngType, strParameter)

    'Populate Collection
    Do While Not m_Recordset.EOF
        objCollection.Add _
            m_Recordset!au_id, _
            m_Recordset!au_lname, _
            m_Recordset!au_fname, _
            m_Recordset!Phone, _
            m_Recordset!Address, _
            m_Recordset!City

        m_Recordset.MoveNext
    Loop

PopulateExit:
    Exit Function

PopulateErr:
    IProxy_Populate = False
    Resume PopulateExit
```

Step 16

The Update function reads all of the entries in the collection and updates a recordset. The recordset is then passed to the business services layer for updating. Listing 5.8 shows the code to add to the Update function of the Proxy class to edit the author data.

LISTING 5.8   CODE FOR THE Update FUNCTION

```
On Error GoTo UpdateErr

    IProxy_Update = True

    'Update Recordset
    Dim objAuthor As UserState.Author

    m_Recordset.MoveFirst
```

continues

LISTING 5.8   CONTINUED

```
    For Each objAuthor In objCollection
        m_Recordset!au_lname = objAuthor.LastName
        m_Recordset!au_fname = objAuthor.FirstName
        m_Recordset!Phone = objAuthor.Phone
        m_Recordset!Address = objAuthor.Address
        m_Recordset!City = objAuthor.City
        m_Recordset.MoveNext
    Next

    'Send Recordset to Server
    IProxy_Update = m_Business.SubmitChanges(m_Recordset)

UpdateExit:
    Exit Function

UpdateErr:
    IProxy_Update = False
    Resume UpdateExit
```

Step 17

After you have finished adding code, the application is complete. The code to display the data is already written for you. Compile the entire project by selecting File, Make Project Group from the menu.

Step 18

When the project is successfully compiled, start the MTS Explorer. In the MTS Explorer, build a new package named Authors. Select to run the package under the common identity "MTSUSER." You should have set up this account earlier.

Step 19

After the package is created, add both the Stub and IStub objects to the new package. You should include the interface definitions with the components that use them. When the components are installed, the application is complete.

Step 20

The application is run by starting the USERDISPLAY.EXE file. This runs the front end and starts up the business object. In the front end, you can try the various queries as well as editing data. Figure 5.12 shows the front end for the application.

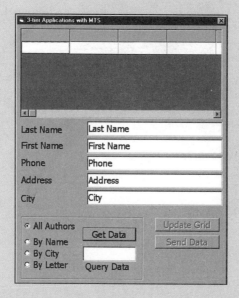

FIGURE 5.12
This is the front end for the application.

MANAGING
TRANSACTIONS WITH MTS

PREREQUISITES

Before beginning this chapter, you should have a firm understanding of the data
access strategies used in MTS. It is also helpful if you have some experience with
transactional applications.

Skills Learned

- MTS(13): Set appropriate values for the `MTSTransactionMode`
  property.
- MTS(14): Enlist MTS components in distributed transactions.
- MTS(15): Use the `TransactionContext` to manage transactions
  in MTS.

One of the key features provided by Microsoft Transaction Server (MTS) is the ability to initiate, monitor, and commit transactions on a single database or across multiple databases. Transactions are a vital part of any database application, but they take on more significance as an application is distributed across an enterprise system. Database transactions are nothing more than a series of actions performed on a database; however, the collection of actions are grouped together to form a single unit of operation. This single unit of operation will succeed or fail as a batch, which is what makes a transaction so important.

The classic example of a database transaction is the transfer of money between accounts at a bank. Suppose, for example, that you want to transfer money from your savings account at one bank to a checking account at another bank. From a database perspective, this operation requires two independent actions. Funds must be removed from the savings account and then added to the checking account. If either of the separate actions fail, money will be created or destroyed—a significant problem for the banking system.

UNDERSTANDING TRANSACTION ATTRIBUTES

Transactions are designed to prevent the problems that arise when related database actions are dependent on each other. When describing transactions, we talk about a set of attributes that define a transaction and prevent catastrophic failures. These transaction attributes are said to be ACID attributes because of the first letter for each key attribute (atomicity, consistency, isolation, and durability). The ACID attributes form the heart of every transaction performed on a database.

The first attribute of a transaction is *atomicity*. Atomicity is an attribute that simply states all parts of a transaction must succeed or fail as a single unit. In the case of the money transfer, if either the debit or the credit operation fails, both actions must be negated. Negating the partial work of a transaction is called a "rollback."

The second attribute of a transaction is *consistency*. Consistency is a concept that says the transaction must take the database from one stable state to another. No operations are left partially complete, and completing a transaction makes the system ready to perform a new transaction. Consistency requires that the system be able to handle any number of transactions in any order without negative impact on the overall system.

The third attribute of transactions is *isolation*. Isolation is an attribute that requires each transaction to operate independently from other transactions. All dependent operations are part of a single transaction. No other transactions operating on the same system at the same time can have a negative effect on the current transaction. Furthermore, other transactions cannot see the intermediate results of an executing transaction. Results are visible to the system only after the transaction succeeds or fails.

The final attribute of transactions is *durability*. Durability means that the results of a transaction are permanent and can only be undone by a subsequent operation. This means that hardware failure must not affect the results of the transaction.

When transactions are performed, they may be executed as several actions against a single database or as a group of actions that spans many databases. When a transaction is performed against a single database, we call that a "single-server" transaction. Transactions against multiple databases are called "distributed transactions." Distributed transactions that conform to the ACID requirements are said to engage in "two-phase commit." Two-phase commit engages in communication between transaction and resource managers to ensure compliance with the ACID principles. You may create both single-server and distributed transactions using ADO, OLEDB, SQL Server, and MTS. The remainder of this chapter is devoted to explaining the techniques for executing transactions.

ADO TRANSACTION SUPPORT

The ActiveX Data Objects also support transactions, but they are only supported natively at the `Connection` level. This means that you can perform transactions against a single data source using ADO, but you cannot perform a distributed transaction without the help of other tools like MTS.

Creating a single-server transaction in ADO is accomplished through the use of methods on the ADO `Connection` object. The ADO `Connection` object utilizes the `BeginTrans`, `CommitTrans`, and `RollbackTrans` methods to start, commit, and undo several operations as a batch. Error handling is normally used to roll back the transaction. If no errors occur, the transaction is committed. The following code shows a simple transaction under ADO with a connection variable `objConnection`:

```
On Error Goto TransErr

    'Execute Transaction
    objConnection.BeginTrans

    objConnection.Execute _
        "EXECUTE sp_AddAuthor '111-11-1111','Hillier','Scot'
    objConnection.Execute _
        "EXECUTE sp_AddTitle 'NTS001','MTS Programming'"

    objConnection.CommitTrans

    Exit Sub
```

```
TransErr:
    objConnection.RollbackTrans
    MsgBox Err.Description & vbCrLf & " Transaction Rolled Back!"

End Sub
```

Although ADO supports methods for use with transactions, not all OLEDB providers support transaction processing with their drivers. If a particular driver supports transactions, a property entitled `Transaction DDL` will be available in the `Properties` collection of the `Connection` object. You can check for transaction support by accessing the `Properties` collection. The following code shows how to access this property:

```
'Verify Transaction Support
Dim objProperty As ADODB.Property
Dim blnExists As Boolean
blnExists = False

For Each objProperty In objConnection.Properties
    If objProperty.Name = "Transaction DDL" Then
        blnExists = True
        Exit For
    End If
Next

If blnExists Then
    MsgBox "Transactions Supported!", vbOKOnly + vbInformation, "ADO"
Else
    MsgBox "Transactions not supported!", vbOKOnly + vbExclamation, "ADO"
End If
```

If a particular driver does not support transactions, you will generate a runtime error if you call any of the transaction methods of the `Connection` object. If a driver supports multiple nested transactions, you can also set up your code to return long integers from the `BeginTrans` method that indicate the level of nesting within the code. This can be useful for tracking multiple transactions within ADO.

QUICK CHECK 6-1:

ADO TRANSACTIONS

1. Using the CD-ROM for the book, locate the directory TEMPLATES\QUICK CHECK6-1. This directory contains a partially completed project you can use to investigate transactions with ADO.

2. On your hard drive, create a new directory with the Windows Explorer named MTS\QUICK CHECK6-1. Copy the contents from the CD-ROM directory into the new directory you just created.

3. Because the CD-ROM will create read-only copies of the project files, select all of the files you copied, right-click them, and select **Properties** from the pop-up menu. In the properties dialog, uncheck the read-only flag. Close the dialog.

4. Start Visual Basic and open the project. You will find that this project is a simple Standard EXE project with a single form. All of the code for the project is placed in this form. This exercise is not intended to run under MTS, but rather is intended to give you an idea of how ADO handles transactions without MTS. This exercise simulates transferring money in a bank account. Figure 6.1 shows the form.

FIGURE 6.1
This form is used to test ADO transactions.

5. Open the code window for the form. This form uses a single Microsoft Access database to simulate accounts at a bank. You can enter an amount to transfer and the application will move the money. The transfer occurs when you click the Transfer button. Add the code in Listing 6.1 to the cmdTransfer_Click event to create an ADO transaction.

LISTING 6.1 CODE FOR THE cmdTransfer_Click EVENT

```
On Error GoTo TransferErr

    'Start Transaction
    objConnection.BeginTrans

    'Credit Account
    If optToChecking.Value = True Then
        objConnection.Execute _
        "UPDATE Accounts SET AccountBalance = _
        AccountBalance + " & txtTransfer.Text & _
        " WHERE AccountID = 1"
```

continues

continued

```
    Else
        objConnection.Execute _
        "UPDATE Accounts SET AccountBalance = _
        AccountBalance + " & txtTransfer.Text & _
        " WHERE AccountID = 2"
    End If

    'Debit Account
    If optToSavings.Value = True Then
        If CCur(txtTransfer) > CCur(lblChecking) _
        Then Err.Raise vbObjectError
        objConnection.Execute _
        "UPDATE Accounts SET AccountBalance = _
        AccountBalance - " & txtTransfer.Text & _
        " WHERE AccountID = 1"
    Else
        If CCur(txtTransfer) > CCur(lblSavings) _
        Then Err.Raise vbObjectError
        objConnection.Execute _
        "UPDATE Accounts SET AccountBalance = _
        AccountBalance - " & txtTransfer.Text & _
        " WHERE AccountID = 2"
    End If

    'Finish Transaction
    objConnection.CommitTrans

TransferExit:
    'Update Displays
    Display
    Exit Sub

TransferErr:
    'Rollback Transaction
    objConnection.RollbackTrans
    MsgBox "Transfer Aborted!", _
    vbOKOnly + vbExclamation, "Transactions"
    Resume TransferExit
```

6. Run the application and try moving money between the accounts.

Although ADO supports transactions, this type of code is not appropriate for mission-critical applications. This is because ADO transactions do not comply with the ACID properties. Instead, an ADO transaction simply executes a batch of SQL statements. You are relying on a specific runtime error to roll back the transaction as opposed to a true transaction control service.

DISTRIBUTED TRANSACTION COORDINATION

ADO is not the only way to create a transaction. SQL Server can initiate both single-server and distributed transactions using Transact SQL statements in stored procedures. Single-server transactions are created with the BEGIN TRANSACTION and COMMIT TRANSACTION statements, whereas distributed transactions rely on the BEGIN DISTRIBUTED TRANSACTION statement.

Beginning with SQL Server 6.5, Microsoft started shipping a product specifically designed to provide scalable, robust distributed transactions. This product is called the Microsoft Distributed Transaction Coordinator (MSDTC). The MSDTC is responsible for initiating, monitoring, and committing distributed transactions that meet the ACID requirements. The MSDTC does this through a process called "two-phase commit." Unlike ADO transactions, the MSDTC is appropriate for mission-critical applications.

Two-phase commit receives its name from the two distinct phases of a distributed transaction. These phases are called the Prepare phase and the Commit phase. When a distributed transaction takes place under two-phase commit, the transaction is controlled through a series of commands and responses that form the two-phase commit protocol. The transaction control is handled by a Transaction Manager that is responsible for sending and receiving messages in the protocol. Individual databases participate in the transaction through their own Resource Manager that guarantees the atomicity of actions on a single database and responds to commands from the Transaction Manager. The Transaction Manager is then responsible for the ACID attributes of the entire distributed transaction, and the Resource Managers are responsible for the ACID attributes of each individual database.

The MSDTC embodies all of the function points necessary to perform two-phase commit protocol across databases. The MSDTC can be both a Transaction Manager and a Resource Manager. Installing SQL Server or the Microsoft Transaction Server will install the MSDTC on the system. After the MSDTC is installed, you can control the MSDTC as a Windows/NT Service using either the services dialog or the SQL Server Services Manager. MTS also provides a menu selection accessible from the Microsoft Management Console (MMC) to start and stop the MSDTC. Figure 6.2 shows the MyComputer menu in the MMC for managing the MSDTC.

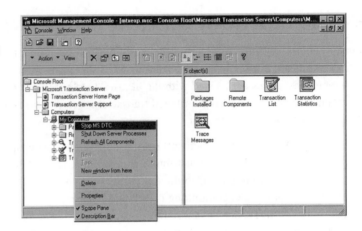

FIGURE 6.2

Use the pop-up
menu in the MTS
Explorer to start
and stop the
MSDTC.

Remote Servers

Because the MSDTC works across SQL Server installations, prior to using the MSDTC
with multiple SQL Server installations, you must enable each SQL Server to call remote
stored procedures in the other installations. Setting up a server to call remote stored
procedures allows the MSDTC to coordinate these calls across servers in a distributed
transaction. The setup itself is performed through the SQL Enterprise Manager. In the
SQL Enterprise Manager, you can set up remote servers by right-clicking the Remote
Servers folder and choosing **New Remote Server** from the pop-up menu. In this dialog,
you provide the name of the remote server where you want to call a stored procedure
along with some key information regarding the user ID and password for the remote
server. Figure 6.3 shows the Remote Servers dialog.

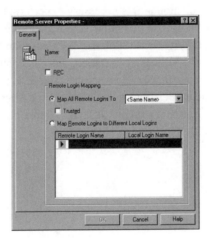

FIGURE 6.3

Use the SQL
Enterprise
Manager to give
one installation of
SQL Server per-
mission to call
stored procedures
in another
installation.

To begin the setup, enter the name of the server where you would like to call remote stored procedures from this installation of SQL Server in the Name box. The RPC option is required for distributed transactions. The MSDTC communicates with Resource Managers involved in the transaction by using Remote Procedure Calls (RPC). Therefore, you have to enable this option. You also must ensure that the RPC service is operating on the computers involved in the distributed transactions. The RPC service can be enabled through the Control Panel using the Services Manager. Figure 6.4 shows the RPC service in the Services Manager.

FIGURE 6.4

Use the Services Manager to turn on the RPC services.

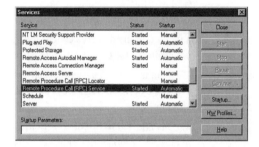

When a remote stored procedure is called, one installation of SQL Server must provide a valid login to the remote installation. In the Remote Logins section, you can specify the login name for use when the remote stored procedure is called. In this box you can map an existing name in your installation to a name in the remote installation. If you have the same set of users in both installations, you simply set up the names by selecting Translate All Remote Logins to <*same name*>, which just uses the same user name to access the remote procedure. After the remote server is established, you can use the `BEGIN DISTRIBUTED TRANSACTION` statement to create a distributed transaction utilizing the MSDTC.

TRANSACTIONAL COMPONENTS UNDER MTS

Transaction support is greatly simplified under the Microsoft Transaction Server through the use of transactional components. Transactional components are business objects that operate in transactional contexts. These business objects are the same Visual Basic ActiveX DLLs that you create for any application; however, MTS allows transactions to be performed across the methods of these objects.

Designating a transactional component inside MTS is done through the properties of the object in the MTS Explorer. Access the properties dialog by clicking an object and selecting Action, Properties from the Explorer menu. The Transaction tab of the properties dialog contains the transaction property options for the selected object. MTS supports four mutually exclusive transaction options. These are Requires a Transaction, Requires a New Transaction, Supports Transactions, and Does Not Support Transactions.

Beginning with Visual Basic 6.0, you can also set the transactional properties for a component directly in the properties window. Each class in an ActiveX component supports a property named MTSTransactionMode. If you set this property using an option shown in Table 6.1, the correct setting will automatically appear in the MTS Explorer when the component is added to a package. If you do not put the class in a package, the property has no effect.

TABLE 6.1 TRANSACTION PROPERTY OPTIONS FOR COMPONENTS

Property	Description
Requires a Transaction	MTS includes the object in a transaction context every time a method in the object is called. If a specific transaction is not available for the object, MTS starts a new one.
Requires a New Transaction	MTS starts a new transaction each time the object is invoked by a client regardless of what other transactions are in progress.
Supports Transactions	MTS is allowed to run the object in a transaction if requested, or alone if no transaction is required.
Does not Support Transactions	MTS will never run the object in a transaction context.

When a component is designated to be inside a transaction, MTS uses the MSDTC to coordinate a transaction between the Resource Managers and Resource Dispensers that perform the work called by the code in the transactional component. Resource Managers are used to manage the state of persistent resources such as database information, whereas Resource Dispensers are used to manage nonpersistent resources such as database connections. In either case, when your business object invokes a Resource Manager or Resource Dispenser from a transaction, the MSDTC serves as the Transaction Manager responsible for ensuring the ACID attributes of the transaction across all involved resources.

The MTS Explorer provides a special view that shows the transactional attributes of components without having to specifically examine the properties dialog. This view is called the Property view. You can shift the Explorer view to Property view by selecting View, Property view from the Explorer menu. The Property view not only shows the transactional attributes, but also displays other key object information such as the CLSID and the threading model supported by the object.

UNDERSTANDING TRANSACTION CONTEXT

MTS manages objects involved in a transaction through the transaction context. The transaction context is a concept used to define whether or not work done by different objects should be considered part of the same transaction. When objects share transaction context, all of their work must succeed or fail as a batch, and the ACID attributes of a transaction are maintained. If the context spans objects that perform work on multiple data sources, the transaction is managed by the MSDTC. Each object involved in the transaction still resides in the same context, even if their Resource Managers are on different machines.

When programming transactions in MTS, developers need to understand the transaction context associated with a particular object. The context is determined by the transaction property of the object as set in the MTS Explorer. Objects that are designated to always begin a new transaction will never inherit the transaction of any other object. The context for these objects is new each time the object is called. Objects that support transactions can inherit the context of another object and thus participate in the overall transaction. If an object does not support transactions, it cannot inherit transaction context or participate in any transaction.

As a simple example of transaction support, assume that we have an Internet StoreFront that is taking orders for flowers. On the Web site, you can order flowers and pay by credit card. The flower orders are written to the ORDERS table of a database, while the credit card information is written to the PAYMENTS table of the database. Because we do not want to have any orders processed that do not have valid payment information, we want to update both tables as an atomic unit. Therefore we'll use a transaction.

The simplest transactional design under MTS uses two objects to perform the transaction. One object serves to manage the transaction, and the second serves to perform the work of the transaction. For ease, we'll call the objects `Manager` and `Transactor`. The `Manager` object has only one method—`OrderFlowers`. This method is called by the application front end when the user is ready to begin the transaction. `Manager` subsequently calls to the `AddOrder` and `AddPayment` methods of the `Transactor` object to accomplish the table updates. If either update fails, the `Manager` object notifies MTS that the transaction must be rolled back. Think of the `Manager` object as the business services layer and the `Transactor` object as the data services layer. Figure 6.5 shows a graphical representation of the transaction sequence.

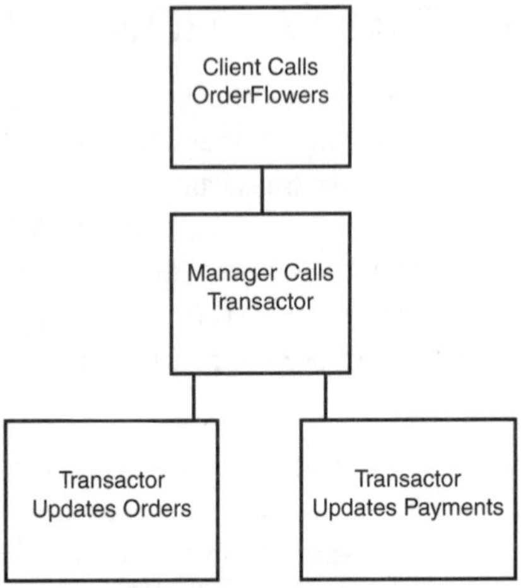

FIGURE 6.5

This diagram represents a transactional process.

```
┌─────────────────┐
│  Client Calls   │
│  OrderFlowers   │
└────────┬────────┘
         │
┌────────┴────────┐
│  Manager Calls  │
│    Transactor   │
└───┬─────────┬───┘
    │         │
┌───┴────┐ ┌──┴──────┐
│Transactor│ │Transactor│
│ Updates  │ │ Updates  │
│ Orders   │ │ Payments │
└──────────┘ └──────────┘
```

TIP

Key Principle: When building transactional components, always use one object as the manager of a transaction. This object should have its transaction property set to always require a new transaction. This object then enlists other objects in the transaction. Enlisted objects should be set to support transactions.

In order for the transaction to meet the ACID attributes, the Manager object must enlist the Transactor object in the same transaction context. Therefore, the Manager object must first create a new transaction context through the transaction attributes in the MTS Explorer. The transaction property for the Manager object is set to Requires a New Transaction to ensure that a new transaction is started each time a new client calls the Manager object.

With the transaction property set to generate a new transaction, the Manager object is ready to enlist the Transactor object in the transaction. In order to share transaction context with the Transactor object, the Manager object uses the CreateInstance method of the ObjectContext object. This method creates an instance of the Transactor and enlists it in the Manager object's transaction, as follows:

```
'Variables
Dim objContext As MTxAS.ObjectContext
Dim objTransactor As Flowers.Transactor

'Create Transactor in my context
Set objContext = GetObjectContext
Set objTransactor = objContext.CreateInstance("Flowers.Transactor")
```

The Transactor object must be able to support transactions when it is invoked; however, we do not want a new transaction started when the object is called. In order to ensure the proper functionality of the components, we set the transaction property of the Transactor object to Requires a Transaction. This allows the Transactor to be enlisted in a transaction started by the Manager object.

After the Manager object creates an instance of the Transactor with the CreateInstance method, all work performed by the Transactor will be involved in the transaction. The Manager object is free to invoke the methods of the Transactor to perform work, which it does through the AddOrder and AddPayment methods.

```
'Call Transactor
blnSuccess = objTransactor.AddOrder(CustomerID, ProductID)
If Not blnSuccess Then Err.Raise vbObjectError

blnSuccess = objTransactor.AddPayment(CustomerID, CardNumber)
If Not blnSuccess Then Err.Raise vbObjectError
```

The methods of the Transactor object are designed to return Boolean success or failure flags that the Manager can use to monitor the transaction progress. If all methods succeed, the transaction is committed, but if either method fails, the transaction is rolled back. Committing and rolling back transactions is accomplished through the SetComplete and SetAbort methods of the ObjectContext:

```
Public Function OrderFlowers(CustomerID As Long, _
CardNumber As String, ProductID As Long) As Boolean

On Error GoTo OrderFlowersErr

    OrderFlowers = True

    'Variables
    Dim objContext As MTxAS.ObjectContext
    Dim objTransactor As Flowers.Transactor
    Dim blnSuccess As Boolean

    'Create Transactor in my context
    Set objContext = GetObjectContext
    Set objTransactor = _
        objContext.CreateInstance("Flowers.Transactor")

    'Call Transactor
    blnSuccess = objTransactor.AddOrder(CustomerID, ProductID)
    If Not blnSuccess Then Err.Raise vbObjectError

    blnSuccess = objTransactor.AddPayment(CustomerID, CardNumber)
    If Not blnSuccess Then Err.Raise vbObjectError
```

```
    'Commit Transaction
    objContext.SetComplete

OrderFlowersExit:
    Exit Function

OrderFlowersErr:
    'Rollback Transaction
    objContext.SetAbort
    OrderFlowers = False
    Debug.Print Err.Description
    Resume OrderFlowersExit

End Function
```

The SetComplete method is called by each method of the Transactor object if the
method is successful. SetComplete notifies MTS that this portion of the transaction was
successful and that the method has left the Transactor object in a condition where it can
be reused. Therefore, the Transactor should not be retaining any state from the method
when the SetComplete method is called.

If any error occurs during the transaction, the Transactor object will call the SetAbort
method. SetAbort notifies MTS that the transaction has failed and the system is not in a
consistent state. Therefore MTS should roll back to the last known consistent state.
Either method of the Transactor object or even the Manager object itself may call
SetAbort if an error occurs. SetAbort is typically called as a normal part of the error-
handling routine for any object.

```
Public Function AddOrder(CustomerID, ProductID As Long) As Boolean

On Error GoTo AddOrderErr

    AddOrder = True

    'Variables
    Dim objContext As MTxAS.ObjectContext

    Dim objConnection As ADODB.Connection
    Dim strSQL As String

    'Get Context
    Set objContext = GetObjectContext

    'Build SQL Statement
    strSQL = "INSERT INTO Orders (CustomerID,ProductID) VALUES (" _
    & CustomerID & "," & ProductID & ")"

    'Open Connection
```

```vb
    Set objConnection = New ADODB.Connection
    objConnection.Open "DSN=Flowers;"

    'Update Data
    objConnection.Execute strSQL
    objConnection.Close
    Set objConnection = Nothing

    'Commit Changes
    objContext.SetComplete

AddOrderExit:
    Exit Function

AddOrderErr:
    'Roll back
    objContext.SetAbort
    AddOrder = False
    Debug.Print Err.Description
    Resume AddOrderExit

End Function

Public Function AddPayment(CustomerID As Long, _
CardNumber As String) As Boolean

On Error GoTo AddPaymentErr

    AddPayment = True

    'Variables
    Dim objContext As MTxAS.ObjectContext
    Dim objConnection As ADODB.Connection
    Dim strSQL As String

    'Get Context
    Set objContext = GetObjectContext

    'Build SQL Statement
    strSQL = "INSERT INTO Payments (CustomerID,CardNumber) VALUES (" _
    & CustomerID & ",'" & CardNumber & "')"

    'Open Connection
    Set objConnection = New ADODB.Connection
    objConnection.Open "DSN=Flowers"

    'Update Data
    objConnection.Execute strSQL
    objConnection.Close
    Set objConnection = Nothing
```

```
        'Commit Changes
        objContext.SetComplete

AddPaymentExit:
        Exit Function

AddPaymentErr:
        'Rollback
        objContext.SetAbort
        AddPayment = False
        Debug.Print Err.Description
        Resume AddPaymentExit

End Function
```

Transactional work in MTS is handled by the MSDTC based on the transactional properties of the component. Generally speaking, transactions are simple to implement and offer an additional layer of error protection. This protection can be extended to any component even if that component only performs a single database operation.

THE `TransactionContext` OBJECT

Although you can easily use an object like the `Manager` object described earlier to initiate and manage a transaction, MTS provides a default transaction management object called the `TransactionContext` object. The `TransactionContext` object is like an object that has its transaction attribute set to Requires a New Transaction except that clients using the `TransactionContext` typically do not run inside MTS. This means that a form in a Standard EXE project can directly initiate transactions in MTS. Obviously this violates our partitioning rules and for this reason, you should not utilize this feature in a typical MTS application. However, it is important to understand this concept because some day you may have to perform maintenance on an application that does use this feature.

In order to use the `TransactionContext` object, you must first set a reference to the Transaction Context Type Library in the References dialog of Visual Basic. With the reference set, you can create an instance of the `TransactionContext` object and use it to create instances of any object running under MTS. Objects created by the `TransactionContext` object will run in the same transaction as long as they are designated to support transactions and not to require a new transaction.

As an example of using the `TransactionContext` object, imagine a new front end to the Flowers application that enlists a transaction directly from a Visual Basic form running outside MTS control. Because the form itself will manage the transaction, the `Manager` object is not required. Instead, the base client may call directly to the `Transactor` object. The following code shows how to create an instance of the `TransactionContext` and enlist an MTS object in the new transaction:

```
On Error GoTo OrderErr

    Dim blnSuccess As Boolean

    'Create TransactionObject
    Set objTransaction = New TxCTx.TransactionContext

    'Enlist the Transactor object
    Set objFlowers = objTransaction.CreateInstance("Flowers.Transactor")

    'Place Order
    blnSuccess = objFlowers.AddOrder
    If Not blnSuccess Then Err.Raise vbObjectError

    blnSuccess = objFlowers.AddPayment
    If Not blnSuccess Then Err.Raise vbObjectError

    'Commit Transaction
    objTransaction.Commit
    MsgBox "Thank You for your order!", _
        vbOKOnly + vbInformation, "Flowers"

OrderExit:
    Exit Sub

OrderErr:
    'Rollback Transaction
    objTransaction.Abort

    MsgBox "Sorry.  Transaction failed!", _
    vbOKOnly + vbExclamation, "Flowers"
    Resume OrderExit
```

QUICK CHECK 6-2:

USING THE TRANSACTIONCONTEXT

1. Using the CD-ROM for the book, locate the directory TEMPLATES\QUICK CHECK6-2. This directory contains a partially completed project you can use to investigate transactions with the TransactionContext object.

2. On your hard drive, create a new directory with the Windows Explorer named MTS\QUICK CHECK6-2. Copy the contents from the CD-ROM directory into the new directory you just created.

3. Because the CD-ROM will create read-only copies of the project files, select all of the files you copied, right-click them, and select **Properties** from the pop-up menu. In the properties dialog, uncheck the read-only flag. Close the dialog.

continues

continued

4. Start Visual Basic and open the project. This project contains a Standard EXE and an ActiveX DLL. The ActiveX DLL project will be placed in MTS and the Standard EXE will use it in a transaction. The transaction simulates moving money between checking and savings accounts.

5. In the Project Explorer, locate the project named `TransContext`. In this project, open the class module named `Transactor`. This class contains two methods. The `GetBalance` method is used to retrieve the account balance based on an `AccountID`. The `AdjustBalance` method is used to change the balance of an account. The key to the transaction is that we can call the `AdjustBalance` method once for the account we credit and once for the account we debit.

6. MTS components that we use with the `TransactionContext` must be designated to at least support transactions. In the properties window, set the `MTSTransactionMode` property for the `Transactor` class to `2- RequiresTransaction`.

7. In the Project Explorer, locate the `FrontEnd` project. In the project, open the code window for the form named `frmTransfer`. This form creates an instance of the `TransactionContext` object when it loads and uses the object to enlist the `Transactor`.

8. The transactions occur through calls to the `AdjustBalance` method of the `Transactor` object. These calls are made when you click the Transfer button. Add the code in Listing 6.2 to the `cmdTransfer_Click` event to generate the transaction and move the money.

LISTING 6.2   CODE FOR THE `cmdTransfer_Click` EVENT

```
'Transfer money
    If optToChecking.Value = True Then
        If objBusiness.AdjustBalance _
        (1, CCur(txtTransfer.Text)) = False _
        Or objBusiness.AdjustBalance _
        (2, -1 * CCur(txtTransfer.Text)) = False Then
                objTransaction.Abort
        Else
                objTransaction.Commit
        End If
    Else
        If objBusiness.AdjustBalance _
        (1, -1 * CCur(txtTransfer.Text)) = False _
        Or objBusiness.AdjustBalance _
        (2, CCur(txtTransfer.Text)) = False Then
                objTransaction.Abort
```

```
        Else
                objTransaction.Commit
        End If
    End If

    Display
```

9. After the code is added, compile the project by selecting File, Make Project Group from the menu. After the project has been compiled, create a package in MTS named TransContext. Add the Transactor class to the package. After the package is built, run the application and try moving money.

Although you can use the TransactionContext object to perform transactions from a base client, doing so removes many of the advantages of using MTS. Because the TransactionContext object runs in process with the base client, MTS must be on the same computer as the base client. This functionality is not always a disadvantage—Active Server Pages uses the TransactionContext object to create transactions that run directly in a Web page—but for most applications, requiring MTS to be on the client computer violates the optimal design of a three-tier application. Additionally, you should note that any work done in the base client itself can never be part of the overall transaction. The TransactionContext object can only enlist MTS components in a transaction and not methods of the base client.

DISTRIBUTED TRANSACTIONS

Creating distributed transactions using MTS components is coded in essentially the same way as a single-server transaction. You can use an object as the Transaction Manager and one or more objects to perform work with the context of the transaction started by the managing object. When you create a distributed transaction, you enlist the services of the Microsoft Distributed Transaction Coordinator (MSDTC). Therefore, you must ensure that the MSDTC is installed and running on all the computers involved in the distributed transaction.

Utilizing the MSDTC from inside MTS is similar to using the service from a SQL Server BEGIN DISTRIBUTED TRANSACTION statement. When the MSDTC is involved in a transaction, the ACID attributes are maintained through a two-phase commit that uses the MSDTC to enlist the services of Resource Managers on other computers to complete the distributed transaction. Any machine running MTS and the MSDTC can initiate and manage a transaction distributed across other MTS/MSDTC computers. The advantage of MTS is that distributed transactions are as simple to perform as single-server transactions.

As developers learn to use transactional components inside MTS, many architectural issues arise that can greatly affect overall system performance. All of the examples so far in this chapter have utilized stateless business objects that do not remember any information between method calls. This architecture allows MTS to reuse system resources as quickly as possible. However, MTS does not require an object to release its state information in order to commit a transaction. An object can allow a transaction to commit or abort while maintaining state through the use of the `EnableCommit` and `DisableCommit` methods of the `ObjectContext`.

For example, we could maintain state between method calls to the `Transactor` object used in the flower shop demo earlier. In this case, we can let the `Transactor` object hold key information required by the transaction through properties. This means that while the transaction is in process, MTS cannot reuse the `Transactor` object for any other client because the state must be preserved for the current transaction.

Although it is possible to maintain state across transactions, doing so can have serious negative impact on performance. Suppose for example, you architect the flower shop to begin a transaction by placing an order and then returning to the user for credit card information. In this case, the users may take a significant amount of time to complete the transaction while they decide what credit card to use and even if they are sure they want to actually buy. The issue here is that the user has entered into the middle of the transaction while an object in MTS is holding state. Because the object is holding state, MTS cannot reuse it, which causes the system performance to grind to a halt while waiting the completion of the transaction. The object does not become available again until it calls `SetComplete` or `SetAbort` following the entry into the Payments table.

Transaction boundaries, therefore, are critical to application performance. Generally speaking, objects should not retain state between method calls in a transaction unless absolutely necessary. State can be maintained on the client and passed as arguments to the method calls involved in the transaction. This type of architecture has a tremendous impact on the success of any MTS application.

MONITORING TRANSACTIONS

While transactions are running under MTS, you can monitor the state of each transaction as well as view statistics regarding the success and failure of each transaction. In the MTS Explorer, transactions can be monitored for any computer in the Explorer. Simply select the desired computer and then click the Transaction Statistics icon. In this view, you can see statistical information regarding the success and failure of previous transactions.

While transactions are running, you may occasionally have to resolve a transaction manually. Transactions can be viewed and resolved manually using the Transaction List view in the MTS Explorer. Using this view, you can monitor the state of each running transaction. Transactions that are in an undefined state due to system resource failure can be manually committed or failed by selecting them in the MTS Explorer and right-clicking for a context menu. Transactions can be in an undefined state when MSDTC prepares all of the system Resource Managers but then fails unexpectedly. In this state, Resource Managers are awaiting a commit or abort command from the Transaction Manager, but it is unavailable.

EXERCISE 6-1: MTS TRANSACTIONS

This exercise uses the skills covered in the chapter to create an application that utilizes transactions. You will be building an application that simulates an online order system.

Step 1
Using the CD-ROM for the book, locate the directory TEMPLATES\EXERCISE6-1. This directory contains a partially completed project you can use to investigate transactions in MTS.

Step 2
On your hard drive, create a new directory with the Windows Explorer named MTS\EXERCISE6-1. Copy the contents from the CD-ROM directory into the new directory you just created.

Step 3
Because the CD-ROM will create read-only copies of the project files, select all the files you copied, right-click them, and select **Properties** from the pop-up menu. In the properties dialog, uncheck the read-only flag. Close the dialog.

Step 4
Start Visual Basic and open the project. This project contains a Standard EXE and an ActiveX DLL. The ActiveX DLL project will be placed in MTS, and the Standard EXE will use it in a transaction. The transaction simulates making a credit card purchase as a transaction.

Creating the Database

In this section, you will create a database for use with the application. The database is created using a SQL script.

Step 5
Before you can create the code for this application, you must build a database in SQL Server. In the EXERCISE6-1 directory, you will find a SQL script file named EXERCISE6-1.SQL. This is a script file that you can run on a database in SQL Server to create the correct structure for this exercise.

Step 6
Before running the SQL script, you must first create a blank database in SQL Server. Creating a blank database is done in the SQL Enterprise Manager. If you are using SQL 6.5, the Enterprise Manager is a separate utility. In SQL 7.0, the Enterprise Manager is run through the Microsoft Management Console. In either case, start the appropriate Enterprise Manager.

Step 7

In the Enterprise Manager, create a new database named Flowers. This database can be small, but make it at least 2M in size. Depending upon which version of SQL Server you are running, you will see different dialogs when creating the database. Figure 6.6 shows the dialog for creating a database in SQL 7.0.

FIGURE 6.6

Create a blank database for this exercise in SQL Server.

Step 8

After the database is created, you can run the script to finish building the structure. In SQL Server 6.5, use the ISQL_w utility. In SQL Server 7.0, this is known as the Query Analyzer. In either case, the command-line utility will allow you to open and run the SQL script. When you run the script, it will create three tables for you to use with the exercise. Figure 6.7 shows a database diagram with the four tables. The Customers table contains customer information; the Orders table contains information about floral arrangements that were ordered by customers; the Payments table contains information about credit cards used by the customers; and the Products table contains the available products you can order. In this example, we want to make an order in the Orders table only when a valid entry exists in the Payments table. Therefore we'll use a transaction to make the entries.

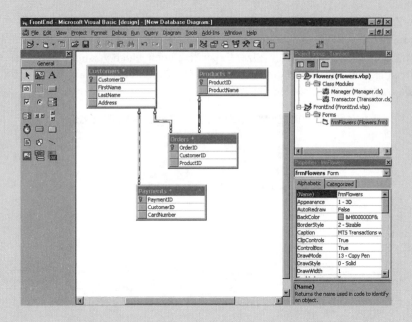

FIGURE 6.7

Three tables are used to take orders in the example.

Building the Business Objects

In this section, you will build the business objects to perform the transaction. One component will manage the transaction while another performs the detailed work. This is a typical setup for MTS transactions.

Step 9

In the Project Explorer, locate the ActiveX DLL project named Flowers. This project contains two class modules: Manager and Transactor. The Manager class is the single point of interface between the MTS components and the client. It will begin and manage the transaction. The Transactor class handles all data access. This is primarily adding data to the tables.

Step 10

Open the code module for the Transactor class. In this class, you will find three data access methods: AddCustomer, AddOrder, and AddPayment. The AddCustomer method is used to enter the name and shipping address for the order. It also generates a unique CustomerID for the transaction. This CustomerID is used in the transaction to form the data relationships. In this example, we generate a GUID as the CustomerID. Add the code in Listing 6.3 to the AddCustomer method to create a new customer entry and generate a CustomerID.

LISTING 6.3   CODE TO ADD TO THE AddCustomer METHOD

```
On Error GoTo AddCustomerErr

    'Get Object Context
    Dim objContext As MTxAs.ObjectContext
    Set objContext = GetObjectContext()

'Open Connection
    Dim strGUID As String
    Dim objConnection As ADODB.Connection
    Set objConnection = New ADODB.Connection

    objConnection.Provider = "SQLOLEDB"
    objConnection.ConnectionString = _
    "Data Source=(local);Database=Flowers;UID=sa;PWD=;"
    objConnection.Open

    'Add Customer
    strGUID = MakeGUID
    AddCustomer = strGUID
    objConnection.Execute _
    "EXECUTE sp_AddCustomer '" & strGUID & "','" _
    & strFirstName & "','" & strLastName & "','" & strAddress & "'"

    'Tell MTS we succeeded
    objContext.SetComplete

AddCustomerExit:
    Exit Function

AddCustomerErr:
    'Tell MTS we failed
    objContext.SetAbort

    'Log errors
    Debug.Print Err.Description
    App.StartLogging App.Path & "\error.log", vbLogToFile
    App.LogEvent Err.Description, vbLogEventTypeError
    Resume AddCustomerExit
```

Step 11

After the CustomerID is generated, we start a transaction to create entries in the Orders
and Payments table. The AddOrder method writes to the Orders table. Add the code in
Listing 6.4 to the AddOrder method to make a new order entry.

LISTING 6.4   CODE FOR THE AddOrder METHOD

```
On Error GoTo AddOrderErr

    AddOrder = True

    'Variables
    Dim objContext As MTxAs.ObjectContext

    'Variables
    Dim objConnection As ADODB.Connection
    Dim strSQL As String

'Get Context
    Set objContext = GetObjectContext

    'Open Connection
    Set objConnection = New ADODB.Connection
    objConnection.Provider = "SQLOLEDB"
    objConnection.ConnectionString = _
    "Data Source=(local);Database=Flowers;UID=sa;PWD=;"
    objConnection.Open

    'Build SQL Statement
    strSQL = "INSERT INTO Orders (CustomerID,ProductID) VALUES ('" _
    & strCustomerID & "'," & lngProductID & ")"

    'Update Data
    objConnection.Execute strSQL

    'Commit Changes
    objContext.SetComplete

AddOrderExit:
    Exit Function

AddOrderErr:
    'Roll back
    objContext.SetAbort
    AddOrder = False
    App.StartLogging App.Path & "\error.log", vbLogToFile
    App.LogEvent Err.Description, vbLogEventTypeError
    Debug.Print Err.Description
    Resume AddOrderExit
```

Step 12

The AddPayment method is used to record credit card information. Along with the
AddOrder method, it comprises the complete transaction. Add the code in Listing 6.5 to
the AddPayment method to save credit card data.

LISTING 6.5   CODE FOR THE AddPayment METHOD

```
On Error GoTo AddPaymentErr

    AddPayment = True

    'Variables
    Dim objContext As MTxAs.ObjectContext
    Dim objConnection As ADODB.Connection
    Dim strSQL As String

    'Get Context
    Set objContext = GetObjectContext

    'Build SQL Statement
strSQL = "INSERT INTO Payments (CustomerID,CardNumber) VALUES ('" _
    & strCustomerID & "','" & strCardNumber & "')"

    'Open Connection
    Set objConnection = New ADODB.Connection
    objConnection.Provider = "SQLOLEDB"
    objConnection.ConnectionString = _
    "Data Source=(local);Database=Flowers;UID=sa;PWD=;"
    objConnection.Open

    objConnection.Execute strSQL

    'Commit Changes
    objContext.SetComplete

AddPaymentExit:
    Exit Function

AddPaymentErr:
    'Rollback
    objContext.SetAbort
    AddPayment = False
    Debug.Print Err.Description
    App.StartLogging App.Path & "\error.log", vbLogToFile
    App.LogEvent Err.Description, vbLogEventTypeError
    Resume AddPaymentExit
```

Step 13

Because the methods in the Transactor will participate in transactions, we must mark the class as transactional. If the AddCustomer is called, we want to start a transaction. If either of the other two methods are called, we want to participate in a transaction started by the Manager. Therefore, set the MTSTransactionMode property of the Transactor class to "2-Requires Transaction."

Step 14

In the Project Explorer, open the Manager class. This class is called by the client and handles the transaction management. It has a single method called "OrderFlowers" that calls all the different methods of the Transactor. Add the code in listing 6.6 to the OrderFlowers method to complete the transaction.

LISTING 6.6   CODE FOR THE OrderFlowers METHOD

```
On Error GoTo OrderFlowersErr

    OrderFlowers = True

    'Variables
    Dim objContext As MTxAs.ObjectContext

Dim objTransactor As Flowers.Transactor
    Dim blnSuccess As Boolean
    Dim strCustomerID As String

    'Create Transactor in my context
    Set objContext = GetObjectContext
    Set objTransactor = objContext.CreateInstance("Flowers.Transactor")

    'Add a Customer
    strCustomerID = _
    objTransactor.AddCustomer(strFirstName, strLastName, strAddress)
    blnSuccess = objTransactor.AddOrder(strCustomerID, lngProductID)
    If Not blnSuccess Then Err.Raise vbObjectError

    blnSuccess = objTransactor.AddPayment(strCustomerID, strCardNumber)
    If Not blnSuccess Then Err.Raise vbObjectError

    'Commit Transaction
    objContext.SetComplete

OrderFlowersExit:
    Exit Function

OrderFlowersErr:
    'Rollback Transaction
    objContext.SetAbort
    OrderFlowers = False
    Debug.Print Err.Description
    App.StartLogging App.Path & "\error.log", vbLogToFile
    App.LogEvent Err.Description, vbLogEventTypeError
    Resume OrderFlowersExit
```

Step 15

Because the Manager class will always initiate transactions, we want to mark it to always require transactions. Therefore, set the MTSTransactionMode property to "4-RequiresNewTransaction."

Step 16

After the code is entered, compile the entire project by selecting File, Make Project Group from the menu. In the MTS Explorer, create a package for the Manager and Transactor classes. Add these classes to the new package.

Step 17

When the components are in the new MTS package, run the front-end executable and test the application. You should be able to order flowers from the application and verify that the data was correctly entered in the database. Figure 6.8 shows the front end.

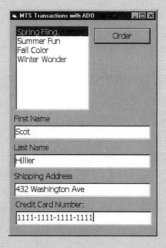

FIGURE 6.8

Use this form to create transactions in MTS.

MTS SECURITY

PREREQUISITES

Before beginning this chapter, you should have a firm understanding of MTS administration facilities. You should also understand the use of the ObjectContext and how to write components in Visual Basic that utilize the ObjectContext.

Skills Learned

- MTS(16): Use the ObjectContext to determine the client's role.
- MTS(17): Use the Security object to determine the client's identity.
- MTS(18): Use roles to prevent access to the methods of a component.
- MTS(19): Use roles to configure the functionality of an application.

Most business applications have the need for some level of security. However, security is a deceivingly simple word that means much more than most application developers realize. We are all familiar, of course, with the notion of a logon screen that requires a user ID and password, which is used to permit access to a network or database, but this is only the beginning of security in Windows/NT. There are many resources besides the database or network directory that may be secured. In many cases, business applications do not have a need for highly sophisticated security features, but when you need them, Windows/NT and MTS can help you access and manage these features.

NETWORK BASICS

Although this book does not attempt to train you as a network administrator, we have found that a firm understanding of network principles helps developers better grasp how their applications fit into a distributed world. This distributed world begins when computers are connected through a network infrastructure. In this environment computers are connected through network cards and hubs, which process signals and allow computers to communicate.

When computers are connected, they can, of course, transfer data between them. However, in order to efficiently transfer data, the computers must have a common language that describes the format and mechanism for data transfer. This transfer language is known as a protocol. Although many different protocols exist—and Windows/NT can run them—the primary protocol of interest in most distributed applications is the Transfer Control Protocol/Internet Protocol (TCP/IP). TCP/IP is important to Windows/NT developers because it is the primary protocol used on the Internet. Therefore understanding how it works is a must for developers.

TCP/IP protocol defines both the manner in which data is transferred between networked computers and the mechanism for addressing the computers on the network. The first half of the protocol—Transfer Control Protocol—defines the data transfer mechanism. The second half—Internet Protocol—defines the addressing mechanism.

Whenever data is transferred between computers using TCP/IP protocol, the data to be transferred is broken into "packets." These packets are a predefined size and contain part of the total information being transferred. This is similar to taking a piece of paper and running it through a shredder. The output is a set of uniform pieces that when reassembled represent the information.

After the data packets are created, they are each individually addressed to the destination machine. This is sort of the equivalent of shredding a letter to your mother and then individually addressing each piece. You could then put a stamp on each piece of shred and drop the whole bunch in the local mailbox.

The address of the destination machine is the function of the Internet Protocol. This protocol defines a set of four numbers that uniquely identify a computer on the face of the planet. Each of the four numbers can be between 0 and 255. Each number is separated from the other by a decimal. Thus the address 38.213.11.8 identifies a unique machine across the entire planet. These addresses can either be dynamically assigned by your network, or hand-coded into each machine. The address is typically entered using the network icon in the Control Panel. Figure 7.1 shows a hand-coded IP address.

FIGURE 7.1

You can configure the TCP/IP protocol through the network applet.

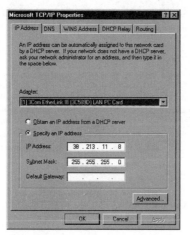

The address of the destination machine is the function of the Internet Protocol. This protocol defines a set of four numbers that uniquely identify a computer on the face of the planet. Each of the four numbers can be between 0 and 255. Each number is separated from the other by a decimal. Thus the address 38.213.11.8 identifies a unique machine across the entire planet. These addresses can either be dynamically assigned by your network, or hand-coded into each machine. The address is typically entered using the network icon in the Control Panel. Figure 7.1 shows a hand-coded IP address.

7

MTS SECURITY

Although you are free to enter any numbers you want into your computer, if your computer participates in a network—especially if it's attached to the Internet—you need to use a unique address. Assigning unique addresses is the job of the InterNIC. The InterNIC is responsible for assigning IP addresses to companies and organizations that want to connect to the Internet. Typically these IP addresses are associated with a plain English "domain name." For example, the domain name vb-bootcamp.com is associated with the IP address 38.213.11.x. Inside this domain, we can specify any valid number for the last of the four numbers. Furthermore, any computer with an IP address that begins with 38.213.11 is said to be a member of the vb-bootcamp.com domain.

Having a valid IP address is not enough, however, to gain access to the resources of a domain. You cannot, for example, simply change your IP address to begin with 38.213.11 and be a member of vb-bootcamp.com. This is because network security is managed by a special computer known as the Primary Domain Controller (PDC). The PDC is responsible for managing all the users and computers that belong to a domain. Therefore domain membership is determined by both user and machine. Both must be recognized and valid members of the domain before the PDC will grant access.

Adding users to a domain is fairly straightforward. This is generally done by a network administrator who belongs to the group of domain administrators as recognized by the PDC. The administrator uses the User Manager for Domains utility to add user names and passwords to the domain. Individuals may also be collected into named groups and permissions assigned at the group level. Figure 7.2 shows the User Manager.

FIGURE 7.2

The User Manager manages individuals and groups.

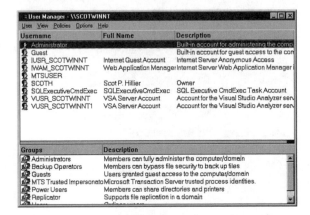

Adding computers to the domain is done by using the name of the computer. Each computer is given a plain English name along with its IP address. These English names can then be used to access the computer and add it to the domain. Managing the computers in the domain is done with the Server Manager utility. Figure 7.3 shows the Server Manager.

FIGURE 7.3

The Server Manager manages computers in the domain.

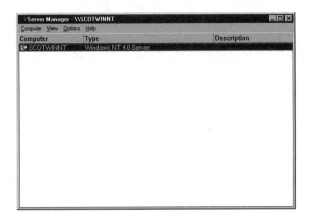

After computers and users are added to the domain, they can be assigned permissions and log on to the network. At this point, they enter the world of Windows/NT security.

This is where your applications can take advantage of the powerful security features in Windows/NT to manage permissions within your own project.

WINDOWS/NT SECURITY

Although Windows/NT appears to manage users by their names, it actually manages them by a unique number. Just as COM components receive a unique number to manage object creation, Windows/NT assigns numbers to users. These numbers are called Security Identifiers (SID).

A SID is used throughout Windows/NT to track users who are logged on to the network. If you are logged on to a Windows/NT network and start an application, the PDC knows that you are the originator of the application because it associates your SID with each process that you start.

Because a single user may actually be a member of many groups, a single SID is not enough to adequately identify all of the permissions assigned to a user. Therefore, Windows/NT creates an "access token" and attaches it to each process a user starts. An access token represents the combination of all security permissions received by the user as a member of any group and permissions assigned directly to the user.

Whenever a process you start needs access to resources under control of the PDC, your access token is used to determine if you have sufficient privileges. Privileges are assigned to a given system resource in the form of an "access control list" (ACL). Windows/NT compares your access token to the ACL for a given resource and determines your level of access—for example read, write, access, or launch. ACLs are kept for each resource in the system registry and in this way Windows/NT can always find out whether to grant or deny permission to access a resource.

DCOM SECURITY

For most business applications, providing credentials to access the database is enough security. However, Windows/NT provides for security when calling distributed components as well. This is done using the Distributed Component Object Model (DCOM) subsystem. DCOM allows network administrators to restrict access to ActiveX components on the system such that permissions can be given for both launch (creating instances) and access (calling methods). To date, very few applications have needed this type of security. There are certainly plenty of functions in the Windows API for accessing security features, but they are tricky to work with, and most applications simply don't care about anything except database security.

MTS Security features are a simple abstraction of DCOM security that makes component security more attractive than it has been in the past. However, understanding MTS security begins with understanding DCOM security. Therefore developers of distributed applications must have a familiarity with the details of DCOM security. DCOM security leverages the security features of Windows/NT to manage user access to components running in the domain. Like the File Explorer, any business object in the domain represents a resource that the administrator should be able to allocate at the individual or group level within the enterprise.

Allocating component permissions is done using the DCOM configuration (DCOMCNFG) utility. DCOMCNFG allows configuration of DCOM security for groups and individuals seeking component access. The utility is run by simply typing **DCOMCNFG** into the command line and running it. When first started, the DCOMCNFG utility shows a list of all the registered components under the Applications tab. Figure 7.4 shows the DCOMCNFG utility.

FIGURE 7.4

The DCOMCNFG utility lists all components on the system.

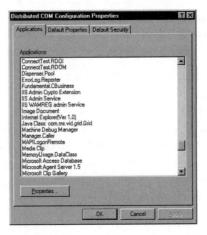

Using the Applications tab, you may configure the security for any individual component. However, DCOMCNFG offers default settings that apply to all components that you can set. These settings are handled through the Default Properties tab and the Default Security tab. The Default Properties tab allows you to set the authentication and impersonation levels for components. Figure 7.5 shows the Default Properties tab.

Default Authentication Level is a setting that determines when the identity of a caller is authenticated. Just as you must be authenticated prior to being logged on to a network,

Windows/NT will authenticate users who are attempting to access the services of a distributed component. The authentication level settings allow authentication at various levels based on how tightly you want to control security. Table 7.1 lists the available settings and explains their effect.

FIGURE 7.5

The Default Properties tab allows you to set the authentication and impersonation levels.

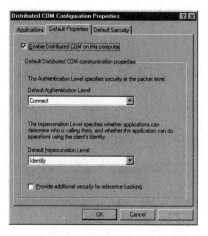

7

MTS SECURITY

TABLE 7.1 DCOM AUTHENTICATION LEVELS

Setting	Explanation
None	No authentication is performed.
Connect	Callers are authenticated only when they first connect to a component.
Call	Callers are authenticated each time they access a method of a component.
Packet	Each data packet is authenticated.
Packet Integrity	Authenticates each packet and ensures no packet data has been modified during transmission.
Packet Privacy	Authenticates each packet, ensures no packet data has been modified during transmission, and encrypts the data.

The Default properties tab also allows you to specify the Impersonation level for a component. Impersonation is a process that allows a component to assume the permissions of a Windows/NT user for the purpose of accessing system resources. DCOMCNFG provides a number of different settings that affect the ability of a component to access the system. Table 7.2 lists the settings and their features.

TABLE 7.2 IMPERSONATION LEVEL SETTINGS

Setting	Explanation
Anonymous	The caller cannot be identified.
Identify	The component can impersonate the caller for identification purposes only.
Impersonate	The component can impersonate the caller to access system resources.
Delegate	The component can impersonate the caller to gain access to system resources and to make calls to other objects.

The Default Security tab specifies the users who are assigned launch, access, and configuration permissions. Using these features, you may assign groups or individuals the right to create instances and call methods of remote components. Assigning these permissions is done through the Windows/NT security system. You can select individuals or whole NT groups for permission. Two special accounts are also listed that affect DCOM security. These accounts are the Interactive and System accounts. The Interactive account represents the current interactive user while the System account represents the operating system itself. Normally, you will leave the Interactive and System accounts as part of the default security settings. Figure 7.6 shows the Default Security tab.

FIGURE 7.6

The Default Security settings allow you to specify launch, access, and configuration permission.

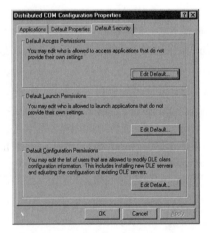

In addition to setting default security features, DCOMCNFG allows you to set security for any individual component as well. In order to set security for a single component, simply select that component from the list shown on the Applications tab and click the Properties button. DCOMDNFG displays a dialog with information about the individual component. This dialog has four tabs starting with the General tab that contains component identification information. Figure 7.7 shows the General tab.

FIGURE 7.7

The General tab contains basic information about a component.

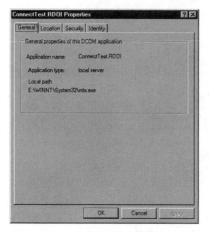

The Location tab allows you to specify whether this component runs on the current machine or somewhere else. If the component is on another machine, you can type the name of the machine and DCOM will invoke the component remotely. Figure 7.8 shows the Location tab.

FIGURE 7.8

The Location tab allows you to specify where the component is to run.

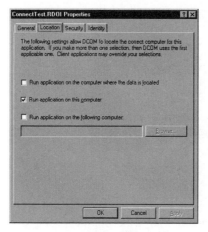

The Security tab allows you to modify the default settings you provided in the main DCOMCNFG dialog. Here you can customize the access and launch options just for this component. You may also choose to simply use the default settings from the main dialog. Figure 7.9 shows the Security tab.

FIGURE 7.9

The Security tab allows you to modify the default settings.

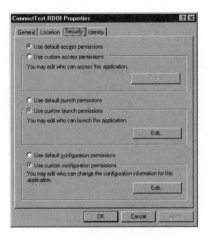

The Identity tab allows you to specify an account that will run the selected component. Using this tab, you can designate that the component should run in the context of the Interactive user. This means that the component will have the same permissions as the calling user according to the Impersonation settings used in the main dialog. You may alternately specify that the component be run in the context of the user who originally launched the component. Finally, you may specify a completely separate account where you want the component to run. Figure 7.10 shows the Identity tab.

FIGURE 7.10

The Identity tab allows you to specify the account under which a component runs.

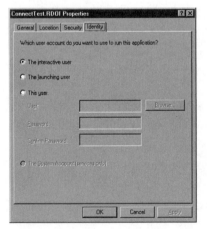

MTS SECURITY

Our experience with the DCOMCNFG utility is that it can be difficult to set up the right combination of settings to get your components to run across the network without problems. Fortunately, this is where MTS security really shines. MTS security is a combination of standard NT security and DCOM security. All of these aspects provide an extremely flexible security system that allows you to control permissions right down to the component interface level. Because MTS abstracts the complexities of DCOM and Windows/NT security, you will find that it is much simpler to distribute and secure your applications with MTS. However, as you learn about MTS security, keep in mind that this security is not about network logins or database security. This type of security is meant to prevent unauthorized use of a component, and in many applications this type of security is simply unnecessary.

The other key issue to understand about MTS and DCOM is that you can change several settings in either utility. However, you should not use the DCOMCNFG utility if you intend to use MTS to manage your distributed components. In fact, MTS only works correctly with DCOMCNFG set up to have a default settings of "Identify" for Impersonation Level and "Connect" for Authentication Level. Any changes to these settings should be done through the Security tab in the properties for a package directly in the MTS Explorer as opposed to using DCOMCNFG.

7

MTS SECURITY

> **TIP**
>
> Key Principle: Ensure that DCOMCNFG is set for a default Impersonation level of "Identity" and a default Authentication level of "Connect."

QUICK CHECK 7-1:

DCOM AND MTS

1. We can examine the relationship between MTS and DCOM by changing properties in MTS and then examining the effect in DCOMCNFG.

2. For this example, you can use any component that you have already placed under MTS control. Open the properties dialog for the package by clicking the package and selecting Action, Properties from the menu. On the Security tab, check the box Enable Authorization Checking. This will activate security for the package.

3. On the Identity tab, change the identity for the package so that it runs under your name.

4. Now run the DCOM configuration utility by clicking the Start button and selecting Run. In the command line, type **DCOMCNFG** and click OK.

continues

continued

> 5. In the DCOMCNFG utility, locate the component you were working with in MTS. Open the properties dialog for this component and examine the Identity tab. Your account should be listed as the identity for the component. This shows that MTS and DCOMCNFG affect many of the same characteristics for a component.

MTS supports two basic kinds of security for objects: declarative and programmatic. Declarative security relies on the definition of roles within the MTS Explorer. It is largely a graphical system of managing permissions. Programmatic security, on the other hand, relies on code within the business object to restrict access to components.

Declarative Security

Declarative security abstracts the security features of DCOM to provide a system that assigns access permissions to Windows/NT users and groups. Access permissions are assigned through the definition of MTS roles that are defined by the MTS Administrator at the package, object, and interface level. A role is a completely arbitrary name that represents a set of users and their permissions. Creating a role is done by selecting the Roles folder underneath any package, component, or interface and choosing Action, New, Role from the menu in the MTS Explorer. Figure 7.11 shows the MTS prompting for the name of a new role.

Figure 7.11

Roles are arbitrary names that you provide to represent a set of users and permissions.

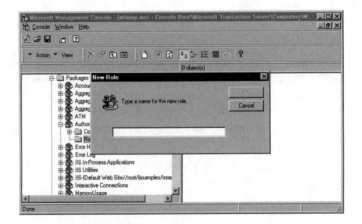

After a new role is created, you may assign Windows/NT users to the role through the Users folder. The Users folder is available for each role defined at the package, component, or interface level. Simply select the folder and choose Action, New, User from the

7

MTS SECURITY

menu in the MTS Explorer. MTS prompts you to choose the individual or group to assign to the role. Figure 7.12 shows how you select Windows/NT users for assignment to a role.

FIGURE 7.12

Windows/NT users are assigned to roles within a package.

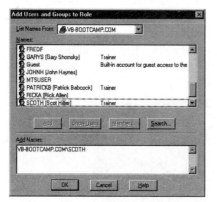

After users are assigned to roles, you must specify the permissions for a role. Each component in a package contains a folder called Role Membership. This folder contains all of the roles in the package that are allowed to access the component. To give permission for a role to access a component, select the Role Membership folder and choose Action, New, Role from the menu. You will then be able to pick from all available roles in the package. Choose the role you want to give permission to access the component. Figure 7.13 shows the role dialog.

FIGURE 7.13

Use this dialog to give permission for a role to access a component.

MTS allows you to specify role membership down to the interface level. If you examine the components in the package carefully, you will see that each interface defined for a component has a Role Membership folder. You may place any role in the package in any folder for any interface. This gives you a high degree of control over permissions.

After you have added the roles to the appropriate folders, you must activate security for the package. Security is activated using the Enable Authorization Checking option in the properties dialog. Checking this option causes the DCOM security features to activate. This means that calling clients must be a member of the Access Control List (ACL) for the given component. If you do not enable security for the package, role membership is meaningless. When security is activated, any caller not on the ACL for the given component will receive a Permission Denied error when he tries to access the component. Figure 7.14 shows the Security tab for the package.

Figure 7.14

Use this dialog to enable security for a package.

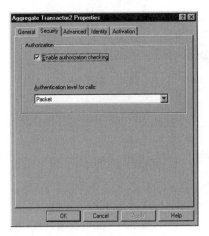

Unlike Windows/NT user management, defining a role in MTS does not explicitly provide rights to a user beyond permission to create instance of the business object. Defining at the package level gives access to all components in the package. The only way to restrict permissions is to define the role at a different level in the hierarchy. This strategy must be implemented carefully, however, to avoid excessive maintenance requirements for users and groups in MTS.

Programmatic Security

In addition to defining roles, MTS also allows you to write code specifically designed to enforce security within an object. When your object takes over the responsibility for managing access to services, that is called Programmatic Security. Although declarative security provides a simple technique for securing an object, it may not be flexible enough for your needs. You can complement declarative security by identifying the role of a particular caller directly in your component. Your component can than take additional action to permit or deny functionality. You can determine what role a user is in by calling the `IsCallerInRole` method of the `ObjectContext`. The `IsCallerInRole` method takes a string with the name of the role and returns a Boolean value indicating True if the user is a member of the role. After you have determined the role membership, your object can manage the permissions inside the current user context.

QUICK CHECK 7-2

DETERMINING ROLE MEMBERSHIP

1. Using the CD-ROM for the book, locate the directory TEMPLATES\QUICK CHECK7-2. This directory contains a partially completed project you can use to investigate roles in MTS.

2. On your hard drive, create a new directory with the Windows Explorer named MTS\QUICK CHECK7-2. Copy the contents from the CD-ROM directory into the new directory you just created.

3. Because the CD-ROM will create read-only copies of the project files, select all of the files you copied, right-click them, and select **Properties** from the pop-up menu. In the properties dialog, uncheck the read-only flag. Close the dialog.

4. Start Visual Basic and open the project group. In this project group you will find a Standard EXE project and an ActiveX DLL project.

5. In the Project Explorer, locate the project named `MTSCaller`. This project contains a single class named `User`. Open the code window for class `User`.

6. Class `User` contains a single method named `WhatsMyRole`. This method returns a String with the name of the role that the caller is in. When you put this component in MTS, you will build roles for this component to check. For now, add the code in Listing 7.1 to the `WhatsMyRole` method to return the role name.

LISTING 7.1   CODE TO RETURN THE ROLE NAME FOR THE `WhatsMyRole` METHOD

```
On Error GoTo WhatsMyRoleErr

    'Get My Context
    Dim objContext As MTxAS.ObjectContext
    Set objContext = AppServer.GetObjectContext()

    'Test for Security
    'Returns False if not running under MTS
    If objContext.IsSecurityEnabled = False Then
        WhatsMyRole = "Unknown!"
        GoTo WhatsMyRoleExit
    End If
```

continues

7

MTS SECURITY

continued

```
    'Test for Role
    If objContext.IsCallerInRole("Student") Then
        WhatsMyRole = "Student"
    Else
        WhatsMyRole = "None"
    End If

    'Release Object
    objContext.SetComplete

WhatsMyRoleExit:
    Exit Function

WhatsMyRoleErr:
    objContext.SetAbort
    WhatsMyRole = Err.Description
    Resume WhatsMyRoleExit
```

7. After the code is added to the method, compile the project group by selecting File, Make Project Group from the menu. When the project group is compiled, close Visual Basic.

8. Start the MTS Explorer. In the Explorer, create a new package named Roles. Place the MTSCaller component in the new package.

9. After the package is created, locate the Roles folder under the package. Create a new role for the package by selecting the folder and choosing Action, New, Role from the menu. Create a new role for the package named "Student."

10. After the role is created, add yourself to the role by selecting the Users folder and choosing Action, New, User from the menu. Locate your Windows/NT account and add it to the role.

11. Under the new component in the package, locate the Role Membership folder. Add the Student role to this folder by right-clicking and selecting New, Role from the pop-up menu.

12. Open the properties tab for the new package by right-clicking the package and selecting **Properties** from the pop-up menu. In the Security tab, check the Enable Authorization Checking box.

13. Locate the FRONTEND.EXE application you compiled earlier. When you run this project, you can call the WhatsMyRole method, which should now return "Student."

Prior to determining a client's role with `IsCallerInRole`, you should make sure that the business object has enabled security; otherwise, the information returned from `IsCallerInRole` may not be reliable. You can see if role checking is enabled by calling the `IsSecurityEnabled` method of the `ObjectContext`. This method returns a Boolean indicating True if role checking is valid. Also role checking is only valid for components that run in a Server Package. Server Packages run in the memory space of MTS. If your package is designated as a Library Package—one that runs in process with the client—role checking is not valid.

In addition to checking the client's role, MTS also allows you to directly determine the client identity. This is done through the `SecurityProperty` object. The `SecurityProperty` object has four methods used to return identification information:

> **`GetDirectCaller`** name returns the identity of the current calling client.
>
> **`GetDirectCreatorName`** returns the identity of the creator of the current object.
>
> **`GetOriginalCallerName`** returns the identity of the client that initiated the series of calls that resulted in the current call.
>
> **`GetOriginalCallerName`** returns the identity of the client that first created the object that initiated the series of calls resulting in the current call.

These methods are ideal for identifying the actual user even when a package is running under a common identity to support features like connection pooling.

QUICK CHECK 7-3

> ### DETERMINING CALLER IDENTITY
>
> 1. Using the CD-ROM for the book, locate the directory TEMPLATES\QUICK CHECK7-3. This directory contains a partially completed project you can use to investigate security in MTS.
>
> 2. On your hard drive, create a new directory with the Windows Explorer named MTS\QUICK CHECK7-3. Copy the contents from the CD-ROM directory into the new directory you just created.
>
> 3. Because the CD-ROM will create read-only copies of the project files, select all of the files you copied, right-click them, and select **Properties** from the pop-up menu. In the properties dialog, uncheck the read-only flag. Close the dialog.
>
> 4. Start Visual Basic and open the project group. In the group, you will find a Standard EXE and an ActiveX DLL project.
>
> *continues*

continued

5. In the Project Explorer, locate the project named "Secure." In this project, you will find a single class named "Identity." Open the code module for this class.

6. The class Identity has a single method named "GetCreator." This method is used to return the Windows/NT account of the person who is actually calling the component. Add the code in Listing 7.2 to the GetCreator method.

LISTING 7.2   CODE FOR THE GetCreator METHOD

```
On Error GoTo GetCreatorErr

    GetCreator = ""

    'Get the Object Context
    Dim objContext As MTxAS.ObjectContext
    Set objContext = GetObjectContext()

    'Get the SecurityProperty Object
    Dim objSecurity As MTxAS.SecurityProperty
    Set objSecurity = objContext.Security

    'Get the name of the caller
    GetCreator = objSecurity.GetDirectCreatorName

    'Tell MTS we are done
    objContext.SetComplete

GetCreatorExit:

    'Destroy objects
    Set objSecurity = Nothing
    Set objContext = Nothing

    Exit Function

GetCreatorErr:

    'Tell MTS we failed
    objContext.SetAbort

    Debug.Print Err.Description
    Resume GetCreatorExit
```

7. After the code is added to the method, compile the project group by selecting File, Make Project Group from the menu. When the project group is compiled, close Visual Basic.

8. Start the MTS Explorer. In the Explorer, create a new package named "Security." Run this package under the MTSUSER identity you set up earlier in the book. This will show you how you can get a user's name even if the package is running under another account. Place the `MTSCaller` component in the new package.

9. After the package is created, locate the Roles folder under the package. Create a new role for the package by selecting the folder and choosing Action, New, Role from the menu. Create a new role for the package named "Student."

10. After the role is created, add yourself to the role by selecting the Users folder and choosing Action, New, User from the menu. Locate your Windows/NT account and add it to the role.

11. Under the new component in the package, locate the Role Membership folder. Add the Student role to this folder by right-clicking and selecting New, Role from the pop-up menu.

12. Open the properties tab for the new package by right-clicking the package and selecting **Properties** from the pop-up menu. In the Security tab, check the Enable Authorization Checking box.

13. Locate the FRONTEND.EXE application you compiled earlier. When you run this project, you can call the `GetCreator` method, which should now return your Windows/NT account.

Determining the appropriate security strategy for your system depends on many factors. The simplest way to implement security is to define roles at the package level for components in your system. Components that share a package should perform functions that are at the same security level. This prevents having to define role membership at the component or interface level. Additionally, you can define roles that correspond directly to your defined domain groups. You can create, for example, an Administrator role and assign the Domain Administrators as members. You can define a Guest role and assign Domain Guests as members. This minimizes the overhead associated with role maintenance and centralizes access control with the MTS Administrator.

If, however, you have many levels of security within an application, some combination of Declarative and Programmatic security may be appropriate. Roles can be defined at the package level for ease of maintenance while business objects use `IsCallerInRole` to define finer grains of security control. The issue here, of course, is that security is buried within the code and will require a recompile to change. Additionally, some network administrators may be uncomfortable with the concept of software managing security. In this case, Programmatic Security may be a tough sell.

EXERCISE 7-1: MTS SECURITY

In this exercise, you will use role-based security to configure an application. The application will support two roles, Administrator and Guest. Administrators will be able to read and write to the database while Guests will have read-only access. This exercise does not include many of the partitioning features we have discussed earlier in the book. Rather, it focuses on providing some ideas for securing MTS applications.

Step 1
Using the CD-ROM for the book, locate the directory TEMPLATES\EXERCISE7-1. This directory contains a partially completed project you can use to investigate roles in MTS.

Step 2
On your hard drive, create a new directory with the Windows Explorer named MTS\ EXERCISE7-1. Copy the contents from the CD-ROM directory into the new directory you just created.

Step 3
Because the CD-ROM will create read-only copies of the project files, select all of the files you copied, right-click them, and select **Properties** from the pop-up menu. In the properties dialog, uncheck the read-only flag. Close the dialog.

Configuring the Application Based on a Role

In this section, you will change the application appearance based on the role. This allows you to limit the functionality available to users based on their Windows/NT account.

Step 4
Start Visual Basic and open the project group. In this project group you will find a Standard EXE project and two ActiveX DLL projects.

Step 5
In the Project Explorer, locate the project named "Security." This project contains a class module named "Configuration." The class Configuration is used to determine what role a user is in. This information is used to configure the front-end application as read-only or updateable. Open the Configuration class module in the code editor.

Step 6
The Configuration class has a single method named GetRole. This method returns a long value, which is from the RolesEnum enumeration. This enumeration signals the role of the user. The value returned is based on testing the client using the IsCallerInRole method of the ObjectContext. Add the code in Listing 7.3 to the GetRole method to return the enumeration.

LISTING 7.3   CODE FOR THE GetRole METHOD

```
On Error GoTo GetRoleErr

    GetRole = ntsUnknown

    'Get Object Context
    Dim objContext As MTxAS.ObjectContext
    Set objContext = GetObjectContext()

    'Check Role
    If objContext.IsCallerInRole("Administrator") Then
        GetRole = ntsAdministrator
    Else
        GetRole = ntsGuest
    End If

     objContext.SetComplete

GetRoleExit:
    Exit Function

GetRoleErr:
     objContext.SetAbort

    Debug.Print Err.Description
    App.StartLogging App.Path & "\error.log", vbLogToFile
    App.LogEvent Err.Description, vbLogEventTypeError
    Resume GetRoleExit
```

7

MTS SECURITY

Step 7
In the Project Explorer, locate the project named "FrontEnd." Configuring the application to be read-only or allow data updating is done as soon as the client logs in. The login screen calls the Security component to retrieve this information. The information is then used to set properties in the main client form. Therefore, we need to modify the login form. The login form also accepts the UserID and password for data access with SQL Server. It's important to recognize that the role of the user is independent of the UserID and password utilized by SQL Server. In the FrontEnd project, locate the form named "frmLogin." Figure 7.15 shows the login form.

Step 8
Open the code window for frmLogin. The application configuration takes place when the user clicks the OK button. In this routine, the form calls the Security component. The Security component return value indicates the role that is used to set properties on the main application form. The UserID and password are also sent to the main client form so it can access the database. Add the code in Listing 7.4 to the cmdOK_Click event to log in the user.

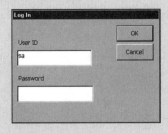

FIGURE 7.15

The login form helps configure the application.

LISTING 7.4   CODE TO LOG IN THE USER FOR THE CMDOK_CLICK EVENT

```
On Error GoTo OKErr

    'Get the users role
    lngConfigure = objSecurity.GetRole

    'Configure the application
    frmClient.strUID = txtUID.Text
    frmClient.strPassword = txtPassword.Text
    Load frmClient

    Select Case lngConfigure
        Case ntsAdministrator
            frmClient.grdPublishers.AllowUpdate = True
            frmClient.cmdUpdate.Visible = True
        Case ntsGuest
            frmClient.grdPublishers.AllowUpdate = False
            frmClient.cmdUpdate.Visible = False
        Case ntsUnknown
            MsgBox "Permission Denied!", vbOKOnly + vbExclamation,
                ➥"Security"
            End
    End Select

    frmClient.Show
    Unload Me
    Exit Sub

OKErr:
    MsgBox Err.Description, vbOKOnly + vbExclamation, "Security"
    End
```

Step 9

In the FrontEnd project, locate the form named `frmClient`. This form is the main form
for the application. It uses a grid to display records from SQL Server. This grid can allow
editing if the `AllowUpdate` property is True. This property is set by the login form based

on the role of the user. This form also supports batch updates with a single
CommandButton named cmdUpdate. The Visible property for this button is set based on
the role of the user. Utilizing the AllowUpdate property of the grid and the Visible
property of the CommandButton, the application can be configured as read-only or updateable based on the user role. Figure 7.16 shows the client form.

FIGURE 7.16
The main form is configured based on the user role.

Creating the User Roles

In this section, you will set up roles for the users of the application. These roles will be
used to determine the configuration at runtime.

Step 10
After the code is added, compile the project group by selecting File, Make Project Group
from the menu. This will create two dynamic link libraries and one EXE.

Step 11
Open the MTS Explorer. In the Explorer, create a new package named Configure. Add
both the Security and the PublisherObject components from the application to the
new package.

Step 12
After the package is created, you must create new roles for the package. Under the package, locate the Roles folder. Click on this folder and select Action, New, Role from the
menu. Add a new role named "Administrator." Repeat the process and add a new role
named "Guest."

Step 13
After the new roles are created, add yourself to the Administrator role. Do this by locat-
ing the Users folder under the Administrator role. Click the folder and select Action,
New, User from the menu. Add your Windows/NT account to the role.

Step 14

Now you must give permission for the roles to access the components. Under both the `Security` component and the `PublisherObject` component, you will find folders named Role Membership. Click the folder under one of the components and select Action, New, Role from the menu. Add both the Administrator and Guest role to the folder. Repeat the process for the other component. Both roles must be in the Role Membership folder for both components.

Step 15

When the roles are added, you can enable security for the package by right-clicking on the package and selecting **Properties** from the pop-up menu. In the Security tab, check the box Enable Authorization Checking.

Step 16

After the package is created and security is established, you can run the application. Run FRONTEND.EXE and you should see the login screen. Enter your credentials for data access and click OK. If you are utilizing standard security, be sure to use the user name and password of your SQL Server account, not your Windows/NT account or you will get an error. Because you are in the role of Administrator, you should be able to edit the records in the grid and update the database.

Step 17

Now go back to the MTS Explorer and remove yourself from the Administrator role. Add yourself instead to the Guest role. Run the application again and verify that the data is read-only now.

BUILDING CUSTOM DATA SOURCES

PREREQUISITES

Before beginning this chapter, you should be able to create ActiveX components from Visual Basic. You should also have a firm understanding of OLEDB fundamentals such as the use of providers and ADO.

Skills Learned

- MTS(23): Create a simple OLEDB provider.

Although ActiveX Data Objects support a wide variety of relational and nonrelational data stores through OLEDB, if you are attempting to access legacy data in a proprietary format, you may run into difficulty. SQL Server is an excellent back end for MTS applications, but we still see many companies who are unable or unwilling to move proprietary data formats into relational databases.

The essential problem with some legacy data is that the format of this data is so unique that developers cannot hope to find an OLEDB provider that will allow them to use ADO in their application. In these situations, developers will have to create their own data sources that deliver the proprietary data in an acceptable format. This may entail building a simple custom conversion routine or even creating a custom OLEDB provider. This chapter provides some ideas for people who want to build custom data providers for proprietary data formats.

DATA SOURCE CLASSES

The simplest custom data source is created in Visual Basic as a "data-aware" class. Data-aware classes in Visual Basic can function as a data provider or a data consumer. A data provider class is essentially a custom data control, whereas a data consumer is a custom bound control. We have already discussed binding data to the properties of a class module in Chapter 5. These types of classes are data consumers. Here we discuss using a class module to serve up data. These types of classes are data providers.

Any class module in Visual Basic may be a data provider. You can accomplish this by setting the DataSourceBehavior property of the class to 1-vbDataSource. Setting this property causes Visual Basic to add a new procedure to the class module named GetDataMember. This method has the following signature:

```
Private Sub Class_GetDataMember(DataMember As String, Data As Object)
End Sub
```

GetDataMember takes a String as an argument and returns an Object. The String is intended to be a query statement, whereas the Object is an instance of a class capable of supporting data access. This means that the input string might be "SELECT * FROM Authors", and the output is an ADO Recordset object. The input might also be some sort of proprietary query language you create yourself. You are certainly not limited to SQL. The key to creating the data source, however, is to understand how the query is turned into data.

After you set the DataSourceBehavior property, you must decide how your data source interacts with the underlying data. As an example, suppose we have some legacy data contained in text files. The format of the text files is such that the first line of the file contains the field names. Each additional line contains field data. The fields are delimited by commas, and the rows are delimited by carriage returns. The following code shows some sample data:

```
ProductID,Supplier,Manufacturer
1,Chai,Exotic Liquids
2,Chang,Exotic Liquids
3,Aniseed Syrup,Exotic Liquids
4,Chef Anton's Cajun Seasoning,New Orleans Cajun Delights
5,Chef Anton's Gumbo Mix,New Orleans Cajun Delights
6,Grandma's Boysenberry Spread,Grandma Kelly's Homestead
7,Uncle Bob's Organic Dried Pears,Grandma Kelly's Homestead
8,Northwoods Cranberry Sauce,Grandma Kelly's Homestead
9,Mishi Kobe Niku,Tokyo Traders
10,Ikura,Tokyo Traders
11,Queso Cabrales,Cooperativa de Quesos 'Las Cabras'
12,Queso Manchego La Pastora,Cooperativa de Quesos 'Las Cabras'
13,Konbu,Mayumi's
14,Tofu,Mayumi's
15,Genen Shouyu,Mayumi's
```

During the `Initialize` event for our data source, we will access the proprietary data and create an ADO `Recordset` object on the fly that contains the tabular data. This is possible because ADO `Recordset` objects can be created independently without any connection to an OLEDB data source; you simply create a new instance.

```
Set MyRecordset = New ADODB.Recordset
```

When an ADO `Recordset` is created this way, it contains no field definitions and no data. Therefore, we have to build the field definitions for the new `Recordset` ourselves. This is simple because the first line of data in the file contains the names of the fields. You can create field definitions in the new `Recordset` by using the `Append` method. This method requires the name of the new field to create and the data type for the field. Thus the following code creates a new field named `Supplier`, which takes 255 characters of text.

```
m_Recordset.Fields.Append "supplier", adBSTR, 255
```

After the field definitions are created, you must fill the new recordset with data from the file. This is done by reading the file out line by line based on the `Query` statement passed into the `GetDataMember` function. Regardless of the particulars of the query, however, we must open the file, read data, add it to the recordset, and close the file. After the recordset is created, it can be returned from the `GetDataMember` function.

```
Open App.Path & "\mydata.txt" For Input As #1
    Do While Not EOF(intFile)

        Line Input #intFile, strTemp
        vData = Split(strTemp, ",")
```

8

```
        m_Recordset.AddNew
        m_Recordset!supplier = vData(0)
        m_Recordset.Update

    Loop
Close #1
```

Data sources that you create in VB class modules are intended to be used with databound elements. This means that you can use databound controls directly to display the data or create a second class module to act as a data consumer. In any case, you must use the Microsoft Data Binding Collection object to bind the recordset returned from the data source to the data consumer. Typically, this binding occurs inside a class module in an MTS application. This class module is created in the user services layer, and the ADO `Recordset` object is transferred from the data source to the client machine for display through the data consumer class. The process of binding ADO recordsets to class modules was discussed in detail in Chapter 5.

QUICK CHECK 8-1:

BUILDING A CUSTOM DATA SOURCE

1. Using the CD-ROM for the book, locate the directory TEMPLATES\QUICK CHECK8-1. This directory contains a partially completed project you can use to create a custom data source.

2. On your hard drive, create a new directory with the Windows Explorer named MTS\QUICK CHECK8-1. Copy the contents from the CD-ROM directory into the new directory you just created.

3. Because the CD-ROM will create read-only copies of the project files, select all the files you copied, right-click them, and select **Properties** from the pop-up menu. In the properties dialog, uncheck the read-only flag. Close the dialog.

4. Start Visual Basic. In the Project Explorer, you should see a Standard EXE project and an ActiveX DLL project. The ActiveX DLL is the custom data source, and the Standard EXE is the front end for the data source.

5. In the Project Explorer, locate the project named PubData. This project contains a class named Publishers. The Publishers class implements a custom data source. In this example, we have converted the Publishers table from SQL Server into a text file to simulate legacy data. This file is named PUBLISHERS.TXT.

6. Open the code window for the Publishers class. In the code window, you will see the Initialize event. The Initialize event is used to read data from the text file and create a stand-alone recordset. Add the code in Listing 8.1 to the Initialize event to create the stand-alone recordset object.

LISTING 8.1 CODE FOR THE Initialize EVENT

```
'Create a new recordset
Set m_Recordset = New ADODB.Recordset
m_Recordset.Fields.Append "pub_id", adBSTR, 255
m_Recordset.Fields.Append "pub_name", adBSTR, 255
m_Recordset.Fields.Append "city", adBSTR, 255
m_Recordset.Fields.Append "state", adBSTR, 255
m_Recordset.Fields.Append "country", adBSTR, 255
m_Recordset.Open

'Populate the Recordset
Dim intFile As Integer
Dim strTemp As String
Dim vData As Variant

intFile = FreeFile

Open App.Path & "\publishers.txt" For Input As #intFile
    Do While Not EOF(intFile)

        Line Input #intFile, strTemp
        vData = Split(strTemp, "¦")
        If UBound(vData) <> 4 Then Exit Do

        m_Recordset.AddNew
        m_Recordset!pub_id = vData(0)
        m_Recordset!pub_name = vData(1)
        m_Recordset!city = vData(2)
        m_Recordset!State = vData(3)
        m_Recordset!country = vData(4)
        m_Recordset.Update

    Loop
Close #1

m_Recordset.MoveFirst
```

7. In order to make the Publishers class a data source, the DataSourceBehavior property must be set appropriately. In the properties window for the Publishers class, set the DataSourceBehavior property to 1-vbDataSource.

continues

8

**BUILDING CUSTOM
DATA SOURCES**

continued

8. Setting the `DataSourceBehavior` property will add the `GetDataMember` function to the class definition. You can add this procedure to your code by dropping the object box in the code window and selecting the `Class` entry. Then select `GetDataMember` from the procedure box.

9. After `GetDataMember` is added to the class, you can use it to receive query requests and return data. This example recognizes only one `Query` statement. It is only capable of returning all entries in the file. Obviously, a more sophisticated data source needs to return data for various queries. We cover this topic in the next section. For now, add the following code to the `GetDataMember` procedure to return the publisher data.

```
If UCase$(DataMember) = "SELECT * FROM Publishers" Then
    Set Data = m_Recordset
End If
```

10. After the code is added to the `Publishers` class, save your work, and open the code window for the `frmClient` form found in the `FrontEnd` project.

11. The client form uses the Microsoft Data Binding Collection to bind `TextBox` controls to the recordset provided by the custom data source. In this way, the data from the source is automatically sent to the display. Add the code in Listing 8.2 to the `Form_Load` event to bind the data source to the display.

LISTING 8.2   CODE TO ADD TO THE `Form_Load` EVENT

```
'Create Objects
Set m_BindCollection = New MSBind.BindingCollection
Set m_DataSource = New PubData.Publishers

'Assign the provider to the binding collection
m_BindCollection.DataMember = "SELECT * FROM Publishers"
Set m_BindCollection.DataSource = m_DataSource

'Bind the text
m_BindCollection.Add txtPubId, "Text", "pub_id"
m_BindCollection.Add txtPubName, "Text", "pub_name"
m_BindCollection.Add txtCity, "Text", "city"
m_BindCollection.Add txtState, "Text", "state"
m_BindCollection.Add txtCountry, "Text", "country"
```

12. After the code is entered in the project, save your work. You should now be able to run the project, display, and navigate the data. Figure 8.1 shows the client form.

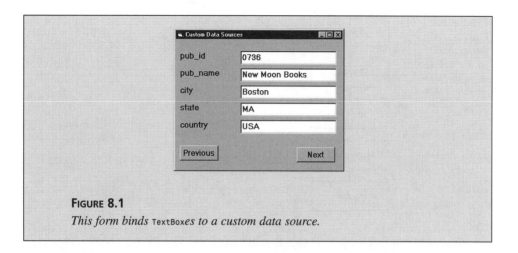

FIGURE 8.1

This form binds TextBoxes *to a custom data source.*

DEVELOPING A CUSTOM QUERY LANGUAGE

In the previous section, we showed that you can create a custom data source using a Visual Basic ActiveX DLL. However, one weakness should be made clear. In the preceding example, we supported only a single simple query statement, SELECT * FROM Publishers. It's obvious that any custom data provider must support a range of query constructs if it has any chance of being productive in an application. Therefore, each custom data source must be supported by a query language engine that can parse query statements for evaluation. This section outlines a simple query language engine you can use in your custom data sources.

The query engine we use is an object-based engine designed to parse query statements into elements and arguments. Elements consist of keywords such as SELECT or WHERE. Arguments are the data fields associated with the element. Our engine creates a collection of elements, and each element has its own collection of arguments. These collections can then be used by the data source to decide what elements to include in the final data set. Figure 8.2 shows the object model for the engine.

FIGURE 8.2

Our query engine parses query strings into elements and arguments collections.

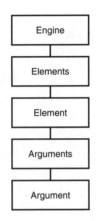

The `Engine` object is the top-level object in the hierarchy. The `Engine` object serves as a controlling object to parse the query string. The `Engine` has a `QueryString` property into which you place the string you want to parse. It also has a `Parse` method that will create the collection of arguments. Therefore, you begin by assigning the query to the `QueryString` property:

```
Dim objEngine As New QueryEngine.Engine
objEngine.QueryString = "SELECT au_lname,au_fname FROM Authors"
```

After the `QueryString` property is set, you must tell the `QueryEngine` about the key elements in your query language. You should note that this engine is capable of creating any kind of proprietary query language you want. We use SQL-like syntax here, but you can use any words for the language elements. Along with the language elements, you must enter the character used as the delimiter for the element. For example, columns that follow the `SELECT` element are separated by a comma. Therefore, the following code can be used to tell the engine how to parse the `SELECT` element:

```
objEngine.Elements.Add "SELECT",","
```

You continue adding elements to the engine until you have defined your entire language. Although this can be quite complex, the essential actions are to add the element and delimiter for each keyword. The delimiter will be used to locate arguments for the element. In our example, `au_lname` and `au_fname` are arguments of the `SELECT` element and will eventually appear in the arguments collection. Some words of warning here; our query engine does not like spaces between the delimiters. This means that the comma-separated arguments should appear without spaces (for example, `au_lname,au_fname`). Additionally, our engine uses only single-character delimiters. This means that we substitute symbols for words such as `LIKE`, which are more than one character.

After all the elements are added to the engine, you are ready to parse the query. This is done by simply calling the `Parse` method. This will create a collection of arguments for each element in the engine. Thus our example query would produce a `"SELECT"` element with an arguments collection containing au_lname and au_fname objects. The following code could be used to examine all the required fields for the `"SELECT"` statement:

```
Dim objArgument As QueryEngine.Argument
For Each objArgument In objEngine.Elements("SELECT").Arguments
    MsgBox objArgument.Value
Next
```

When you have access to the required fields for the query, you can use them to create an ADO `Recordset` object by appending fields. You can also use the data to retrieve the appropriate data from the proprietary file and populate the stand-alone ADO `Recordset` object.

QUICK CHECK 8-2:

USING A CUSTOM QUERY ENGINE

1. Using the CD-ROM for the book, locate the directory TEMPLATES\QUICK CHECK8-2. This directory contains a partially completed project you can use to test our query engine.

2. On your hard drive, create a new directory with the Windows Explorer named MTS\QUICK CHECK8-2. Copy the contents from the CD-ROM directory into the new directory you just created.

3. Because the CD-ROM will create read-only copies of the project files, select all the files you copied, right-click them, and select **Properties** from the pop-up menu. In the properties dialog, uncheck the read-only flag. Close the dialog.

4. Start Visual Basic. In the Project Explorer, you should see a Standard EXE project and two ActiveX DLL projects. The ActiveX DLL projects contain the query engine and the custom data source. The Standard EXE is the front end for the data source.

5. In the Project Explorer, locate the project named FrontEnd. In this project, open the code window for the form named frmClient. This form creates an instance of a custom data source named AuthorData, which reads a text file full of author information. Figure 8.3 shows the form.

6. The form allows you to query for author information based on a partial match of characters with the last name. This simulates a LIKE clause in SQL. The query is run when you click the Search button. Add the code in Listing 8.3 to the click event of cdmSearch to run the query.

continues

continued

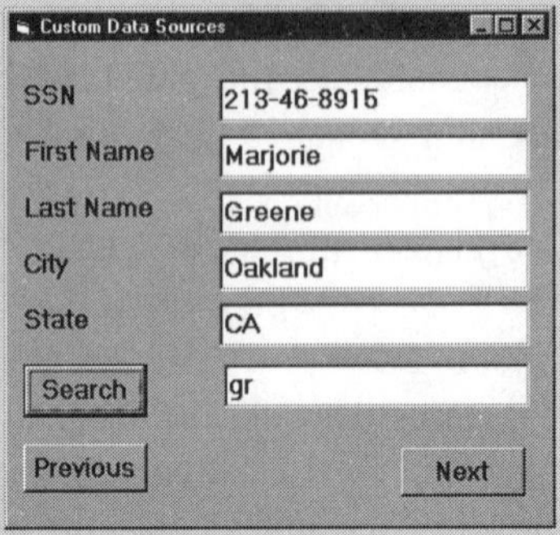

FIGURE 8.3

This form binds TextBoxes *to a custom data source.*

LISTING 8.3   CODE FOR THE click EVENT OF cdmSearch

```
'Create Objects
    Set m_BindCollection = New MSBind.BindingCollection
    Set m_DataSource = New AuthorData.Authors

    'Assign the provider to the binding collection
    m_BindCollection.DataMember = _
        "SELECT * FROM Authors WHERE au_lname?" & txtSearch.Text
    Set m_BindCollection.DataSource = m_DataSource

    'Bind the text
    m_BindCollection.Add txtId, "Text", "au_id"
    m_BindCollection.Add txtFirstName, "Text", "au_fname"
    m_BindCollection.Add txtLastName, "Text", "au_lname"
    m_BindCollection.Add txtCity, "Text", "city"
    m_BindCollection.Add txtState, "Text", "state"
```

7. In the Project Explorer, locate the project named AuthorData. This is the custom data source. Open the code window for the class named Authors. When the new query statement is set by the client, the GetDataMember procedure is called in the Authors class. When this procedure is called, the query is parsed using the engine found in the QueryEngine project. Add the code in Listing 8.4 to the GetDataMember procedure to parse and run the query.

LISTING 8.4   CODE TO PARSE AND RUN THE QUERY

```
'First parse SQL statement
m_QueryEngine.QueryString = DataMember
```

```
m_QueryEngine.Elements.Add "SELECT", ","
m_QueryEngine.Elements.Add "FROM", ","
m_QueryEngine.Elements.Add "WHERE", "?"
m_QueryEngine.Parse

'Create a new recordset
Set m_Recordset = New ADODB.Recordset
m_Recordset.Fields.Append "au_id", adBSTR, 255
m_Recordset.Fields.Append "au_lname", adBSTR, 255
m_Recordset.Fields.Append "au_fname", adBSTR, 255
m_Recordset.Fields.Append "city", adBSTR, 255
m_Recordset.Fields.Append "state", adBSTR, 255
m_Recordset.Open

'Populate the Recordset
Dim intFile As Integer
Dim strTemp As String
Dim vData As Variant

intFile = FreeFile

'Open Data File
Open App.Path & "\authors.txt" For Input As #intFile
    Do While Not EOF(intFile)

        Line Input #intFile, strTemp
        vData = Split(strTemp, "¦")
        If UBound(vData) <> 8 Then Exit Do

        'Test data against query
        With m_QueryEngine.Elements("WHERE")
            If .Arguments(1).Value = "au_lname" And _
            InStr(vData(au_lname), .Arguments(2).Value) > 0 Then


            'Add the record
            m_Recordset.AddNew
            m_Recordset!au_id = vData(au_id)
            m_Recordset!au_lname = vData(au_lname)
            m_Recordset!au_fname = vData(au_fname)
            m_Recordset!city = vData(city)
            m_Recordset!State = vData(State)
            m_Recordset.Update

        End If

    End With
    Loop
```

continues

8

**BUILDING CUSTOM
DATA SOURCES**

continued

```
Close #1

'Return Data
If m_Recordset.RecordCount > 0 Then m_Recordset.MoveFirst
Set Data = m_Recordset
```

8. After the code is added, run the project. Try searching for author information using the search box.

OLEDB PROVIDERS

If a simple data source object does not provide enough features, you may need to develop your own OLEDB provider. When you create your own OLEDB provider, you have two options for building it. If your provider requires all the features of OLEDB, then you should create a fully featured OLEDB provider. If, however, you do not need all the OLEDB interfaces, but want a provider that has just the fundamentals of OLEDB, you can use the OLEDB Simple Provider (OSP) toolkit. The difference between the fully featured provider and the simple provider is not just the features supported, but also the skills necessary to construct them. Fully featured providers can only be written in C++. If you want to write a simple provider, you can create your own in Visual Basic. In either case, you will need the OLEDB SDK, which contains all the tools necessary for a fully featured provider or a simple provider. The toolkit is available at
`www.microsoft.com/data`.

When you install the OLEDB SDK, you can install the entire contents or just install the OLEDB Simple Provider (OSP) Toolkit. The OSP Toolkit has everything you need to make an OLEDB provider in Visual Basic. In order to decide whether a simple provider written in Visual Basic is sufficient for your needs, you should examine the help file that ships with the OSP toolkit. This file lists the limitations of the OSP. The OSP toolkit is ideal for creating your own provider that wraps simple data stores like text files, collections, and memory arrays. This means that you can easily create custom providers that can be called directly from ADO.

The heart of the OSP toolkit is a special DLL named MSDAOSP.DLL that contains most of the functionality necessary to interface with an OLEDB consumer like ADO. Your job is simply to implement the appropriate interfaces for interacting with MSDAOSP.DLL. Through these interfaces, MSDAOSP.DLL is capable of requesting data from your provider as well as writing information to your custom data store. The OSP toolkit does not provide all the functionality of OLEDB, but it does provide the foundation for exposing a set of data as an OLEDB `Recordset` object that may be read and written through the `ADODB.Recordset` object.

Creating an OSP generally requires two classes. The first class, called the `Provider` class, is used to implement a set of interfaces that MSDAOSP.DLL can call for manipulating an OLEDB `Recordset`. The second class, called the `DataSource` class, is used by MSDAOSP.DLL to request a reference to the first `Provider` class. This is remarkably similar to the `GetDataMember` functionality we worked with before. Essentially, you must provide a set of data in response to a query string. Therefore, we will have to use our query engine once again to access the data. Figure 8.4 shows the process.

FIGURE 8.4

This diagram shows how MSDAOSP.DLL interacts with a simple OLEDB provider.

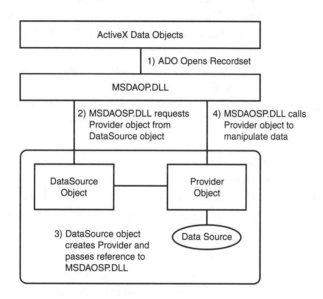

The process of accessing the data begins when a client uses ADO to open a connection and create a `Recordset` object. When the connection is open, the ADO client passes a connection string of the form `Provider=Name;`. The `Provider` name is created by the designer of the OSP and is placed in the System Registry. The Registry associates the name with the CLSID of the `DataSource` object so that MSDAOSP.DLL can access the simple provider. When MSDAOSP.DLL has access to the `DataSource` object, it passes the query string sent by the client. The `DataSource` object uses this information to initialize the `Provider` class. The `DataSource` object then creates an instance of the `Provider` class and passes the reference to MSDAOSP.DLL. Now MSDAOSP.DLL can call the provider directly through the interfaces implemented in the `Provider` class. The `Provider` in turn manipulates the data in the custom data store. This is very similar to the way in which the `GetDataMember` function works in the custom VB data source shown earlier.

8

BUILDING CUSTOM DATA SOURCES

In order to build a provider, we begin by setting a reference to two Type Libraries that come with the OSP toolkit. These are "Microsoft Data Sources Interfaces" contained in the file MSDATSRC.TLB and "OLE-DB Simple Provider Types Library" contained in the file SIMPDATA.TLB. These type libraries contain all the interfaces your provider may need. They are available to you after you install the OLEDB SDK.

In order to communicate with MSDAOSP.DLL, the `Provider` class must implement the `OLEDBSimpleProvider` interface. Implementing this interface means that you must provide code for all the methods in the interface. In some cases, you need only provide a comment, but other methods are critical for the OSP functionality. The key methods for a provider are `getVariant`, `setVariant`, and `Find`. The `getVariant` and `setVariant` methods are fairly straightforward. These methods are called by MSDAOSP.DLL whenever it needs to read or write data. The data is identified by a row and column and is sent or returned as a `Variant`. Your job is simply to read or write the data at the current location in the data store. The `Find` method is a little bit more complex. Essentially, the `Find` method allows MSDAOSP.DLL to locate data within the data store.

The `DataSource` class is fairly simple and implements only two methods: `msDataSourceObject` and `addDataSourceListener`. The first method is used by MSDAOSP.DLL to request an instance of the `Provider` class. The second method is used to add listeners who want to receive notification when the underlying data store is changed.

After the OSP is created, it must be properly registered so that a client can invoke the functionality. Registering the OSP associates a provider name you assign with the CLSID of the `DataSource` object. Registering also associates your provider with MSDAOSP.DLL so that when your provider is called, MSDAOSP.DLL is loaded as well. The OSP toolkit contains a template that you can use to create a REG file to enter the appropriate information in the Registry. You simply take this template and modify it for your project. When the provider is registered, you may call it from a client using ADO.

```
REGEDIT4

[HKEY_CLASSES_ROOT\<INSERT:  ProgID for OLE DB Provider>]
@="<INSERT:  Name of OLE DB Provider>"

[HKEY_CLASSES_ROOT\<INSERT:  ProgID for OLE DB Provider>\CLSID]
@="<INSERT:  GUID for OLE DB Provider>"

[HKEY_CLASSES_ROOT\CLSID\<INSERT:  GUID for OLE DB Provider>]
@="<INSERT:  ProgID of OLE DB Provider>"

[HKEY_CLASSES_ROOT\CLSID\<INSERT:  GUID for OLE DB
Provider>\InprocServer32]
@="<INSERT:  Path to OLE DB Directory  —>
"ThreadingModel"="Both"
```

```
[HKEY_CLASSES_ROOT\CLSID\<INSERT:  GUID for OLE DB Provider>\ProgID]
@="<INSERT:  ProgId of OLE DB Provider>.1"

[HKEY_CLASSES_ROOT\CLSID\
<INSERT:  GUID for OLE DB Provider>\VersionIndependentProgID]
@="<INSERT:  ProgId of OLE DB Provider>"

[HKEY_CLASSES_ROOT\CLSID\<INSERT:  GUID for OLE DB Provider>\
➥OLE DB Provider]
@="<INSERT:  Name of OLE DB Provider>"

[HKEY_CLASSES_ROOT\CLSID\<INSERT:  GUID for OLE DB Provider>\
➥OSP Data Object]
@="<INSERT:  ProgID for OSP Data Object>"

Example Notes ==========================================>
ProgID for OLE DB Provider = TestPWProv
Name of OLE DB Provider = Microsoft Test OLE DB Provider for OSP
GUID for OLE DB Provider = {6B94E051-E170-11d0-94EA-00C04FB66A50}
ProgId for OSP Data Object= MyOSPProject.OSPClass


Example ================================================>
REGEDIT4


[HKEY_CLASSES_ROOT\TestPWProv]
@="Microsoft Test OLE DB Provider for OSP"

[HKEY_CLASSES_ROOT\TestPWProv\CLSID]
@="{6B94E051-E170-11d0-94EA-00C04FB66A50}"

[HKEY_CLASSES_ROOT\CLSID\{6B94E051-E170-11d0-94EA-00C04FB66A50}]
@="TestPWProv"

[HKEY_CLASSES_ROOT\CLSID\{6B94E051-E170-11d0-94EA-00C04FB66A50}\
➥InprocServer32]
@="c:\\Program Files\\Common Files\\System\\OLE DB\\MSDAOSP.DLL"
"ThreadingModel"="Both"

[HKEY_CLASSES_ROOT\CLSID\{6B94E051-E170-11d0-94EA-00C04FB66A50}\ProgID]
@="TestPWProv.1"

[HKEY_CLASSES_ROOT\CLSID\
{6B94E051-E170-11d0-94EA-00C04FB66A50}\VersionIndependentProgID]
@="TestPWProv"

[HKEY_CLASSES_ROOT\CLSID\{6B94E051-E170-11d0-94EA-00C04FB66A50}\
➥OLE DB Provider]
@="Microsoft Test OLE DB Provider for OSP"

[HKEY_CLASSES_ROOT\CLSID\{6B94E051-E170-11d0-94EA-00C04FB66A50}\
➥OSP Data Object]
@="MyOSPProject.OSPClass"
```

8

BUILDING CUSTOM
DATA SOURCES

EXERCISE 8-1: CREATING AN OLEDB SIMPLE PROVIDER

This exercise creates an OLEDB simple provider that accesses data in flat files. The provider is created through the OLEDB SDK Simple Provider Toolkit. When the provider is created, you will be able to issue text query commands in ADO that return Recordset objects.

Installing the OLEDB SDK

In this section, you will install the OLEDB SDK. The install contains the OLEDB Simple Provider Toolkit to build the provider.

Step 1

Before you can begin this exercise, you must install the OLEDB SDK, which contains the OLEDB Simple Provider Toolkit. You can access the OLEDB SDK from the CD-ROM or at http://www.microsoft.com/data/download.htm. Locate and run the self-extracting setup. Figure 8.5 shows the setup splash screen.

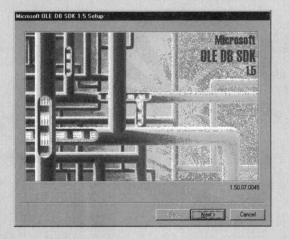

FIGURE 8.5

The OLEDB SDK contains the OLEDB Simple Provider Toolkit.

Step 2

The OLEDB SDK setup contains several different screens where you must provide information. Generally, these screens are simple question-and-answer screens. However, you should note a few details as you proceed. The first screen of interest is the installation directory. You will need to locate files later in this directory, so record below the directory where you installed the OLEDB SDK. Figure 8.6 shows the screen where you set the installation path.

Installation Path: _____

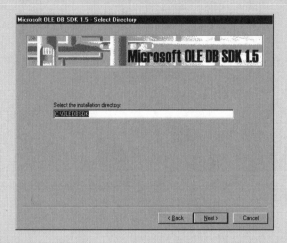

FIGURE 8.6
Record the installation path for the OLEDB SDK.

Step 3
The next critical step is the selected installation options. In this screen, select to perform a custom installation. This will allow you to ensure that you select to install the Simple Provider Toolkit. The OLEDB SDK contains many features for C++ programmers that are not required to build a simple provider. Figure 8.7 shows the installation options screen.

Step 4
After the OLEDB SDK is installed, run the Windows File Explorer and locate the installation directory you recorded earlier. In this directory you will find several subfolders. The Simple Provider Toolkit is in the directory \OLEDBSDK\OSPTK. Here you will find complete documentation as well as examples.

Step 5
In the OLEDB SDK, you will also find two critical files for use with a simple provider called MSDATSRC.TLB and SIMPDATA.TLB. These files, which are located in the \OLEDBSDK\BIN directory, contain the interface definitions that your OLEDB provider

must implement in order to interact with the ActiveX Data Objects. Record the complete path to these files below.

MSDATSRC.TLB/SIMPDATA.TLB File Path: _____

Step 6

The last file of interest installed by the OLEDB SDK is MSDAOSP.DLL, which is the heart of any simple provider. This DLL provides the essential recordset functionality required by ADO. This file is always installed in the path \PROGRAM FILES\ COMMON FILES\SYSTEM\OLEDB. Locate this file using the File Explorer. This file along with the MSDATSRC.TBL and SIMPDATA.TLB files must be distributed with your provider in order for a client to use it. After you verify the files are all properly installed, you are ready to create your provider.

Creating the Provider

In this section, you will create the actual provider. This provider will work with ADO to access data.

Step 1

Using the CD-ROM for the book, locate the directory TEMPLATES\EXERCISE8-1. This directory contains a partially completed OLEDB simple provider. The provider accesses text files we created from the Authors, Titles, and Publishers tables in SQL Server.

Step 2

On your hard drive, create a new directory with the Windows Explorer named MTS\EXERCISE8-1. Copy the contents from the CD-ROM directory into the new directory you just created.

Step 3

Because the CD-ROM will create read-only copies of the project files, select all the files you copied, right-click them, and select **Properties** from the pop-up menu. In the properties dialog, uncheck the read-only flag. Close the dialog.

Step 4

Start Visual Basic and open the file EXERCISE8-1.VBG. In the Project Explorer, you should see a Standard EXE project and two ActiveX DLL projects. The ActiveX DLL projects contain the query engine and the OLEDB Simple Provider. The Standard EXE is the front end for the provider.

Step 5

In the Project Explorer, locate the project named `PubsProvider`. This project contains the two class modules needed to build the OLEDB simple provider. The `DataSource` class is used as an interface to the simple provider. The `Provider` class is used to implement the functionality of the simple provider.

Step 6

Open the code window for the `DataSource` class. In this class, you will find a function named `msDataSourceObject`. This function is used to create an instance of the `Provider` class and return it to MSDAOSP.DLL. MSDAOSP.DLL calls this class when your provider is invoked and passes the query string created in the client code. Add the code in Listing 8.5 to the `msDataSourceObject` function to create the instance of the `Provider` class.

LISTING 8.5   CODE TO CREATE THE INSTANCE OF THE Provider CLASS

```
On Error GoTo DataSourceErr

    'Create an instance of the provider
    Dim objOSP As Provider
    Set objOSP = New Provider

    If objOSP.InitProvider(strQuery) = False Then
        Set objOSP = Nothing
    End If

DataSourceExit:
```

continues

LISTING 8.5   CONTINUED

```
    'Return provider object
    Set msDataSourceObject = objOSP
    Exit Function

DataSourceErr:
    Set objOSP = Nothing
    App.StartLogging App.Path & "\error.log", vbLogToFile
    App.LogEvent Err.Source & "; " & Err.Description
    Debug.Print
    Resume DataSourceExit
```

Step 7

Open the code window for the `Provider` class. In this class locate the `InitProvider` procedure. This procedure is called by the `DataSource` class to initialize the provider instance. This procedure opens the appropriate text file and reads the file into an array. The members read into the array are based on the query passed into the provider. This essentially uses an array like a cursor to keep the data requested by the query. The requested data is identified by using the query engine to parse the query string. Add the code in Listing 8.6 to the `InitProvider` procedure to build the array of requested data.

LISTING 8.6   CODE TO ADD TO THE `InitProvider` PROCEDURE

```
On Error GoTo InitProviderErr

    InitProvider = True

    'Local Variables
    Dim intFile As Integer
    Dim strTemp As String
    Dim vTemp As Variant
    Dim intTemp As Integer
    Dim intCols As Integer
    Dim strFile As String
    Dim strTable As String

    'Program the Parsing engine
    'for a SELECT statement
    Set m_objEngine = New QueryEngine.Engine
    With m_objEngine.Elements
        .Add "SELECT", ","
        .Add "FROM", ","
    End With

    'Save and Parse the QueryString
    With m_objEngine
        .QueryString = strQuery
        .Parse
```

```
    End With

    'Get Data from engine
    strTable = m_objEngine.Elements("FROM").Arguments(1).Value
    strFile = App.Path & "\" & strTable & ".txt"
    intCols = m_objEngine.Elements("SELECT").Arguments.Count

    intFile = FreeFile

    'Open the selected table
    Open strFile For Input As #intFile

        ReDim strData(intCols - 1, 0)

        Do While Not EOF(intFile)

            'Get a line
            Line Input #intFile, strTemp
            vTemp = Split(strTemp, "¦")

            'Add it to the array
            For intTemp = 1 To
m_objEngine.Elements("SELECT").Arguments.Count
                If strTemp = "" Then Exit For
                strData(intTemp - 1, UBound(strData, 2)) = _
                    vTemp(GetInitialOrdinalPosition(strTable, _

m_objEngine.Elements("SELECT").Arguments(intTemp).Value))
            Next

            'Add a new row to the array
            ReDim Preserve strData(intCols - 1, UBound(strData, 2) + 1)

        Loop

    Close #intFile

    'Remove unused array row
    ReDim Preserve strData(intCols - 1, UBound(strData, 2) - 2)

InitProviderExit:
    Exit Function

InitProviderErr:
    InitProvider = False
    Debug.Print Err.Description
    App.StartLogging App.Path & "\error.log", vbLogToFile
    App.LogEvent "InitProvider: " & Err.Description
    Resume InitProviderExit
```

Step 8

The `Provider` class implements the `OLEDBSimpleProvider` interface. If you have
installed the OLEDB SDK correctly, you should be able to open the references dialog
and verify that references are set to the files MSDATSRC.TLB and SIMPDATA.TLB. In
the References dialog, these files appear as "Microsoft OLEDB Simple Provider 1.5" and
"Microsoft Data Source Interfaces" respectively. If these references are not set, you can
use the Browse button to locate the files in the paths you recorded earlier. Figure 8.8
shows the References dialog.

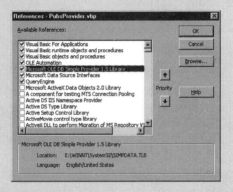

FIGURE 8.8

The simple provider needs references set to MSDATSRC.TLB and SIMPDATA.TLB.

Step 9

The `Provider` class already lists all the methods required to implement the
`OLEDBSimpleProvider` interface. We will concentrate on filling in the code in just a few
of the procedures. The first key procedure is `OLEDBSimpleProvider_find`. This procedure is called whenever a piece of data needs to be located. This procedure is most often
called when a user is attempting to access fields in your data by name (for example,
`MyRecordset.Fields("Field1")`). When fields are accessed by name, the name must be
translated into an ordinal number. The `OLEDBSimpleProvider_find` procedure takes the
string name as an input and returns the row where the data was found. By design, the
zero row always contains the names of the fields. Add the code in Listing 8.7 to the
`OLEDBSimpleProvider_find` procedure to implement the functionality.

LISTING 8.7   CODE FOR THE `OLEDBSimpleProvider_find` PROCEDURE

```
On Error GoTo FindErr

    OLEDBSimpleProvider_find = -1
```

```
    Dim c As Integer
    Dim r As Integer

    'Check column values for each row
    For r = 0 To UBound(strData, 2)
        For c = 0 To UBound(strData, 1)
            If strData(c, r) = val Then OLEDBSimpleProvider_find = r
            Exit For
        Next
    Next

    Exit Function

FindErr:
    App.StartLogging App.Path & "\error.log", vbLogToFile
    App.LogEvent "Find: " & Err.Description
    Exit Function
```

Step 10

When data is written to the provider, the SetVariant procedure is called. This procedure receives row and column values as arguments and sets the data for the selected cell. When the array is built, this functionality is simple to implement. Add the code in Listing 8.8 to the SetVariant procedure to write a field value.

LISTING 8.8 CODE FOR THE SetVariant PROCEDURE

```
On Error GoTo SetVariantErr

    'This function sets a new value
    strData(iColumn - 1, iRow) = Var

    Exit Sub

SetVariantErr:
    App.StartLogging App.Path & "\error.log", vbLogToFile
    App.LogEvent "SetVariant: " & Err.Description
    Exit Sub
```

Step 11

When data is read from the provider, the GetVariant procedure is called. This procedure receives row and column values as arguments and returns the data for the selected cell. When the array is built, this functionality is simple to implement. Add the code in Listing 8.9 to the GetVariant procedure to return a field value.

LISTING 8.9   CODE FOR THE GetVariant PROCEDURE

```
On Error GoTo GetVariantErr

    'This function returns a value
    OLEDBSimpleProvider_getVariant = strData(iColumn - 1, iRow)

    Exit Function

GetVariantErr:
    OLEDBSimpleProvider_getVariant = Err.Description
    App.StartLogging App.Path & "\error.log", vbLogToFile
    App.LogEvent "GetVariant: " & Err.Description
    Exit Function
```

Creating the Registry File

In this section, you'll create the registry file for the new provider. This file will allow you to register and use the provider with ADO.

Step 12

After you have added all the code for the Provider class, minimize Visual Basic. Now start Notepad. Use Notepad to locate and open the file PROVIDER.REG, which is located in the same directory as your project. This file is used to automatically create the appropriate registry entries to make your simple provider recognizable to ADO clients. Listing 8.10 shows the file as it looks when you open it in Notepad.

LISTING 8.10   A FILE USED TO AUTOMATICALLY CREATE APPROPRIATE REGISTRY ENTRIES

```
REGEDIT4

[HKEY_CLASSES_ROOT\PubsProvider]
@="OLEDB Simple Provider for delimited file"

[HKEY_CLASSES_ROOT\PubsProvider\CLSID]
@="{C0A5CFE0-7369-11D2-B5C4-0060088D02A3}"

[HKEY_CLASSES_ROOT\CLSID\{C0A5CFE0-7369-11D2-B5C4-0060088D02A3}]
@="PubsProvider"

[HKEY_CLASSES_ROOT\CLSID\{C0A5CFE0-7369-11D2-B5C4-
0060088D02A3}\InprocServer32]
@="E:\\Program Files\\Common Files\\System\\OLE DB\\MSDAOSP.DLL"
"ThreadingModel"="Both"

[HKEY_CLASSES_ROOT\CLSID\{C0A5CFE0-7369-11D2-B5C4-0060088D02A3}\ProgID]
@="PubsProvider.1"
```

```
[HKEY_CLASSES_ROOT\CLSID\
{C0A5CFE0-7369-11D2-B5C4-0060088D02A3}\VersionIndependentProgID]
@="PubsProvider"

[HKEY_CLASSES_ROOT\CLSID\{C0A5CFE0-7369-11D2-B5C4-0060088D02A3}\OLE DB
Provider]
@="OLEDB Simple Provider for delimited file"

[HKEY_CLASSES_ROOT\CLSID\{C0A5CFE0-7369-11D2-B5C4-0060088D02A3}\OSP Data
Object]
@="PubsProvider.DataSource"
```

Step 13

Examine the file carefully and you will see multiple registry entries that will be made for your provider. The description for each entry is explained in the registry template file found in the OLEDB SDK. This template was also listed earlier in the chapter. Most of the entries do not need changing; however, you must modify one setting to successfully register the simple provider. Carefully locate the following line in the file.

```
[HKEY_CLASSES_ROOT\CLSID\{C0A5CFE0-7369-11D2-B5C4-
0060088D02A3}\InprocServer32]
@="E:\\Program Files\\Common Files\\System\\OLE DB\\MSDAOSP.DLL"
"ThreadingModel"="Both"
```

Step 14

The code in Step 13 shows the location of the MSDAOSP.DLL file on your system. Edit this line by hand to reflect the true file path you noted earlier in the exercise. If you installed the OLEDB SDK correctly, you will probably only have to change the drive letter. After you have made the change, save the file and close Notepad. You will use this file later.

8

BUILDING CUSTOM
DATA SOURCES

WARNING

File paths in registry entries require two backslashes between folders. Do not alter this syntax or the registry file will not work.

Creating the Front End

In this section, you will create a user interface to access the data with your new provider. The code here will be similar to any ADO coding you have done with standard databases like SQL Server.

Step 15

Now return to Visual Basic. In the Project Explorer, locate the project named FrontEnd. This is the project that will call the simple provider through ADO. Open the code window for the form frmClient found in the project. Figure 8.9 shows the form.

FIGURE 8.9

This form uses ADO to call the simple provider and fill a grid.

Step 16

The client code is quite simple. A user can create a query in a TextBox and run it by pushing a button. In the Click event of the button cmdQuery, add the following code to run the query and display the results:

```
On Error Resume Next
objRecordset.Close
objRecordset.Open txtQuery.Text, "Provider=PubsProvider"
Set grdData.DataSource = objRecordset
```

Finalizing the Provider

Step 17

After all the code is written, compile the entire application by choosing File, Make Project Group from the menu. At this point, the components are created; however, the provider is not yet registered. You can register the provider by running the registry file you created earlier.

Step 18

Locate the file PROVIDER.REG using the Windows Explorer. Run this file by double-clicking it in the File Explorer. When the file runs, it will register your provider under the name `PubsProvider`. This is what allows the client code to call your provider by using the string `Provider=PubsProvider`. If the registry entries are made correctly, you will see a confirmation dialog.

Step 19

After all the steps are complete, locate and run the FRONTEND.EXE file. This is the compiled front end. Try creating `Query` statements to run in the front end. Here are some statements to try:

```
SELECT au_lname,au_fname FROM Authors
SELECT pub_name,city FROM Publishers
```

Step 20

This exercise implements only a portion of a truly complete simple provider. Examine the code for the `Provider` class, and you will see several methods where you can add new features. Research some of these features in the OLEDB SDK and implement them in the provider later.

MTS AND THE INTERNET

PREREQUISITES

Before beginning this chapter, you should be completely familiar with creating components in MTS. Although not specifically required, some familiarity with Internet Information Server is helpful. Work in related technologies like Active Server Pages is also helpful.

Skills Learned

- MTS(20): Use Active Server Pages to call components in MTS.
- MTS(21): Use MTS components to create HTML in Active Server Pages.
- MTS(22): Use transactional Web pages to create transactions in Active Server Pages.

With the release of Internet Information Server (IIS) version 4.0, Internet applications created with Microsoft development tools are now tightly integrated with MTS. This integration provides both scalability and fault tolerance to Internet solutions, which were unavailable in previous versions of IIS. The IIS/MTS integration is so complete that Web applications run with MTS by default. In fact, simply installing IIS will cause MTS to be installed as well. The two servers are essentially inseparable. In this chapter, we examine the relationship between IIS and MTS and how to use them to create scalable Web applications.

WEB PROJECTS

Before you can begin to take advantage of the IIS/MTS integration, you must understand how VBScript and ASP work together with IIS to create Internet solutions. IIS is the primary Web server used to create Internet applications with Microsoft products. Like all Web servers, IIS does more than simply pass Web pages to calling clients. IIS also allows clients to start executable processes on the server. These processes can then be used to perform advanced functions such as data access. Server-side processes form the heart of any Web application.

In the past, Web applications have relied on out-of-process executables that ran independently of the Web server. These EXEs would be started by the Web server, perform a function, and return the results to the server. These types of applications typically used the Common Gateway Interface (CGI) to provide the communication between the Web server and out-of-process EXE.

When IIS was introduced, it presented a vastly different architecture for performing server-side functions. Instead of out-of-process EXEs, IIS allowed developers to create in-process components that ran in the same memory space as the Web server itself. This change directly contributed to major performance improvements because in-process components can run significantly faster than out-of-process EXEs. In order to facilitate the development of these new in-process components, IIS provided a programming interface known as the Internet Services API (ISAPI). ISAPI allowed developers to create applications that directly communicated and controlled IIS.

As IIS developed, Microsoft created several ISAPI applications. Many of these applications are no longer supported products, but through the trial and error of development, Microsoft produced one ISAPI application that proved superior. That application is known as Active Server Pages (ASP). ASP is an ISAPI application that allows developers to create Web pages dynamically and populate the pages with information from any data source. ASP uses scripting languages to make simple decisions and format pages. ASP also has the ability to call any COM component including ActiveX DLLs created in Visual Basic.

The scripting languages recognized by ASP are VBScript and JScript. VBScript is a subset of the Visual Basic for Applications (VBA) language, which is the same language utilized in Visual Basic. Therefore, VB developers will find ASP to be a natural extension to their skills. JScript is a Microsoft version of the Netscape JavaScript language, which uses Java style syntax. Both languages are extremely simple tools used primarily as glue between Web pages and COM objects.

QUICK CHECK 9-1

ASP FUNDAMENTALS

1. This exercise shows some fundamental ASP programming principles. If you are already familiar with ASP, you can skip this exercise.

2. Using the CD-ROM for the book, locate the directory TEMPLATES\QUICK CHECK9-1. This directory contains a Web page with some ASP code that you can modify.

3. On your hard drive, create a new directory with the Windows Explorer named MTS\QUICK CHECK9-1. Copy the contents from the CD-ROM directory into the new directory you just created.

4. Because the CD-ROM will create read-only copies of the project files, select all the files you copied, right-click them, and select **Properties** from the pop-up menu. In the properties dialog, uncheck the read-only flag. Close the dialog.

5. Start Notepad. Locate and open the file QUICK CHECK 9-1.ASP, which you copied from the CD-ROM. This file contains some simple ASP code that you will enhance. When this page is called, we will create a simple display dynamically using a VBScript For...Next Loop. Locate the comment in the file where you should place code, and add the following code to the page:

```
<%For i=1 To 7%>

<P>
<FONT FACE="ARIAL" SIZE=<%=i%>>
SCALABLE
</FONT>
</P>

<%Next%>
```

6. Save your work and close Notepad.

continues

continued

7. Start the Internet Services Manager in the MMC. This will allow you to create a new Internet application to run the ASP page. In order to create a new Internet application, you must create a new "virtual directory." A virtual directory is an Internet address associated with your application.

8. In the Internet Services Manager, locate the Default Web Site. This is the reference to your Web server. Right-click this item and select **New, Virtual Directory** from the pop-up menu. Figure 9.1 shows the menu to select.

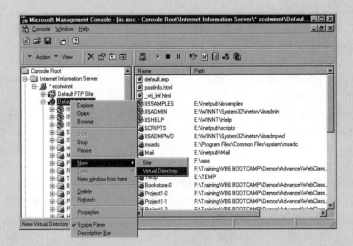

FIGURE 9.1
Use the Internet Services Manager to create a virtual directory.

9. When you select to create a virtual directory, this starts the New Virtual Directory Wizard. In this wizard, you must first provide an alias name for your new directory. Name your new directory QuickCheck. Figure 9.2 shows the first step of the wizard.

10. In the second step of the wizard, you must provide the path to the new application you are creating. Using this step, enter the path to the exercise directory you created earlier. Figure 9.3 shows the path in the wizard.

FIGURE 9.2

Enter a name for the new virtual directory.

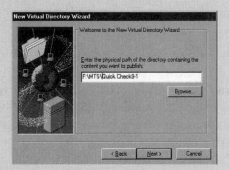

FIGURE 9.3

Enter a path for the new virtual directory.

11. In the third step, you must specify the access features for the new directory. In order to run ASP code, the directory must allow Script Access. This permission is set by default. Figure 9.4 shows the permissions.

12. Click Finish to create the new directory. You should now see the ASP file you created in the Internet Services Manager.

13. In order to run the ASP page, you can simply right-click the file in the MMC and select **Browse** from the pop-up menu.

continues

continued

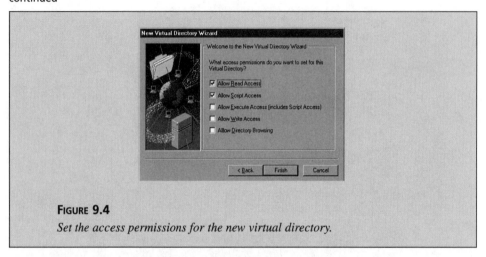

FIGURE 9.4
Set the access permissions for the new virtual directory.

ASP offers some significant advantages to developers that make it an attractive technology. Unlike many other solutions, ASP can be platform-independent. Depending upon the HTML code you use, you can create pages that work in any number of different browsers. ASP also runs in the same process as IIS, which makes it faster than other solutions. However, the advantages brought by running in process also result in a serious disadvantage. When in-process applications crash, they also crash the host application. This means that if ASP should crash, IIS would also fail. Fortunately, this problem is handled nicely by integrating ASP processes with MTS packages.

We already know that we can administer MTS through the MTS Explorer, which is hosted in the Microsoft Management Console (MMC), but you can also administer IIS from the MMC. In fact, if you start the Internet Service Manager, the MMC will display the Explorer for both MTS and IIS. This shows the strong integration of the two products.

Part of the IIS/MTS integration causes all ASP applications to run with packages in MTS. When you install MTS, one package is created by default for all ASP applications. This package is called IIS In-Process Applications. You can examine this package in the Microsoft Management Console (MMC) under the Packages Installed folder. In this package, MTS creates a component entry for each Web project running under IIS. Figure 9.5 shows the package in the MMC.

FIGURE 9.5

ASP applications run with MTS packages by default.

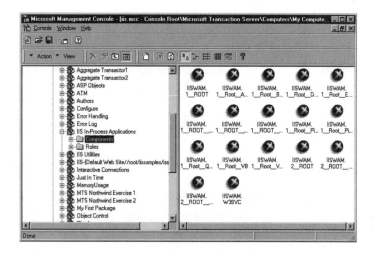

Using the MMC, you can access the properties of any Web project and affect how it is run under MTS. To access the properties of the Web project, you must select the project in the IIS Explorer portion of the MMC. You can view the property sheet for the selected project by selecting Action, Properties from the menu. The property sheet contains several tabs. The Directory tab is used to change how the project is handled by MTS. On the Directory tab, the checkbox Run in Separate Memory Space (Isolated Process) determines whether the project runs in the memory space of IIS or a separate process. Figure 9.6 shows the property sheet for a Web project.

FIGURE 9.6

ASP applications can be run in the memory space of IIS or a separate memory space.

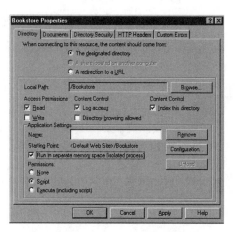

9

MTS AND THE INTERNET

Checking the Run in Separate Memory Space option causes MTS to remove the project from the IIS In-Process Applications package and create a new package. The new package is set to run as a Server package, which provides process isolation and fault tolerance. Running applications this way is safer, but does require slightly more memory than in-process applications because MTS has to provide a separate process for the application.

Because the new package runs as a Server Package, it must be started separately as a new process. Starting the process requires that a valid security context be in force. However, IIS does not inherently have permission to start new processes. Therefore, MTS and IIS use a special UserID that is trusted to start applications. This is created when you install IIS and can be found in the User Manager for Domains. The UserID is IWAM_*machinename* where *machinename* is the name of the computer where IIS is installed. Figure 9.7 shows the IWAM account.

FIGURE 9.7

This account is used to start new MTS packages that contain ASP projects.

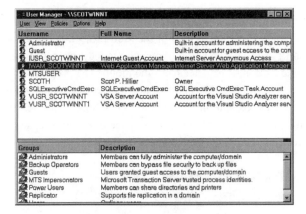

QUICK CHECK 9-2

PROCESS ISOLATION

1. This exercise shows how to create an isolated Web application process. It uses the project created in Quick Check 9-1. Therefore, you must complete Quick Check 9-1 before performing this exercise.

2. Start the Internet Service Manager. In the MMC, locate the virtual directory you created for Quick Check 9-1. This application is currently run in the memory space of IIS. This is the default for all new ASP applications. You can verify this by locating the package IIS In-Process Application. In the Components folder, you will see a component labeled IISWAM.1_Root_Quick Check. This is the placeholder for an in-process ASP application. Figure 9.8 shows the component.

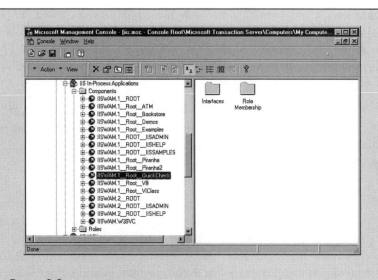

FIGURE 9.8

New ASP applications run in-process.

3. After you examine the MTS package, return to the virtual directory you located earlier. Now, you will change the package to run out of process. Right-click the virtual directory and select **Properties** from the pop-up menu. This will open the properties dialog.

4. Click the **Run in Separate Memory Space** box in the Virtual Directory tab. This will create a separate MTS package just for this application.

5. The new package will not show up in the MTS Explorer until the view is refreshed. In the MTS Explorer, right-click the Packages Installed folder and select **Refresh** from the pop-up menu. Now locate the package named IIS-{Default Web Site//Root/QuickCheck}.

6. When you have located the package, right-click it and select **Properties** from the pop-up menu. In the properties dialog, click the Activation tab. You will now see that the application is running as a Server package, which means the process will be isolated inside MTS.

ASP OBJECTS

One of the most powerful features of ASP is the ability to access scripting and business objects from within the page. These objects provide a high degree of extensibility that allows ASP to go beyond simple pages to more complex applications that can provide access to databases, mail servers, and other resources. ASP provides several scripting objects that are "built-in" to the technology. That is, you can call them from your ASP page without specifically creating an instance. Additionally, you can use special features to create instances of any ActiveX component and call its functionality from an ASP application.

We'll start our examination of these objects with the built-in scripting objects provided by ASP itself. These objects make it simple to receive input from a browser and format response pages. ASP also provides scripting objects for managing state variables in your applications, which allows you to remember information and share it among various Web pages.

Perhaps the greatest difficulty encountered when trying to create Web applications is the inherent statelessness of the Internet. By that we mean that the Internet itself was never designed to remember user information such as names, passwords, credit card numbers, and so on. In fact, the Internet model is one of a server simply passing requested Web pages to a browser and then forgetting that the browser was ever at the site. Each Web page that is passed from the server to the client is a separate, distinct, and stateless transaction between the two machines.

This stateless relationship makes it nearly impossible to even define what constitutes a Web application. Unlike a standard Windows application, Web apps do not have a clear definition of the beginning and ending of a program. There is no icon to click on the Web nor is there a File, Exit command to select when you are done. Without a clear definition of the beginning and end of an application, you cannot determine how long to remember a user's information.

Consider this scenario. Imagine you are creating an on-line shopping site. This site has ten pages that represent ten different departments where merchandise is maintained. This department includes Men's, Women's, Sports, Shoes, and so on. The objective is to allow the users to fill a virtual shopping cart as they move from page to page. On the last page of the application, we want to recall all the items selected in each department and complete the transaction.

Now imagine that a user is shopping on our new site. The user works through three or four pages and then decides to quickly browse to a favorite financial site to check a stock quote. So the user places a bookmark on page four of our application and leaves. Sometime later, the user returns by selecting the bookmark. When the user returns, should our application remember what was in her cart? Maybe. But what if the user is gone for an hour and then returns? What about a day? You can see that it is not a simple matter to determine when an application begins and ends or how long to maintain information. These state issues are an integral part of Internet development that is solved by ASP.

Among the scripting objects provided by ASP, two of them are responsible for maintaining state. These objects are known as the `Application` object and the `Session` object. The `Application` object creates a variable that is available to all users of an application, and the `Session` object creates variables that are available only to an individual user. Along with these objects, ASP also provides a convenient definition for Web applications and sessions.

Applications that run under ASP are defined as all Web pages contained in the same site subdirectory. This means that when you create a new project with Visual InterDev through the Web Project Wizard, all the pages contained under the project directory constitute a single application. If a user selects any page under this directory, the application is said to start.

Sessions in ASP are defined with an arbitrary time limit. Although you can change the definition, by default a user session is said to last as long as the user continues to request Web pages from within a given application without waiting more than 20 minutes. If a user fails to select a Web page from within an application for 20 minutes, the individual session is said to end and all `Session` variables are destroyed.

Creating both `Application` and `Session` variables is remarkably simple in ASP. In order to create the variables, just address the `Application` or `Session` object directly and set the value of the new variable. The following code shows how to simultaneously define and set the value for two variables in ASP:

```
Session("var1") = value1
Application("var2") = value2
```

Along with the objects for managing state, ASP also provides objects for receiving data input from a browser and formatting a response page. These objects are known as the `Request` and `Response` object respectively. The `Request` object is used to retrieve information sent to the server from a form in a Web page submitted by a browser. When a form is submitted, each field of the form is given a name, which allows the `Request` object to retrieve the information. The following code shows a typical HTML form with several text fields. Each field is defined with an `<INPUT>` tag and the names are designated through the `NAME` attribute:

```
<HTML>
<HEAD>
<BASEFONT FACE="ARIAL" SIZE=5>
```

```
<TITLE>Request Object</TITLE>
</HEAD>

<BODY BGCOLOR="WHITE">
<CENTER>
Echo a Request<P>
<FORM NAME="frmRequest" METHOD="POST"
ACTION="request.asp">

<TABLE>
    <TR>
        <TH>
        Name
        </TH>
        <TD>
        <INPUT TYPE="TEXT" NAME="txtName">
        </TD>
    </TR>
    <TR>
        <TH>
        Phone
        </TH>
        <TD>
        <INPUT TYPE="TEXT" NAME="txtPhone">
        </TD>
    </TR>
    <TR>
        <TH>
        E-Mail
        </TH>
        <TD>
        <INPUT TYPE="TEXT" NAME="txtEMail">
        </TD>
    </TR>
</TABLE>
<INPUT TYPE="SUBMIT" VALUE="Send Data">
</FORM>

</CENTER>
</BODY>
</HTML>
```

When the form is submitted, the data is sent to the Web page designated by the ACTION attribute of the <FORM> tag. This page is an Active Server Page called REQUEST.ASP. In this page, we can access any of the submitted fields through the Request object. The following code fragment shows how to retrieve a field called txtEMail from the submitted form:

```
MyVariable = Request.Form("txtEMail")
```

Formatting a response to a browser is the function of the `Response` object. The `Response` object has a method called `Write`, which writes data directly into a Web page and returns it to the client. The `Write` method is used constantly in ASP applications and has special shorthand notation. To use the `Write` method, we simply place an equal sign in the page. For example, the ASP code `<%=i%>` is shorthand for the `Write` method. The following code is therefore equivalent:

```
<%Response.Write i %>
```

QUICK CHECK 9-3

RESPONDING TO USER INPUT

1. Using the CD-ROM for the book, locate the directory TEMPLATES\QUICK CHECK9-3. This directory contains a Web page with some ASP code that you can modify.

2. On your hard drive, create a new directory with the Windows Explorer named MTS\QUICK CHECK9-3. Copy the contents from the CD-ROM directory into the new directory you just created.

3. Because the CD-ROM will create read-only copies of the project files, select all the files you copied, right-click them, and select **Properties** from the pop-up menu. In the properties dialog, uncheck the read-only flag. Close the dialog.

4. Start Notepad. Locate and open the file QUICK CHECK 9-3.HTM, which you copied from the CD-ROM. This file contains a simple HTML form, which you can fill out with your name, phone number, and email. The fields in the form are named `txtName`, `txtPhone`, and `txtEMail` respectively. When the form is submitted, this data is sent to file QUICK CHECK 9-3.ASP.

5. Locate and open the file QUICK CHECK 9-3.ASP, which you copied from the CD-ROM. This file contains some HTML to which you will add ASP code. The ASP code will create a response page by examining the submitted data and simply sending it back to the browser. Add the ASP code in Listing 9.1 to the page to send the submitted data back to the sender as a simple response.

continues

continued

LISTING 9.1 CODE TO CREATE A RESPONSE PAGE

```
<TABLE>
    <TR>
        <TH>
        Name
        </TH>
        <TD>
        <%=Request.Form("txtName")%>
        </TD>
    </TR>
    <TR>
        <TH>
        Phone
        </TH>
        <TD>
        <%=Request.Form("txtPhone")%>
        </TD>
    </TR>
    <TR>
        <TH>
        E-Mail
        </TH>
        <TD>
        <%=Request.Form("txtEMail")%>
        </TD>
    </TR>
</TABLE>
```

---

6. In the Internet Services Manager, locate the Default Web Site. This is the reference to your Web server. Right-click this item and select **New, Virtual Directory** from the pop-up menu.

7. Create a new virtual directory in the Internet Services Manager for your new project. In order to run the application page, right-click the file QUICK CHECK 9-3.HTM in the MMC and select **Browse** from the pop-up menu.

The last of the scripting objects provided by ASP is the Server object. The Server object has no direct relation to specific parts of a Web application like the other objects—rather, the Server object is a collection of utility functions that did not fit well anywhere else. The Server object has several useful utilities, but the most important method is the CreateObject method. This method allows you to create an instance of any ActiveX component for use in ASP. This means that you can use existing objects like ADO and RDO or create your own objects with Visual Basic.

CALLING ASP OBJECTS WITH THE `ObjectContext`

When you have an understanding of the scripting objects provided by ASP, you quickly discover that Internet development absolutely depends on their functionality. The problem with the objects, however, is that ASP pages can become quite lengthy and complex if you perform all your functionality directly in script. Fortunately, a new feature of IIS/MTS integration significantly eases the scripting burden on ASP applications. Specifically, all the ASP scripting objects are now available to ActiveX components running under MTS.

MTS exposes the ASP scripting objects through the `ObjectContext`. You can access the objects in any ActiveX component placed in an MTS package by simply getting a reference to the `ObjectContext`. All that is required is to use the `CreateObject` method of the ASP Server object to create an instance of your business object. The business object in turn calls the `GetObjectContext` function to access the `ObjectContext`. After the `ObjectContext` is retrieved, individual ASP objects are accessed as follows:

```
Dim MyContext As MTxAS.ObjectContext
Set MyContext = GetObjectContext()
MyContext("Session")
MyContext("Application")
MyContext("Request")
MyContext("Response")
MyContext("Server")
```

> **TIP**
>
> Key Principle: Web applications should perform the bulk of their work in MTS objects called from the page. Avoid coding large amounts of functionality directly into the page. VBScript code is much harder to maintain than a set of ActiveX DLL components.

TRANSACTIONAL WEB PAGES

Along with scalability and fault tolerance, MTS also provides for the creation of transactional Web pages. Transactional Web pages are unique to ASP pages and should not be confused with calling transactional business objects from an ASP page. Unlike pages that call business objects, transactional Web pages can be created completely within an ASP page using nothing but VBScript. This technology allows Web masters to take advantage of transaction processing without having to create a separate COM component.

The key to creating transactional Web pages lies in a special MTS component created when you install MTS 2.0. This component is the ASP ObjectContext. Figure 9.9 shows the ASP ObjectContext, which is contained inside the IIS Utilities package. This package is designated as a Library package, which means that transactional Web pages will enlist the ASP ObjectContext inside their own memory space, which may or may not be inside the IIS memory space, depending upon the project settings.

FIGURE 9.9

The IIS Utilities package contains the ASP ObjectContext.

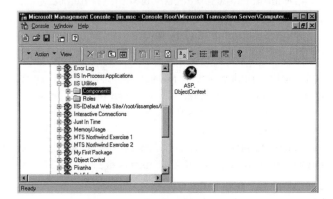

The IIS utilities package is initially installed so that changes and deletions to the package are not allowed. Although you could certainly change these settings, this could adversely affect the operation of transaction pages within ASP. If you examine the properties of the ASP ObjectContext, you will note that the object is set to require a transaction. This means that each time an ASP page enlists the ASP ObjectContext, a new transaction will be started if one does not already exist.

The secret to starting a transaction in an ASP page is a matter of using the new @TRANSACTION directive. This directive is analogous to the transaction properties you set for an MTS object in a package. The @TRANSACTION directive is always placed as the first line in any ASP page or else an error is generated. When you use the directive, the operations performed in any page are treated as a unit and function in much the same way as work performed by a conventional MTS component. The @TRANSACTION directive has the following values:

@TRANSACTION=REQUIRED: The ASP page will initiate a new transaction if one does not already exist. Because it is not possible to enlist multiple ASP pages in a single transaction context, a new transaction is always started.

@TRANSACTION=REQUIRES_NEW: The ASP page will always initiate a new transaction. Although Microsoft distinguishes between the REQUIRES and REQUIRES_NEW values, they are functionally equivalent in the current release of ASP. Maybe in the future, Microsoft will create a way to enlist several ASP pages in a single transaction, but for now, it is not possible.

@TRANSACTION=NOT_SUPPORTED: The Web page never initiates a transaction using the ASP `ObjectContext`. This is the default for all ASP pages that do not specify an @TRANSACTION directive. The page can, of course, still create separate business objects running in MTS, which may or may not create new transactions. The @TRANSACTION directive applies specifically to work done by VBScript and has no effect on work done by external components.

@TRANSACTION=SUPPORTED: This value seems to imply that a transaction context can be used, however, because ASP cannot enlist multiple pages in a transaction, the net effect of this setting is that a transaction is never initiated for the script in this page. Once again, the distinction between SUPPORTED and NOT_SUPPORTED may become meaningful in a future release of ASP.

When the ASP page is set to start a transaction, all work done by script code in the page is part of a new transaction. All work performed by the page will succeed or fail as a batch. Commits and rollbacks of the work are automatic. Unlike a conventional MTS component, script pages are not required to specifically call a `SetComplete` or `SetAbort` method to commit or rollback transactions. Instead, ASP provides transaction events, which notify the page of success or failure. These two events are `OnTransactionCommit` and `OnTransactionAbort`. A transactional Web page simply codes both an `OnTransactionCommit` and `OnTransactionAbort` event handler, which is automatically executed when the transaction succeeds or fails. This means that you can format response pages to users that indicate success or failure. The code in Listing 9.2 performs a transaction between two databases simulating a money transfer.

LISTING 9.2   CODE PERFORMING A TRANSACTION BETWEEN TWO DATABASES

```
<%@TRANSACTION="REQUIRED" LANGUAGE="VBSCRIPT" %>

<html>
<head>
<meta NAME="GENERATOR"
Content="Microsoft Visual InterDev 1.0">

<title>Transactional Web Pages</title>
</head>
<body>

<!--This example shows  Transactional -->
<!--web page support under IIS 4.0 and MTS 2.0-->

<%
Dim objSavings
Dim objChecking
Dim txtAmount
```

continues

9

MTS AND THE
INTERNET

LISTING 9.2   CONTINUED

```
Dim objResultset
Dim txtSavingsBalance
Dim txtCheckingBalance

Const rdUseClientBatch = 3
Const rdDriverNoPrompt = 1
Const rdSavings = 1
Const rdChecking =2

'Get Amount
txtAmount = Request.Form("txtAmount")
If txtAmount = "" Then txtAmount = 0

'Debit Savings
Set objSavings = Server.CreateObject("ADODB.Connection")
objSavings.Open _
"Provider=SQLOLEDB;Data Source=(local);Database=federal;UID=sa;PWD=;"
objSavings.Execute _
"EXECUTE sp_AdjustAccount " & rdSavings & ", -" & txtAmount

'Credit Checking
Set objChecking = _
    Server.CreateObject("ADODB.Connection")
objChecking.Open _
"Provider=SQLOLEDB;Data Source=(local);Database=national;UID=sa;PWD=;"
objChecking.Execute _
"EXECUTE sp_AdjustAccount " & rdChecking & ", " & txtAmount

'Get Savings balance
Set objResultset = _
    Server.CreateObject("ADODB.Recordset")
objResultset.Open _
    "EXECUTE sp_GetBalance " & rdSavings,objSavings
txtSavingsBalance = objResultset("AccountBalance")

'Get Checking balance
Set objResultset = _
    Server.CreateObject("ADODB.Recordset")
objResultset.Open _
    "EXECUTE sp_GetBalance " & rdChecking,objChecking
txtCheckingBalance = objResultset("AccountBalance")

'Close Connections
objSavings.Close
objChecking.Close

Set objSavings = Nothing
Set objChecking = Nothing

'Format Response
Sub OnTransactionCommit()
```

```
%>
<h1>Thank You!</h1>
<table>
    <tr>
    <td>
    Savings
    </td>
    <td>
    <%=txtSavingsBalance%>
    </td>
    </tr>
    <tr>
    <td>
    Checking
    </td>
    <td>
    <%=txtCheckingBalance%>
    </td>
    </tr>
</table>

<%
End Sub

Sub OnTransactionAbort()
%>
<h1>Sorry, your transaction
cannot be completed at this time.</h1>
<%
End Sub

%>

</body>
</html>
```

REMOTE DATA SERVICES

While ASP allows developers to utilize MTS components through server-side processing, these applications often result in a user experience that is less satisfying than it should be. Because ASP pages must always return to the server for modification, the user is forced to tolerate an endless series of redrawn pages. This results in an interface that appears to blink every time the user makes a change.

As an alternative to server-side processing, Microsoft offers Internet developers Remote Data Services (RDS). RDS is a technology that allows a single page to access data and components on the server without redrawing the page. The result is that the interface looks and feels much more like a standard Windows application than an equivalent application written with ASP.

RDS, like ASP, is an ISAPI application, meaning that it works in concert with IIS. The proper name of the application that implements RDS is Advanced Data ISAPI (ADIS-API). Like many technologies, RDS can be utilized in ways ranging from the simple to the sophisticated. In all cases, however, the underlying technology relies on COM objects that communicate across the Internet. RDS utilizes COM objects on both the server and the browser. These objects can pass arguments and data across the Internet without navigating between Web pages. Think of the Web page as a user interface and RDS as the data to place in the interface.

When you install Internet Information Server, you have the option to install the RDS server-side components. When you install Internet Explorer, you automatically install the client-side components. Therefore, every client using IE 4.0 or later can utilize RDS technology. At this point, we should mention that RDS only works with the Internet Explorer and IIS. You cannot use RDS solutions for Netscape Navigator. This is a significant disadvantage if you need cross-browser support and is the primary reason to develop in ASP.

RDS Fundamentals

At its simplest, RDS operates using a single component on the server and a single component on the client. The client-side component is known as the Advanced Data Control (ADC) and functions similarly to any data control in Visual Basic. On the server, a component named the Advanced Data Factory (ADF) is installed. The ADC has the capability to call the ADF across the Internet and instruct it to retrieve data from a relational database. The data is retrieved when the ADC calls the ADF and passes a connect string and SQL statement. The ADF responds by packing the data and sending it to the browser. After the data arrives at the browser, it can be bound to controls such as HTML text fields or tables for display. Figure 9.10 shows how the ADC and ADF communicate.

FIGURE 9.10

Remote Data Services uses COM components to transfer data.

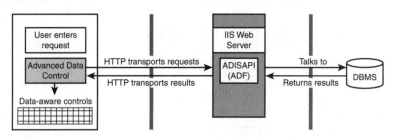

Although RDS is a sophisticated data transport strategy, using it from a Web page can be remarkably simple. Because every installation of Internet Explorer contains the ADC, you can assume its presence and use it to access the ADF on a server. The ADC is created through the use of the HTML <OBJECT> tag.

```
<!-- The Advanced Data control -->
<object ID="Data1" WIDTH="11" HEIGHT="11"
CLASSID="clsid:BD96C556-65A3-11D0-983A-00C04FC29E33">
    <param NAME="Server" VALUE="http://www.vb-bootcamp.com">
    <param NAME="Connect" VALUE="DSN=Biblio">
    <param NAME="SQL" VALUE="SELECT * FROM Authors>
</object>
```

The <OBJECT> tag is the HTML equivalent of the CreateObject function in Visual Basic. If you examine the <OBJECT> tag carefully, you will see all information necessary to create the object and assign properties. In this tag, you will first notice the ID attribute. This attribute assigns a name to the data control. This name can then be used elsewhere in the page to bind fields to the control. Next, you'll notice the CLSID attribute. This attribute is the class identifier for the object to create. Just like you must specify the programmatic identifier (ProgID) when using the CreateObject function, the <OBJECT> tag uses the CLSID to indicate the object to create. Finally, notice the <PARAM> tags contained within the <OBJECT> tag. These tags are field/value pairs that set properties for the control when it is created. These tags represent the three critical properties you must set to get RDS to function.

The Server property designates the Web server where the ADF is located. By setting this property, the ADC can call across the Internet to the location specified and attempt to contact the ADF. If the ADF is found at the specified location, a request for data is made. When the request is passed from the ADC to the ADF, the Connect and SQL properties are included in the request. These properties tell the ADF what database to query and what SQL statement to run. Obviously, this information must be meaningful to the ADF. In other words, the DSN or Data Link specified in the connect string must represent a database that is accessible to the ADF. Keep in mind that all queries are run by the ADF for the ADC. Therefore, the database must be within the domain shared by the web server. The simplest solution, therefore, is to use a database on the same machine as the Web server.

After the query is run, the resulting data is returned to the client and stored in the ADC. At this moment, the data is available for binding to elements in the page. Data binding is accomplished through the use of the DATASRC and DATAFLD attributes of HTML elements. For example, the following code will bind a field from the ADC to an HTML text field.

```
<INPUT id=txtName DATASRC=#Data1 DATAFLD="Name">
```

9

MTS AND THE
INTERNET

Notice how the DATASRC attribute contains the name of a valid ADC control in the page preceded by a # sign. The DATAFLD attribute specifies the field in the ADC recordset that should be bound to this control. After the data set returns from the ADF, it will appear automatically in the text field. In fact, once populated, the ADC behaves much like an ADO Recordset object. The Recordset property of the ADC exposes many familiar properties and methods such as BOF, EOF, MoveFirst, MoveLast, MoveNext, and MovePrevious, which you can access from client-side script code for navigation. The code in Listing 9.3 shows how to use the ADC and bind the results to a grid.

LISTING 9.3   CODE THAT BINDS ADC TO A GRID CONTROL

```
<html>
<head>
<meta NAME="GENERATOR" Content="Microsoft Developer Studio">

<title>Document Title</title>

<script LANGUAGE="VBScript">
<!--

  Sub MSFlexGrid1_Click()
    'Reference the Form
    Dim MyForm
    Set MyForm = Document.frmData
    If MyForm.MSFlexGrid1.Row = 1 Then
      'Sort by Column
      MyForm.Data1.SortColumn = _
      MyForm.MSFlexGrid1.TextArray(MyForm.MSFlexGrid1.Col)
      MyForm.Data1.SortDirection = True
      MyForm.Data1.Reset
      'Refresh Grid
      'MyForm.MSFlexGrid1.Refresh
    End If
  End Sub

-->
</script>

</head>
<body>

<form NAME="frmData">

<!-- The Advanced Data control -->
<OBJECT height=11 id=Data1 width=11
classid=clsid:BD96C556-65A3-11D0-983A-00C04FC29E33 >

  <PARAM NAME="SQL" VALUE="SELECT Authors.Author, Titles.Title,
  Titles.Subject FROM Authors, `Title Author`, Titles
```

```
   WHERE Authors.Au_ID = `Title Author`.Au_ID
   AND `Title Author`.ISBN = Titles.ISBN
   AND (Titles.Title LIKE '%Internet%')">
   <PARAM NAME="Connect" VALUE="DSN=Biblio">
   <PARAM NAME="Server" VALUE="http://localhost">
</OBJECT>

<!-- A Data-Bound Grid -->
<OBJECT dataSrc=#Data1  height=400
id=MSFlexGrid1 width=600
classid=CLSID:6262D3A0-531B-11CF-91F6-C2863C385E30>
</OBJECT>

</form>

</body>
</html>
```

Calling MTS Components

Although the ADC is a useful mechanism for exploiting RDS, it is limited to use with
SQL statements and recordsets. If you want, however, you can take more control over
RDS and call other components besides the ADF. In fact, RDS is capable of calling any
method on any COM component. This includes MTS components you create.

The Advanced Data Space

To call a COM component other than the ADF, you must utilize a different client-side
component than the ADC. Along with the ADC, Internet Explorer also installs a component known as the Advanced Data Space (ADS). The ADS is a client-component that can
call server-side components other than the ADF. To use the ADS, you must create an
instance of the component by using the <OBJECT> tag just as you did for the ADC. The
following code shows how to create an instance of the ADS from a Web page.

```
<!-- DataSpace -->
<OBJECT ID=DataSpace1
CLASSID=clsid:BD96C556-65A3-11D0-983A-00C04FC29E36>
</OBJECT>
```

Notice that the <OBJECT> tag utilizes the CLSID for the ADS just as it did for the ADC. In
this case, however, you do not have to supply any <PARAM> tags. The whole reason to create the ADS is to take advantage of a single method. Once created, the ADS allows you
to use the CreateObject method to create an instance of any object on the server. This
will give you a reference to a COM component in the browser that is actually running on
the server! This means that you can create server-side MTS components and call them
from client-side Web pages. When you call the CreateObject method, you must pass the

ProgID of the component you want to create and the Web address of the server where the component resides. The code in Listing 9.4 shows an example of creating a component named `SimpleObject.Simple` and calling a method named `Process`.

LISTING 9.4   CODE THAT CALLS AN MTS COMPONENT FROM THE ADS

```
<HTML>
<HEAD>
<META name=VI60_defaultClientScript content=VBScript>
<META NAME="GENERATOR" Content="Microsoft Visual Studio 6.0">
<TITLE></TITLE>
</HEAD>
<BODY>

<!-- RDS.DataSpace -->
<OBJECT classid=CLSID:BD96C556-65A3-11D0-983A-00C04FC29E36 height=1
id=DataSpace1 width=1 VIEWASTEXT></OBJECT>

<SCRIPT LANGUAGE="VBScript">

Dim MTSObject1
Set MTSObject1 = DataSpace1.CreateObject("SimpleObject.Simple",
"http://localhost")

Sub Button1_OnClick
    Msgbox MTSObject1.Process
End Sub

</SCRIPT>
<INPUT type="button" value="Push me!" id=button1 name=button1>

</BODY>
</HTML>
```

RDS Security Issues

When you call an MTS component using the ADS, you can create any valid component and call any valid method. Unlike the ADC, you are free to call methods that return not only ADO Recordset objects, but you can also pass primitive data types as well as arrays. This makes the technology much more powerful while preserving a highly interactive interface. However, nothing in programming comes for free. Before you can use the ADS to call a COM component, you must wrestle with a few security issues.

Whenever you call a component across the Internet, you have the potential for contracting a virus. That's because MTS components represent executable content that can damage a client machine if they are written by a malicious author. Therefore, Internet Explorer does not allow these components to run by default. Additionally, ADISAPI does not have permission to create an instance of a component by default.

Solving the security problems is accomplished by making three registry entries on the server where the MTS components reside. Two of these entries are relayed to the calling client to indicate that the component is safe while a third gives ADISAPI permission to launch the component on the server. These entries are:

Safe for Initialization: This registry entry is made on the machine where MTS and IIS are running. It tells the client browser that the MTS component can be launched safely. The following registry key marks the component as safe for initialization:

```
[HKEY_LOCAL_MACHINE\SOFTWARE\Classes\CLSID\{Component CLSID}\
➡Implemented Categories\{7DD95801-9882-11CF-9FA9-00AA006C42C4}]
```

Safe for Scripting: This registry entry is made on the machine where MTS and IIS are running. It tells the client browser that the MTS component methods can be called safely. The following registry entry marks the component as safe for scripting:

```
[HKEY_LOCAL_MACHINE\SOFTWARE\Classes\CLSID\{Component CLSID}\
➡Implemented Categories\{7DD95802-9882-11CF-9FA9-00AA006C42C4}]
```

Permission to Launch: This registry entry is made on the machine where MTS and IIS are running. It gives ADISAPI permission to create the MTS component for the requesting client. The following registry entry gives IIS permission to launch the component:

```
[HKEY_LOCAL_MACHINE\SYSTEM\CurrentControlSet\Services\W3SVC\
➡Parameters\ADCLaunch\Component ProgID]
```

When you first examine the registry entries required to enable RDS, the task looks daunting. However, the CD-ROM for this book comes with a wizard that can make these entries for you automatically. The RDS Wizard is a utility that enables you to select an MTS component from a list and make the necessary registry entries for use with RDS. We have found this to be a simple and straightforward way to successfully implement RDS solutions. Figure 9.11 shows the wizard interface.

FIGURE 9.11

The RDS Wizard makes registry entries necessary to use MTS components with RDS.

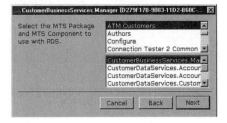

9

MTS AND THE
INTERNET

After you have made all the server-side registry entries, you are still not quite through. Even though the components are marked as safe, Internet Explorer still will not allow them to be created under its default security configurations. In fact, you must establish custom security configurations that allow the components to be created. This requires utilizing the options panel in the browser to allow the creation of unsigned ActiveX components. Figure 9.12 shows the security options for Internet Explorer.

FIGURE 9.12

You must alter the default security settings of IE to run MTS components with ADS.

ADS Checklist

With all of the issues surrounding the use of ADS, you might conclude that it is too complicated for use in a real application. However, we have been successful implementing these solutions once all of the developers on the team have been trained on the requirements. Additionally, the client-side security issues can be solved easily if the application is on an intranet. With that in mind, here is a checklist to help you be successful with ADS and MTS applications.

1. Create MTS components that you want to call from a Web page.
2. Run the RDS Wizard on all of the components that you want to call from the Web page.
3. Establish custom settings for Internet Explorer that allow unsigned ActiveX components to be created.
4. Create a Web page that contains the <OBJECT> tag for the Advanced Data Space.
5. Use the CreateObject method of the ADS to create an instance of the server-side MTS component. For those developers using Visual InterDev, you will find a special design-time control on the CD-ROM which helps write the required RDS code for you.
6. Call methods on the component and manipulate data with client-side script.

EXERCISE 9-1: MTS AND ACTIVE SERVER PAGES

This exercise creates a Web-based search engine for a hypothetical online bookstore called Piranha.Com. You can search by author, title, or publisher to locate books. The search is conducted by components running under the Microsoft Transaction Server.

Step 1

Using the CD-ROM for the book, locate the directory TEMPLATES\EXERCISE9-1. This directory contains a partially completed project you can use to create the Web-based bookstore. This directory contains two subdirectories. One is labeled \WEB and the other \VB.

Step 2

On your hard drive, create a new directory with the Windows Explorer named MTS\ EXERCISE9-1. Copy the contents from the TEMPLATES\EXERCISE9-1\VB directory into the new directory you just created. This exercise builds projects in both Visual Basic and Visual InterDev. You will start by building the MTS components in Visual Basic.

Step 3

Because the CD-ROM will create read-only copies of the project files, select all the files you copied, right-click them, and select **Properties** from the pop-up menu. In the properties dialog, uncheck the read-only flag. Close the dialog.

Building the MTS Components

In this section, you will build the MTS components. These components will be utilized in the ASP page.

Step 4

Open the Visual Basic project EXERCISE9-1.VBP. This project contains two class modules named Results and Query. Together, these classes perform the search and build a results table.

Step 5

In the Project Explorer, locate the Query class. This class is used to run a query on the pubs database in SQL Server. The class has a single method named GetBooks. It takes as arguments the search criteria you want to run and returns a firehose cursor. Add the code in Listing 9.5 to the GetBooks method to run the query:

LISTING 9.5   CODE TO ADD TO THE GetBooks METHOD

```
On Error GoTo GetBooksErr

    'Get Object Context
    Dim objContext As MTxAs.ObjectContext
    Set objContext = GetObjectContext()

    'Build SQL Statement
    Dim strSQL As String
    strSQL = ""
    strSQL = strSQL & _
    "SELECT authors.au_lname, titles.title, publishers.pub_name "
    strSQL = strSQL & _
    "FROM authors INNER JOIN titleauthor "
    strSQL = strSQL & _
    "ON authors.au_id = titleauthor.au_id "
    strSQL = strSQL & _
    "INNER JOIN titles ON titleauthor.title_id = titles.title_id "
    strSQL = strSQL & _
    "INNER JOIN publishers ON titles.pub_id = publishers.pub_id "
    strSQL = strSQL & _
    "WHERE authors.au_lname LIKE '%" & strAuthor & "%' "
    strSQL = strSQL & _
    "AND titles.title LIKE '%" & strTitle & "%' "
    strSQL = strSQL & _
    "AND publishers.pub_name LIKE '%" & strPublisher & "%' "

    'Open the connection
    Dim objRecordset As ADODB.Recordset
    Set objRecordset = New ADODB.Recordset

    objRecordset.Source = strSQL
    objRecordset.ActiveConnection = _
    "Provider=SQLOLEDB;Data Source=(local);Database=pubs;UID=sa;PWD="
    objRecordset.CursorLocation = adUseServer
    objRecordset.CacheSize = 1
    objRecordset.CursorType = adOpenForwardOnly
    objRecordset.Open
    Set GetBooks = objRecordset

    'Tell MTS we succeeded
    objContext.SetComplete

GetBooksExit:
    Exit Function

GetBooksErr:
    'Tell MTS we failed
    objContext.SetAbort
```

```
'Log Error
Debug.Print Err.Description
App.StartLogging App.Path & "\error.log", vbLogToFile
App.LogEvent Err.Description, vbLogEventTypeError

Resume GetBooksExit
```

Step 6

The Query class should initiate a transaction when it is called. Therefore, set the
MTSTransactionMode property of this class to 4-RequiresNewTransaction.

Step 7

Now locate the class named Results. This class is called by an Active Server Page. This
class has a single method named BuildResultsPage. This method uses the ASP object
model accessed through the ObjectContext. It builds a table in the calling page based on
a recordset. Add the code in Listing 9.6 to the BuildResultsPage method to create the
table of results from the search.

LISTING 9.6 CODE FOR THE BuildResultsPage METHOD

```
On Error GoTo BuildPageErr

    'Get Object Context
    Dim objContext As MTxAs.ObjectContext
    Set objContext = GetObjectContext()

    'Get search criteria
    Dim strAuthor As String
    Dim strTitle As String
    Dim strPublisher As String

    strAuthor = _
        objContext.Item("Request").Form("txtAuthor")
    strTitle = _
        objContext.Item("Request").Form("txtTitle")
    strPublisher = _
        objContext.Item("Request").Form("txtPublisher")

    'Create Query object
    Dim objQuery As Piranha.Query
    Set objQuery = New Piranha.Query

    'Run Query
    Dim objRecordset As ADODB.Recordset
```

continues

LISTING 9.6 CONTINUED

```
    Set objRecordset = _
        objQuery.GetBooks(strAuthor, strTitle, strPublisher)

    'Build Table
    With objContext.Item("Response")
        .Write "<TABLE ALIGN=center BORDER=1>"
        .Write "<TR>"
        .Write "<TD>Author</TD>"
        .Write "<TD>Title</TD>"
        .Write "<TD>Publisher</TD>"
        .Write "</TR>"

        Do While Not objRecordset.EOF
            .Write "<TR>"
            .Write "<TD>" & _
            objRecordset!au_lname & "</TD>"
            .Write "<TD>" & _
            objRecordset!Title & "</TD>"
            .Write "<TD>" & _
            objRecordset!pub_name & "</TD>"
            .Write "</TR>"
            objRecordset.MoveNext
        Loop

        .Write "</TABLE>"
    End With

    'Tell MTS we succeeded
    objContext.SetComplete

BuildPageExit:
    Exit Sub

BuildPageErr:
    'Tell MTS we failed
    objContext.SetAbort

    'Print Error Message
    objContext.Item("Response").Write Err.Description

    Resume BuildPageExit
```

Step 8

When the code is added to the project, compile the classes by selecting File, Make Project Group from the menu. This will create a single DLL that you can add to MTS.

Step 9

Start the MTS Explorer. In the Explorer, create a new package named Piranha for the components you just coded. Add the components you compiled to this new package.

Building the Web Project

In this section you will build a Web project for the application. This project is created using Visual InterDev.

Step 10

The MTS components will be called from a new Visual InterDev Web project. Visual InterDev is a development environment that simplifies the process of creating Web pages and virtual directories. If you have experience with Visual InterDev, this project will be straightforward. If you are new to Visual InterDev, follow the next few steps carefully. Start Visual InterDev. Choose to create a new Web project under the MTS\EXERCISE9-1 directory you created earlier. Figure 9.13 shows the New Project dialog in Visual InterDev.

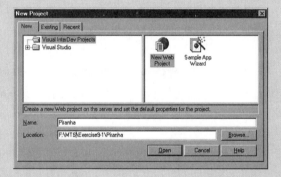

FIGURE 9.13
Start a new Visual InterDev project.

Step 11

When you create the new project, the Web Project Wizard will start. In the first step of the wizard, type the name of the server to use for the project. If IIS is installed on your local machine, you may simply use the keyword localhost. Choose to work in Master Mode. Figure 9.14 shows step 1 of the Web Project Wizard.

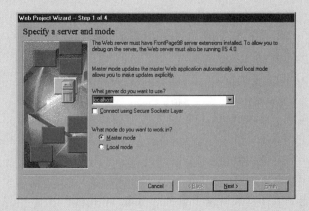

FIGURE 9.14

Enter the name of the Web server in Step 1.

Step 12

In step 2 of the Web Project Wizard, accept the default settings to create your new project. Figure 9.15 shows step 2 of the wizard.

FIGURE 9.15

Accept the default name for your new project.

Step 13

In step 3 of the Web Project Wizard, you will be asked to choose a layout. Accept the default setting of None. Figure 9.16 shows step 3 of the wizard.

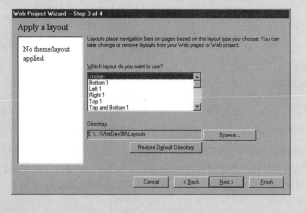

FIGURE 9.16
Accept the default of None for the layout.

Step 14

In step 4 of the Web Project Wizard, you will be asked to pick a theme for the site. Select the Blue Mood theme. When you have selected the theme, you may click Finish to build your new project. Figure 9.17 shows step 4 of the wizard.

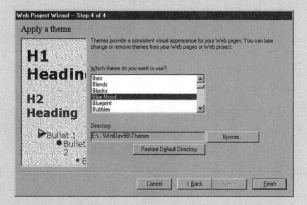

FIGURE 9.17
Select the Blue Mood theme.

Step 15

When the project is successfully created, you can add the Web pages from the CD-ROM. From the Visual InterDev menu, select Project, Add Item. This will open the Add Item dialog. Click the Existing tab and add the files DEFAULT.HTM and SEARCH.ASP to the project from the CD-ROM directory TEMPLATES\EXERCISE9-1\WEB.

Step 16

DEFAULT.HTM is the home page for the bookstore. It presents a search table you can fill out. The search is done in the file SEARCH.ASP, which calls MTS components. Open the SEARCH.ASP file in Visual InterDev.

Step 17

Calling the MTS components is done by creating an instance of the `Results` object. Add the following code to SEARCH.ASP just under the heading Search Results:

```
<%Set objBusiness = Server.CreateObject("Piranha.Results")%>
<%objBusiness.BuildResultsPage%>
```

Step 18

Save your work. Run the application by right-clicking the DEFAULT.HTM page in the Project Explorer and selecting **View in Browser** from the pop-up menu. This will bring up a home page with a search criteria form. Figure 9.18 shows the home page.

FIGURE 9.18
Enter search criteria in this Web page.

Step 19

On the search criteria form, enter **Moon** in the Publisher field. Then click the Search button. This will cause the MTS components to query the database and format a table of results. Figure 9.19 shows the results page.

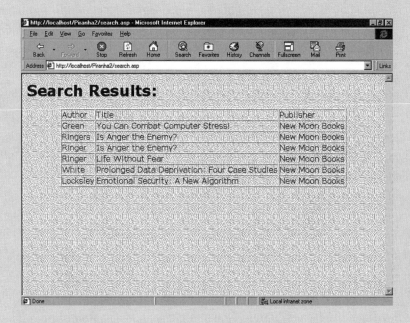

FIGURE 9.19

View results in this Web page.

DEBUGGING AND DISTRIBUTING MTS APPLICATIONS

PREREQUISITES

Before beginning this chapter, you should have a complete understanding of how to create MTS components. You should also be familiar with fundamental SQL Server administration concepts such as security and scripts. Additionally, you should understand Windows/NT networking concepts such as security permissions and groups.

Skills Learned

- 70-175(8): Configure a client computer to use an MTS component.
- 70-175(9): Create packages that install or update MTS components on a client computer.
- 70-175(18): Debug Visual Basic code that uses objects from a COM server.
- 70-175(21): Use the Package and Deployment Wizard to create a package.
- 70-175(36): Debug DLLs in process.
- 70-175(37): Use the Package and Deployment Wizard to create a setup program that installs a distributed application, registers the COM components, and allows for uninstall.
- 70-175(40): Plan and implement floppy disk-based deployment or compact disc-based deployment for a distributed application.
- 70-175(41): Plan and implement Web-based deployment for a distributed application.
- 70-175(42): Plan and implement network-based deployment for a distributed application.
- 70-175(44): Fix errors, and take measures to prevent future errors.
- 70-175(45): Deploy application updates for distributed applications.

When you create enterprise applications with MTS, you encounter a whole new level of troubleshooting issues. You have to deal not only with the validity of your code solution, but with issues of network traffic and bottlenecks. Additionally, application deployment is complicated proportionally. You must create setups for the client, MTS components, and database objects.

DEBUGGING MTS COMPONENTS

Historically, debugging MTS components in Visual Basic has been difficult primarily because code running outside MTS has never been capable of returning meaningful information in the `ObjectContext`. In fact, previous versions of Visual Basic return `Nothing` from the `GetObjectContext` function. Because the `ObjectContext` is not set, any call to a method such as `SetComplete` results in a runtime error.

Debugging in Visual Basic 6.0

Because of recent enhancements in Visual Basic 6.0, debugging ActiveX DLL components in MTS can now be as simple as debugging any Visual Basic application. The key to successful debugging is to install Windows/NT Service Pack 4. When you install Service Pack 4, it upgrades MTS 2.0 to Service Pack 1. This Service Pack enables complete debugging of MTS components within Visual Basic 6.0. This means that you can run ActiveX DLL components directly in Visual Basic and still gain useful information from the `ObjectContext`.

In order to take advantage of MTS debugging features in Visual Basic 6.0, you must meet a very specific set of conditions. First, you must compile the MTS component as an ActiveX DLL and install it in an MTS package. Second, you must set the version compatibility to Binary Compatibility for the ActiveX DLL project in Visual Basic. The compatible project should be the compiled DLL that you already installed in MTS. Finally, you must run the ActiveX DLL in a separate copy of Visual Basic 6.0 from the calling client project. When you meet all these conditions, you can set breakpoints in the ActiveX DLL project that will now receive meaningful information from the `ObjectContext`.

QUICK CHECK 10-1:

DEBUGGING VB 6.0 COMPONENTS

1. Using the CD-ROM for the book, locate the directory TEMPLATES\QUICK CHECK10-1. This directory contains an MTS component that you can use to test out debugging principles.

2. On your hard drive, create a new directory with the Windows Explorer named MTS\QUICK CHECK10-1. Copy the contents from the CD-ROM directory into the new directory you just created.

3. Because the CD-ROM will create read-only copies of the project files, select all the files you copied, right-click them, and select **Properties** from the pop-up menu. In the properties dialog, uncheck the read-only flag. Close the dialog.

4. Start Visual Basic and open the file DEBUGGER.VBP. This project is an ActiveX DLL that is already coded. However, it is intended to run under MTS, so set the MTSTransactionMode property to 4-RequiresNewTransaction.

5. After you set the MTSTransactionMode, compile the project into an ActiveX DLL. When you compile the project, Visual Basic will automatically set the version compatibility to Project Compatibility; however, in order to debug the component, you must set the version compatibility to Binary Compatibility. Figure 10.1 shows the version compatibility setting in the Project Properties dialog.

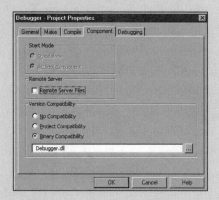

FIGURE 10.1
Set the version compatibility to Binary Compatibility.

6. In order to debug the component, you must place it in an MTS package. Start the MTS Explorer and create a new empty package. After you create the package, install the new component into the package.

7. So that you can fully test debugging facilities, set up a role for the new package. The exact name of the role is unimportant, but you should place your Windows/NT user ID under the role and add the role to the Role membership folder of the component. Finally, turn on security for the package after the role is configured.

8. After the package is complete, return to Visual Basic and run the ActiveX DLL. The running code will supersede the component in MTS and allow you to debug the code. The component code already has a `Stop` statement coded into it so it will break when you call it.

9. Return to the Windows File Explorer and locate the project FRONTEND.VBP. Open this project in a separate copy of Visual Basic.

10. Open the References dialog and ensure the project has a reference set to the ActiveX DLL component. When the reference is set, run the front end. You can call the MTS component by clicking the button on the form. Figure 10.2 shows the client form.

NOTE

If you receive an "Error 91 object variable or with block variable not set," this is indicative of your machine being improperly set up for debugging. Make sure you have Windows/NT Service Pack 4 installed and that you have carefully followed all steps in the exercise.

FIGURE 10.2
Use this form to call the MTS component.

11. When the component is called, it will break on the `Stop` statement. You can now single-step through the code and examine some features of the `ObjectContext`.

Debugging in Visual Basic 5.0

If you are creating MTS components in Visual Basic 5.0, you will not be able to run the components in the VB environment for debugging as you can with VB 6.0. Instead, you must compensate for the fact that the `ObjectContext` cannot return meaningful information when the code is run in the VB environment. Without some form of compensation, this means that all references to context or security through the `ObjectContext` will result in runtime errors.

The simplest way to compensate for lost information in the `ObjectContext` is to place MTS in a special debug mode that can be enabled through a registry key. In the debug mode, MTS will return a special debug version of the `ObjectContext` that is suitable for use in the VB environment. Using the registry editor, you can create the following key to enable this mode:

```
HKEY_LOCAL_MACHINE\SOFTWARE\Microsoft\Transaction Server\Debug\
➥RunWithoutContext
```

When the debug registry key is created, calls to `GetObjectContext` return the special debug `ObjectContext`. The debug `ObjectContext` cannot return any significant information; however, it is set to return information that will at least prevent a runtime error in Visual Basic. The purpose of the debug `ObjectContext` is only to allow you to debug the business logic in your component. You cannot do anything meaningful with the return values from such methods as `IsCallerInRole`. All the `ObjectContext` methods return fixed values according to the information in Table 10.1.

TABLE 10.1   THE DEBUG `ObjectContext`

Debug `ObjectContext`	*Resulting Changes*
`CreateInstance`	Simply creates a new instance
`SetComplete`	Does nothing
`SetAbort`	Does nothing
`EnableCommit`	Does nothing
`DisableCommit`	Does nothing
`IsInTransaction`	Always returns FALSE
`IsSecurityEnabled`	Always returns FALSE
`IsCallerInRole`	Always returns TRUE

Although setting the `RunWithoutContext` registry key will allow you to run MTS code in the VB environment, developers should be concerned about repeatedly creating and deleting registry keys. Anytime you open the registry editor with the intention of modifying or deleting keys, you have the possibility of damaging the registry due to an accidental deletion. Because of this, we prefer to use conditional compilation to run VB 5.0 code. Utilizing conditional compilation, you can hide the `ObjectContext` code when debugging. For example, the following code hides the `CreateInstance` method and uses the `New` keyword to create an instance during debugging:

```
#Const MTS = True

#If MTS Then
    Set MyObject = New MyProject.MyClass
#Else
    Set MyObject = objContext.CreateInstance("MyProject.MyClass")
#End If
```

Using conditional compilation results in more code within the component than simply using the `RunWithoutContext` registry key, but it is safer. The simplest answer of all, however, is to upgrade to Visual Basic 6.0 where possible. If running under Windows/NT, be sure to install Service Pack 4.

DEPLOYING MTS APPLICATIONS

Because network connectivity issues can cause problems during the debugging process, we have always found it easier to develop MTS applications on a single machine. However, after you debug the components in your MTS application, you will need to deploy them to machines on the enterprise. Deploying an MTS application is significantly more complex than a traditional application and requires some thought and planning to be successful.

Deploying Data Services

Deploying the data services layer means creating SQL Server database structures, establishing permissions, and connecting remote servers. The simplest way to begin this deployment is to create a database script from your test installation of SQL Server. This script can then be used to generate the new database structure on another installation of SQL Server. The script you create may contain appropriate security information, or you may have to modify the settings. In any case, you should be sure to establish a single Windows/NT account if you intend to utilize connection pooling. Figure 10.3 shows the SQL Server script generation dialog.

FIGURE **10.3**
Generate SQL scripts to deploy the database structure.

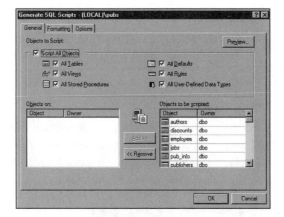

If multiple SQL Server installations are involved, you may need to connect remote servers through the Remote Servers dialog. If you intend to connect remote servers, be sure that you have the RPC service running. You will also need the Microsoft Distributed Transaction Coordinator running on all machines. Figure 10.4 shows the Remote Server Properties dialog.

FIGURE **10.4**
Connect remote servers for distributed transactions.

Deploying Business Services

Deploying the business services layer is all about deploying MTS components. Although other layers, most notably data services, may also contain MTS components, the mechanics for deploying the components do not change. Therefore, we will cover all the information in this section.

If you have built your distributed application on a single machine or in a separate testing environment, you already have MTS components installed and working. Deploying these components is a matter of moving them from one installation of MTS to another. The simplest way to move a package is to create a PAK file. Exporting an existing package creates a PAK file. You may then use the PAK file to import the package to another MTS installation.

Exporting the package is done by simply right-clicking the package of interest and selecting **Export** from the menu. When you select this menu, the MTS Explorer presents the Export Package dialog. This dialog allows you to select a location for the PAK file you want to create. Figure 10.5 shows the Export Package dialog.

FIGURE 10.5

Use this dialog to create exported PAK files.

After a PAK file is created, you can take it to any MTS installation and use it to create a new package. You utilize the PAK file in the Package Wizard. Up to this point, we have always selected the Create an Empty Package option on the Package Wizard. When you import from a PAK file, select the option **Install Pre-Built Package**. The Package Wizard will then present the Select Package Files dialog, which will let you browse for PAK files to install. Figure 10.6 shows the Select Package Files dialog.

FIGURE 10.6

Use this dialog to import packages from PAK files.

QUICK CHECK 10-2:

EXPORTING PACKAGES

1. On your hard drive, create a new directory with the Windows Explorer named MTS\QUICK CHECK10-2.

2. Start the MTS Explorer. Select any package that you have previously installed. Right-click the package in the MTS Explorer and select **Export** from the pop-up menu. This will display the Export Package dialog.

3. In the Export Package dialog, select to create a PAK file named QUICK CHECK10-2.PAK. Place this file in the directory you created earlier.

4. After the PAK file is exported, open the Windows File Explorer and examine the directory where you created the PAK file. In the directory, you will find a PAK file as well as a DLL file that contains the components you are exporting. Along with the DLL, you can use the PAK file to create a new package in another installation of MTS. Note that the DLL file will require supporting files including the Visual Basic runtime engine MSVBVM60.DLL. You cannot simply use a DLL file alone.

5. In addition to the DLL and PAK files, you will also see a directory called CLIENTS. This directory contains an executable you can use to help setup client machines. We discuss the use of this EXE file later in the chapter.

Along with exporting and importing packages, you can also deploy MTS components by building a traditional setup with the Visual Basic Package and Deployment Wizard. You can then run the setup on the machine where you want to deploy the component. This is much less efficient, however, because Visual Basic does not know how to create MTS packages. Therefore, you will have to build the package by hand for the components installed by your setup.

Deploying User Services

Deploying the user services layer entails building a setup for the client machine that contains the GUI and components necessary to run the application. This is done using the Visual Basic Package and Deployment Wizard. Creating a setup for a distributed application, however, is a little different than a traditional setup.

The key to creating a distributed client setup is to remember that the ActiveX components required by the client are not present on the client machine—they are under MTS. Therefore, your setup must create the appropriate registry entries to reference the deployed components.

Visual Basic recognizes the need to establish client-side registry entries to facilitate distributed application setups and supports a special file called a VBR file to assist. A VBR file can be generated from any ActiveX DLL component you create. The VBR is specific to a particular ActiveX component, so you must create one for each ActiveX DLL that the client will call directly. You can tell Visual Basic to create a VBR file for an ActiveX component by checking the Remote Server Files box under the Component tab of the Project Properties dialog. Figure 10.7 shows the dialog.

FIGURE 10.7

VBR files are generated when the Remote Server Files box is checked.

If the Remote Server Files box is checked for a component, Visual Basic will generate a VBR file for that component when the component is compiled. The VBR file contains all the registry entries necessary for a client computer to call the component, with one notable exception. The VBR file does not contain any information for the RemoteServerName entry. This is because Visual Basic cannot possibly know where the ActiveX DLL component will reside. Instead, we will enter this information during the client installation. Listing 10.1 shows a typical VBR file.

LISTING 10.1 A TYPICAL VBR FILE

```
VB5SERVERINFO
VERSION=1.0.0
APPDESCRIPTION=MTS Book, ATM Project Objects
HKEY_CLASSES_ROOT\Typelib\{3F763B5A-6950-11D2-B5A7-0060088D02A3}
\1.0 = MTS Book, ATM Project Objects
HKEY_CLASSES_ROOT\Typelib\{3F763B5A-6950-11D2-B5A7-0060088D02A3}
\1.0\0\win32 = ATM.dll
HKEY_CLASSES_ROOT\Typelib\{3F763B5A-6950-11D2-B5A7-0060088D02A3}
\1.0\FLAGS = 0
HKEY_CLASSES_ROOT\ATM.Manager\CLSID = {3F763B5C-6950-11D2-B5A7-
➥0060088D02A3}
HKEY_CLASSES_ROOT\CLSID\{3F763B5C-6950-11D2-B5A7-0060088D02A3}
\ProgID = ATM.Manager
```

```
HKEY_CLASSES_ROOT\CLSID\{3F763B5C-6950-11D2-B5A7-0060088D02A3}
\Version = 1.0
HKEY_CLASSES_ROOT\CLSID\{3F763B5C-6950-11D2-B5A7-0060088D02A3}
\Typelib = {3F763B5A-6950-11D2-B5A7-0060088D02A3}
HKEY_CLASSES_ROOT\CLSID\{3F763B5C-6950-11D2-B5A7-0060088D02A3}
\LocalServer32 = ATM.dll
HKEY_CLASSES_ROOT\INTERFACE\{3F763B5B-6950-11D2-B5A7-0060088D02A3} =
➡Manager
HKEY_CLASSES_ROOT\INTERFACE\{3F763B5B-6950-11D2-B5A7-0060088D02A3}
\ProxyStubClsid = {00020420-0000-0000-C000-000000000046}
HKEY_CLASSES_ROOT\INTERFACE\{3F763B5B-6950-11D2-B5A7-0060088D02A3}
\ProxyStubClsid32 = {00020420-0000-0000-C000-000000000046}
HKEY_CLASSES_ROOT\INTERFACE\{3F763B5B-6950-11D2-B5A7-0060088D02A3}
\Typelib = {3F763B5A-6950-11D2-B5A7-0060088D02A3}
HKEY_CLASSES_ROOT\INTERFACE\{3F763B5B-6950-11D2-B5A7-0060088D02A3}
\Typelib\"version" = 1.0
```

Although the VBR is created when you compile the MTS component, the file is actually used by the client setup. When you use the Package and Deployment Wizard to create an installation for the client project, the Wizard will naturally identify the ActiveX DLL components as being required for setup. If you do nothing, the wizard would actually deploy the ActiveX DLL components onto the client machine. Instead, you must uncheck the DLL files and add the VBR file to the setup. Adding the VBR file causes the wizard to make the registry entries in the file during setup instead of installing the associated component on the client machine. And what about that critical RemoteServerName entry? Simple—the setup will prompt you during the client setup for the name of the machine where the distributed component has been installed.

QUICK CHECK 10-3:

CREATING CLIENT SETUPS

1. Using the CD-ROM for the book, locate the directory TEMPLATES\QUICK CHECK10-3. This directory contains an complete project you can build a setup with.

2. On your hard drive, create a new directory with the Windows Explorer named MTS\QUICK CHECK10-3. Copy the contents from the CD-ROM directory into the new directory you just created.

3. Because the CD-ROM will create read-only copies of the project files, select all the files you copied, right-click them, and select **Properties** from the pop-up menu. In the properties dialog, uncheck the read-only flag. Close the dialog.

continues

10

DEBUGGING AND
DISTRIBUTING
MTS APPS

4. Start Visual Basic and open the file QUICK CHECK10-3.VBG. This project contains an ActiveX DLL and a Standard EXE. In the Project Explorer, select the ActiveX DLL file. Then open the Project Properties dialog and check the box **Remote Server Files** under the Component tab.

5. Now compile the ActiveX DLL project by selecting **File, Make Bookquery.dll.** When you compile the project, a file named BOOKQUERY.VBR will be created. This file is used to build the client setup.

6. Now select the Standard EXE project. In the References dialog, set a reference to the BookQuery project. With this project selected, start the Package and Deployment Wizard in Visual Basic. Build a setup package for the Standard EXE. When prompted to add and remove files from the setup, remove BOOKQUERY.DLL from the setup and add BOOKQUERY.VBR.

NOTE

You may have to make the Package and deployment Wizard available via the Add-In Manager.

7. After the VBR file is added, continue building the setup disks in the normal fashion. You may now run the setup on a client machine. If you did not specify a remote server when using the Package and Deployment Wizard, you will be prompted for a server name during the client installation.

As we have said before, the RemoteServerName entry is critical to the successful communication between the client and deployed MTS components. Because of this critical relationship, MTS also provides a way to set this entry. When you export a package from MTS, you not only get a PAK file, but you also get a an EXE file that you can run on a client machine. When you run the EXE file, it will update the RemoteServerName entry on any client to point to the machine where you did the package export. This way, you can change the entry should an MTS component be moved to another machine.

Internet Deployments

If you intend to call your MTS components from the Internet, then you must still deploy the components as stated earlier. However, you must keep several special concerns in mind. MTS components may be called from Internet Information Server through Active Server Pages technology or Remote Data Services.

If you intend to use ASP, you can call the components without issue. However, you will want to be certain that you evaluate the need to run your ASP pages in a separate memory space. All ASP pages initially run in the memory space of IIS, which is usually optimal, but if you have concerns about your application misbehaving, you might want to isolate it.

RDS, on the other hand, requires some special considerations. In order to call an MTS component from RDS, you must set the appropriate registry entries on the machine where the component resides. These entries include Safe for Scripting, Safe for Initialization, and IIS permission to launch the component. Use the RDS Wizard included on the CD-ROM to set these entries.

Deployment Checklist

This is a checklist of items to perform during an MTS deployment.

- **Data Services**

  Build SQL scripts for database structures.

  Create Windows/NT and SQL Server accounts.

  Enable the MSDTC service on all SQL Server installations.

  Enable the RPC service on all SQL Server installations.

- **Business Services**

  Build PAK files or separate setups for components.

  Ensure roles are established with appropriate membership.

  Ensure package security is enabled where appropriate.

  Turn on security for the System package.

  Disable component editing and deletion.

- **User Services**

  Build setups for front end.

  Ensure that each client has an appropriate `RemoteServerName` entry for each distributed component accessed.

- **Internet Checklist**

  Run ASP applications in a separate memory space, if necessary.

  If using Remote Data Services, mark each component as Safe for Scripting, Safe for Initialization, and give IIS permission to launch.

ANALYZING MTS APPLICATIONS

When an MTS application is debugged and deployed, you will want to determine how it performs. The Visual Studio Analyzer is a tool that allows you to build a special project just for analyzing applications. After the Analyzer is installed, you can find it as a project type in the Visual InterDev environment. Figure 10.8 shows the New Project dialog in Visual InterDev.

FIGURE 10.8

Use the New Project dialog to start a new Analyzer project.

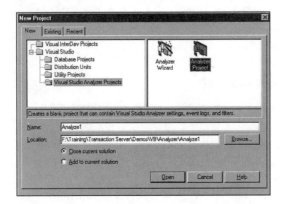

The Visual Studio Analyzer works by recording events that are generated by components on your system. These events are not the classic events that you program in Visual Basic. Instead these events are MTS and ADO events that indicate when objects are created and destroyed or when database connections are made and broken. The events that are collected by an Analyzer project can be generated by any distributed component in your application. The only catch is that each machine participating in the Analyzer project must be running the Visual Studio Analyzer server. This server can be installed from the Visual Studio CD-ROM set and is located with the server components.

Creating a new Analyzer project can be done using the Visual Studio Analyzer Project Wizard or by manually creating a new project. In either case, you must perform several essential tasks before you can begin analysis. First, you must select the machines that will participate in the project. After you identify the machines, you create a new event log to record events. Finally, you can establish filters to show only certain sets of events in your application.

When the new project is created, you can add new machines to the project. When added, your Analyzer project will collect events from these new machines. To add a new machine, right-click the Analyzer project in the Project Explorer and select **Connect to Machine** from the pop-up menu. This will display the Connect to Machine dialog.

In this dialog, you can type the name of a machine or use the Browse button to locate a machine. Figure 10.9 shows the dialog.

Event logs are the heart of an Analyzer project. An event log gathers events from all the machines in the distributed application and records them so you can perform analysis. You can add an event log to your Analyzer project. To add an event log, select **Project, Add Item** from the menu. This displays the Add Item dialog from which you can select a new event log. Figure 10.10 shows the Add Item dialog.

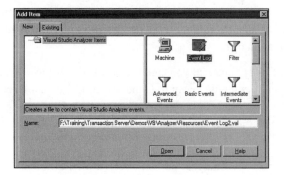

Filters allow you to focus on the events that are most important to you. You can add multiple filters to your Analyzer project to reflect different views of the events. You can add a filter to your project by using the Add Item dialog. The Add Item dialog contains several predefined filters that you can choose from, or you can select to create your own filter. When you create your own custom filter, you use the Edit Filter dialog to specify the events in your filter. Figure 10.11 shows the dialog.

After a filter is created, you may use the filter to limit the events that are recorded or to view a subset of events that are already recorded in the event log. To set the filter as a recording filter, right-click the filter and choose **Set Record Filter** from the pop-up menu. You can use a broad filter as the recording filter and then view a subset of events with a different filter later by right-clicking the filter and selecting **Apply Filter to View** from the pop-up menu.

FIGURE **10.11**

Use this dialog to create custom filters for your Analyzer project.

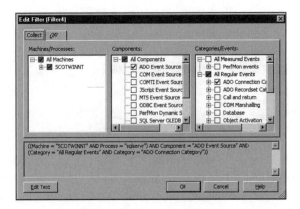

After you have identified the machines, created the event log, and enabled the filters, you are ready to begin recording events. Start recording by right-clicking the event log and selecting **Record Events** from the pop-up menu. Then the event log begins recording. At this point, you can minimize the running Analyzer project and start running the MTS application you want to analyze.

After you run your MTS application, you can stop recording events by returning to the Analyzer project, right-clicking the event log, and selecting **Record Events** again. This menu item works like a two-state button. It pops out and event recording stops. Now you can double-click the event log and examine the recorded events. Figure 10.12 shows a typical event log.

After events are recorded, the Analyzer project offers several different views of the data that can identify potential trouble spots. Perhaps the most useful view is the event chart. This view shows all the events and the time each event took to execute. This is valuable because you can easily identify events that took a long time to complete. This may indicate areas where you need to tune your application. You can select the chart view from the menu under **View, Analyzer, Chart**. Figure 10.13 shows a typical event chart.

FIGURE 10.12
The event log records events from all the machines in an MTS application.

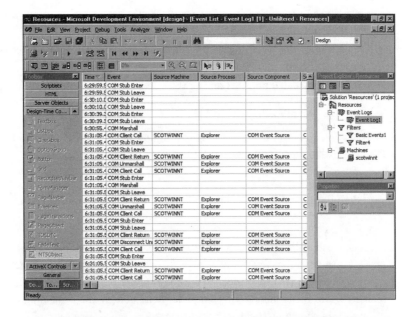

FIGURE 10.13
The event chart allows visual analysis of the collected events.

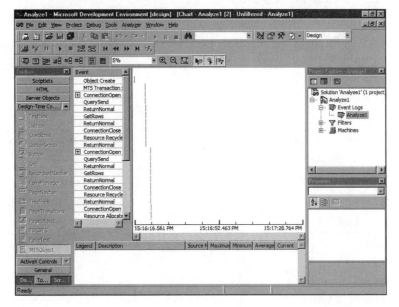

EXERCISE 10-1: ANALYZING MTS APPLICATIONS

The Visual Studio Analyzer is a tool that helps find and solve network issues associated with your MTS application. This exercise uses the Visual Studio Analyzer to locate bottlenecks in a distributed application.

Creating the Application

In this section, you will create an application that you can analyze. This application will simulate distributed components under test.

Step 1

Using the File Explorer, create a new directory named MTS\EXERCISE10-1.

Step 2

Start a new Standard EXE project in Visual Basic. To simulate the distributed components, we use three ActiveX DLL projects in a project group with the Standard EXE. Add three ActiveX DLL projects to your project group by selecting **File, Add Project** from the Visual Basic menu. After you add them, change the project names and component names as shown in Table 10.2.

TABLE 10.2 THE PROJECT EXPLORER

Old Name	New Name
Project1	Client
Project1.Form1	frmClient
Project2	Manager
Project2.Class1	Caller
Project3	Transactor1
Project3.Class1	Aggregate
Project4	Transactor2
Project4.Class1	Aggregate

Step 3

This project creates a simple set of objects that you can use to investigate the Analyzer project in Visual Studio. Transactor1 and Transactor2 are going to perform simple aggregate functions on the PUBS database of SQL Server. The idea is to measure the difference in performance between calling an aggregate function and running a calculation manually in Visual Basic. Both Transactor1 and Transactor2 will use the ADO object model to access the database. Select these projects and set a reference to the Microsoft ActiveX Data Objects 2.0 and Microsoft Transaction Server Type Library using the References dialog.

Step 4

Select `Transactor2` in the Project Explorer and open the code window for class `Aggregate`. This class will have a single method in it to run the aggregate function. Add a new method to the class by selecting **Tools, Add Procedure** from the menu. In the Add Procedure dialog, select to add a new function. Name the function `Calculate`. Make it a `Public` function and add it to the code window. After the procedure is added to the class, modify the function signature to return a `Double`. The complete function signature should appear as follows:

```
Public Function Calculate() As Double

End Function
```

Step 5

In the `Calculate` method, you will connect to the PUBS database using ADO and run an aggregate function to find the average price of all the books in the database. Add the code in Listing 10.2 to the `Calculate` method to return the average price.

LISTING 10.2   CODE FOR THE `Calculate` METHOD TO RETURN THE AVERAGE PRICE

```
On Error GoTo CalculateErr

    Dim objContext As MTxAS.ObjectContext

    Dim objConnection As New ADODB.Connection
    Dim objRecordset As ADODB.Recordset

    'Get Object Context
    Set objContext = GetObjectContext

    'Open Connection
    objConnection.Provider = "SQLOLEDB"
    objConnection.ConnectionString = _
        "Data Source=(local);Database=pubs;;UID=sa;PWD=;"
    objConnection.Open
    Set objRecordset = objConnection.Execute("SELECT AVG(Price) FROM
        ➥Titles")

    Calculate = objRecordset.Fields(0).Value

    objContext.SetComplete
```

continues

LISTING 10.2   CONTINUED

```
    Exit Function

CalculateErr:
    Calculate = 0
    App.StartLogging App.Path & "\mts.log", vbLogToFile

    objContext.SetAbort

    Exit Function
```

Step 6

Set the `MTSTransactionMode` property for class Aggregate to `2-Requires Transaction`.

Step 7

Select `Transactor1` in the Project Explorer and open the code window for class `Aggregate`. This class will have a single method just like the `Transactor2`. The difference is that the average price will be calculated differently in this method so you can see any performance differences. Add a `Calculate` method to this class and add the following code to the method:

LISTING 10.3   THE Calculate METHOD FOR THE Aggregate CLASS

```
On Error GoTo CalculateErr

    Dim objContext As MTxAS.ObjectContext

    Dim objConnection As New ADODB.Connection
    Dim objRecordset As ADODB.Recordset
    Dim lngTemp As Long
    Dim lngCount

    'Get Object Context
    Set objContext = GetObjectContext

    'Open Connection
    objConnection.Provider = "SQLOLEDB"
    objConnection.ConnectionString = _
        "Data Source=(local);Database=pubs;UID=sa;PWD=;"
    objConnection.Open
    Set objRecordset = objConnection.Execute("SELECT Price FROM Titles")

    'Calculate Value
    lngCount = 0
    Do While Not objRecordset.EOF
        If Not (IsNull(objRecordset!Price)) Then
```

```
                lngTemp = lngTemp + objRecordset!Price
                lngCount = lngCount + 1
            End If
            objRecordset.MoveNext
        Loop

        'Return Value
        Calculate = lngTemp / lngCount

        objContext.SetComplete

        Exit Function

CalculateErr:
        Calculate = 0
        App.StartLogging App.Path & "\mts.log", vbLogToFile

        objContext.SetAbort

        Exit Function
```

Step 8

Set the `MTSTransactionMode` property for class `Aggregate` to `2-Requires Transaction`.

Step 9

Select `Manager` in the Project Explorer. This project is the transaction manager for the application. It will create instances of both `Transactor1` and `Transactor2` and call their respective `Calculate` methods. Open the References dialog by selecting **Project, References** from the menu. In the References dialog, set a reference to `Transactor1`, `Transactor2`, and the Microsoft Transaction Server Type Library.

Step 10

Open the code window for class `Caller`. Add a new method to this class by selecting **Tools, Add Procedure** from the menu. In the Add Procedure dialog, select to add a new `Public Sub`. Name the routine `Process`. The following code shows the function signature for the new method:

```
Public Sub Process()

End Sub
```

Step 11

In the `Process` method, class `Caller` will create an instance of `Transactor1.Aggregate` and `Transactor2.Aggregate`, enlist them in a transaction, and call the `Calculate` methods. Add the code in Listing 10.4 to the `Process` method to carry out the function.

LISTING 10.4 THE Process METHOD FOR THE Caller CLASS

```
On Error GoTo ProcessErr

    Dim objContext As MTxAS.ObjectContext
    Dim objTransactor1 As Transactor1.Aggregate
    Dim objTransactor2 As Transactor2.Aggregate
    Dim dblReturn As Double

    'Create Objects
    Set objContext = GetObjectContext
    Set objTransactor1 =
objContext.CreateInstance("Transactor1.Aggregate")
    Set objTransactor2 =
objContext.CreateInstance("Transactor2.Aggregate")

    'Run methods
    dblReturn = objTransactor1.Calculate
    dblReturn = objTransactor2.Calculate

    objContext.SetComplete

    Exit Sub

ProcessErr:
    App.StartLogging App.Path & "\mts.log", vbLogToFile

    objContext.SetAbort

    Exit Sub
```

Step 12
Set the `MTSTransactionMode` property for `Manager.Caller` to `4-Requires New Transaction`.

Step 13
Select the `Client` project in the Project Explorer. We will use this form to create an instance of `Manager.Caller` and call the `Process` method. Set a reference to `Manager` in the References dialog.

Step 14
Add a single `CommandButton` to `Form1`. Rename the `CommandButton` `cmdGO`. Change the `Caption` of the button to `GO!`.

Step 15

Add the following code to the `click` event of `cmdGO` to create the objects and call the methods:

```
Dim objManager As New Manager.Caller
objManager.Process
MsgBox "Processing Complete!"
```

Step 16

Save your projects. Compile the entire project group by selecting **File, Make Project Group** from the menu. Close Visual Basic when your projects are compiled.

Step 17

Open the Microsoft Transaction Server Explorer. In the MTS Explorer, create a new package for each of the three classes you built. Using the Package Wizard, name the new packages `Manager`, `Transactor1`, and `Transactor2`. Add the three ActiveX DLL components you made in Visual Basic to the new packages that have the same name. Close the MTS Explorer.

Creating the Analyzer Project

In this section, you will create the Analyzer project. This will allow you to investigate the tools available for analyzing distributed applications.

Step 18

Start Visual InterDev. When Visual InterDev starts, you will be presented with the New Project dialog. If you do not see the dialog, select **File, New** from the menu.

Step 19

In the New Project dialog, select to start a new Visual Studio Analyzer project. Be sure to select the Analyzer Wizard from the right side of the dialog. Select to make the new project in the same directory you created at the beginning of the exercise. Name the new project `Aggregates` and click the Open button to start the wizard. Figure 10.14 shows the New Project dialog.

Step 20

Step 1 of the wizard asks if you would like it to search for machines that can participate in the project. Answer Yes to this question and click the Next button. Figure 10.15 shows step 1 of the wizard.

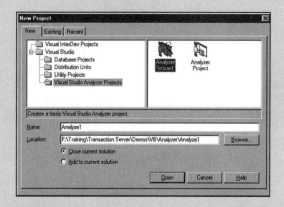

FIGURE 10.14

Use the New Project dialog to start a new Analyzer project.

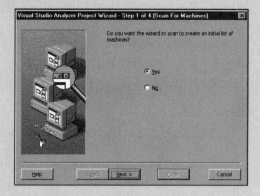

FIGURE 10.15

Search for machines to participate in the project.

Step 21

Step 2 of the wizard lists machines that can participate in the project. If you have set up your test machine to stand alone, the wizard will only list one machine. Accept this entry by clicking the Next button. Figure 10.16 shows the list of machines.

Step 22

Step 3 of the wizard asks what components you want to record events for. Select to view events for ADO Event Source, SQL Server OLEDB, COM Event Source, and MTS Event Source. Click Next. Figure 10.17 shows step 3.

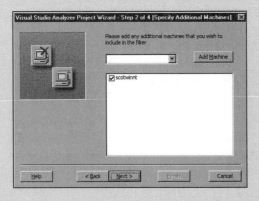

FIGURE 10.16
The wizard lists all the machines that can participate in the project.

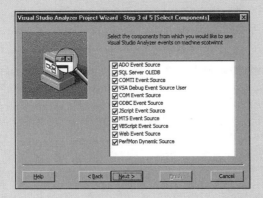

FIGURE 10.17
Select the components to provide events.

Step 23

Step 4 of the wizard asks you what filters you want in the project. Filters record certain types of events. Select Basic Database Events, Basic COM (and MTS) Events, Basic Object Events, and Basic Events. Click the Next button. Figure 10.18 shows the list of filters.

Step 24

The wizard then shows you a summary of the project specifications you have entered. Simply click Finish to build the new project. The Project Explorer shows the new project, filters, and event logs for the project.

FIGURE **10.18**
Select the filters for the project.

Step 25

When the project is first created, it is automatically recording events. Minimize Visual
InterDev and run the project you created. Click the button to process the aggregate functions and then end the application.

Step 26

Return to Visual InterDev. Right-click the event log and choose Record Events. This will
pop up the record button and stop event recording. Now double-click the event log
named Aggregates in the Project Window to see the events that the Analyzer recorded.
Any time you are viewing analyzer data, you may right-click on the filters in the Project
Explorer and select **Apply to View** from the pop-up menu. This will show only the
events for the selected filter.

Step 27

The event log lists the events in chronological order. You can also see a graphical representation of the events and their duration by opening a chart. The chart is opened by
selecting **View, Analyzer, Chart** from the menu. When the chart opens, examine the
timelines carefully for any operation that took longer than other operations. Depending
upon many factors, you may see noticeable delays in connection or processing times.
You should also take note of key events in the life of the components you created and
destroyed.

Step 28

Select **View, Analyzer, Process Diagram** from the menu. The Analyzer project now shows a graphical representation of all the event sources for the project. Using this representation, you can walk through the events that were recorded. Select **Analyzer, Replay Events** from the menu to watch the analyzer play the recorded events in the order they occurred. This type of playback can help you understand the processes that underlie your application.

SCRIPTING ADMINISTRATION IN MTS

PREREQUISITES

Before beginning this chapter, you should have a complete understanding of MTS administration through the MTS Explorer. A familiarity with VBScript is also useful, but not required.

Skills Learned

- MTS(24): Use the MTS Scripting Administration objects to identify packages, components, interfaces, and roles.
- MTS(25): Use the MTS Scripting Administration objects to create and export packages.
- MTS(26): Use the MTS Scripting Administration objects to install components.
- MTS(27): Use the MTS Scripting Administration objects through the Windows Scripting Host.

The MTS Explorer, like virtually every other application, is made up of COM objects. These COM objects can be programmed to automate administrative tasks or assist in the setup of a distributed system. Administering MTS through its objects is known as Scripting Administration.

Writing applications that use Scripting Administration is a matter of understanding the objects exposed by the MTS Explorer. Throughout the book, we have worked with the MTS Explorer and the various collections located inside folders. In the MTS Administration model, these folders are known as catalogs. Using the MTS Administration model, you can access administrative functionality for any computer or component contained inside a catalog.

THE MTS ADMINISTRATION OBJECT MODEL

Scripting Administration begins by setting a reference to the MTS Administration objects. These objects are contained in a library known as the MTS 2.0 Admin Type Library. When the reference is set, you can use the library objects to completely control all facets of administration within MTS. As with all object models, you must have a strong understanding of the objects within the model before you can begin. Figure 11.1 shows the MTS Administration Object Model.

FIGURE 11.1

Use the MTS Administration Object Model to automate tasks.

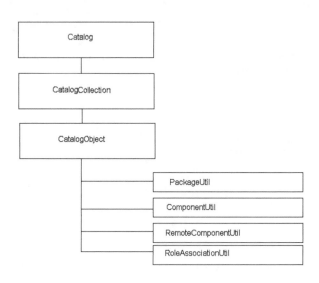

The `Catalog` Object

Scripting Administration begins with the `Catalog` object. A catalog in MTS is a source of information. This information can come from any computer on your network where MTS is running. Using the `Connect` method of the `Catalog` object, you can open a connection with a local or remote server running MTS. The `Connect` method takes the name of the server as an argument. If you leave the argument as an empty string, a connection with the local server is opened. After a connection is established, you can use the `Catalog` object to return `CatalogCollection` objects, which are discussed in the next section. The following code shows how to connect to a server running MTS:

```
Private objCatalog As MTSAdmin.Catalog
Private objRoot As MTSAdmin.CatalogCollection

Set objCatalog = New MTSAdmin.Catalog
Set objRoot = objCatalog.Connect("MachineName")
```

The `CatalogCollection` Object

The `CatalogCollection` object represents a collection of information in MTS. This information corresponds to the folders in the MTS Explorer. Using `CatalogCollection` objects, you can return information about such items as computers, packages, components, roles, interfaces, and methods.

`CatalogCollection` objects can be returned from `Catalog` objects, as when you make an initial connection to an MTS server, or they can be returned from other `CatalogCollection` objects. Returning a `CatalogCollection` from either object is done using the `GetCollection` method. The `GetCollection` method uses a string argument to identify the collection to return. The string is a predefined value as shown in Table 11.1.

TABLE 11.1 VALID ARGUMENTS FOR THE `GetCollection` METHOD

Argument	Collection Returned
`Packages`	A collection of all packages in the Packages Installed folder.
`ComputerList`	A collection of all computers in the Computers folder.
`LocalComputer`	A collection of specific information about the particular computer you are accessing.

continues

TABLE 11.1 CONTINUED

Argument	Collection Returned
RemoteComponents	A collection of all the components in the Remote Components folder.
RelatedCollectionInfo	A list of available collections under the collection you are accessing. This allows you to identify additional collections in the MTS Explorer hierarchy.
ComponentsInPackage	A collection of components for a given package identifier.
InterfacesForComponent	A collection of interfaces for a given component identifier.
InterfacesForRemoteComponent	A collection of interfaces for a given remote component identifier.
RolesForPackageComponent	A collection of roles associated with a particular component.
RolesForPackageComponentInterface	A collection of roles associated with a particular component interface.
MethodsForInterface	A collection of methods for a particular interface.
RolesInPackage	A collection of all roles defined for a particular package identifier.
UsersInRole	A collection of all users who are in a particular role.
ErrorInfo	Returns extended error information.
PropertyInfo	Returns information about properties supported by a particular collection.

Using the GetCollection method returns a reference to the desired collection; however, the collection is initially empty. To fill a collection you have accessed, you must call the Populate method of the returned CatalogCollection object. In this way, you can move through the MTS Explorer hierarchy to get to the information you want. The following code shows how to retrieve all of the packages from a server:

```
Private objCatalog As MTSAdmin.Catalog
Private objRoot As MTSAdmin.CatalogCollection
Private objPackages As MTSAdmin.CatalogCollection

Set objCatalog = New MTSAdmin.Catalog
Set objRoot = objCatalog.Connect("MachineName")

Set objPackages = objRoot.GetCollection("Packages", "")
objPackages.Populate
```

QUICK CHECK 11-1:

CATALOG COLLECTIONS

1. Using the CD-ROM for the book, locate the directory TEMPLATES\QUICK CHECK11-1. This directory contains a partially completed project you can use to investigate catalog collections in MTS.

2. On your hard drive, create a new directory with the Windows Explorer named MTS\QUICK CHECK11-1. Copy the contents from the CD-ROM directory into the new directory you just created.

3. Because the CD-ROM will create read-only copies of the project files, select all of the files you copied, right-click them, and select **Properties** from the pop-up menu. In the properties dialog, uncheck the read-only flag. Close the dialog.

4. Start Visual Basic. Open the project named QUICK CHECK11-1.VBP. This project contains a single Standard EXE with a form. Figure 11.2 shows the form.

FIGURE 11.2
This form shows information about related collections in MTS.

5. This project is designed to allow you to see some of the collections associated with MTS. To view the collections, you must first connect to an MTS server. You can do this in the project by typing the name of a server in the TextBox and clicking the Connect button. Add the code in Listing 11.1 to the `Click` event for the button to connect to a server and show an initial list of collections:

continues

continued

LISTING 11.1 CODE TO ADD THE Click EVENT FOR THE CONNECT BUTTON

```
On Error GoTo ConnectErr
    Screen.MousePointer = vbHourglass

    'Connect to Server
    Set objCatalog = New MTSAdmin.Catalog
    Set objItem = objCatalog.Connect(txtServer.Text)
    lblStatus = txtServer.Text & "\"

    'Get the Related Collections
    Set objCollections = objItem.GetCollection _
        ("RelatedCollectionInfo", "")
    objCollections.Populate

    'Show Related Collections in List
    lstCollections.Clear
    Dim i As Integer
    For i = 0 To objCollections.Count - 1
        lstCollections.AddItem objCollections.Item(i).Name
    Next

ConnectExit:
    Screen.MousePointer = vbDefault
    Exit Sub

ConnectErr:
    MsgBox Err.Description
    Resume ConnectExit
```

6. After the initial list of collections is presented, you can click on one and see any other collections below it. The form builds a path for you as you click so you can follow your progress. Listing 11.2 shows the code to add to the Click event for the list to view additional collections:

LISTING 11.2 CODE TO ADD THE Click EVENT FOR THE COLLECTION LIST

```
On Error GoTo ClickErr

    lblStatus = lblStatus & _
        lstCollections.List(lstCollections.ListIndex) & "\"

    'Get Selected Collection
    Set objItem = objItem.GetCollection _
        (lstCollections.List(lstCollections.ListIndex), "")
    objItem.Populate
```

Scripting Administration in MTS

CHAPTER 11

325

11

SCRIPTING
ADMINISTRATION
IN MTS

```
    'Get the Related Collections
    Set objCollections = _
        objItem.GetCollection("RelatedCollectionInfo", "")
    objCollections.Populate

    'Show Related Collections in List
    lstCollections.Clear
    Dim i As Integer
    For i = 0 To objCollections.Count - 1
        lstCollections.AddItem objCollections.Item(i).Name
    Next

    Exit Sub

ClickErr:
    MsgBox "No more related collections to show!"
    Exit Sub
```

7. After you add the code, run the project and try clicking on collections in the list.

The `CatalogObject` Object

The `CatalogObject` represents an individual member of the `CatalogCollection`. If, for example, the `CatalogCollection` contains packages, a `CatalogObject` contains an individual package. Similarly, if you are examining a `CatalogCollection` of roles, a single role is represented by a `CatalogObject`.

Because `CatalogObjects` are members of the `CatalogCollection`, you may return a reference to a `CatalogObject` through the `Item` method. The `Item` method of the `CatalogCollection` requires you to provide a `Long Integer` for the index. Unlike most collections, however, the `Item` method does not accept a key value. Instead of looking for particular information through the `Item` method, the `CatalogCollection` provides various methods for populating the collection. These methods are listed in Table 11.2.

TABLE 11.2 POPULATION METHODS FOR THE `CatalogCollection`

Method	*Description*
`Populate`	Fills a `CatalogCollection` with all valid members.
`PopulateByKey(vGUID)`	Populates a `CatalogCollection` using an array of variants. Each variant contains the key for an item to include in the collection.
`PopulateByQuery`	Reserved for future use.

Obtaining a reference to a particular `CatalogObject` is accomplished by populating the `CatalogCollection` with the items of interest. If you want to see what components are in a package, simply use the `Populate` method. If you want to see only a particular component, populate a collection by key and provide the Class Identifier (CLSID) of the component you want. MTS provides easy access to the CLSID for a component from the property sheet. Figure 11.3 shows the CLSID for a component.

FIGURE 11.3

Use the key on the property sheet to find particular `CatalogObjects`.

QUICK CHECK 11-2:

`CatalogObjects`

1. Using the CD-ROM for the book, locate the directory TEMPLATES\QUICK CHECK11-2. This directory contains a partially completed project you can use to investigate catalog objects in MTS.

2. On your hard drive, create a new directory with the Windows Explorer named MTS\QUICK CHECK11-2. Copy the contents from the CD-ROM directory into the new directory you just created.

3. Because the CD-ROM will create read-only copies of the project files, select all of the files you copied, right-click them, and select **Properties** from the pop-up menu. In the properties dialog, uncheck the read-only flag. Close the dialog.

4. Start Visual Basic. Open the project named QUICK CHECK11-2.VBP. This project contains a single Standard EXE with a form. Figure 11.4 shows the form.

Scripting Administration in MTS

CHAPTER 11

327

11

SCRIPTING
ADMINISTRATION
IN MTS

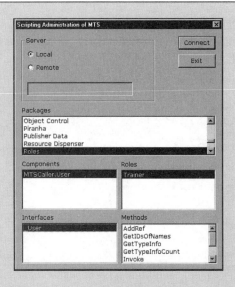

FIGURE 11.4
This form allows you to navigate the MTS Explorer through code.

5. Open the code window for the form. In this project, you will build an MTS Explorer from Visual Basic. You will be able to see the various packages, components, roles, and interfaces installed in MTS.

6. Before you can view information, you must connect to an MTS server. This is done by selecting either "local" or "remote" from the form. If you select "remote," you must provide the name of the MTS server. Then you can click the Connect button to establish a connection. When you are connected, the project builds a list of packages found on the MTS server. Add the code in Listing 11.3 to the cmdConnect_Click event to connect and get a list of packages:

LISTING 11.3 CODE TO ADD THE Click EVENT FOR SERVER CONNECT

```
On Error GoTo ConnectErr
    Screen.MousePointer = vbHourglass

    'Connect to Server
    Set objCatalog = New MTSAdmin.Catalog
    If optLocal Then
```

continues

continued

```
        Set objRoot = objCatalog.Connect("")
    Else
        Set objRoot = _
            objCatalog.Connect(txtServer.Text)
    End If

    'Get the Packages Collection
    Set objPackages = _
        objRoot.GetCollection("Packages", "")
    objPackages.Populate

    'Show Packages in List
    lstPackages.Clear
    lstComponents.Clear
    lstRoles.Clear

    For Each objPackage In objPackages
        lstPackages.AddItem objPackage.Name _
        & Space$(100) & objPackage.Key
    Next

ConnectExit:
    Screen.MousePointer = vbDefault
    Exit Sub

ConnectErr:
    MsgBox Err.Description
    Resume ConnectExit
```

7. After the package list is created, you can select any package to view the components and roles associated with the package. Each item is tracked, where appropriate, by its GUID so we can get more detailed information for an item. Add the code in Listing 11.4 to the lstPackages_Click event to get role and component information:

LISTING 11.4 ADDITIONAL CODE FOR PACKAGE'S List Click EVENT

```
'Get Components for this package
Set objComponents = objPackages.GetCollection _
    ("ComponentsInPackage", _
    Trim$(Right$(lstPackages.List(lstPackages.ListIndex), _
    Len(lstPackages.List(lstPackages.ListIndex)) - _
    InStr(lstPackages.List(lstPackages.ListIndex), Space$(100)))))
objComponents.Populate

'Get Roles for this package
```

Scripting Administration in MTS

CHAPTER 11

329

11

SCRIPTING
ADMINISTRATION
IN MTS

```
Set objRoles = objPackages.GetCollection _
    ("RolesInPackage", _
    Trim$(Right$(lstPackages.List(lstPackages.ListIndex), _
    Len(lstPackages.List(lstPackages.ListIndex)) - _
    InStr(lstPackages.List(lstPackages.ListIndex), Space$(100)))))
objRoles.Populate

'FillList
lstComponents.Clear
lstRoles.Clear

For Each objComponent In objComponents
    lstComponents.AddItem objComponent.Name _
    & Space$(100) & objComponent.Key
Next

For Each objRole In objRoles
    lstRoles.AddItem objRole.Name & Space$(100) & objRole.Key
    Next
```

8. After the components list is populated, you may click any component to view
the interfaces associated with the component. The interfaces are then listed
in a ListBox. Listing 11.5 shows the code to add to the 1stComponents_Click
event to get the component interfaces:

LISTING 11.5 CODE TO ADD TO COMPONENTS TO THE Click EVENT

```
'Get Interfaces for this component
Set objInterfaces = objComponents.GetCollection _
("InterfacesForComponent", _
Trim$(Right$(lstComponents.List(lstComponents.ListIndex), _
Len(lstComponents.List(lstComponents.ListIndex)) - _
InStr(lstComponents.List(lstComponents.ListIndex), Space$(100)))))
objInterfaces.Populate

'FillList
lstInterfaces.Clear

For Each objInterface In objInterfaces
    lstInterfaces.AddItem objInterface.Name _
    & Space$(100) & objInterface.Key
    Next
```

continues

continued

---

9. Finally, after the interface list is populated, you can click on any item to view the methods for the interface. Add the code in Listing 11.6 to the `lstInterfaces_Click` event to show the members for an interface:

LISTING 11.6   CODE TO SDD THE INTERFACE'S Click EVENT

```
'Get Members for this package
Set objMethods = objInterfaces.GetCollection _
("MethodsForInterface", _
Trim$(Right$(lstInterfaces.List(lstInterfaces.ListIndex), _
Len(lstInterfaces.List(lstInterfaces.ListIndex)) - _
InStr(lstInterfaces.List(lstInterfaces.ListIndex), Space$(100)))))
objMethods.Populate

'FillList
lstMethods.Clear

For Each objMethod In objMethods
    lstMethods.AddItem objMethod.Name
    Next
```

10. After the code is added, run the project. Try connecting to an MTS server and navigating the information on packages and components.

Utility Objects

In addition to browsing packages and components, the MTS Admin model also supports objects that install, edit, and delete packages, components, and roles. These objects are the `PackageUtil`, `ComponentUtil`, `RemoteComponentUtil`, and `RoleAssociationUtil` objects. Using these objects, you may perform administrative tasks in the MTS Explorer programmatically.

Each of the utility objects is accessed through the `GetUtilInterface` method of a `CatalogCollection` object. The `GetUtilInterface` method takes no arguments and determines which utility object to provide based on the items in the `CatalogCollection`. Therefore, the `GetUtilInterface` method is only valid for the `Packages`, `ComponentsInPackage`, `RemoteComponents`, `RolesForPackageComponent`, and `RolesForPackageComponentInterface` collections. Table 11.3 shows the relationship between `CatalogCollection` and utility object.

TABLE 11.3   UTILITY OBJECT RETURNED BY GetUtilInterface

Collection	*Object Returned*
Packages	PackageUtil
ComponentsInPackage	ComponentUtil
RemoteComponents	RemoteComponentUtil
RolesForPackageComponent	RoleAssociationUtil
RolesForPackageComponentInterface	RoleAssociationUtil

After you obtain a reference to the utility object, you can use the methods of the object to perform basic administrative tasks. Each object has methods related to its particular area. For example, you can import and export packages with the `PackageUtil` object.

The `PackageUtil` Object

The `PackageUtil` object contains three methods: `InstallPackage`, `ExportPackage`, and `ShutdownPackage`.

The `InstallPackage` method takes a PAK file and installs it on the server where you have established a connection.

```
PackageUtil.InstallPackage(Filename, Path, Options)
```

Filename is the name of a PAK file. All of the ActiveX DLL components addressed by the PAK file must reside in the same directory as the PAK file. *Path* is the complete path to the location of the PAK file. The *Options* parameter is a zero if you want to use the Windows/NT security information in the PAK file for the package you are installing.

The `ExportPackage` method allows you to create a PAK file from a package.

```
PackageUtil.ExportPackage(PackageID, Filename, Options)
```

PackageID is a string that corresponds to the package identifier for the package you want to export. The package identifier is available from the property sheet in the MTS Explorer. Figure 11.5 shows the property sheet.

Filename is the name of the PAK file you want to create. The *Options* parameter is zero if you want to export Windows/NT security information with the package.

The `ShutdownPackage` method allows you to unload a package from memory:

```
PackageUtil.ShutdownPackage(PackageID)
```

PackageID is a string that corresponds to the package identifier for the package you want to shut down.

FIGURE 11.5

*Use the package
ID on the proper-
ty sheet to export
a particular
package.*

The `ComponentUtil` Object

The `ComponentUtil` object contains four methods: `InstallComponent`,
`ImportComponent`, `ImportComponentByName`, and `GetCLSIDs`.

The `InstallComponent` method installs a component from an ActiveX DLL file.

```
ComponentUtil.InstallComponent(Filepath, TypeLibrary, Proxy-Stub)
```

Filepath is the complete path to the ActiveX DLL you want to install. *TypeLibrary* is
the name of the Type Library for this component. For VB ActiveX DLLs, use an empty
string for this argument. *Proxy-Stub* is a custom proxy/stub combination for this component. For VB ActiveX DLLs, use an empty string for this argument.

The `ImportComponent` method imports a registered component into a package:

```
ComponentUtil.ImportComponent(CLSID)
```

CLSID is a `String` that contains the CLSID for the registered component that you want to
install.

The `ImportComponentByName` method imports a registered component into a package
using its programmatic identifier:

```
ComponentUtil.ImportComponentByName(ProgID)
```

ProgID is a `String` that contains the `ProgID` for the registered component that you want
to install.

The `GetCLSIDs` method returns an array filled with CLSIDs for components registered on
the server:

```
ComponentUtil.GetCLSIDs
```

The `RemoteComponentUtil` Object

The `RemoteComponentUtil` object contains two methods: `InstallRemoteComponent` and `InstallRemoteComponentByName`.

The `InstallRemoteComponent` method installs a component onto the local server from a remote server:

`RemoteComponentUtil.InstallRemoteComponent(MachineName, PackageID., CLSID)`

MachineName is the name of the remote computer where the component resides. *PackageID* is a `String` containing the package identifier for the package where the component resides. *CLSID* is the Class Identifier for the component you want to install.

The `InstallRemoteComponentByName` method installs a component onto the local server from a remote server using the programmatic identifier:

`RemoteComponentUtil.InstallRemoteComponentByName(MachineName, PackageID., ProgID)`

MachineName is the name of the remote computer where the component resides. *PackageID* is a `String` containing the package identifier for the package where the component resides. *ProgID* is the programmatic identifier for the component you want to install.

The `RoleAssociationUtil` Object

The `RoleAssociationUtil` object contains two methods: `AssociateRole` and `AssociateRoleByName`.

The `AssociateRole` method associates a role with a component:

`RoleAssociationUtil.AssociateRole(RoleID)`

RoleID is the role identifier of the role to associate with the current component.

The `AssociateRole` method associates a role with a component using the name of the role:

`RoleAssociationUtil.AssociateRoleByName(RoleName)`

RoleName is the name of the role to associate with the current component.

THE WINDOWS SCRIPTING HOST

Do you remember the old DOS batch files? These files had a BAT extension and were used for creating batch processes. Someone might, for example, create a BAT file to copy files from one drive to another. This BAT file could then be used on any machine to manage files. The Windows Scripting Host (WSH) is an updated batch processing engine that administrators can use to automate tasks. Along with the MTS scripting objects, administrators will find WSH to be a valuable tool for maintaining MTS installations.

WSH is not a native part of the Windows/NT installation. However, it can be installed along with the new services found in the NT4 Option Pack. When WSH is installed, you will not see any changes to your operating system because WSH is a batch engine that has no user interface. It is intended to run batch programs directly from the desktop or through the command-line console. WSH recognizes two different languages for batch operations: VBScript and JScript. Both batch files are created using Notepad. Saving a file from Notepad with a VBS extension tells WSH that VBScript is the batch language for the file, whereas an extension of JS indicates JScript.

Understanding VBScript

Although WSH is more than happy to utilize scripts written in JScript, the most natural scripting language for Visual Basic developers is VBScript. VBScript is a subset of the full VB language found in the Visual Basic product. Its purpose is to provide a generalized lightweight macro language for automating tasks. As a language, VBScript is supported not only in WSH, but can be used in the Internet Explorer and Microsoft Outlook as well.

Using VBScript in WSH is a simple matter of writing batch code in Notepad and saving the file with a VBS extension. After the file is created, you can run the file directly by double-clicking it or you can execute it from the command line by typing its filepath and name. Additionally, you can run it from the console just like an old BAT file.

When writing batch files, you will face limitations from the VBScript language. For example, VBScript does not support data types. All variables in VBScript are of type `Variant`. In fact the `As [DataType]` syntax that you use in Visual Basic will cause an error if used in WSH. Variables are all simply declared with the `Dim` keyword and a variable name. Many keywords you take for granted in Visual Basic are not supported such as `With...End With`, `Declare Function`, and others.

So why care about WSH for task automation if VBScript is so limiting? Simple—WSH supports a `CreateObject` method that can be used to access object models. Therefore, you can rapidly write scripts that operate against the MTS scripting objects to perform automated tasks. Administrators can create these batch operations as simple files that can easily be deployed and executed without the effort of creating setup files.

WSH Objects

WSH goes beyond simply using VBScript for task automation by providing a set of objects that you can use to assist in administrative tasks. Through the use of these objects, you can perform fundamental administration as well as access the MTS scripting objects.

The `WScript` Object

The `WScript` object is the center of all operations involving COM components. Using the `CreateObject` method of the `WScript` object, you can create an instance of any COM object using its `ProgID`. This includes not only MTS scripting objects, but other useful components such as ADO `Connections`, `Commands`, and `Recordsets`. Because all variables in VBScript are `Variants`, the following code can be used to create any instance from a `ProgID`:

```
Dim MyObject
Set MyObject = WScript.CreateObject("ProgID")
```

After the instance is created, you can call the properties and methods of the object just as you would in Visual Basic. If the component has the capability to return events, WSH will allow you to receive the events by providing an event prefix as the second argument of the `CreateObject` method. The prefix is used to create an event handler for the component. The event handler is created in the format `Sub Prefix_EventName`.

In addition to the `CreateObject` method, the `WScript` object also provides methods such as the `Echo` method for displaying information in a message box and the `Quit` method for terminating the script. Together, these methods provide essential functionality for the batch program. Table 11.4 lists the methods and their purposes.

TABLE 11.4 METHODS OF THE `WScript` OBJECT

Method	Description
CreateObject(*ProgID*,*KeyName*)	Creates an object instance based on a `ProgID`
DisconnectObject *VarName*	Disconnects an object that was connected for the purpose of receiving events
Echo *Message*	Outputs information in a message box
GetObject(*Path*,*ProgID*,*KeyName*)	Gets an object instance that is already created
Quit *Code*	Ends the current script

Along with the WScript methods, several properties are also supported. Perhaps the most useful of the available properties is the Arguments property, which allows you to access command-line arguments that were passed in when the script was started. The Arguments property returns a zero-based array of the arguments passed in to the script. Table 11.5 lists all of the properties supported by the WScript object.

TABLE 11.5 PROPERTIES OF THE WScript OBJECT

Property	Description
Application	References the WSH application object
Arguments	A collection of arguments passed in to the script
FullName	The full path to the scripting engine
Name	A friendly name for the scripting engine
Path	The path to the scripting engine
ScriptFullName	Complete path to the running script
ScriptName	Name of the running script
Version	Current version of WSH

The Shell Object

As we have shown, WSH has the ability to create an instance of any ActiveX component on your system. Because WSH is intended for use by administrators, a special ActiveX component ships with WSH design to help automate administrative tasks. This component is contained in the file WSHOM.OCX, which contains the Shell object. The Shell object contains properties and methods that allow such administrative functions as creating shortcuts or interacting with the system registry. Table 11.6 lists the members of the Shell object.

Obtaining an instance of the Shell object is accomplished through the use of the CreateObject method, just as you would for any component. The ProgID for the WshShell object is WScript.Shell. Using the ProgID, the following code will create an instance of the object:

```
Set MyShell = WScript.CreateObject("WScript.Shell")
```

When you have an instance of the Shell object, it can be used to perform some simple tasks. As an example, it could be used to turn on and off MTS debugging for a Visual

Basic 5.0 environment. In this environment, we support debugging through the `RunWithoutContext` registry key. The following code uses the `RegWrite` method of the `Shell` object to create the appropriate registry key to enable debugging:

```
Set WshShell = Wscript.CreateObject("Wscript.Shell")
WshShell.RegWrite _
    "HKLM\Software\Microsoft\Transaction
Server\Debug\RunWithoutContext\",""
MsgBox "Debug Mode Enabled"
```

You could also write a script to turn debugging mode back off by using the `RegDelete` method. These scripts are a vast improvement over manually editing the system registry. Manual editing always leaves the possibility of incorrectly altering data, which can cause tremendous problems for your system. The following code shows a script for deleting the debugging registry key:

```
Set WshShell = Wscript.CreateObject("Wscript.Shell")
WshShell.RegDelete _
    "HKLM\Software\Microsoft\Transaction Server\Debug\RunWithoutContext\"
WshShell.RegDelete _
    "HKLM\Software\Microsoft\Transaction Server\Debug\"
MsgBox "Debug Mode Disabled"
```

TABLE 11.6 MEMBERS OF THE `Shell` OBJECT

Member	Description
Environment	Returns environment information such as the processor type and available memory
SpecialFolders	Returns a reference to special folders such as the Desktop or Start menu
CreateShortcut	Creates a shortcut to a file
ExpandEnvironmentStrings	Returns environment variables
Popup	Pops up a message box
RegDelete	Deletes a registry key or value
RegRead	Reads a registry value
RegWrite	Writes a registry key or value
Run	Starts an executable program

QUICK CHECK 11-3:

THE WINDOWS SCRIPTING HOST

1. The Windows Scripting Host is useful for creating scripts that can quickly and easily automate tasks. In this exercise, you will create a script that can shut down all packages in a given MTS installation. This is useful for when you want to update components running under MTS with a new compiled version. Create a new folder for your scripts in the File Explorer as MTS\QUICK CHECK11-3.

2. Start Notepad. WSH applications can be written directly in Notepad and saved with a VBS extension for VBScript or a JS extension for JScript.

3. In this example, we will pass the name of the server as an argument to the script. The script will connect with the server and then shut down all packages it finds on the server. Add the code in Listing 11.7 to Notepad to create the script:

LISTING 11.7   CODE FOR THE SCRIPT TO SHUT DOWN PACKAGES ON THE SERVER

```
Set Args = WScript.Arguments

'Connect to server
Set objCatalog = WScript.CreateObject("MTSAdmin.Catalog")
Set objRoot = objCatalog.Connect(Args(0))

If objRoot Is Nothing Then
    MsgBox "No Server Available!"
Else

    'Get the Packages Collection
    Set objPackages = objRoot.GetCollection("Packages", "")
    objPackages.Populate

    'Shutdown each package
    For i=0 To objPackages.Count - 1
        WScript.Echo "Shutting Down " _
        & objPackages.Item(i).Name
        Set objPackUtil = objPackages.GetUtilInterface
        objPackUtil.ShutdownPackage(objPackages.Item(0).Key)
    Next

    WScript.Echo Args(0) & " shutdown!"

        End If
```

4. When the code is entered, save the Notepad file to the directory you created earlier as SHUTDOWN.VBS.

5. Now you can run the script from the command line. Select Start, Run from the Windows Start menu. In the command line, type the complete file path to the VBS file. After the path, type a space and the name of the server to shut down. Run the script, and all the packages on that server should shut down. The following code shows an example of the line you would type into the command prompt:

   E:\MTS\Quick Check11-3\shutdown.vbs scotwinnt

6. You can also create the script for shutting down the server in JScript. JScript is the Microsoft version of JavaScript. This language is much more like Java or C++ than Visual Basic. Try adding the code in Listing 11.8 to a new copy of Notepad:

LISTING 11.8 JSCRIPT CODE, EQUIVALENT TO LISTING 11.7

```
Args = WScript.Arguments;

//Connect to server
objCatalog = WScript.CreateObject("MTSAdmin.Catalog");
objRoot = objCatalog.Connect(Args(0));

if(objRoot==null)
    WScript.Echo("No Server Available!");
else{

    //Get the Packages Collection
    objPackages = objRoot.GetCollection("Packages", "");
    objPackages.Populate();

    //Shutdown each package
    for(i=0;i<objPackages.Count;i++){
        WScript.Echo("Shutting Down " + objPackages.Item(i).Name);
        objPackUtil = objPackages.GetUtilInterface();
        objPackUtil.ShutdownPackage(objPackages.Item(0).Key);
    }

    WScript.Echo(Args(0) + " shutdown!");

    }
```

7. Save the new file as SHUTDOWN.JS and run it from the command line. It should also shut down packages for the selected server.

EXERCISE 11-1: SCRIPTING ADMINISTRATION

The Scripting Administration objects can be used to create many different tools for MTS development. This includes design-time controls for Visual InterDev and code generators for Visual Basic. In this exercise, you will create a simple wizard that creates a new class module file based on an interface found in MTS.

Step 1

Using the CD-ROM for the book, locate the directory TEMPLATES\EXERCISE11-1. This directory contains a partially completed project you can use to create the interface wizard.

Step 2

On your hard drive, create a new directory with the Windows Explorer named MTS\EXERCISE11-1. Copy the contents from the CD-ROM directory into the new directory you just created.

Step 3

Because the CD-ROM will create read-only copies of the project files, select all of the files you copied, right-click them, and select **Properties** from the pop-up menu. In the properties dialog, uncheck the read-only flag. Close the dialog.

Step 4

Start Visual Basic. Open the project named EXERCISE11-1.VBP. This project contains a single Standard EXE with a form named `frmWizard`. Figure 11.6 shows the form.

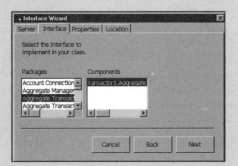

FIGURE **11.6**
This form is used to create the code wizard.

Scripting Administration in MTS

CHAPTER 11

341

11

SCRIPTING
ADMINISTRATION
IN MTS

Step 5

Open the code window for frmWizard. In the [General][Declarations] section, you will notice several sets of variables and enumerations. The variables are used to access the scripting objects. The enumerations are used to track the steps in the wizard. If you examine the frmWizard form carefully, you will see it is built on a tabbed dialog. Each step in the wizard is a tab on the dialog. Each tab has a set of three buttons for Cancel, Back, and Next operations. These buttons are all part of control arrays. Therefore, we can use the index of the buttons to determine what step the wizard is on.

Step 6

The control array for the Next operations is named cmdNext. Each of the four steps has a button named cmdNext. These buttons are indexed 0 through 3. When the button is clicked, we can use the index of the selected button to determine what action to take. These actions include connecting to the MTS server, retrieving component information, and generating code. Add the code in listing 11.9 to the cmdNext_Click event to handle forward navigation in the wizard:

LISTING 11.9 CODE TO ADD THE NEXT Click

```
On Error GoTo NextErr

    'Navigate Forward
    Select Case Index
        Case ntsServer

            'Connect to server
            Set objCatalog = New MTSAdmin.Catalog
            Set objRoot = objCatalog.Connect(txtServer.Text)

            If objRoot Is Nothing Then
                MsgBox "No Server Available!", _
                vbOKOnly + vbExclamation, "Interface Wizard"
            Else
                'Get the Packages Collection
                Set objPackages = objRoot.GetCollection("Packages", "")
                objPackages.Populate

                'Show Packages in List
                lstPackages.Clear
                lstComponents.Clear

                For Each objPackage In objPackages
                    lstPackages.AddItem objPackage.Name _
                    & Space$(100) & objPackage.Key
                Next
```

continues

LISTING 11.9   CONTINUED

```
                    'Move to Next step
                    tabWizard.Tab = ntsInterface
            End If

        Case ntsInterface

            If lstComponents.Text = "" Then
                MsgBox "Select a Component!", _
                vbOKOnly + vbExclamation, "Interface Wizard"
            Else
                'Move to Next step
                tabWizard.Tab = ntsProperties
            End If

        Case ntsProperties
                'Move to Next step
                tabWizard.Tab = ntsLocation
                ChDrive Left$(App.Path, 1)
                ChDir App.Path
        Case ntsLocation
                GenerateCode
    End Select

    Exit Sub

NextErr:
    MsgBox Err.Description
    Exit Sub
```

Step 7

When all of the required information is retrieved, the wizard generates a class module
that you can add to a project. The code generation is done by opening a new file and
printing out the class file definition. In the wizard, a custom function named
GenerateCode takes care of writing the code. Locate this function in the project and add
the code in listing 11.10.

LISTING 11.10   CODE TO ADD THE GenerateCode FUNCTION

```
On Error GoTo GenerateCodeErr

    Dim intFile As Integer
    intFile = FreeFile

    strComponent =
Trim$(Left$(lstComponents.List(lstComponents.ListIndex),
InStr(lstComponents.List(lstComponents.ListIndex), " ")))
```

```
'open new class file
Open lblFilename For Output As #intFile

    'Write Out the Header
    Print #intFile, "VERSION 1.0 CLASS"
    Print #intFile, "BEGIN"
    Print #intFile, "  MultiUse = -1  'True"
    Print #intFile, "  Persistable = 0  'NotPersistable"
    Print #intFile, "  DataBindingBehavior = 0  'vbNone"
    Print #intFile, "  DataSourceBehavior = 0   'vbNone"


    'Transaction Mode
    If optTransactionMode(NotAnMTSObject).Value = True Then
        Print #intFile, _
        "  MTSTransactionMode = 0  'NotAnMTSObject"
    ElseIf optTransactionMode(NoTransactions).Value = True Then
        Print #intFile, _
        "  MTSTransactionMode = 1  'NoTransaction"
    ElseIf optTransactionMode(RequiresTransactions).Value = True Then
        Print #intFile, _
        "  MTSTransactionMode = 2  'RequiresTransaction"
    ElseIf optTransactionMode(UsesTransactions).Value = True Then
        Print #intFile, _
        "  MTSTransactionMode = 3  'UsesTransactions"
    ElseIf optTransactionMode(RequiresNewTransaction).Value = True Then
        Print #intFile, _
        "  MTSTransactionMode = 4  'RequiresNewTransaction"
    End If


    'Attributes
    Print #intFile, "End"
    Print #intFile, "Attribute VB_Name = " _
        & Chr$(34) & txtName.Text & Chr$(34)
    Print #intFile, "Attribute VB_GlobalNameSpace = False"
    Print #intFile, "Attribute VB_Creatable = True"
    Print #intFile, "Attribute VB_PredeclaredId = False"
    Print #intFile, "Attribute VB_Exposed = True"


    'Code
    Print #intFile, "Option Explicit"
    Print #intFile, "Implements " & strComponent
    Print #intFile, ""

Close intFile

MsgBox "Code Complete!", _
vbOKOnly + vbInformation, "Interface Wizard"
End
```

continues

LISTING 11.9 CONTINUED

```
GenerateCodeExit:
    Exit Sub

GenerateCodeErr:
    MsgBox Err.Description, _
    vbOKOnly + vbExclamation, "Interface Wizard"
    Debug.Print Err.Description
    Resume GenerateCodeExit
```

Step 8

When the code is added, you should be able to run the wizard. Fill in the information for each step and generate a class module. Then open the class module in VB to examine the results. This wizard is fairly simple, but gives you an idea what is possible with the Scripting Administration objects.

THE MICROSOFT
MESSAGE QUEUE

PREREQUISITES

Before beginning this chapter, you should be familiar with transactional concepts in distributed applications. You must also have a complete understanding of how to program object models using Visual Basic.

Skills Learned

- MTS(28): Explain how to set up MSMQ on an enterprise.
- MTS(29): Use the MSMQ Explorer to create and manage message queues.
- MTS(30): Send and receive messages from MSMQ using Visual Basic.
- MTS(31): Use MSMQ to create an internal transaction.
- MTS(32): Use MSMQ to create an external transaction.

As you build larger and more complex enterprise systems, fault tolerance becomes a larger concern. Particularly where mission-critical data is handled, you will want to guarantee that certain layers of your application will always be able to communicate even if a network failure occurs. The Microsoft Message Queue (MSMQ) is a store-and-forward service that enables distributed objects to communicate asynchronously either by design or because of a failure. Adding MSMQ to your architecture can significantly improve the overall reliability of your system.

MSMQ uses a system of queues to support asynchronous messaging. These queues act as storage areas for messages that can consist of either text or binary information. Messages can be delivered to a queue by one distributed object and retrieved later by a different object. Messages can be as simple as plain text or as complex as a COM object.

MSMQ INSTALLATION AND ADMINISTRATION

Although the overall concept of message queuing is fairly straightforward, organizations that want to employ MSMQ technology should plan carefully to avoid problems. Chief among your planning concerns should be how many MSMQ installations you need, where they will be located, and how the installations will interact to achieve the design goals for an application. In this section, we cover some of the larger issues surrounding MSMQ setup and administration.

MSMQ Enterprise Architecture

Unlike many services you use in conjunction with distributed applications, any application using message queuing is likely to employ several servers running MSMQ. An enterprise installation of MSMQ consists of a hierarchy of servers having relationships to each other. MSMQ servers are typically installed to connect outbound offices to the main network as well as to route messages within a local area network (LAN).

In MSMQ terminology, an enterprise is the set of all computers belonging to an organization. This might consist of a single LAN or it could be a global network of separate domains. In any case, each enterprise consists of a top-level installation of MSMQ known as the Primary Enterprise Controller (PEC). The PEC is an installation of MSMQ that is associated with a SQL Server database called MQIS. The MQIS database consists of information about the network topology as well as information about other installations of MSMQ on the enterprise.

If you have a simple LAN, a single PEC may be enough for your entire network. However, if you have a Wide-Area Network (WAN), you should install additional Primary Site Controllers (PSC) that provide local message services for the computers in different physical locations. The PSC provides local control of messaging for physically separated networks in the enterprise. Generally, MSMQ site boundaries should be closely related to the physical grouping of computers in your enterprise. This is because message routing is more expensive when machines are separated by long distances.

For additional safety, sites may deploy Backup Site Controllers (BSC). BSC servers contain read-only replicas of the PSC information and can provide fail-safe operation if a PSC goes down. MSMQ routing servers can also be deployed to provide alternate message paths that can be used to ensure message delivery. In general, MSMQ installations depend upon the size and number of sites as well as your fail-safe requirements. Figure 12.1 shows a typical MSMQ installation architecture.

FIGURE 12.1

A typical queuing installation consists of many MSMQ servers.

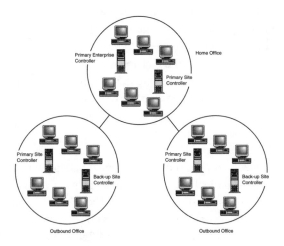

MSMQ Administration

After you have established the queuing architecture for your enterprise, you will have to create and manage queues for the enterprise. MSMQ administration is fairly straightforward and is accomplished through the MSMQ Explorer (see Figure 12.2). The MSMQ Explorer is a typical tree view and list view combination that allows you to see the MSMQ servers, queues, and messages. MSMQ divides your enterprise into sites and connected networks (CN). Sites are groups of computers where messages can be passed inexpensively. A CN is a group of computers that can communicate directly. The difference between a site and a CN is that a site is generally defined by the physical location of computers, such as in an outbound office. A CN, on the other hand, is defined by network protocol. All computers using TCP/IP protocol, for example, are considered part of the same CN.

FIGURE 12.2

The MSMQ Explorer is used to administer message queues.

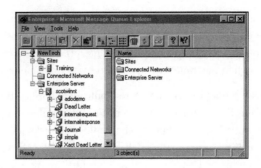

Creating a queue can be done for any installation of MSMQ through the MSMQ Explorer. Simply right-click on the server where you want to create the new queue and select **New, Queue** from the pop-up menu. You will then be prompted to name the queue and indicate whether or not you want the queue to be "transactional." We will have more to say about MSMQ transactions later in the chapter. After the queue is created, however, you can examine its properties by right-clicking the queue and selecting **Properties** from the pop-up menu. The MSMQ Explorer responds by showing a tabbed Queue Properties dialog where you can set several key attributes for the queue.

The General Tab

The General tab of the Queue Properties dialog presents fundamental information about the new queue. This information includes the queue name, path, and creation date. You will also find two GUIDs in this tab: ID and TypeID. The ID GUID cannot be modified and is the unique identifier for your queue. You can use this number to programmatically locate a specific queue. The TypeID GUID can be modified and is an identifier for a family of queues. This allows you to create several unique queues that provide a certain kind of service. For example, you might create a family of queues responsible for querying a database. In your applications, you can then search for any queue on the enterprise with this capability. Figure 12.3 shows the General tab of the Queue Properties dialog.

The Advanced Tab

The Advanced tab of the Queue Properties dialog presents additional options for the queue. In this tab, you can specify a limit for the queue size by limiting message storage to a certain size. When you specify a queue size, this is referred to as the queue quota. When the queue quota is reached, no new messages can be sent to the queue.

The Advanced tab also allows you to specify that the queue will accept only authenticated messages. Authenticating messages ensures that a user has not been impersonated by someone else. Authentication in MSMQ is established through the use of digital certificates. Digital certificates can be either internal or external. Internal certificates are generated by MSMQ for users through the MSMQ applet in the Control Panel. Internal certificates are simply a guarantee that the Security Identifier (SID) of the message sender is valid. For additional security, you can implement external certificates.

External certificates are issued separately by a Certificate Authority (CA). These authorities grant a certificate after verifying identification information for a user. These personal certificates are then registered on the client machine and can be used to authenticate messages. External certificates are stored in conjunction with the Internet Explorer browser, so users must install IE 3.0 or later to utilize certificate information with MSMQ.

FIGURE 12.3

The General tab gives fundamental queue information.

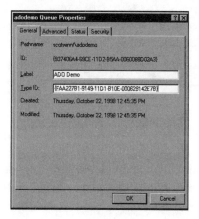

QUICK CHECK 12-1:

INTERNAL CERTIFICATES

1. Internal certificates are used to validate the SID of a sending user. Internal certificates are created using the MSMQ applet in the Control Panel. Locate this applet and run it. Figure 12.4 shows the MSMQ Properties dialog that results.

2. Use the MSMQ Properties dialog to create an internal certificate by clicking the Renew Internal Certificate button. This will generate an internal certificate just for you. Note: To create an internal certificate, you must be logged on to a Windows/NT domain and validated by a Primary Domain Controller (PDC).

3. Before using an internal certificate, it must be registered with the MQIS database. You can register your new internal certificate by clicking the Register button on the security tab.

continues

continued

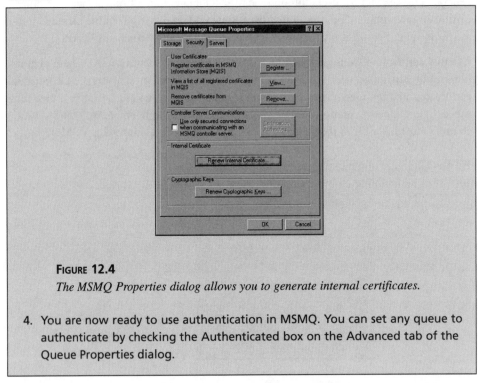

FIGURE 12.4
The MSMQ Properties dialog allows you to generate internal certificates.

4. You are now ready to use authentication in MSMQ. You can set any queue to authenticate by checking the Authenticated box on the Advanced tab of the Queue Properties dialog.

The Advanced tab also allows you to set up queue "journaling." Journaling allows you to store a copy of all messages entering a queue. You can also specify a size limit for the queue.

Queues can also be set up to accept encrypted messages. This option is set using the Privacy Level option. Queues set to a privacy level of None do not accept encrypted messages. Queues set to a privacy level of Optional will accept encrypted and plain messages. A privacy level of Body accepts only encrypted messages. Queue encryption requires a knowledge of cryptography beyond the scope of this chapter. See the MSMQ help for more information on implementing encryption.

The last option on the Advanced tab is the Base Priority. Base priority establishes a significance for this queue. Priority numbers help MSMQ establish the order in which message routing occurs. Queue priority can be set between -32768 and +32767. When a message is sent to a queue, the message can also have a priority set between 0 and 7. The MSMQ system routes messages based on queue priority first and then message priority. Figure 12.5 shows the Advanced tab of the Queue Properties dialog.

FIGURE 12.5

The Advanced tab is used to set attributes of a queue.

The Status Tab

The Status tab of the Queue Properties dialog is used to view various performance counters for the MSMQ server. You can view all available MSMQ counters by clicking the Performance Monitor button. This button starts the Windows/NT performance monitor. Figure 12.6 shows the Status tab of the Queue Properties dialog.

FIGURE 12.6

The Status tab is used to monitor queue performance.

The Security Tab

The Security tab is used to set security levels for a queue. You can restrict access to a queue in a variety of ways. You can allow full control for sending and receiving messages, or you can simply allow users to read messages. You can also set up various combinations of processing. For example, you can allow a user Peek access, which lets the user read messages, but not remove them from a queue. Figure 12.7 shows the Security tab of the Queue Properties dialog.

FIGURE 12.7
The Security tab is used to set permissions for queue access.

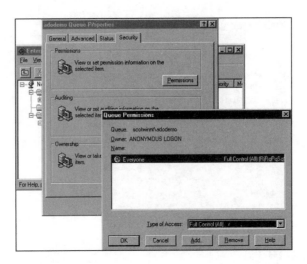

MSMQ APPLICATIONS

Programming applications to use MSMQ is done through the MSMQ Object Model. The model allows you to programmatically manage queues and messages. You can create, locate, and delete queues as well as send and receive messages. You may programmatically control MSMQ directly from an application or as a function of a business object running under MTS control. Figure 12.8 shows the MSMQ object model.

FIGURE 12.8
MSMQ applications are created using the MSMQ object model.

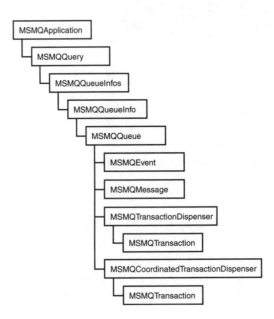

MSMQApplication Object

The MSMQApplication object contains only a single method named MachineIdOfMachineName. This method is used to return the GUID for an MSMQ server. This allows you to locate a server by name and then subsequently locate queues on that server. The syntax for the MachineIdOfMachineName method is shown following:

```
MachineID = MSMQApplication. MachineIdOfMachineName("machinename")
```

MSMQQuery Object

The MSMQQuery object is used to locate queues on the enterprise. Using this object, your application can find the proper queue to send a message. The MSMQQuery object has only a single method, the LookUpQueue method. This method accepts a number of optional arguments that allow you to search for queues based on known characteristics. When a queue or queues are located that match the criteria, they are returned through an MSMQQueuesInfo object. The syntax for locating a queue with the LookUpQueue method is shown following:

```
Set MSMQQueuesInfo = MSMQQuery.LookupQueue _
([QueueGuid] [, ServiceTypeGuid] [, Label] _
[, CreateTime] [, ModifyTime] [, RelServiceType] _
[, RelLabel] [, RelCreateTime] [, RelModifyTime])
```

QueueGuid is a Globally Unique Identifier (GUID) that is used to uniquely identify a queue. ServiceTypeGUID is a GUID that is used to identify a family of queues. If you search for queues based on the ServiceTypeGUID, you may return multiple queues from which you will pick a specific queue to receive a message. Label is a text label for the queue. You can search by Label, but you cannot guarantee that a label is unique in the same way as a GUID. CreateTime is the time when the queue was first created. ModifyTime is the time when the queue properties were last changed. RelServiceType is the relationship parameter for the ServiceTypeGUID, which allows you to specify a Boolean operator for use in the search. This allows you to search for all queues that do not have a certain ServiceTypeGUID, for example. RelLabel is the relationship parameter for Label. RelCreateTime is the relationship parameter for CreateTime. RelModifyTime is the relationship parameter for ModifyTime. The following code shows how an application might perform a simple search for queues that meet a specified criterion:

```
'Declare MSMQ Objects
Dim objQuery As MSMQ.MSMQQuery
Dim objQueueInfos As MSMQ.MSMQQueueInfos

'The following is the ServiceTypeGUID we
'want to search for
Const msmqServiceTypeGUID$ = "{581EA041-8D8E-11d1-B101-000629142E7B}"
```

```
'Locate all queues that meet the criteria.
Set objQuery = New MSMQ.MSMQQuery

Set objQueueInfos = objQuery.LookupQueue _
(ServiceTypeGuid:=msmqServiceTypeGUID)
```

MSMQQueueInfos Object

The MSMQQueueInfos object is the return object from the LookUpQueue method of the MSMQQuery object. This object contains all the queues that met the search criteria. You may move through this collection to examine and select a particular queue from the set. The collection has only two methods associated with it: Next and Reset. The Next method moves the collection to the next queue, and the Reset method returns the collection to the first queue in the set.

The collection of queues returned to the MSMQQueueInfos collection is dynamic and can change as queues are created and destroyed. Because of this, you cannot depend on the count of the collection remaining constant. Therefore, you use the Next method to work through the collection while checking each operation to ensure a valid queue is returned. The following code shows how to walk through a collection of MSMQQueueInfo objects:

```
'List the Create Times for all queues that
'are of a certain ServiceType.
Dim objQuery As new MSMQQuery
Dim objQueueInfo As MSMQQueueInfo

'Get queues.
Dim objQueueInfos As MSMQQueueInfos

Set objQueueInfos = objQuery.LookupQueue _
(ServiceTypeGuid := "{581EA041-8D8E-11d1-B101-000629142E7B}")

'Start with First queue in collection
objQueueInfos.Reset

Set objQueueInfo = objQueueInfos.Next

While Not objQueueInfo Is Nothing
    lstQueues.AddItem objQueueInfo.CreateTime
    Set objQueueInfo = objQueueInfos.Next
Wend
```

MSMQQueueInfo Object

The MSMQQueueInfo object represents information for a single message queue. Using this object, you can create, destroy, open, and close message queues. All of the queue parameters are also available as properties of this object. The MSMQQueueInfo object represents a queue, but does not represent an open queue in use by an application. Open queues are returned as MSMQQueue objects from the Open method of the MSMQQueueInfo object. The Open method of the MSMQQueueInfo object has the following syntax:

```
Set MSMQQueue = MSMQQueueInfo.Open (Access, ShareMode)
```

The Access argument determines what type of access is allowed to the queue. Access can be granted for sending, receiving, or peeking. Peeking at messages in the queue means that they can be examined, but cannot be removed from the queue. The Access argument is specified by the constants MQ_PEEK_ACCESS, MQ_SEND_ACCESS, and MQ_RECEIVE_ACCESS.

The ShareMode argument determines how multiuser access is handled to a queue. When set to MQ_DENY_NONE, the queue is available to everyone without restriction. This setting is required if the Access argument is set to MQ_PEEK_ACCESS or MQ_SEND_ACCESS. When the ShareMode argument is set to MQ_DENY_RECEIVE_SHARE, two applications cannot receive messages from the queue simultaneously. The option is only valid if the Access argument is set to MQ_RECEIVE_ACCESS.

MSMQQueue Object

The MSMQQueue object represents an instance of an open connection to a message queue. Using this object, your application can send and receive messages from queues. When a queue is open, message receipt is performed asynchronously as a runtime event that fires in Visual Basic code.

MSMQEvent Object

The MSMQEvent object is used to trap asynchronous events that occur as the result of message activity in a queue. The MSMQEvent object is declared WithEvents in Visual Basic code and provides two events as a result: Arrived and ArrivedError. The events are received when you call the EnableNotification method for a queue.

The Arrived event fires when a queue of interest receives an event. The ArrivedError fires when a queue has an error delivering a message. MSMQ events function slightly differently than a standard Visual Basic event handler. In Visual Basic, using the WithEvents keyword normally establishes an event handler that lasts for the life of the handling object. In MSMQ, however, an event handler is connected for a single event only. After an event is received by your application, you must explicitly call the EnableNotification method to receive additional events. The following code shows how the recipient of a message connects to a queue for asynchronous notification through the MSMQEvent object:

```
'Declare an event object to receive
'notification of new messages in
'the queue
Private WithEvents objEvents As MSMQ.MSMQEvent

REM: ******************************************
REM: The following snippet connects the events!
REM: ******************************************

'Declare MSMQ Objects
Dim objQuery As MSMQ.MSMQQuery
Dim objQueueInfos As MSMQ.MSMQQueueInfos
Dim objQueueInfo As MSMQ.MSMQQueueInfo
Dim objQueue As MSMQ.MSMQQueue

Const msmqServiceTypeGUID$ = "{581EA041-8D8E-11d1-B101-000629142E7B}"

'Before we can receive a message, we must
'locate the correct queue
Set objQuery = New MSMQ.MSMQQuery

Set objQueueInfos = objQuery.LookupQueue _
(ServiceTypeGuid:=msmqServiceTypeGUID, Label:="Simple Demo")
objQueueInfos.Reset

Set objQueueInfo = objQueueInfos.Next

'Now that we have found the queue,
'we can open it for receiving
Set objQueue = objQueueInfo.Open(MQ_RECEIVE_ACCESS, MQ_DENY_NONE)

'Since we receive asynchronously,
'we have to connect the queue to
'the event object
Set objEvents = New MSMQEvent
objQueue.EnableNotification objEvents
```

MSMQMessage Object

The MSMQMessage object is the object used to send and receive data from queues.
MSMQMessage objects are flexible objects that contain properties to describe the message
as well as the actual message data. The MSMQMessage object carries the message data in
the Body property. The Body property may contain a string; an array of bytes; any numeric, date, and currency type that a variant can contain; or any persistent ActiveX object.
The following code sends a message to an open queue:

```
Set objMessage = New MSMQ.MSMQMessage

With objMessage
```

```
.Priority = 4
.Body = txtMessage.Text
.Label = "My Messageî
.Send objQueue
End With
```

QUICK CHECK 12-2:

A SIMPLE MSMQ EXAMPLE

1. To examine the fundamental requirements for using MSMQ successfully, we will create a simple application that uses a client to send a simple text message asynchronously to a receiving application. Before we discuss any Visual Basic code, we will create a new queue for this example. With the MSMQ Explorer running, simply select the site where you want the new queue created. Right-click on the server and select **New, Queue** from the pop-up menu.

2. When you select the menu item, the Queue Name dialog will appear and you can enter a name for the queue. After you enter a name and click the OK button, the new queue will be created in MSMQ.

3. You can view the properties for your new queue by selecting the queue in the MSMQ Explorer and right-clicking the icon. When the pop-up menu appears, select **Properties**.

4. One thing you will notice immediately is that the new queue has a `ServiceTypeGUID` set to "`{00000000-0000-0000-0000-000000000000}`". This setting is unacceptable if you want to search for queues using unique numbers. Therefore, you will have to generate a GUID for this new queue type. The easiest way to generate a new GUID is to use the GUIDGEN.EXE utility. This utility is available with both Visual C++ and Visual J++.

5. When you run GUIDGEN.EXE, you generate new GUIDs for use in any application. These numbers are unique and can never be exhausted. Simply run the utility and copy the resulting GUID into the properties sheet for your new queue. You will also need to be able to access this number later for use by applications that want to connect to the new queue. Therefore, be sure to record this number before continuing. When the queue is created, you are ready to write an MSMQ application.

6. Using the CD-ROM for the book, locate the directory TEMPLATES\QUICK CHECK12-2. This directory contains a partially completed MSMQ project.

continues

continued

7. On your hard drive, create a new directory with the Windows Explorer named MTS\QUICK CHECK12-2. Copy the contents from the CD-ROM directory into the new directory you just created.

8. Because the CD-ROM will create read-only copies of the project files, select all the files you copied, right-click them, and select **Properties** from the pop-up menu. In the properties dialog, uncheck the read-only flag. Close the dialog.

9. Start Visual Basic. Open the project group named QUICK CHECK12-2.VBG. This group contains two Standard EXE projects. The Client project sends data to the newly created queue, and the Server project will read the data.

10. In the Project Explorer, locate the Client project. This project contains a single form named frmClient. Figure 12.9 shows the form.

FIGURE 12.9
Use this form to send data to the new queue.

11. In the form, a message is sent to the queue by clicking the Send button. In this code, we first locate the queue using the LookUpQueue method. The GUID for the ServiceTypeGUID is supplied as an argument; therefore, you will have to insert your new GUID into the code. Because we are sure that this is the only queue using the GUID, we simply connect to the first queue in the MSMQQueueInfos collection. The queue is opened for sending, and the message is sent as plain text. Add the following code to the cmdSend_Click event to send the message:

```
On Error GoTo SendErr

    'Declare MSMQ Objects
    Dim objQuery As MSMQ.MSMQQuery
    Dim objQueueInfos As MSMQ.MSMQQueueInfos
    Dim objQueueInfo As MSMQ.MSMQQueueInfo
    Dim objQueue As MSMQ.MSMQQueue
    Dim objMessage As MSMQMessage
```

```
            'A GUID is used to uniquely identify
            'queues associated with a particular
            'type of application
            'INSERT YOUR GUID FOR THE ONE SHOWN HERE!!!
            Const msmqServiceTypeGUID$ = _
                "{581EA041-8D8E-11d1-B101-000629142E7B}"

            'Before we can send a message, we must
            'locate the correct queue to send it to.  This
            'demo assumes the queue already exists
            Set objQuery = New MSMQ.MSMQQuery

            Set objQueueInfos = objQuery.LookupQueue _
            (ServiceTypeGuid:=msmqServiceTypeGUID, Label:="Simple")
            objQueueInfos.Reset

            Set objQueueInfo = objQueueInfos.Next

            'Now that we have found the queue,
            'we can open it for sending
            Set objQueue = objQueueInfo.Open _
            (MQ_SEND_ACCESS, MQ_DENY_NONE)

            'Now we can send the message
            Set objMessage = New MSMQ.MSMQMessage

            With objMessage
                .Priority = 4
                .Body = txtMessage.Text
                .Label = "Simple Test " & Format$(Now)
                .Send objQueue
            End With

            'Close the Queue
            objQueue.Close

    SendExit:
        Exit Sub

    SendErr:
        MsgBox Err.Description
        Resume SendExit
```

12. In the Project Explorer, locate the Server project. This project contains a single form named frmServer. This form is used to connect to the queue and retrieve the message sent by the Client project. Figure 12.10 shows the form.

continues

12

THE MICROSOFT
MESSAGE QUEUE

continued

FIGURE 12.10

Use this form to retrieve messages from the new queue.

13. The `Server` project retrieves messages when the user clicks the Connect to Queue button. Just like the client portion, the server must locate and open the desired queue. In this case, however, the queue is opened for receiving messages. Because receiving is done asynchronously, the code provides an `MSMQEvent` object, which is notified when a new message appears for the server. When received, the message is processed for display in the server application. Add the following code to the `cmdConnect_Click` event to retrieve the messages:

```
On Error GoTo ConnectErr

    'Before we can receive a message, we must
    'locate the correct queue
    Set objQuery = New MSMQ.MSMQQuery

    'INSERT YOUR GUID FOR THE ONE SHOWN HERE!!!
    Const msmqServiceTypeGUID$ = _
        "{581EA041-8D8E-11d1-B101-000629142E7B}"

    Set objQueueInfos = objQuery.LookupQueue _
    (ServiceTypeGuid:=msmqServiceTypeGUID, Label:="Simple")
    objQueueInfos.Reset

    Set objQueueInfo = objQueueInfos.Next

    'Now that we have found the queue,
    'we can open it for receiving
    Set objQueue = objQueueInfo.Open(MQ_RECEIVE_ACCESS, MQ_DENY_NONE)

    'Since we receive asynchronously,
    'we have to connect the queue to
    'the event object
    Set objEvents = New MSMQEvent
```

```
        objQueue.EnableNotification objEvents

ConnectExit:
    Exit Sub

ConnectErr:
    MsgBox Err.Description
    Resume ConnectExit
```

14. When the code is added to the projects, compile both projects by selecting **File, Make Project Group** from the menu. You can then run the two applications and send messages through the queue.

MSMQ TRANSACTIONS

Along with application programming, MSMQ also supports the use of transactions. Transactional programming in MSMQ begins by marking a new queue as transactional. Setting a queue as transactional is done when the queue is created. Marking a queue as transactional means that sending messages to a queue can be part of an overall transaction. MSMQ supports two different types of transactions: internal and external.

The `MSMQTransactionDispenser` Object

The `MSMQTransactionDispenser` is responsible for beginning a new internal transaction. An internal transaction is a transaction that involves nothing except messages. This type of transaction allows you to send multiple messages to multiple queues as part of a transaction. In this type of transaction, if one of the messages in the transaction is not delivered, all the messages can be rolled back.

The `MSMQTransactionDispenser` object supports a single method—`BeginTransaction`. This method starts a new internal transaction and returns an `MSMQTransaction` object. The `MSMQTransaction` object can then be used to coordinate the sending of messages to queues. The following code shows how a new internal transaction might be created:

```
Dim objDispenser As New MSMQ.MSMQTransactionDispenser
Dim objTransactor As MSMQ.MSMQTransaction
Set objTransactor = objDispenser.BeginTransaction
```

The `MSMQCoordinatedTransactionDispenser` Object

The `MSMQCoordinatedTransactionDispenser` object is responsible for beginning a new external transaction. An external transaction allows MSMQ to participate in a transaction with other operations, such as updating a database. In this way, you can coordinate the sending of messages with the accomplishment of data access tasks. For example, you might want to coordinate the completion of a product order entry to a database with a confirmation message to a client. Like the `MSMQTransactionDispenser`, the `MSMQCoordinatedTransactionDispenser` supports only the `BeginTransaction` method. Similarly, it also returns an `MSMQTransaction` object.

The `MSMQTransaction` Object

When a transaction is started, committing and aborting the transaction is accomplished through the `MSMQTransaction` object. This object works on either an internal or external transaction. This object has two methods: `Commit` and `Abort`. Quite simply, these methods commit or abort the internal or external transaction. Using this object, you can send multiple messages and coordinate with external database operations. The `Commit` method can then be called to send all the messages and commit the database operations. `Abort`, on the other hand, rolls back all messages and database operations.

QUICK CHECK 12-3:

MSMQ TRANSACTIONS

1. This exercise investigates transactions by using a request queue for a client application and a response queue for a server application. Start the MSMQ Explorer so you can create the request and response queues for this exercise.

CAUTION

The data access code in this exercise assumes that you are using the SQL Server administrator credentials. If not, you may have to edit the database connect string.

2. Select the site where you want to set up the request and response queues. Right-click the site and select **New, Queue** from the pop-up menu. Create a new queue named `InternalRequest`. Mark this queue as transactional. Repeat this process and create a transactional queue named `InternalResponse`.

3. This exercise searches for request and response queues by TypeID. The TypeID can be set by examining the properties for each queue. Access the properties

for each queue by right-clicking the queue and selecting **Properties** from the pop-up menu. Change the TypeID GUID for each queue as follows:

InternalRequest: {50527B80-8463-11D2-B5F7-0060088D02A3}

InternalResponse: {6EBD8F00-8463-11D2-B5F7-0060088D02A3}

4. Using the CD-ROM for the book, locate the directory TEMPLATES\QUICK CHECK12-3. This directory contains a partially completed MSMQ project that will allow you to investigate transactions.

5. On your hard drive, create a new directory with the Windows Explorer named MTS\QUICK CHECK12-3. Copy the contents from the CD-ROM directory into the new directory you just created.

6. Because the CD-ROM will create read-only copies of the project files, select all the files you copied, right-click them, and select **Properties** from the pop-up menu. In the properties dialog, uncheck the read-only flag. Close the dialog.

7. Start Visual Basic. Open the project group named QUICK CHECK12-3.VBG. This group contains two Standard EXE projects. The Client project creates an internal transaction that requests a query to be run on a database. The Server project creates an external transaction that runs a query on a database and sends the results to a queue as a disconnected recordset.

8. In the Project Explorer, locate the InternalClient project. This project has a user interface to examine a set of records returned from the pubs database. The recordset is returned in response to a request message sent by the project to a queue. This project contains a single form named frmClient, which is shown in Figure 12.11.

FIGURE 12.11
This form is used to send a query request to a queue.

continued

9. Open the code window for `frmClient`. This form sends a query request to a queue to return a disconnected recordset based on a company name entered in the form. When a company name is entered, the GO! button is used to send the query request. After the request is sent, the form attaches to the response queue and waits for a recordset to return. Add the following code to the `cmdGO_Click` event to send a query request:

```
On Error GoTo GoErr

    'Open the queue
    Set objRequestQueue = objRequestQueueInfo.Open _
    (MQ_SEND_ACCESS, MQ_DENY_NONE)

    'Create a new Internal Transaction
    Dim objTransactor As MSMQ.MSMQTransaction
    Set objTransactor = objDispenser.BeginTransaction

    'Now we can send the message
    Set objMessage = New MSMQ.MSMQMessage

    With objMessage
        .Priority = 4
        .Body = txtFields(ntsCompanyName).Text
        .Label = "Query Request: " & Now
        .Send objRequestQueue, objTransactor
    End With

    'Clear the Form
    Dim objControl As Control
    For Each objControl In Controls
        If TypeOf objControl Is TextBox Then
            objControl.Text = ""
        End If
    Next

    'Connect for events
    objResponseQueue.EnableNotification _
        objEvents, MQMSG_FIRST, 5000

    'Commit Transaction
    objTransactor.Commit

GoExit:

    'Close the Queue
    objRequestQueue.Close
    Exit Sub
```

```
GoErr:
    objTransactor.Abort
    MsgBox Err.Description
    Resume GoExit
```

10. In the Project Explorer, locate the project named InternalServer. This project contains a single form named frmServer. This form is not intended for user interaction. Instead, this form is used to track the number of query requests, committed transactions, and aborted transactions. Figure 12.12 shows the form.

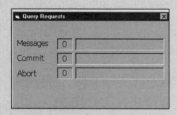

FIGURE 12.12

This form is used to track MSMQ transactions.

11. Open the code window for frmServer. This form waits for request messages to arrive in the request queue. When a request is received, a query is run and a disconnected recordset is created. This recordset is then returned to the response queue for the front end to retrieve. Add the code in Listing 12.1 to the Arrived event to process query requests in a transaction.

LISTING 12.1 CODE TO ADD TO THE Arrived EVENT

```
On Error GoTo EventErr

    'Get request message
    Dim objMessage As MSMQMessage
    Set objMessage = Queue.Receive
    lblTotal = lblTotal + 1

    'Open the Response queue
    Set objResponseQueue = objResponseQueueInfo. _
        Open(MQ_SEND_ACCESS, MQ_DENY_NONE)

    'Start a new external transaction
    Dim objTransactor As MSMQ.MSMQTransaction
```

continues

continued

```
        Set objTransactor = objDispenser.BeginTransaction

        'Create query
        Dim strSQL As String
        strSQL = "SELECT titles.title, authors.au_lname, "
        strSQL = strSQL & "publishers.pub_name, "
        strSQL = strSQL & "titleauthor.title_id,titles.pubdate "
        strSQL = strSQL & "From authors INNER JOIN titleauthor "
        strSQL = strSQL & "ON authors.au_id = titleauthor.au_id "
        strSQL = strSQL & "INNER JOIN titles "
        strSQL = strSQL & "ON titleauthor.title_id = titles.title_id "
        strSQL = strSQL & "INNER JOIN publishers ON "
        strSQL = strSQL & "titles.pub_id = publishers.pub_id "
        strSQL = strSQL & "WHERE pub_name LIKE '%" _
        strSQL = strSQL & objMessage.Body & "%'"

        'Create connection string
        Dim strConnect As String
        strConnect = "Provider=SQLOLEDB;"
        strConnect = strConnect & "Data Source=(local);"
        strConnect = strConnect & "UID=sa;"
        strConnect = strConnect & "PWD=;"
        strConnect = strConnect & "Database=pubs;"

        'Run the requested query
        Set objRecordset = New ADODB.Recordset
        objRecordset.CursorLocation = adUseClient
        objRecordset.CursorType = adOpenStatic
        objRecordset.LockType = adLockBatchOptimistic
        objRecordset.Source = strSQL
        objRecordset.ActiveConnection = strConnect
        objRecordset.Open
        Set objRecordset.ActiveConnection = Nothing

        'Fail if no records
        If objRecordset.BOF And objRecordset.EOF Then
            Err.Raise vbObjectError
        End If

        'Now we can send the message
        Set objMessage = New MSMQ.MSMQMessage

        With objMessage
            .Priority = 4
            .Body = objRecordset
            .Label = "Query Response: " & Now
            .Send objResponseQueue, objTransactor
        End With
```

```
        'Commit Transaction
        objTransactor.Commit
        lblCommit = lblCommit + 1

EventExit:

        'Update Progress Bars
        UpdateProgress

        'Close the Queue
        objResponseQueue.Close

        'Re-enable events
        Queue.EnableNotification objEvents

        Exit Sub

EventErr:

        'Roll back transaction
        objTransactor.Abort
        lblAbort = lblAbort + 1

        Resume EventExit
```

12. After the code is added, compile both projects by selecting **File, Make Project Group** from the menu. After the files are compiled, run both projects simultaneously. Use the client form by typing a company name in the text field and clicking GO!. Try using the company name "Moon." The server should register the request and return a result.

12

THE MICROSOFT MESSAGE QUEUE

EXERCISE 12-1: MSMQ AND ADO

As an example of a more complex MSMQ solutions, we have put together an application that uses ADO to query and edit a disconnected recordset object. This disconnected recordset is then sent to MSMQ for storage until a server application is started. The server application retrieves the disconnected recordset from the queue and reconnects to SQL Server to commit the stored changes.

CAUTION

The data access code in this exercise assumes that you are using the SQL Server administrator credentials. If not, you may have to edit the database connect string.

Creating the Client

In this section, you will create a client application. This application will allow you to edit records and send them to a queue.

Step 1

Using the CD-ROM for the book, locate the directory TEMPLATES\EXERCISE12-1. This directory contains a partially completed MSMQ project that utilizes disconnected recordsets.

Step 2

On your hard drive, create a new directory with the Windows Explorer named MTS\ EXERCISE12-1. Copy the contents from the CD-ROM directory into the new directory you just created.

Step 3

Because the CD-ROM will create read-only copies of the project files, select all the files you copied, right-click them, and select **Properties** from the pop-up menu. In the properties dialog, uncheck the read-only flag. Close the dialog.

Step 4

Start Visual Basic. Open the project group named EXERCISE12-1.VBG. This group contains two Standard EXE projects. The Client project retrieves records in a disconnected recordset and allows the user to edit them. The Server project receives the modified recordset and commits the changes to SQL Server.

Step 5

In the Project Explorer, locate the Client project. This project contains a single form named frmClient. This form runs a query to return all the authors in the pubs database. This recordset can then be edited locally and sent to a queue for updating. Figure 12.13 shows the client form.

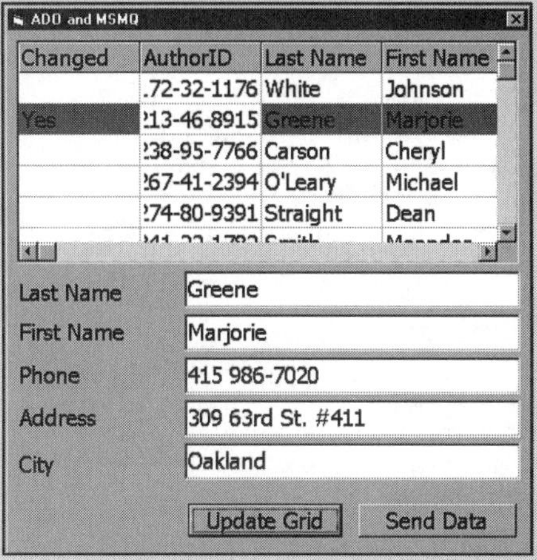

FIGURE 12.13

This form is used to edit a disconnected recordset.

Step 6

Open the code window for frmClient. When this form loads, it runs a query to return the set of all authors in the pubs database. The records are returned using a disconnected recordset. Add the code in Listing 12.2 to the Form_Load event to run the query and return the records.

LISTING 12.2 CODE TO ADD TO THE Form_Load EVENT

```
'Create SQL Statement
Dim strSQL As String
strSQL = "SELECT * FROM Authors"

'Run Query
Set objRecordset = New ADODB.Recordset
objRecordset.Source = strSQL
objRecordset.CursorLocation = adUseClient
objRecordset.CursorType = adOpenStatic
objRecordset.LockType = adLockBatchOptimistic
```

continues

LISTING 12.2   CONTINUED

```
objRecordset.ActiveConnection = _
"Provider=SQLOLEDB;Data source=(local);database=pubs;uid=sa;pwd=;"
objRecordset.Open
Set objRecordset.ActiveConnection = Nothing

If objRecordset Is Nothing Then Exit Sub

'Fill Grid from Recordset
grdClient.Clear
grdClient.Rows = 0
grdClient.AddItem "Changed" & vbTab & "AuthorID" _
& vbTab & "Last Name" & vbTab & "First Name" _
& vbTab & "Phone" & vbTab & "Address" & vbTab _
& "City" & vbTab & "State" & vbTab & "Zip" _
& vbTab & "Contract"

Do While Not objRecordset.EOF
    grdClient.AddItem "" _
    & vbTab & objRecordset!au_id _
    & vbTab & objRecordset!au_lname _
    & vbTab & objRecordset!au_fname _
    & vbTab & objRecordset!phone _
    & vbTab & objRecordset!address _
    & vbTab & objRecordset!city _
    & vbTab & objRecordset!State _
    & vbTab & objRecordset!zip _
    & vbTab & objRecordset!contract
    objRecordset.MoveNext
Loop

grdClient.FixedRows = 1
grdClient.Row = 1
grdClient_Click
```

Step 7

After the data is edited, it is sent to a queue for updating. In this exercise, you do not
have to explicitly create the queue because the code will create the queue if it does not
already exist. The queue is created when the data is sent. The data is sent to the queue by
simply setting the body of the message to the disconnected recordset. This means that
you can save any disconnected recordset in a queue indefinitely. Add the code in Listing
12.3 to the cmdSend_Click event to send the recordset to the queue.

LISTING 12.3 CODE TO ADD TO THE cmdSend_Click EVENT

```
On Error GoTo SendErr

    'Declare MSMQ Objects
    Dim objQuery As MSMQ.MSMQQuery
    Dim objQueueInfos As MSMQ.MSMQQueueInfos
    Dim objQueueInfo As MSMQ.MSMQQueueInfo
    Dim objQueue As MSMQ.MSMQQueue
    Dim objMessage As MSMQMessage

    'A GUID is used to uniquely identify
    'queues associated with a particular
    'type of application
    Const msmqServiceTypeGUID$ = _
    "{FAA227B1-9149-11d1-B10E-000629142E7B}"

    'Before we can send a message, we must
    'locate the correct queue to send it to.
    Set objQuery = New MSMQ.MSMQQuery

    Set objQueueInfos = objQuery.LookupQueue _
    (ServiceTypeGuid:=msmqServiceTypeGUID, Label:="ADO Demo")
    objQueueInfos.Reset

    Set objQueueInfo = objQueueInfos.Next

    If objQueueInfo Is Nothing Then
        'Queue does not exist, so create it
        Set objQueueInfo = New MSMQQueueInfo
        objQueueInfo.PathName = ".\ADODemo"
        objQueueInfo.Label = "ADO Demo"
        objQueueInfo.ServiceTypeGuid = msmqServiceTypeGUID
        objQueueInfo.Create
    End If

    'Now that we have found the queue,
    'we can open it for sending
    Set objQueue = objQueueInfo.Open _
    (MQ_SEND_ACCESS, MQ_DENY_NONE)

    'Now we can send the message
    Set objMessage = New MSMQ.MSMQMessage

    With objMessage
        .Priority = 4
        .Body = objRecordset
        .Label = "ADO Test " & Format$(Now)
```

12

THE MICROSOFT
MESSAGE QUEUE

continues

LISTING 12.3 CONTINUED

```
        .Send objQueue
    End With

    'Close the Queue
    objQueue.Close
    MsgBox "Data Sent to Queue!", _
    vbOKOnly + vbInformation, "MSMQ"

SendExit:
    Exit Sub

SendErr:
    MsgBox Err.Description
    Resume SendExit
```

Creating the Server Application

In this section, you will build a server application. The server application will receive queued records from the client. These records will then be sent to the database for updating.

Step 8

In the Project Explorer, locate the Server project. This project connects to the queue where the disconnected recordset is located and retrieves it for updating. The UpdateBatch method is used on the recordset to commit the changes made in the Client project. The resulting recordset is then displayed in a grid. Figure 12.14 shows the server form.

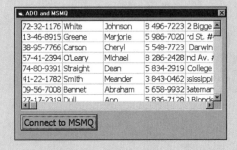

FIGURE 12.14

This form is used to commit changes from a disconnected recordset.

Step 9

The Server project connects to the queue when the user clicks the Connect to MSMQ button. The queue is located and an MSMQEvent object is used to connect to the queue. Add the code in Listing 12.4 to the cmdConnect_Click event to connect to the queue and wait for a recordset to be delivered.

LISTING 12.4   CODE TO ADD TO THE cmdConnect_Click EVENT

```
On Error GoTo ConnectErr

    'Before we can receives a message, we must
    'locate the correct queue
    Set objQuery = New MSMQ.MSMQQuery

    Set objQueueInfos = objQuery.LookupQueue _
    (ServiceTypeGuid:=msmqServiceTypeGUID, Label:="ADO Demo")
    objQueueInfos.Reset

    Set objQueueInfo = objQueueInfos.Next

    'Now that we have found the queue,
    'we can open it for receiving
    Set objQueue = objQueueInfo.Open _
    (MQ_RECEIVE_ACCESS, MQ_DENY_NONE)

    'Since we receive asynchronously,
    'we have to connect the queue to
    'the event object
    Set objEvents = New MSMQEvent
    objQueue.EnableNotification objEvents

ConnectExit:
    Exit Sub

ConnectErr:
    MsgBox Err.Description
    Resume ConnectExit
```

Step 10

When the event handler is connected, the events are received in the Arrived event. In this event, the disconnected recordset is retrieved and the UpdateBatch method is used to commit the changes. Add the code in Listing 12.5 to the Arrived event to update the database with the changes in the recordset.

LISTING 12.5 CODE TO ADD TO THE Arrived EVENT

```
'This event fires every time
'we have a new message
'in the queue

Dim objMessage As MSMQMessage
Set objMessage = objQueue.Receive

'Create Recordset
Dim objRecordset As ADODB.Recordset
Set objRecordset = objMessage.Body

'Fill Grid
Dim i As Integer
Dim strTemp As String

objRecordset.MoveFirst
Do While Not objRecordset.EOF
    strTemp = ""
    For i = 0 To objRecordset.Fields.Count - 1
        strTemp = strTemp & objRecordset.Fields(i).Value
        If i < objRecordset.Fields.Count - 1 _
        Then strTemp = strTemp & vbTab
    Next
    grdServer.AddItem strTemp
    objRecordset.MoveNext
Loop

'Update Data
objRecordset.ActiveConnection = _
"Provider=SQLOLEDB;Data source=(local);database=pubs;uid=sa;pwd=;"
objRecordset.UpdateBatch
MsgBox "Data Updated!"
```

Step 11

When the code is written, compile both projects by selecting **File, Make Project Group** from the menu. After the projects are compiled, run the Client project and edit some records. Then send the records to the update queue. Now run the Server project and commit the changes.

INTERFACING MICROSOFT OUTLOOK AND MTS

PREREQUISITES

Before beginning this chapter, you should be a user of Microsoft Outlook. This chapter shows you how to build collaborative applications with Outlook '98, so it requires that you have Microsoft Exchange services available to your Outlook '98 client.

Skills Learned

- MTS(33): Customize Outlook views.
- MTS(34): Customize Outlook forms.
- MTS(35): Write VBScript code to manipulate Outlook forms and controls.
- MTS(36): Write VBScript code to create and route Outlook items.
- MTS(37): Create applications that access MTS components from Outlook.

Microsoft Outlook is a powerful personal information manager (PIM) that can easily be customized to create collaborative applications. You can use the built-in features of Outlook including contact management, schedule management, and email facilities to provide collaboration and workflow features while simultaneously interacting with MTS components to provide sophisticated transactional capabilities. Together, Outlook and MTS enable you to create scalable, transactional applications that can control workflow in a large organization.

Although Outlook is capable of operating as a standalone PIM, it is most often used as a front-end to the Microsoft Exchange Server. Microsoft Exchange offers a variety of services to the Outlook client. It can provide internal and Internet email, common scheduling and tasking, and threaded discussion groups. All these features can be enhanced through the use of MTS components and Outlook scripting.

As Outlook users know, Outlook is divided into a series of folders. Folders in Outlook represent data stores that contain related information. Outlook provides generic folders that you can use to organize schedules, contacts, email, and several other families of personal information. In many ways, you can think of a folder as a predefined database structure. The structure is created by Outlook, but you add the data.

Folders in Outlook can be stored directly on the Microsoft Exchange server or in a local file on your system. The default installation gives you folders managed by Exchange. However, creating local files gives you the advantage of being able to control the location of files and back up your information. Local files also make excellent development environments for Outlook applications. Local data files in Outlook are called personal folders. Personal folders are kept as PST files on your local machine. This chapter uses PST files to create several applications.

QUICK CHECK 13-1:

ADDING A NEW PST FILE

1. Before you can begin working the exercises for this chapter, you must locate the PST file on the CD-ROM that contains the project templates. PST files are used in Outlook to contain folders and their associated information. On the CD-ROM, locate the file EXERCISE13.PST.

2. Using the File Explorer, create a new directory on your hard drive called MTS/ EXERCISE13. Copy the PST file from the CD-ROM into the new directory you created.

3. Because the CD-ROM creates read-only versions of the files, right-click the PST file and select **Properties** from the pop-up menu. Uncheck the read-only flag and close the properties dialog.

4. Start Microsoft Outlook. If the folder list is not already visible, open it by selecting **View, Folder List** from the menu.

5. Add the new PST file to your Outlook view by selecting **File, New, Personal Folders File** from the menu. Locate the EXERCISE13.PST file on your hard drive and click the Create button. The PST file should now be visible in your folder list. This PST is named "Outlook and MTS" and contains templates for the Outlook exercises in this chapter.

In addition to personal folders, when used in conjunction with Exchange, Outlook also supports public folders. Public folders are folders that can be shared by all users of Exchange on the Enterprise. Creating a new folder under the public area immediately creates groupware, albeit extremely simplified, that clients can use to collaborate. Moving an Outlook application you create locally into a public folder is the equivalent of deploying the application.

CUSTOMIZING MICROSOFT OUTLOOK

Microsoft Outlook provides a large number of customizable components that can be modified without ever writing a single line of code. Customizing these components allows you to quickly create new data sets or even completely new applications. Customizable components in Outlook include data views and forms. Data views are presentations of data in a grid format. This is the default data presentation style in Outlook. Figure 13.1 shows a typical Outlook view.

Outlook forms are tabbed dialogs that contain more information than is normally found in a view. Outlook forms are displayed when adding or editing a record. A single form represents one record in an Outlook folder. Figure 13.2 shows a typical Outlook form.

Outlook views and forms may be customized at any time by a user. Views can be customized by adding or removing fields from the view. This can be accomplished by selecting **View, Current View, Define Views** from the menu. This action presents the Define Views dialog. In the Define Views dialog, you can select any of the views defined for the current folder. You can then add or remove fields from the view. You can also set up sorts and filters for the view from this dialog. Figure 13.3 shows the Define Views dialog.

FIGURE **13.1**

Outlook views are grid-based data presentations.

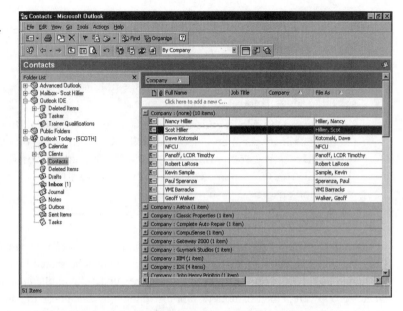

FIGURE **13.2**

Outlook forms show all the fields for a single record.

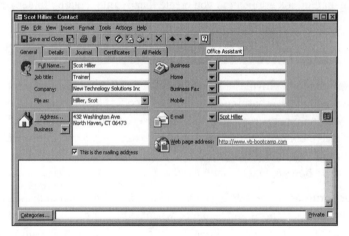

FIGURE 13.3

Use the Define Views dialog to customize a view.

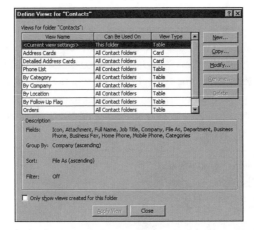

Forms can be customized in Outlook only when the form is visible. You can customize any visible form by selecting **Tools, Forms, Design This Form** from the menu on an open form. This action places the form into design mode where you can use a control toolbox and script editor to completely customize the form's appearance and behavior. Open the control toolbox by selecting **Form, Control Toolbox**. The script editor can be displayed by selecting **Form, View Code**. Figure 13.4 shows a form in design mode.

FIGURE 13.4

Forms can be customized through a toolbox and script editor.

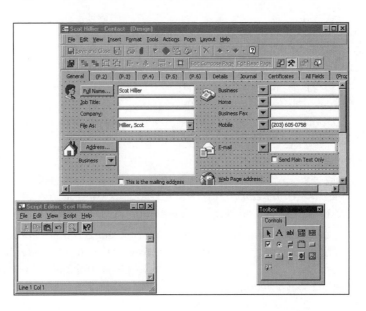

Although you may customize the standard Outlook views and forms at any time, typically you will create a new folder for custom forms and views. When you create a new folder in Outlook, you are creating a new copy of one of the predefined databases. This allows you to build custom applications based on the predefined elements in Outlook. You can create a new folder at any time by right-clicking in the Folder view and selecting **New Folder** from the pop-up menu. When you select to create a new folder, Outlook prompts you to name the new folder and base it on one of the predefined folder types. Figure 13.5 shows the Create New Folder dialog.

Figure 13.5

Use this dialog to create a new Outlook folder.

QUICK CHECK 13-2:

CUSTOMIZING VIEWS AND FORMS

1. Outlook applications can be created with no code at all by simply customizing existing components. In this exercise, you will create a custom view and custom form for managing the qualification progress of employees at a training company.

2. In your Outlook folder list, locate the PST file you installed earlier. In this folder, you will find a second folder named Trainer Qualifications. This folder was created based on the standard Outlook contacts module. In this folder, you will find several contacts already defined.

3. You will begin by customizing the view to make it more appropriate for tracking qualifications. Click on the Trainer Qualifications folder and then select **View, Current View, Define Views** from the menu. This will open the Define Views dialog.

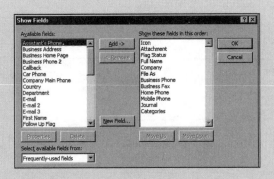

FIGURE **13.6**

Use this dialog to change the fields in a view.

7. In the Show Fields dialog, remove all the fields from the Show These Fields in This Order list except for the Full Name field.

8. In addition to changing the fields in a view, you can also add new fields. Add a new field to the view by clicking the New Field button. This will display the New Field dialog. Name the new field "Visual Basic" and change the type to Yes/No. This will create a check box that can be used to indicate that a trainer is qualified to teach Visual Basic. Save the new field definition by clicking the OK button. Figure 13.7 shows the New Field dialog.

FIGURE **13.7**

Use this dialog to define new fields.

9. Add two additional Yes/No fields to the view for "Visual InterDev" and "Transaction Server." Close the Show Fields dialog by clicking the OK button. Close the View Summary dialog by clicking the OK button.

10. To activate your new view, click the Apply View button in the Define Views dialog. Your new view should enable you to easily track qualifications for the personnel in your list. Figure 13.8 shows the completed view.

continues

13

INTERFACING MS
OUTLOOK AND
MTS

continued

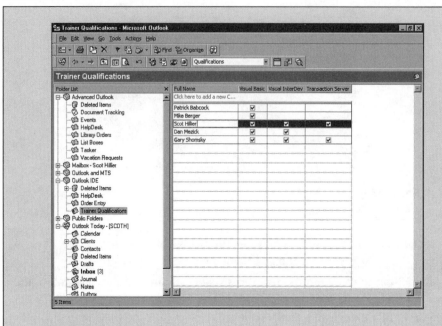

FIGURE **13.8**
This view is used to track trainer qualifications.

11. At this point, you have a new view, but the form associated with the view does not contain your new fields. You can customize the form associated with this folder to show the new fields by selecting **File, New, Contact** from the menu. This will open the contact form for the folder.

12. With the contact form open, select **Tools, Forms, Design This Form** from the menu. This will place the form in design mode. Notice in design mode that the form displays several tabs that are normally not visible. Click the tab labeled (P.2).

13. The P.2 tab is a blank tab you can use to display new information. Normally this tab is not visible; however, you can make it visible by selecting **Form, Display This Page** from the menu. You can also change the caption on the tab by selecting **Form, Rename Page**. Rename this page to Qualifications.

14. With the form in design mode, you should also see the Field Chooser dialog. The Field Chooser lists all the fields that are available for display on the form. In the Field Chooser, select User-Defined Fields in Folder. This will display the three custom fields you created earlier.

15. Using the Field Chooser, drag each of your custom fields to the Qualifications tab. Outlook will respond by creating check boxes for the new fields.

16. When the form is complete, you will need to save the form. Saving the form is known as "publishing" the form in Outlook. You can publish the form by selecting **Tools, Forms, Publish Form**. This will bring up the Publish Form As dialog. Choose to publish the form into the Trainer Qualifications folder.

17. Close the form. Your published form is now available at the bottom of the **Actions** menu. You can select this item to create new contacts for the folder that have the new fields available.

CODING OUTLOOK FORMS

Although Outlook allows a high degree of customization, serious application development will require you to write code. Coding in Outlook is accomplished by writing VBScript in a script editor associated with an Outlook form. As we know from using VBScript in other products like Internet Explorer or Internet Information Server, it is a fairly limited language that primarily offers simple structures and loops for the purpose of communicating with COM objects. This is also true in Microsoft Outlook. You will not write a tremendous amount of code in VBScript, but you will call out to existing object models to accomplish business functions.

When coding Outlook applications, you begin by writing code to the Outlook object model itself. Just like many Microsoft applications, Outlook is built on COM objects. These COM objects represent everything from forms to email messages. Using the Outlook object model, you can manipulate form interfaces, create and send email, assign tasks, and interact with MTS components. Figure 13.9 shows the Outlook object model.

The Outlook object model is extensive, and a complete examination of all the objects is beyond the scope of a single chapter. However, there are some objects that are critical to the MTS programmer wanting to integrate with Outlook. When you first start to manipulate Outlook through the object model, you will want to access controls that are on the form. The following paragraphs describe the key objects necessary to manipulate a form. Complete help on the Outlook object model is available from the Help menu in the Outlook script editor.

FIGURE 13.9

The Outlook object model is accessible through VBScript code.

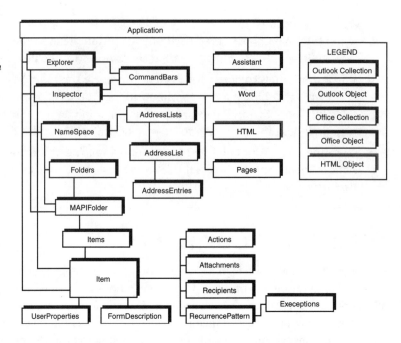

The **Application** Object

The top-level object in the Outlook model is the Application object. This object provides access to all other objects in the model. You never have to explicitly create an instance of the Application object—it is available directly by name. However, the Application object may also be created externally by Visual Basic code. This means that you can choose to either manipulate the Outlook product from VBScript inside an Outlook form or externally through a Visual Basic program. The following code could be used to create an instance of Outlook in a Visual Basic program:

```
Dim MyApplication As Outlook.Application
Set MyApplication = CreateObject("Outlook.Application")
```

The **Item** Object

The workhorse of the object model is the Item object. The Item object represents the currently open item in Outlook. This means that if you are running code within an email message form, Item is the current email form. If the code is within a task, then Item is the current task. The Item is the equivalent of the Form object in Visual Basic.

In keeping with the similarity between Items in Outlook and Forms in Visual Basic, Outlook Items are event-driven and have several predefined events associated with them.

For example, when an Item is first opened, it will fire the Open event. This event is the equivalent of a Form_Load event in Visual Basic. You can write code for this event directly in the Outlook script editor. Outlook will even prepare the event handler for you when you select **Script, Event Handler** from the script editor menu. Unfortunately, Outlook's debugging environment is considerably less robust than Visual Basic's, but you can easily leverage your knowledge of VB to write code in Outlook. Table 13.1 lists all the events supported by the Item object.

TABLE 13.1 ITEM EVENTS

Event	Description
Open	Fires when an item is opened
Read	Fires when an item is opened for editing
Write	Fires when changes to an item are saved
Close	Fires when an item is closed
Send	Fires when an item is sent
Reply	Fires when a user replies to this item
ReplyAll	Fires when a user replies to all recipients of this item
Forward	Fires when this item is forwarded
PropertyChange	Fires when a property of the item is changed
CustomPropertyChange	Fires when a user-defined property is changed
CustomAction	Fires when a user-defined action is executed

The `Inspector` Object

Although the Item object is similar to the Visual Basic form, the Inspector object has no real parallel in Visual Basic. The Inspector object in Outlook represents the frame around the current form. In this sense, the Inspector acts as a container object for all the tabs and controls on the form. You can access the Inspector object for the current Item by calling the GetInspector method of the Item object. The following code shows how this is done:

```
Set MyInspector = Item.GetInspector
```

The `Page` Object

The Page object in Outlook represents one of the pages in the set of tabbed pages on the form. The Page object acts as a container for all the controls that are on it. Accessing an individual page is done by using the name of the page as it appears on the tab. All the pages you have customized in Outlook are members of the `ModifiedFormPages` collection. The following code shows how you can gain a reference to a customized tab named Qualifications:

```
Set MyPage = _
Item.GetInspector.ModifiedFormPages("Qualifications")
```

Controls Objects

All the controls that you place on a customized page in Outlook are members of the `Controls` collection. These controls can be accessed by name in the collection. The names of controls can be set by simply right-clicking the control and selecting **Advanced Properties** from the pop-up menu. This gives you a standard properties window where you can name a control. The following code shows how you could access a `TextBox` named `TextBox1`, which is on a page named `Page1`:

```
Set MyPage = _
    Item.GetInspector.ModifiedFormPages("Page1") _
    .Controls("TextBox1").Text
```

Just as with controls in Visual Basic, you can create event handlers for controls in Outlook. The event handlers generally take the same form as they do in VB. However, because the Outlook environment is limited, the script editor will not create event handlers for controls. Instead, you must enter the event handler yourself. When doing this, simply follow the Visual Basic convention.

CODING OUTLOOK ITEMS

Along with directly manipulating controls on a form, you will want to use the Outlook object model to create and manage Outlook Items. Using the model, you can create new mail items and task items, locate folders, and send information. This will allow you to automate communication and tasking among several members of a team. Creating any item is accomplished through the use of the `CreateItem` method of the `Application` object. When you use this method, you specify an argument for the method that indicates which item to create. The following code shows how to create a new instance of a `MailItem` (for example, an email message):

```
Set MyMessage = Application.CreateItem(0)
```

The preceding code assumes that you are coding in VBScript in the script editor for an Outlook form. Because Outlook uses VBScript, it does not support named constants. Therefore, we have to use the constant 0, which indicates that a new `MailItem` should be created. If you control the Outlook model externally from Visual Basic, you can use the named constants found in the Outlook object model. Table 13.1 lists the named constants for creating items and their associated enumerated values. Although you can create a new item of any type supported by Outlook, in this chapter, we will focus on several key items including the `MailItem`, `TaskItem`, and `ContactItem` objects.

TABLE 13.2 CREATE ITEM CONSTANTS

Constant	*Value*
olMailItem	0
olAppointmentItem	1
olContactItem	2
olTaskItem	3
olJournalItem	4
olNoteItem	5
olPostItem	6

The NameSpace Object

When working with Outlook `Items`, you will want to access the underlying data system that stores the `Items` in folders. This underlying system is called the `NameSpace` object. The `NameSpace` object acts as an entry point to the folder system. Using the `NameSpace` object, you can access any folder under Outlook. This allows you to create new items for the folders. With this capability, you can easily create new tasks, for example, and place them on a task list. The `NameSpace` object is returned through the `GetNameSpace` method. The `GetNameSpace` method takes as an argument the data store you want to return. Currently, only one data store is supported—MAPI. The following code returns the MAPI `NameSpace`:

```
Set MyNameSpace = Application.GetNameSpace("MAPI")
```

The Folders Collection

When you have access to the MAPI `NameSpace`, you will want to use it to locate folders in Outlook. You can use the `GetDefaultFolder` method to return any of the default folders in Outlook. Default folders refer to the set of folders associated with the client's inbox. The `GetDefaultFolder` takes as an argument an integer constant that specifies what folder to return. Table 13.3 lists the named constants and their values. The following code shows how to return a reference to the default inbox:

```
Set MyInBox = MyNameSpace.GetDefaultFolder(6)
```

TABLE 13.3 CONSTANTS FOR THE GetDefaultFolder METHOD

Constant	Value
olFolderDeletedItems	3
olFolderOutbox	4
olFolderSentMail	5
olFolderInbox	6
olFolderCalendar	9
olFolderContacts	10
olFolderJournal	11
olFolderNotes	12
olFolderTasks	13

In addition to default folders, you can locate any folder in the list through the Folders collection. Each folder in the list also has a subsequent Folders collection. Imagine you have a PST file named My Projects and a folder in the PST file named Test Application. You can locate the Test Application folder with the following code:

```
Set MyNameSpace = Application.GetNameSpace("MAPI")
Set MyPSTFolder = MyNameSpace.Folders("My Projects")
Set MyTestFolder = MyPSTFolder.Folders("Test Application")
```

The TaskItem Object

The TaskItem object is one of several different items you can create with the Outlook object model. This item is particularly useful in applications because it allows you to assign tasks to members of a group. Assigning a task is accomplished by locating the folder where you want to add the new task and then adding the TaskItem to the Items collection of the folder. The following code locates the default Task folder and adds a new TaskItem:

```
'Locate the Tasks Folder
Set MyTasks = MAPINameSpace.GetDefaultFolder(13)

'Add a new task
Set NewTask = MyTasks.Items.Add("IPM.Task")
NewTask.Categories = "TO DO"
NewTask.Subject = "Web Page Updates"
NewTask.Display
```

When you add any item to a folder, you specify the message class of the Item that you want to add. In the preceding code, you can see that the message class for a standard task is IPM.Task. Every form you create has a message class. The message class is a combination of the default message class and the name under which you publish the form. Thus, if you modify a standard task and publish it as MyTask, the Message class for the custom form will be IPM.Task.MyTask.

The ContactItem Object

The ContactItem object is an object that represents a new contact in Outlook. Contacts normally represent personal and business contacts, phone numbers, and addresses. However, they are also very useful for creating applications that deal with information about people. We can use them to create Outlook applications that handle customers, employers, or vendors. Contacts are added to folders in much the same way as tasks. After you have added the contact to a folder, you can set key information such as the name and address. The following code adds a new contact to the default contacts folder and sets some information:

```
'Locate the Contacts Folder
Set MyContacts = MAPINameSpace.GetDefaultFolder(10)

'Add a new contact
Set NewContact = MyContacts.Items.Add("IPM.Contact")
NewContact.LastName = "Hillier"
NewContact.FirstName = "Scot"
NewContact.Save
```

The MailItem Object

The MailItem object is an object that represents an email message. Using the Outlook object model, you can create new messages, edit their content, and send the messages to others. The MailItem has dozens of properties associated with it that allow you to completely manage the new message. When you create a MailItem, you can use the Subject and Body properties to edit the basic message content. The Send method is used to send the message to a recipient.

Addressing the MailItem is done through the Recipients collection. When you add a recipient to the Recipients collection, you can use any valid text that can be resolved by Exchange. This includes full names, user names, and mail addresses. When you have added the appropriate recipients to the collection, you can have Exchange resolve the addresses using the ResolveAll method of the Recipients collection. The ResolveAll method returns True if all the recipients were satisfactorily resolved. The following code creates a new MailItem, adds several recipients, and sends the message:

```
Set NewMailItem = Application.CreateItem(0)

NewMailItem.Recipients.Add("SCOTH")
NewMailItem.Recipients.Add("PATRICKB")
NewMailItem.Recipients.Add("GARYS")
```

```
If NewMailItem.Recipients.ResolveAll Then
    NewMailItem.Subject = "Test Mail Item"
    NewMailItem.Body = "This is a test of the Outlook object model."
    NewMailItem.Send
Else
    MsgBox "Sorry, all recipients were not resolved!" _
End If
```

QUICK CHECK 13-3:

OUTLOOK ITEMS

1. Creating items in Outlook is a powerful way to control workflow. In this exercise, you will create a Help Desk application that submits help desk requests to a common pool where technicians can pick up and accept assignments. Locate the HelpDesk folder in Outlook to find this project already partially completed.

2. Click on the HelpDesk project in Outlook. This project folder was created based on the mail items module. Applications based on the mail items module are capable of acting like newsgroups where people can post messages for others to read. In this application, we have already defined part of a custom form for posting help desk requests. When forms are defined in a folder, they are available under the **Actions** menu. Select **Actions, New Helpdesk Request** to view the form. Figure 13.10 shows the form.

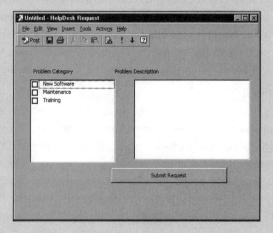

FIGURE **13.10**
This form is used to post help desk requests.

3. When the form is visible, enter design mode by selecting **Tools, Form, Design This Form** from the menu. Now open the script editor for the form by selecting **Form, View Code** from the menu.

4. In the form, users can select a category for their request and type a description. When the form is filled out, it is sent with the Submit button. When the form is submitted, it is posted to the folder where it can be examined by all the help desk technicians. Additionally, a new mail item is sent to the general technical support mailbox announcing that a new request has been placed in the queue. Add the following code to the `Click` event of the Submit button. Note that the code uses the address Support for the general tech support mailbox. You should replace this address with a valid address for your system.

```
'Get the MAPI Namespace
Set MAPINameSpace = Application.GetNameSpace("MAPI")

'Create a new mail item
Set NewMailItem = Application.CreateItem(0)
NewMailItem.Recipients.Add("Support")
If NewMailItem.Recipients.ResolveAll Then
    NewMailItem.Subject = "Help Desk Request Submission"
    NewMailItem.Body = "A new request has been posted."
    NewMailItem.Send
Else
    MsgBox "We cannot process your request at this time."
End If

'Post the Request
Item.Post
```

5. Close the script editor and return to the form. Every Outlook form you customize will actually have two different views: Compose and Read. The Compose page is the view of the form when a user creates a new item. The Read page is the form view when a recipient opens the form. Switch the form to the Read view by clicking the button marked Edit Read Page. Figure 13.11 shows the Read view of the form.

13

INTERFACING MS OUTLOOK AND MTS

continued

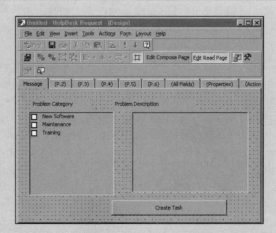

FIGURE 13.11
This view is seen by the recipient of the mail message.

6. When the help desk receives the request, the Read page allows them to create a new task item for the submitted request. The technician simply clicks
the Create Task button. This creates a new task in the default task folder and
sends an email confirmation to the original sender of the request. Open the
script editor and add the following code to the click event of the Create
Task button:

```
'Get the MAPI Namespace
Set MAPINameSpace = Application.GetNameSpace("MAPI")

'Create a new mail item
Set NewMailItem = Application.CreateItem(0)
NewMailItem.Recipients.Add(Item.SenderName)
If NewMailItem.Recipients.ResolveAll Then
    NewMailItem.Subject = "Help Desk Request Confirmation"
    NewMailItem.Body = "We have received your request."
    NewMailItem.Send
Else
    MsgBox "Cannot find recipient"
End If

'Locate the Tasks Folder
Set MyTasks = MAPINameSpace.GetDefaultFolder(13)

'Add a new task
Set NewTask = MyTasks.Items.Add("IPM.Task")
NewTask.Categories = Item.Categories
```

```
NewTask.Subject = Item.Subject
NewTask.Display

'Close this form
Item.Close False
```

7. After the code is added, publish the form to the folder by selecting **Tools, Forms, Publish Forms** from the menu. When the form is published, close the form.

8. Now you should be able to send a request. Open the form by selecting **Action, New Helpdesk Request** from the menu. Type up a request and submit it. Locate the sent email message and try accepting the task.

INTEGRATING OUTLOOK AND MTS

When you have a strong understanding of the workflow and groupware capabilities of Outlook, you are ready to integrate them with MTS. Using these two technologies together, we can take advantage of the familiar interface and flow of Outlook with the strong resource management capabilities of MTS. This allows us to utilize SQL Server databases and ActiveX components while providing a message-based user interface.

The primary strategy for integrating Outlook and MTS is to use Outlook to route assignments in a workflow environment while MTS handles the data access. All our interaction, however, will occur through Outlook forms. As an example, consider a home loan approval process. In this type of system, we need to move an applicant through several layers of approval. At the same time, we need to keep track of a large amount of data. This is a perfect Outlook/MTS application. Outlook will route the approval requests while SQL Server and MTS track all the applicant's information.

13

> **NOTE**
>
> When designing these types of systems, many people attempt to actually route the data along with the approval request. This is an inefficient use of Outlook and should be avoided. Instead, use Outlook to simply route the notification of status.

All the applicant's information should be kept in SQL Server. In this way, you can keep all data centralized, which is safer, and also allows you to easily build management tracking systems that report on the overall process. Figure 13.12 shows an overview of the standard application architecture.

FIGURE 13.12

This diagram shows the standard parts of an MTS/Outlook application.

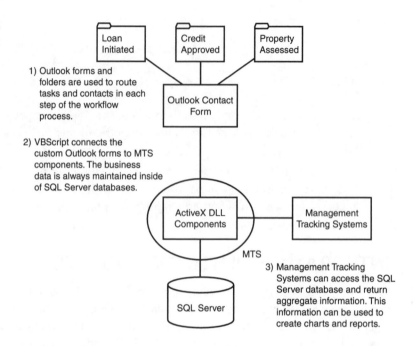

1) Outlook forms and folders are used to route tasks and contacts in each step of the workflow process.

2) VBScript connects the custom Outlook forms to MTS components. The business data is always maintained inside of SQL Server databases.

3) Management Tracking Systems can access the SQL Server database and return aggregate information. This information can be used to create charts and reports.

Creating a Folder System

As part of any workflow application, you will have to create a set of folders that represent work queues for the application. These folders should be defined by the discrete steps in the application. For our mortgage process we might define folders for Loan Initiation, Credit Check, and Property Assessed. Each customer would work through the series of folders until a decision was made.

Along with the folders, you will want to create a custom form. The custom form can be based on any of the standard Outlook forms; however, we have found that the Contacts module makes the best template for such systems. Therefore, your folders would be created as contact folders and you would customize the standard Contact form for your own application. The customized form should contain information necessary to route the form in Outlook as well as empty fields that will be filled by calling to MTS components.

When the form is routed, you will use logic based on the status of the item to find the next folder. When you determine what folder to place the item in, route the item and remove it from the current folder. As an example, if we are moving an item from the Initiated folder to the Cancelled folder, the following code could be used:

```
'Locate Key Folders
Set MAPINameSpace = Application.GetNameSpace("MAPI")
Set MTSFolder = MAPINameSpace.Folders("My Application")
```

```
Set OrderFolder = MTSFolder.Folders("Order Entry")

Select Case pgStatus.cboStatus.Text
  Case "Initiated"
    Set TargetFolder = OrderFolder.Folders("Initiated Items")
  Case "Processing"
    Set TargetFolder = OrderFolder.Folders("Processing Items")
  Case "Approved"
    Set TargetFolder = OrderFolder.Folders("Approved Items")
  Case "Cancelled"
    Set TargetFolder = OrderFolder.Folders("Cancelled Items")
End Select

'Create New Item
Set NewItem = TargetFolder.Items.Add("IPM.Contact.MyForm")

'Save New Item
NewItem.Save

'Delete This Item
Item.Delete
```

In the preceding code, notice that we never actually send an Outlook item from one form to another. Instead, we locate the target folder and add a new item to the folder. This gives the impression that the item was sent, while giving you the flexibility to create the new item in any way you see fit. Users of the application see the item moving from folder to folder while your code processes it in the background.

Interacting with MTS

Calling MTS components from Outlook is a simple matter of using the CreateObject method. There are no special requirements to call an MTS component from Outlook other than the required registry entries. Outlook simply behaves as another VBScript front end, which is similar to using DHTML as a front end. Perhaps the biggest problem when writing the Outlook code is the fact that Outlook has a fairly primitive development environment. We have suffered at length to track down simple typographical errors in our code. But when the application is complete, the results have been worth the effort.

Creating Management Systems

An application that uses Outlook and MTS will undoubtedly have reporting requirements. This is perhaps the greatest strength of this system. Along with the strong workflow features, you can easily write Visual Basic applications that track the overall system. You can query the database by status to reflect the number of items in each Outlook folder, who has responsibility for that item, and its current status. You can also use Visual Basic's report designer to create professional reports on the system.

13

INTERFACING MS
OUTLOOK AND
MTS

EXERCISE 13-1: MTS AND OUTLOOK

This exercise integrates Outlook and MTS to create an order entry system. The system contains four folders that track an order. The system recognizes four valid states for an order: new, paid, shipped, and canceled. Before you can create this exercise, you must have Outlook installed on your machine.

Creating the PST File

In this section, you will create a PST file. This file will function as a design environment for the new Outlook application.

Step 1

If you have already installed the PST file for this chapter, you may skip this section. If not, you must install the PST file before you can begin the exercise. PST files are used by Outlook to create new folders and forms. On the CD-ROM, locate the file EXERCISE13.PST.

Step 2

Using the File Explorer, create a new directory on your hard drive called MTS/ EXERCISE13. Copy the PST file from the CD-ROM into the new directory you created.

Step 3

Because the CD-ROM creates read-only versions of the files, right-click the PST file and select **Properties** from the pop-up menu. Uncheck the read-only flag and close the properties dialog.

Step 4

Start Microsoft Outlook. If the folder list is not already visible, open it by selecting **View, Folder List** from the menu.

Step 5

Add the new PST file to your Outlook view by selecting **File, New, Personal Folders File** from the menu. Locate the EXERCISE13.PST file on your hard drive and click the Create button. The PST file should now be visible in your folder list. This PST is named "Outlook and MTS" and contains templates for the Outlook exercises in this chapter.

Copying the Visual Basic Projects

After the PST file is installed on your system, you will need to copy the Visual Basic files from the CD-ROM. These files are also contained on the CD-ROM in the EXERCISE13 directory.

Step 6

Copy all the files from the EXERCISE13 directory into the MTS\ EXERCISE13 directory you created earlier. You must copy all the files including the ORDERS.MDB database, which is used to for maintaining order information. You will need to record the complete path to ORDERS.MDB for later.

Path to
ORDERS.MDB:_____\ORDERS.MDB

Step 7

Because the CD-ROM creates read-only versions of the files, right-click the PST file and select **Properties** from the pop-up menu. Uncheck the read-only flag and close the properties dialog.

Creating the MTS Component

In this section, you will create an MTS component to call from Outlook. You will also create a separate application to perform reporting.

Step 8

On your hard drive, locate the Visual Basic project group named EXERCISE13.VBG. Open this file in Visual Basic. This project group contains an ActiveX DLL project named OutlookMTS and a Standard EXE project named OutlookEIS. The ActiveX DLL project is the MTS component that we will use to read and write information to the ORDERS.MDB database. The Standard EXE project is an Executive Information System (EIS) used to track the overall status of the application.

Step 9

In the Project Explorer, locate the OutlookMTS project. This project contains a single class named Orders. Open the code window for the Orders class.

Step 10

This component contains three key methods, which you will code: Query, Update, and GetCounts. The Query method is used to retrieve information from the database about a current Order. The method uses a firehose cursor to return a Variant array full of information based on an OrderID. This method is called by a customized Outlook form any time the form is opened. Locate the Query method and add the following code to return the Variant array:

```
On Error GoTo QueryErr

    'Get Object Context
    Dim objContext As MTxAs.ObjectContext
```

```
    Set objContext = GetObjectContext()

    'Get Data for this order
    Dim objRecordset As ADODB.Recordset
    Set objRecordset = New ADODB.Recordset

    objRecordset.CursorLocation = adUseServer
    objRecordset.CursorType = adOpenForwardOnly
    objRecordset.LockType = adLockReadOnly
    objRecordset.CacheSize = 1

    objRecordset.ActiveConnection = "Data Source=<Your database path>"
    objRecordset.Source = "SELECT * FROM Orders WHERE OrderID =" _
        & SQ & strOrderID & SQ

    objRecordset.Open
    If objRecordset.BOF And objRecordset.EOF Then
        ReDim vData(7, 0)
        vData(0, 0) = MakeGUID
        Query = True
    Else
        vData = objRecordset.GetRows
        Query = False
    End If

    'Tell MTS we succeeded
     objContext.SetComplete

QueryExit:
    Exit Function

QueryErr:
    'Tell MTS we failed
     objContext.SetAbort

    'Get Error Code
    ReDim vData(7, 1)
    vData(0, 1) = "ERROR:" & Err.Description

    Debug.Print Err.Description
    App.StartLogging App.Path & "\error.log", vbLogToFile
    App.LogEvent Err.Description, vbLogEventTypeError
    Resume QueryExit
```

Step 11

When a user opens the customized Outlook form, he will see all the pertinent data from the database. He is then free to edit information as the order progresses through the system. When he closes the form, we have to write the data back to the database. This is done by sending the Variant array back to the Update method. The Update method then builds a SQL statement to update the database. Add the following code to update the database from the `Variant` array:

```
On Error GoTo UpdateErr

    Update = True

    'Get Object Context
    Dim objContext As MTxAs.ObjectContext
    Set objContext = GetObjectContext()

    'Build SQL String
    Dim strSQL As String

    If blnNew Then
        strSQL = "INSERT INTO Orders (OrderID,LastName,FirstName,"
        strSQL = strSQL & "Address,Phone,EMail,Product,Status) VALUES "
        strSQL = strSQL & "(" & SQ & vData(OrderID, 0) & SQ
        strSQL = strSQL & "," & SQ & vData(LastName, 0) & SQ
        strSQL = strSQL & "," & SQ & vData(FirstName, 0) & SQ
        strSQL = strSQL & "," & SQ & vData(Address, 0) & SQ
        strSQL = strSQL & "," & SQ & vData(Phone, 0) & SQ
        strSQL = strSQL & "," & SQ & vData(EMail, 0) & SQ
        strSQL = strSQL & "," & SQ & vData(Product, 0) & SQ
        strSQL = strSQL & "," & SQ & vData(Status, 0) & SQ & ")"
    Else
        strSQL = "UPDATE Orders  SET LastName = " _
            & SQ & vData(LastName, 0) & SQ
        strSQL = strSQL & ", FirstName = " _
            & SQ & vData(FirstName, 0) & SQ
        strSQL = strSQL & ", Address = " _
            & SQ & vData(Address, 0) & SQ
        strSQL = strSQL & ", Phone = " _
            & SQ & vData(Phone, 0) & SQ
        strSQL = strSQL & ", EMail = " _
            & SQ & vData(EMail, 0) & SQ
        strSQL = strSQL & ", Product = " _
            & SQ & vData(Product, 0) & SQ
        strSQL = strSQL & ", Status = " _
            & SQ & vData(Status, 0) & SQ
        strSQL = strSQL & " WHERE OrderID = " _
            & SQ & vData(OrderID, 0) & SQ
    End If

    'Execute Query
    Dim objConnection As ADODB.Connection
    Set objConnection = New ADODB.Connection
    objConnection.ConnectionString = _
    "Provider=Microsoft.Jet.OLEDB.3.51;Data Source=" _
    & "<Your database path>\Orders.mdb"
    objConnection.Open
```

```
    objConnection.Execute strSQL

    'Tell MTS we succeeded
    objContext.SetComplete

UpdateExit:
    Exit Function

UpdateErr:
    'Tell MTS we failed
    objContext.SetAbort

    Update = False

    Debug.Print Err.Description
    App.StartLogging App.Path & "\error.log", vbLogToFile
    App.LogEvent Err.Description, vbLogEventTypeError
    Resume UpdateExit
```

Step 12

After the code is entered, set a reference to OutlookMTS from OutlookEIS. Once the reference is set, compile both projects by selecting **File, Make Project Group** from the menu. This will create a DLL file for use with MTS and a complete EIS that you can run to examine the database.

Step 13

Start the MTS Explorer. In the Explorer, create a new empty package named Outlook. Install the OutlookMTS component into the new package.

Creating the Outlook Application

In this section, you will create the Outlook application. This application will call the MTS component.

Step 14

Return to Microsoft Outlook and locate the folder named Outlook and MTS. In this folder, you will see a subfolder named Order Entry. Open this folder and you will see four additional folders. Each of these folders is based on the Contacts module and represents a step in the order entry process.

Step 15

Click the Order Entry folder. In this folder, you will find a customized form named Order form. This is the form we will use to route the order and interact with the MTS component. Open this form by holding down the Shift key and selecting **Actions, New Order Form** from the menu. Note: Holding down the Shift key while opening the form prevents any code in the form from running.

Step 16

Enter design mode for the form by selecting **Tools, Forms, Design This Form** from the menu. Notice that the form has two active tabs: Order and Status. The Order tab contains essential information about the order while the status tab tracks the progression of the item through the folder system. The information on these tabs is stored in the database and returned when the form is opened. However, you should note that the First Name, Last Name, and OrderID are also stored in Outlook. This is necessary because Outlook needs some information in order to manage the item. Figure 13.13 shows the form.

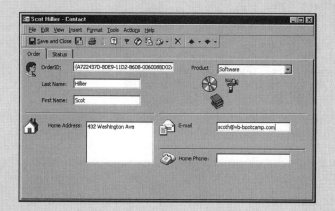

FIGURE 13.13

This form is used to route the order through the folder system.

Step 17

Open the script editor for this form by selecting **Form, View Code** from the menu. This form contains two event handlers: `Item_Open`, and `cmdProcess_Click`. The `Open` event fires when the form is opened by a user. This event initializes the form and returns key information from the database through the MTS component. Add the following code to the `Item_Open` event to read the database:

```
'Get Pages References
Set pgOrder = Item.GetInspector.ModifiedFormPages("Order")
Set pgStatus = Item.GetInspector.ModifiedFormPages("Status")

'Fill Combo Boxes
pgOrder.cboProducts.AddItem "Software"
pgOrder.cboProducts.AddItem "Books"
pgOrder.cboProducts.AddItem "Movies"
pgStatus.cboStatus.AddItem "New Order"
pgStatus.cboStatus.AddItem "Paid Order"
pgStatus.cboStatus.AddItem "Shipped Order"
```

```
pgStatus.cboStatus.AddItem "Cancelled Order"

'Get Data From Database
Set objBusiness = Application.CreateObject("OutlookMTS.Orders")
blnNew = objBusiness.Query(Item.UserProperties("OrderID").Value,vData)

'Fill Form with Data
If UCase(Left(vData(0,0),5)) = "ERROR" Then
  MsgBox "Data Access Error!"
Else
  Item.UserProperties("OrderID").Value = vData(0,0)
  Item.LastName = vData(1,0) & ""
  Item.FirstName = vData(2,0) & ""
  pgOrder.txtAddress.Text = vData(3,0) & ""
  pgOrder.txtPhone.Text = vData(4,0) & ""
  pgOrder.txtEMail.Text = vData(5,0) & ""
  pgOrder.cboProducts.Text = vData(6,0) & ""
  pgStatus.cboStatus.Text = vData(7,0) & ""
End If
```

Step 18

The cmdProcess_Click event fires when the user of a form clicks the Process Order button. This button causes the item to be routed based on its status and then update the database with new information. Add the following code to the cmdProcess_Click event to route the form and update the database through the MTS component:

```
'Update the Database
vData(0,0) = Item.UserProperties("OrderID").Value & ""
vData(1,0) = Item.LastName & ""
vData(2,0) = Item.FirstName & ""
vData(3,0) = pgOrder.txtAddress.Text & ""
vData(4,0) = pgOrder.txtPhone.Text & ""
vData(5,0) = pgOrder.txtEMail.Text & ""
vData(6,0) = pgOrder.cboProducts.Text & ""
vData(7,0) = pgStatus.cboStatus.Text & ""

blnResults = objBusiness.Update(vData,blnNew)

'Route the Order
If blnResults = False Then
  MsgBox "Data Access Error!"
Else

  'Locate Key Folders
  Set MAPINameSpace = Application.GetNameSpace("MAPI")
  Set MTSFolder = MAPINameSpace.Folders("Outlook and MTS")
  Set OrderFolder = MTSFolder.Folders("Order Entry")

  Select Case pgStatus.cboStatus.Text
    Case "New Order"
```



```
        Set TargetFolder = OrderFolder.Folders("New Orders")
    Case "Paid Order"
        Set TargetFolder = OrderFolder.Folders("Paid Orders")
    Case "Shipped Order"
        Set TargetFolder = OrderFolder.Folders("Shipped Orders")
    Case "Cancelled Order"
        Set TargetFolder = OrderFolder.Folders("Cancelled Orders")
    End Select

    'Create New Item
    Set NewItem = TargetFolder.Items.Add("IPM.Contact.OrderForm")

    'Fill New Item
    Set pgNewOrder = NewItem.GetInspector.ModifiedFormPages("Order")
    pgNewOrder.txtOrderID.Text = vData(0,0) & ""
    pgNewOrder.txtLastName.Text = vData(1,0) & ""
    pgNewOrder.txtFirstName.Text = vData(2,0) & ""

    'Save New Item
    NewItem.Save

    'Delete This Item
    Item.Delete
End If
```

Step 19

When your work is complete, close the script editor by selecting **File, Close**. Publish the form by selecting **Tools, Forms, Publish Form** from the menu. You should also make a backup copy of your form by selecting **File, Save As**. This will allow you to save the form as an Outlook template. Outlook templates are saved with an OFT extension. If you make a mistake with your form or lose it, you can recover by opening the OFT file. Save the form as ORDERFORM.OFT in the EXERCISE13 directory. If a form exists in this directory by the same name, overwrite it.

Running the Application

In this section, you run the application. You will create new orders and track them. You will also get to try out the reporting application.

Step 20

When you have finished the form, you are ready to run the application. In Outlook, open a new copy of the Order Form by selecting **Actions, New Order Form**. This time, do not hold down the Shift key. The form should open and a new OrderID will be visible. Fill out the form for a new order. On the Status tab, select New Order for the status. Then click the Process Order button. The order should appear in the New Orders folder. Create several more new orders.

13

INTERFACING MS OUTLOOK AND MTS

Step 21

Now open an item in the New Orders folder. Try changing the status of the item and processing it. The item should move to a new folder. Now try changing some information on the order. The database should update accordingly.

Step 22

When the system is working, try running the EIS. The EIS was compiled earlier and should exist as OUTLOOKEIS.EXE. When you run this application, you should see a pie chart showing the relative volumes in each of the folders. Try out the reporting mechanism as well by clicking the Report button. Figure 13.14 shows the EIS form.

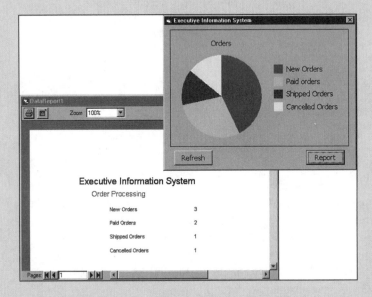

FIGURE **13.14**

The EIS tracks the overall system performance.

PROJECTS

PART III

IN THIS PART

THE DATA SERVICES LAYER PROJECT

Throughout this book, we have taught the fundamental concepts and skills necessary to create distributed applications with Microsoft Transaction Server. In the last three chapters, we will put this knowledge to use by constructing a moderately sophisticated application. This application will simulate some typical banking functions including customer account management and automated teller services. The beauty of this type of application is that we can assume you are already familiar with the business rules surrounding banking. This allows us to concentrate on the design process and the actual code.

PROJECT DESCRIPTION

Before beginning to design any application, you should create a narrative description of the project. This serves as a high-level definition that is responsible for drawing boundaries beyond which the application will not grow. Even though most members of the team will feel that a project description is a statement of the obvious, defining the scope of your project as soon as possible is a key to success.

The MTS Bank is designed to be a training application that simulates several banking processes. The total application will consist of two separate business processes. The first one is a customer management process that allows a bank employee to manage customer account information. The second process is an automated teller system that allows customers with accounts to perform common transactions. These transactions include balance inquiry, deposit, withdrawal, and funds transfer.

Because the application is a training application, we can simplify some of the processes to enhance the educational aspects of the project. The application should focus on utilizing the skills taught throughout the book. Writing the application should be achievable by a student within the context of a week-long class.

CREATING USE CASES

After the project description, we will need to create a set of "use cases" for our applications. Use cases, for those who are not familiar with the term, are documents that identify the key roles played by a user of an application and sequence of events through which the user interacts with the software. Use cases are critical for successfully creating a distributed application. In this section, we will create some simplified use cases for our project, just to give you an idea of how to proceed. The topic of use cases alone is larger than a single chapter will allow, but they are relatively straightforward, and you will get the idea quickly.

The ATM Customers Module

"ATM Customers" is our official title for the module that will allow bank employees to manage customer and account information. For this module, we have identified a single role for the application user. This is the role of "Employee." Employees will use the ATM Customers module to add new customers, add new accounts, edit customer information, and edit account information. The following sections contain the simplified use cases that come from the combination of role and function.

Use Case 1-1: Add a New Customer

PREREQUISITES
Before adding a customer, the employee must have logged into the ATM Customers module.

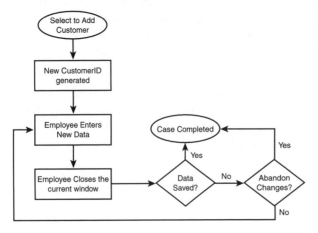

Sequence of events:

1. The employee selects to add a new customer to the system.

2. A new customer identifier is generated by the system.

3. The employee enters personal customer information into the system.

FIGURE 14.1

4. The employee enters a new Personal Identification Number (PIN) for the customer.

5. The employee selects to close the current window.

6. The new customer information will automatically be added to the database when the window is closed. This application does not require an explicit save action.

7. If an error occurs while updating the database, the user can choose to keep the window open and correct the error, or close the window and abandon the changes.

Outcome: A new customer is added to the database.

Use Case 1-2: Add a New Account

PREREQUISITES

Before adding an account, the employee must have logged into the ATM Customers module. The employee must also have a valid customer window open.

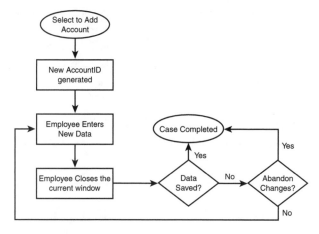

FIGURE **14.2**

Sequence of events:

1. The employee selects to add a new savings or checking account to a customer.

2. A new account number is generated by the system.

3. The employee enters a new balance for the account.

4. The employee selects to close the current window.

5. The new customer information will automatically be added to the database when the window is closed. This application does not require an explicit save action.

6. If an error occurs while updating the database, the user can choose to keep the window open and correct the error, or close the window and abandon the changes.

Outcome: A new customer account is added to the database.

14

THE DATA
SERVICES LAYER
PROJECT

Use Case 1-3: Edit Customer Information

PREREQUISITES

Before editing a customer, the employee must have logged into the ATM Customers module.

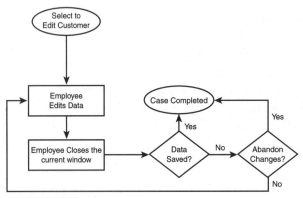

FIGURE 14.3

Sequence of events:

1. The employee selects to retrieve information about a customer.

2. The employee fills out a search screen to locate the customer information.

3. A new application window opens listing all customer identifiers that matched the search criteria.

4. The employee selects the customer to edit.

5. When the customer is selected, the window displays the essential customer information such as name and address. Additional tabs in the window allow access to account information.

6. The employee edits the data in the window. The edited data is saved automatically when the window is closed.

7. If the employee makes the PIN field blank, an error occurs and the window will not close.

8. If an error occurs while updating the database, the user can choose to keep the window open and correct the error, or close the window and abandon the changes.

Outcome: The database is updated with the edited information.

Use Case 1-4: Edit Account Information

PREREQUISITES

Before editing an account, the employee must have logged into the ATM Customers module. The employee must also have searched for and located valid customer information.

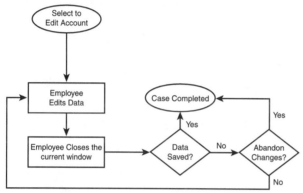

FIGURE 14.4

Sequence of events:

1. The employee selects the account to edit.

2. When the account is selected, an open window displays the essential account information such as balance. Additional tabs in the window allow access to customer information.

3. The employee edits the data in the window. The edited data is saved automatically when the window is closed.

4. If an error occurs while updating the database, the user can choose to keep the window open and correct the error, or close the window and abandon the changes.

Outcome: The database is updated with the edited information.

The ATM Module

"ATM module" is the name for the portion of the application that will allow customers to interact with our simulated bank. This module will allow balance inquiries, deposits, withdrawals, and transfers. Transfers can be between accounts in the same bank or between accounts in different banks. For simplicity, we define two banks for the system: First Federal Banks and First National Bank. This module has only the Customer role associated with it.

Use Case 2-1: Getting an Account Balance

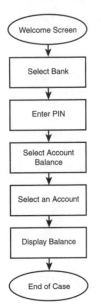

FIGURE 14.5

Sequence of events:

1. The ATM displays a welcome screen and the customer selects a bank.
2. Customer enters PIN number for selected bank.
3. The customer selects to return an account balance.
4. The customer selects to check the balance of either the savings or checking account.

Outcome: The system displays the current balance of the selected account.

Use Case 2-2: Depositing Funds to an Account

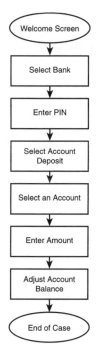

FIGURE **14.6**

Sequence of events:

1. The ATM displays a welcome screen and the customer selects a bank.
2. Customer enters PIN number for selected bank.
3. The customer selects to perform an account deposit.
4. The customer selects to deposit money into the savings or checking account.
5. The customer enters the amount of the deposit.

Outcome: The system adds the deposited amount to the account balance.

Use Case 2-3: Withdrawing Funds from an Account

PREREQUISITES
The ATM module is running.

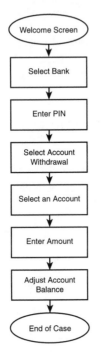

FIGURE 14.7

Sequence of events:

1. The ATM displays a welcome screen and the customer selects a bank.
2. Customer enters PIN number for selected bank.
3. The customer selects to perform an account withdrawal.
4. The customer selects to withdraw money from the checking or savings account.
5. The customer enters the amount to withdraw.

Outcome: The system subtracts the withdrawn funds from the account balance.

Use Case 2-4: Transferring Funds with the Same Bank

PREREQUISITES
The ATM module is running.

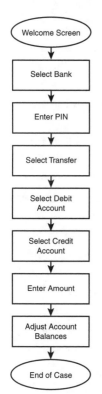

FIGURE 14.8

Sequence of events:

1. The ATM displays a welcome screen and the customer selects a bank.
2. Customer enters PIN number for selected bank.
3. The customer selects to transfer funds between accounts in the same bank.
4. The customer selects the account to be debited.
5. The customer selects the account to be credited.
6. The customer enters the amount of the transfer.

Outcome: The transfer amount is subtracted from the debit account balance and added to the credit account balance.

Use Case 2-5: Transferring Funds to Another Bank

> **PREREQUISITES**
> The ATM module is running.

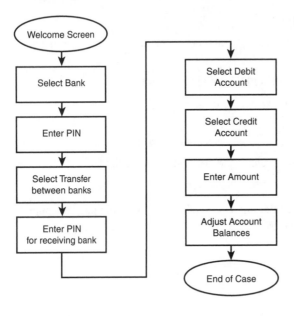

FIGURE 14.9

Sequence of events:

1. The ATM displays a welcome screen and the customer selects a bank.

2. Customer enters PIN number for selected bank.

3. The customer selects to transfer funds between accounts in different banks.

4. The customer enters the PIN number for the bank to receive funds.

5. The customer selects the account to be debited.

6. The customer selects the account to be credited.

7. The customer enters the amount of the transfer.

Outcome: The transfer amount is subtracted from the debit account balance and added to the credit account balance.

CREATING A PAPER PROTOTYPE

After the use cases are defined and the sequence of events is understood, you should have a good idea of the boundaries of your system. The next step is to create a "paper prototype" of your system. A paper prototype is a series of screen shots that you can use to walk through the sequence of events that you described in each use case.

We cannot emphasize enough the need to create a paper prototype; however, most project teams fail to create one. One of the primary reasons that a paper prototype is never created is because Visual Basic itself is often used to fill this gap. Project teams mistakenly believe that they can perform research and development in Visual Basic at this stage and use the results as a conceptual prototype.

It would be acceptable to use Visual Basic to create a conceptual prototype if you threw all the code away when you were done. The reality, however, is that when you have some working code, it is impossible to throw it away. Managers and customers who see working software are not likely to appreciate that the internals of the code may be poorly constructed. They will simply see the software and ask why you cannot deliver it sooner. Therefore, you should never use Visual Basic code as a substitute for a paper prototype.

The ATM Customers Module

The ATM Customers module utilizes a multiple-document interface (MDI) to allow employees to open multiple windows. Each individual window in the MDI environment represents the results of a search for customer information. The application uses standard database security and requires a login when the employee starts the application. The following sections show the screens for this module.

The Login Screen

FIGURE 14.10

The Login screen is used to enter a user name and password for data access.

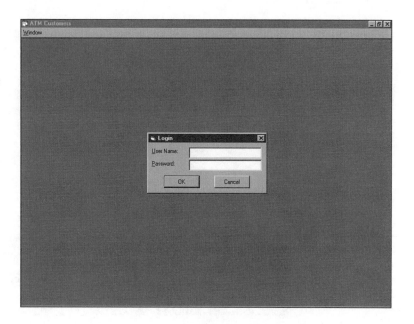

The Main Screen

FIGURE 14.11

The Main screen is an MDI form with a single menu allowing an employee to start a new search.

The Search Screen

FIGURE 14.12

The Search screen is used to set the search parameters for customer and account information.

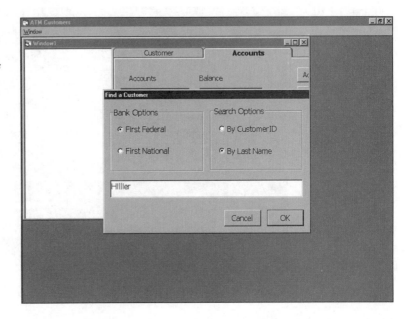

The Data Screen

FIGURE **14.13**

The Data screen is used to display the results of a search.

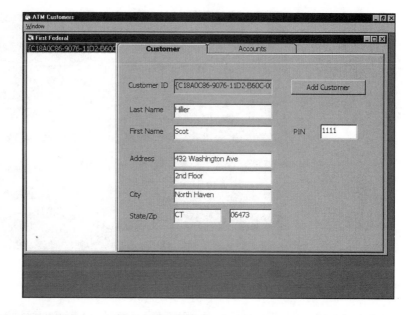

The ATM Module

The ATM module uses a Visual Basic form as an interface. This form is designed to simulate the look and feel of a standard ATM machine. The form has a black background with a green letter display. The flow of this application mimics a standard ATM in that it uses several control buttons on a single screen to control the workflow. The following sections show the ATM in various modes.

The Welcome Screen

FIGURE **14.14**
The Welcome screen is the launch point for the application.

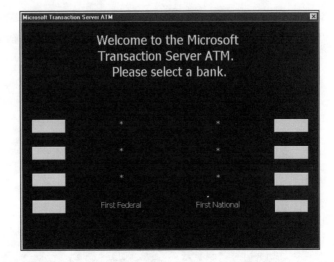

The PIN Screen

FIGURE **14.15**
The PIN screen is used to enter the PIN number for the customer.

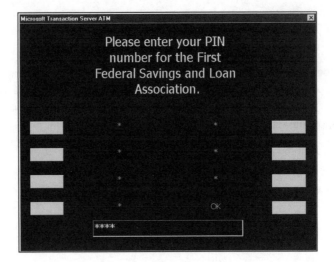

The Transaction Selection Screen

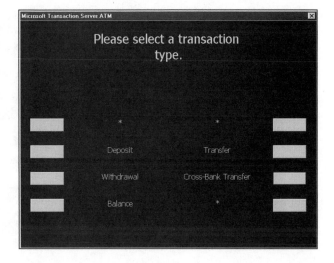

The Account Selection Screen

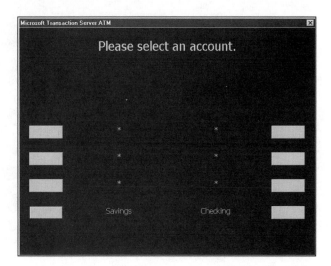

14

THE DATA
SERVICES LAYER
PROJECT

The Balance Screen

FIGURE 14.18

The Balance Selection screen displays an account balance.

The Deposit Amount Screen

FIGURE 14.19

The Deposit Amount screen allows the Customer to enter the amount of the deposit.

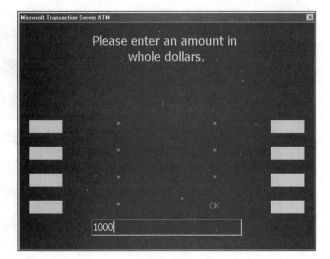

The Withdrawal Amount Screen

FIGURE 14.20
The Withdrawal Amount screen allows the customer to enter the amount of the withdrawal.

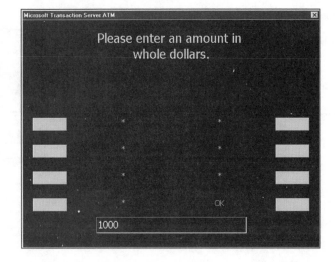

The Credit Account Selection Screen

FIGURE 14.21
The Credit Account screen allows the customer to select the account to credit with a funds transfer.

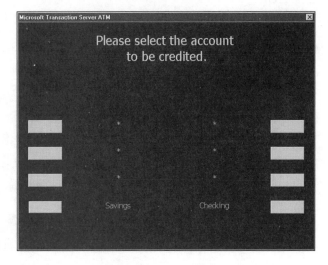

The Debit Account Selection Screen

FIGURE 14.22

The Debit Account screen allows the customer to select the account to debit from a funds transfer.

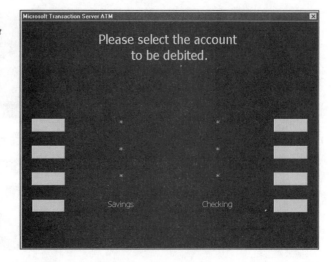

The Transaction Completed Screen

FIGURE 14.23

The Transaction Completed screen tells the user that a transaction is completed.

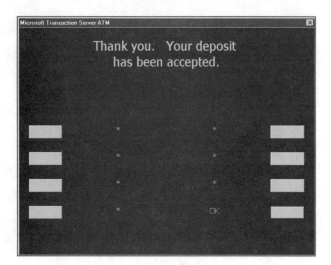

The New Transaction Screen

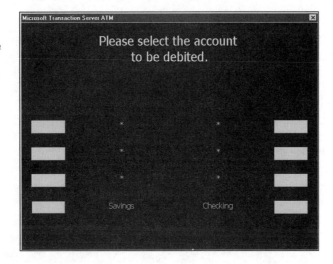

THE LOGICAL MODEL

When you have created the paper prototype and used it to verify the use cases, you are ready to create the logical model for the application. The logical model is a component-based view of the application you are trying to create. This model will be divided into the three tiers and show building blocks within the tiers. The output should be tested against the use cases to verify that you have included all the components necessary to meet the functional requirements of the application.

We create our models using the Microsoft Visual Modeler. This tool forms the boundary between design requirements and code. Because Visual Modeler supports round-trip engineering, we can use the model we create as a starting point for coding the application.

The ATM Customers Module

The ATM Customers module is far and away the more complicated of the two modules in our application. Figure 14.25 shows the model for the ATM Customers module. This module utilizes many of the features discussed throughout this book. For instance, this module uses several Data Services components to wrap stored procedure calls. These components consist of `CustomersByID`, `CustomersByName`, `AccountsByID`,

AccountsByName, TransactionsByID, TransactionsByName, and DataWrite. These components implement the standard Data Services interfaces IReadData and IWriteData. Notice the open-arrow symbol showing how the classes implement a particular interface.

The Business Services layer component called Manager helps to manage database transactions by calling the Data Services components and offering a single point of interface to the User Services. The Manager class is set to require a new transaction, whereas all the Data Services components are set to require transactions.

The User Services layer consists not only of forms (for example, frmSearch and frmChild), but also an object model. The objects Bank, Customers, Accounts, and Transactions are used to model the business process. Notice how several of these classes implement the ICollection interface, which defines the characteristics of objects that hold data sets in this application. The objects in the model are then used as a data source for the forms.

FIGURE 14.25

The logical model for the ATM Customers module.

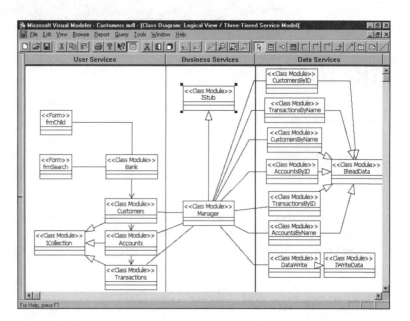

The ATM Module

The ATM module is considerably simpler than the ATM Customers module. This project is designed to show several key aspects of MTS application while sparing many of the more difficult details. If you are looking for an easier place to start, you might want to try constructing the ATM module before you build the ATM Customers module.

The ATM module utilizes the same transactional architecture as the ATM Customers module. The Data Services layer consists of two classes, `Reader` and `Transactor`. Each Data Services class is set to require a transaction. The Business Services layer consists of just one class named `Manager`, which offers a single point of contact to the User Services. The User Services layer is simplified because it contains only a single component, named `Controller`, for managing state and flow as opposed to a full object model. This module also does not utilize any interfaces. Figure 14.26 shows the logical model for the ATM module.

FIGURE 14.26

The logical model for the ATM module.

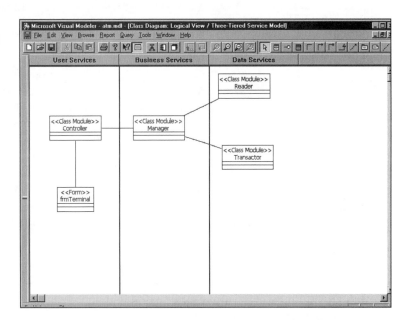

COMPONENT DESCRIPTIONS

When you have completed the logical model, you are ready to create the component descriptions. The component descriptions will detail the exact components that must be constructed to complete the application. In a detailed specification, you should name each component and describe its functions. You should also indicate exactly how the classes and forms would be grouped into Visual Basic projects. Because we will cover all the components in later chapters, we will limit ourselves to a single table that groups the classes and forms from the logical model into Visual Basic projects. Table 14.1 lists the classes and forms from the logical models and designates their respective Visual Basic project.

TABLE 14.1   CLASSES, FORMS, AND PROJECTS

	Project Name	*Class/Form*
ATM Customers	CustomerUserInterfaces	ICollection
	CustomerApp	frmChild
		frmSearch
	CustomerModel	Bank
		Customers
		Accounts
		Transactions
	CustomerBusinessInterfaces	IStub
	CustomerBusinessServices	Manager
	CustomerDataInterfaces	IReadData
		WriteData
	CustomerDataServices	CustomerByID
		CustomersByName
		AccountsByID
		AccountsByName
		TransactionsByID
	TransactionsByName	
		DataWrite
ATM	TerminalManager	Controller
	Terminal	frmTerminal
	ATM	Manager
	DataManager	Reader
		Transactor

THE PROJECT SCHEDULE

The final output of the specification should be a project schedule. Using the table of components we created earlier, assign personnel and schedule time to complete each component. You should create the schedule to build the application one module at a time. For example, plan on completing the ATM Customers module, releasing it to quality assurance, and then proceeding with the ATM module. This process allows you to complete a unit of work so that you can provide a prototype to marketing and management. As you work on the modules, you can roll changes and bug fixes back into previously released modules. Using this methodology, a project manager can easily track the progress of the application.

THE BUSINESS SERVICES LAYER PROJECT

In Chapter 14, we presented the overview and functional specification for the ATM Customers module. In this chapter, we will build the complete module. Completing this module requires that you construct an appropriate test environment. After the test environment is complete, you will build the Data Services, Business Services, and User Services respectively.

ESTABLISHING A TEST CONFIGURATION

Although the design of the system is envisioned as a distributed application running across multiple machines, most readers of this book will not have access to a dedicated test bed with several machines. Therefore, the project is designed to be created on a variety of test setups. Before you begin any work, you should create a suitable testing environment. When creating this environment, you have your choice of several different installations. You may use a single machine with all the required software installed, or you may use multiple machines in various configurations. The project uses one of four different types of installations, which we reference by a letter designation. You may choose from any of these installations to create the project.

Type A Configuration

Type A configurations are single-machine installations. In this case, you will install Windows/NT 4.0 Server, IIS 4.0, MTS 2.0, SQL Server 7.0, Internet Explorer 4.0, and Visual Basic 6.0 on the same machine. This is the simplest installation and is recommended for users who are not intimately familiar with network and domain administration. Readers of this book will find Type A installations to be the most convenient.

Type B Configuration

Type B configurations consist of two machines. In this case, you will have a single Windows/NT 4.0 Server on one machine and a client installation on a second machine. This setup allows you to investigate thin client setups or simulate remote Web access. Figure 15.1 shows the architecture for Type B configurations.

FIGURE 15.1

*Type B configura-
tions utilize a
client machine
and a server
machine.*

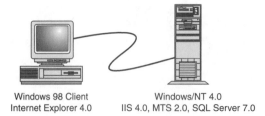

Windows 98 Client
Internet Explorer 4.0

Windows/NT 4.0
IIS 4.0, MTS 2.0, SQL Server 7.0

Type C Configuration

Type C configurations consist of three machines. In this case, one machine is a
Windows/NT 4.0 Server functioning as a middle-tier server. This machine has IIS 4.0
and MTS 2.0 installed. A second machine is also running Windows/NT 4.0 Server, but is
set up as a standalone server with SQL Server 7.0 installed. The third machine is a
domain client consisting of Windows 98 or Windows/NT Workstation with Internet
Explorer 4.0. This configuration allows you to investigate true three-tier applications.
Figure 15.2 shows the architecture for Type C configurations.

FIGURE 15.2

*Type C configura-
tions allow true
three-tier applica-
tions to be
created.*

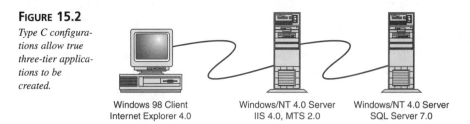

Windows 98 Client
Internet Explorer 4.0

Windows/NT 4.0 Server
IIS 4.0, MTS 2.0

Windows/NT 4.0 Server
SQL Server 7.0

Type D Configuration

Type D installations consist of more than three machines. This configuration may have
multiple MTS installations or multiple SQL Server installations. This configuration is the
most flexible and offers you the chance to investigate concepts such as distributed transactions. This configuration is recommended for individuals with extensive knowledge of
network and domain administration. You may have this configuration if your company
has a dedicated development network. True business applications that you create with
MTS will probably have this configuration. Figure 15.3 shows the architecture for Type
D configurations.

FIGURE 15.3

Type D configurations consist of several machines on a network.

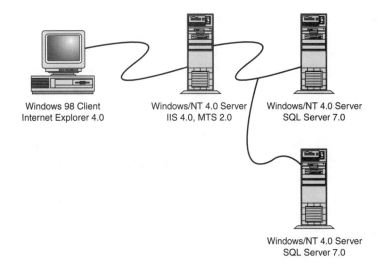

Windows 98 Client
Internet Explorer 4.0

Windows/NT 4.0 Server
IIS 4.0, MTS 2.0

Windows/NT 4.0 Server
SQL Server 7.0

Windows/NT 4.0 Server
SQL Server 7.0

DATA SERVICES

The Data Services layer for the ATM Customers module begins with the construction of the SQL Server database. This database consists of tables for bank customers, accounts, and a record of transactions for each account. Figure 15.4 shows the data model for the project.

FIGURE 15.4

The data model shows the various tables for the database.

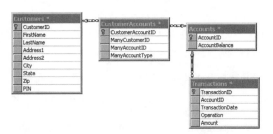

Although the database for the project is fairly simple, you should note one feature of the structure. A many-to-many relationship exists between customers and accounts. This means that a single customer may have many accounts (for example, savings and checking), and a single account may be related to many customers (for example, spouses with joint accounts). This relationship is modeled in the database by an intermediate table named CustomerAccounts.

The idea of using an intermediate table to form a many-to-many relationship is generally well understood by developers and is needed to create a normalized database. However, you should never confuse the structure of a normalized database with the way an end user wants to view data. In most database applications, developers simply reflect the underlying database structure into the front end. This often results in views of the data that are not of interest to the end user.

As an example, consider the use cases we created for the ATM Customers module. All of these use cases dealt with searching for customers and then viewing account information. We say that the ATM Customers module is "customer-centric." The use cases we described never indicated that our bank employee needed to find an account and then identify all the customers that belong to the account. The ATM Customers module is not "account-centric." Therefore, the use cases we defined do not require a many-to-many relationship. The business process, as described, dictates just a one-to-many relationship between one customer and many accounts.

This idea that the database structure may be vastly different from the presentation of the data in the front end should not surprise you. After all, database structure exists solely to satisfy the demands of normalization. Most end users have no concern in the world for normalization, so why should we force a normalized data presentation on them when they don't need it?

But wait, you say. Wouldn't it be nice to be able to add a customer to an existing account? What if a customer already exists in the bank and suddenly the spouse needs to be added? Shouldn't our application allow this? The answer is: If you want the software to allow adding customers to existing accounts, you should create the appropriate use cases and design for it. If the functionality is not required and not described by a use case, do not add it. This is the very definition of "scope creep." Many projects have been doomed by adding functionality that was not required.

If we ultimately decided to include functionality that will add new customers to an existing account, we should update our specification. This may result in an enhancement to the ATM Customers module, or it may result in a new module perhaps called ATM Accounts. For our project, however, this functionality is not in scope.

CREATING THE SQL SERVER DATABASES

Now that you understand the data model, you can create the databases for the project in SQL Server. Because the project simulates two banks, you will build two identical databases. On the CD-ROM, you will find a SQL script to help you build the database structures; however, you will have to create the new databases before you can run the script. Use the following steps to create the databases and run the SQL script.

Step 1

Start the SQL Server 7.0 Enterprise Manager. When the Enterprise Manager is running, expand the tree view and locate the Databases folder. Figure 15.5 shows the Enterprise Manager running and the Databases folder selected.

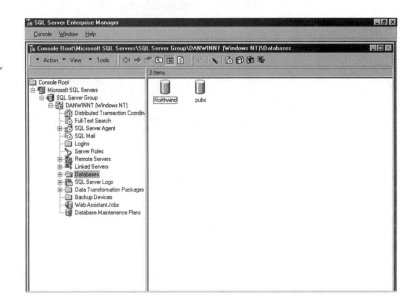

Step 2

With the Databases folder selected, create a new database by clicking **Action, New Database** from the menu. This will bring up the Database Properties dialog. In this dialog, name the new database Federal. If you are an advanced user, you may want to change some of the database properties at this point, but the default values should be acceptable for our project. Repeat this process to create a second database named National. Figure 15.6 shows the Database Properties dialog.

NOTE

Users with Type D configurations should set up the Federal database on one installation of SQL Server and the National database on a separate installation.

FIGURE 15.6
Create two new SQL Server databases for the project.

Step 3

Now that you have created the databases, you are ready to run the SQL script to create the actual database structure. To run the SQL script, you will need to start the SQL Server Query Analyzer. Start this tool by selecting **Tools, SQL Server Query Analyzer** from the menu.

When the Query Analyzer starts, you will see a command-line window where you can enter SQL statements to run against a database. The Query Analyzer contains a drop-down list of all the databases in your SQL Server installation. Open this list and select the Federal database. Figure 15.7 shows the Query Analyzer with the Federal database selected.

FIGURE 15.7
The SQL Server Query Analyzer is used to execute SQL statements against databases.

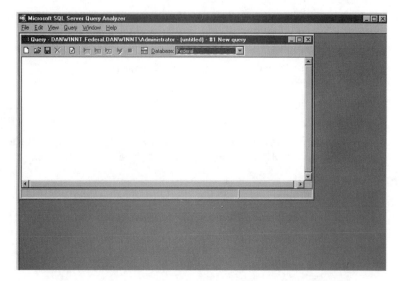

Step 4

In the SQL Server Query Analyzer, open the SQL Script for creating the databases by selecting **File, Open** from the menu. Using the Open File dialog, locate the SQL script on the CD-ROM in the directory EXERCISE15\DATA SERVICES\BANK.SQL. Open this file in the Query Analyzer.

> **NOTE**
>
> If you are using SQL Server 6.5 for the project, you must utilize a separate script file. Instead of opening BANK.SQL, copy BANKA.SQL from the CD-ROM and use this script instead.

The SQL Script is a series of statements that will build the tables and stored procedures to create a bank database. This script can be used to create both the Federal and National databases. Run this script on the Federal database by selecting **Query, Execute Query** from the menu. When the script is complete, you will see the message "The command(s) completed successfully." When you have built the Federal database, select the National database from the drop-down list and run the script again. Close the Query Analyzer when you are finished.

> **NOTE**
>
> Users with a Type D configuration should run the BANK.SQL script on each installation of SQL Server.

Step 5

When you have finished building the database, you should be able to return to the SQL Enterprise Manager and view the tables and stored procedures. Examine these items by clicking the Tables and Stored Procedures folders respectively beneath the Federal and National databases.

Step 6

This project expects to use SQL Server standard security. This means that access to SQL Server databases is determined by a separate user name and password from the Windows/NT account. Ensure that your SQL Server installation is set up to use standard security by right-clicking your server in the SQL Enterprise Manager and selecting **Properties** from the pop-up menu. This will open the SQL Server Properties dialog. In the Properties dialog, click the Security tab. Verify that the authentication is set to SQL

Server and Windows NT. Figure 15.8 shows the Properties dialog with the correct settings for standard security.

FIGURE 15.8

Ensure that your SQL Server uses standard security.

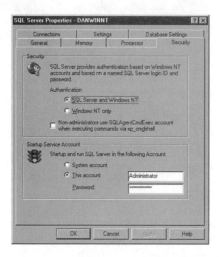

Step 7

In this application, we will utilize standard database security by requesting a user name and password from an Employee when he logs in to the system. This user name and password are utilized on read operations to verify permission to access data. However, write operations are done as a batch update with a single common database account. Additionally, the ATM project in the next chapter requires a common database account to handle all database operations. Therefore, we will need to establish a special MTS system account for accessing data in SQL Server.

In the SQL Enterprise Manager, click the Logins folder to see the available logins that are defined. In this folder, we need to create a new login for the MTS Data Services components. Create a new login by selecting **Action, New Login** from the menu. This opens the SQL Server Login Properties dialog.

In this dialog, add a new login named MTSDATA. Select to authenticate the login using SQL Server Authentication. Enter a new password for this account as **mtspassword**. Set the default database to Federal. Figure 15.9 shows the dialog with the correct information.

FIGURE 15.9
Set up a new login for MTS components.

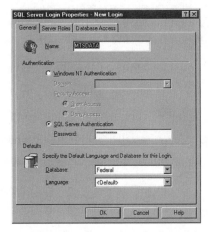

With the SQL Server Login Properties dialog still open, click the Database Access tab to assign permissions to the new login. In the Database Access tabs, permit access to the Federal and National databases for the new login. For each database you permit, assign the new login the roles of public and db_owner. Figure 15.10 shows the dialog with the correct settings.

FIGURE 15.10
Assign permissions and roles for the new login.

After you have set up a new MTS system login, repeat the process to create a personal login that you can use to access the databases. This login will be used when you run the ATM Customers module. When you are done, click the OK button to close the dialog.

> **NOTE**
>
> Users with a Type D configuration will need to set up the MTSDATA account and any personal accounts on both installations of SQL Server. Be sure to use the same name and password configurations on each installation.

Step 8 (Type D Configurations Only)

If you are using a Type D configuration for the project, you will be able to create true distributed transactions across SQL Server installations. However, you must tell each installation of SQL Server about the other. You can accomplish this by adding a remote SQL Server installation to the Remote Servers folder.

In the SQL Enterprise Manager, click the Remote Servers folder and select **Action, New Remote Server**. This opens the Remote Server Properties dialog. In this dialog, add the name of the other SQL Server installation in your configuration. Also be sure to check the RPC box to communicate via remote procedure calls. Figure 15.11 shows the dialog with the correct settings. Repeat this process for both installations of SQL Server.

FIGURE 15.11

Add a new remote server to enable distributed transactions.

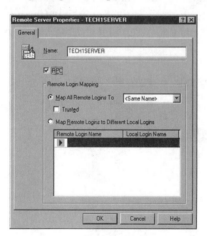

Remote servers communicate via RPC; therefore, you should ensure that the RPC services are running on both machines where SQL Server is installed. The RPC services are enabled through the Control Panel in the Services applet. In the Services applet, ensure that the RPC services are set to start automatically on start up. Figure 15.12 shows the Services applet with the correct settings.

FIGURE 15.12

Enable RPC to support distributed transactions.

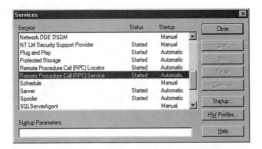

BUILDING DATA SERVICES COMPONENTS

The Data Services components in the ATM Customers module are classes that wrap the calls to the various stored procedures in the SQL Server database. These classes are very similar to each other and primarily read or write to the database. In this section, you will set up the template for the project and complete the Data Services layer.

Step 1

Before you can begin assembling this project, you must locate the project template on the CD-ROM and copy it to your machine. Using the Windows File Explorer, create a new directory on your machine named MTS\EXERCISE15. On the CD-ROM, locate the directory named EXERCISE15, and copy the contents of this directory and all subdirectories into the directory you just created on your machine.

As with all the project templates you use from the CD-ROM, the files will be flagged as read-only. Use the properties dialog for the files to remove the read-only flag. Leaving any project file marked read-only will prevent you from making changes to the template.

Step 2

After you have copied the template to your computer, locate the Visual Basic project group named ATMCUSTOMERS.VBG. Open this file in Visual Basic. When the project opens, you should see several ActiveX DLL projects and a Standard EXE project. You should immediately see that the ATM Customers module is far from trivial even though the scope of the project is small.

Step 3

In the Project Explorer, locate the project named CustomerCommon. This project contains a single class named Enumerations. Open this class and examine the code it contains. You will see that the class contains several enumerations. These enumerations are used throughout the project to provide a standard set of constants that allow the various layers to communicate effectively. Close this project.

Step 4

In the Project Explorer, locate the project named CustomerDataInterfaces. This project contains two classes that define the interfaces for use by the Data Services components. These classes are named IReadData and IWriteData. Every component in the Data Services layer implements one of these classes.

This project requires that you set a reference to ADO. Open the References dialog for this project and set a reference to Microsoft ActiveX Data Objects 2.0 Library. Close the project when you are done.

Step 5

In the Project Explorer, locate the project named `CustomerDataServices`. This project contains a class module for each stored procedure in the SQL Server database. It also contains a single class to perform batch updates, called `DataWrite`.

This project requires that you set a reference to several components. Open the References dialog for this project and set a reference to Microsoft ActiveX Data Objects 2.0 Library, Microsoft Transaction Server Type Library, `CustomerDataInterfaces`, and `CustomerCommon`. Close the project when you are done.

Most of the Data Services components are written; however, we will write one to see how it is done. In the `CustomerDataServices` Project, locate the class named `CustomersByName`. This is the class responsible for returning customers that match a search criteria for the last name. Open this class in Visual Basic.

Because this class reads data, it implements the interface `IReadData`. In this method, we call a stored procedure and return a disconnected recordset to the business layer. Notice that the `Update Criteria` property is set to perform subsequent batch updates based on the primary key. This means that we have little concern about collision handling in this application. Instead, we will perform all updates that are sent back to the system. Add the following code to the `GetRecordset` method of the `IReadData` interface in the `CustomersByName` class:

```
On Error GoTo ReadDataErr

    'Assertions
    Debug.Assert UBound(vArgs) = 3

    'Variables
    Dim strConnect As String
    Dim m_Recordset As ADODB.Recordset

    'Get Object Context
    Dim objContext As MTxAs.ObjectContext
    Set objContext = GetObjectContext()

    'Connect to appropriate data source
    strConnect = atmDatabaseConnect & _
        "UID=" & vArgs(atmUserID) & _
        ";PWD=" & vArgs(atmPassword) & ";"
    Select Case vArgs(atmBankID)
        Case atmFirstFederal
            strConnect = strConnect & _
            atmFederalConnect$ & atmDatabaseConnect$
        Case atmFirstNational
            strConnect = strConnect & _
            atmNationalConnect$ & atmDatabaseConnect$
```

```
    End Select

    'Run Query
    Set m_Recordset = New ADODB.Recordset
    m_Recordset.CursorLocation = adUseClient
    m_Recordset.Properties("Update Criteria") = adCriteriaKey
    m_Recordset.Open _
        "EXECUTE atm_GetCustomersByLastName '%" _
        & vArgs(atmQueryData) & "%'", _
        strConnect, adOpenStatic, adLockBatchOptimistic

    Set IReadData_GetRecordset = m_Recordset

    'Tell MTS we succeeded
    objContext.SetComplete

ReadDataExit:
    Exit Function

ReadDataErr:
    'Tell MTS we failed
    objContext.SetAbort

    Debug.Print Err.Description
    App.StartLogging App.Path & "\error.log", vbLogToFile
    App.LogEvent Err.Description, vbLogEventTypeError
    Resume ReadDataExit
```

Step 6

The DataWrite class implements the IWriteData interface. This component is the only component in the module that writes to the database. It writes data by performing a batch update. Because the Update Criteria property was set to adCriteriaKey when the recordset was originally created, we do not concern ourselves with detailed collision handling. Instead, this component returns a simple Boolean value to indicate success or failure. Add the following code to the PutRecordset method of the IWriteData interface in the DataWrite class:

```
On Error GoTo PutRecordsetErr

    Dim strConnect As String
    IWriteData_PutRecordset = True

    'Get Object Context
    Dim objContext As MTxAs.ObjectContext
    Set objContext = GetObjectContext()

    'Build Connect String
    strConnect = atmDatabaseConnect
    Select Case lngBankID
```

```
        Case atmFirstFederal
            strConnect = strConnect & _
            atmFederalConnect$ & atmDatabaseConnect$
        Case atmFirstNational
            strConnect = strConnect & _
            atmNationalConnect$ & atmDatabaseConnect$
    End Select

    'Reconnect to the database
    objRecordset.ActiveConnection = strConnect

    'Batch Update
    objRecordset.UpdateBatch

    'Tell MTS we succeeded
    objContext.SetComplete

PutRecordsetExit:
    Exit Function

PutRecordsetErr:
    'Tell MTS we failed
    objContext.SetAbort

    IWriteData_PutRecordset = False

    'Log the error
    Debug.Print Err.Description
    App.StartLogging App.Path & "\error.log", vbLogToFile
    App.LogEvent Err.Description, vbLogEventTypeError
    Resume PutRecordsetExit
```

BUILDING BUSINESS SERVICES COMPONENTS

The Business Services layer of the ATM Customer module consists of an interface that defines the behavior of a component and a single business object. In this section you will examine the interface and build the business object.

Step 1

In the Project Explorer, locate the project named CustomerBusinessInterfaces. This project contains a single class module named IStub. IStub defines the methods Query and Update. These methods are called by the User Services layer to request data or submit changes.

This project requires that you set a reference to two components. Open the References dialog for this project and set a reference to Microsoft ActiveX Data Objects 2.0 Library and CustomerCommon. Close the project when you have set the references.

Step 2

In the Project Explorer, locate the project named `CustomerBusinessServices`. This project contains a single class module named `Manager`. This project requires that you set a reference to several components. Open the References dialog for this project and set a reference to Microsoft ActiveX Data Objects 2.0 Library, Microsoft Transaction Server Type Library, `CustomerBusinessInterfaces`, `CustomerDataInterfaces`, `CustomerDataServices`, and `CustomerCommon`.

The `Manager` class implements the `IStub` interface. Notice that the `Query` method takes as an argument an enumerated type of `QueryTypeEnums`. This enumeration is used to specify one of several different queries that can be run. Based on the value of this argument, the `Manager` will call an appropriate Data Services component. All work done by the `Manager` class is within a transaction. The `Manager` class has its `MTSTransactionMode` property set to `4 - RequiresNewTransaction`. It enlists each Data Services object in the transaction as necessary through the `CreateInstance` method. Each Data Services component in turn has its `MTSTransactionMode` property set to `2 - RequiresTransaction`. Add the following code to the `Query` method of the `IStub` interface in class `Manager` to call the Data Services components and return data:

```
On Error GoTo QueryErr

    'Assertions
    Debug.Assert UBound(vArgs) > 0

    'Get Object Context
    Dim objContext As MTxAS.ObjectContext
    Set objContext = GetObjectContext()

    'Data Object
    Dim objDataObject As _
        CustomerDataInterfaces.IReadData

    'Call Data Services Layer
    'Based on query type
    Select Case lngType
        Case atmGetCustomersByID
            Set objDataObject = objContext.CreateInstance _
                ("CustomerDataServices.CustomersByID")
            Set IStub_Query = objDataObject.GetRecordset(vArgs)
        Case atmGetCustomersByLastName
            Set objDataObject = objContext.CreateInstance _
                ("CustomerDataServices.CustomersByName")
            Set IStub_Query = objDataObject.GetRecordset(vArgs)
        Case atmGetAccountsByID
            Set objDataObject = objContext.CreateInstance _
                ("CustomerDataServices.AccountsByID")
```

```
            Set IStub_Query = objDataObject.GetRecordset(vArgs)
        Case atmGetAccountsByLastName
            Set objDataObject = objContext.CreateInstance _
                ("CustomerDataServices.AccountsByName")
            Set IStub_Query = objDataObject.GetRecordset(vArgs)
        Case atmGetTransactionsByID
            Set objDataObject = objContext.CreateInstance _
                ("CustomerDataServices.TransactionsByID")
            Set IStub_Query = objDataObject.GetRecordset(vArgs)
        Case atmGetTransactionsByLastName
            Set objDataObject = objContext.CreateInstance _
                ("CustomerDataServices.TransactionsByName")
            Set IStub_Query = objDataObject.GetRecordset(vArgs)
    End Select

    'Tell MTS we succeeded
    objContext.SetComplete

QueryExit:
    Exit Function

QueryErr:
    'Tell MTS we failed
    objContext.SetAbort

    Debug.Print Err.Description
    App.StartLogging App.Path & "\error.log", vbLogToFile
    App.LogEvent Err.Description, vbLogEventTypeError
    Resume QueryExit
```

Step 3

Along with the Query method, the Manager also uses the Update method to call the DataWrite component in the Data Services layer. This method is fairly simple and just passes the disconnected recordset back to the Data Services layer for updating. In a more complex application, some business rules may be applied to the data at this point. In any case, the call is handled through a transaction just as it is when the data is originally returned through the Query method. Add the following code to the Update method of the IStub interface in the Manager class:

```
On Error GoTo UpdateErr

    'Get Object Context
    Dim objContext As MTxAS.ObjectContext
    Set objContext = GetObjectContext()

    'Call for Update
    Dim objDataObject As CustomerDataInterfaces.IWriteData
    Set objDataObject =
objContext.CreateInstance("CustomerDataServices.DataWrite")
```

```
        IStub_Update = objDataObject.PutRecordset(objRecordset, lngBankID)

        'Tell MTS we succeeded
        objContext.SetComplete

UpdateExit:
    Exit Function

UpdateErr:
    'Tell MTS we failed
    objContext.SetAbort

    Debug.Print Err.Description
    App.StartLogging App.Path & "\error.log", vbLogToFile
    App.LogEvent Err.Description, vbLogEventTypeError
    Resume UpdateExit
```

BUILDING USER SERVICES COMPONENTS

The User Services layer consists of an interface to define the behavior of data collections, an object model used to model the customer management, and a GUI to display the data. These components provide all the state management and workflow control for the application. In this section, you will build part of the object model.

Step 1
In the Project Explorer, locate the project named `CustomerUserInterfaces`. This project has a single class that defines the behavior of stateful objects in the User Services layer. This interface is called `ICollection`. The `ICollection` interface defines a collection class that wraps a disconnected recordset. Wrapping a disconnected recordset in a class allows you to add new features. The `ICollection` class defines two methods: `Populate` and `BatchUpdate`. These methods get data and send changes back to the Business Services layer. The interface also defines a property called `DataSource` that gives the GUI direct access to the disconnected recordset. This allows the user interface to display the data through data binding with the Microsoft Data Binding Collection.

This project requires that you set a reference to two components. Open the References dialog for this project and set a reference to Microsoft ActiveX Data Objects 2.0 Library and `CustomerCommon`. Close the project when you are done.

Step 2

In the Project Explorer, locate the project named CustomerModel. This project contains several classes that model the business data received from the database. These objects include Bank, Customers, Accounts, and Transactions. The CustomerModel is used to manage the state of the application and convert disconnected recordsets into objects that are easier to manage in the front end.

This project requires that you set a reference to several components. Open the References dialog for this project and set a reference to Microsoft ActiveX Data Objects 2.0 Library, CustomerUserInterfaces, CustomerBusinessInterfaces, CustomerBusinessServices, and CustomerCommon.

Step 3

In the CustomerModel project, most of the classes are already coded; however, we will code one collection class to see how it is done. Locate the class named Customers and open it in Visual Basic.

The Customers class implements the ICollection interface. As such, the class knows how to call the Business Services layer and return data. This is done through the Populate method. Add the following code to the Populate method of the ICollection interface in the Customers class:

```
On Error GoTo PopulateErr

    'Assertions
    Debug.Assert lngType = atmByID _
    Or lngType = atmByLastName

    'Run Query
    Select Case lngType
        Case atmByID
            Set m_Recordset = _
            m_Manager.Query(atmGetCustomersByID, vArgs)
        Case atmByLastName
            Set m_Recordset = _
            m_Manager.Query(atmGetCustomersByLastName, vArgs)
    End Select

    'Flag collection
    Populated = True

PopulateExit:
    Exit Function

PopulateErr:
    Debug.Print Err.Description
    App.StartLogging App.Path & "\error.log", vbLogToFile
```

```
App.LogEvent Err.Description, vbLogEventTypeError
Resume PopulateExit
```

Step 4

Data changed by the GUI can be sent back to the Business Services layer by calling the BatchUpdate method. This method simply passes the underlying recordset back to the Manager class in the Business Services layer. Add the following code to the BatchUpdate method of the ICollection interface for the Customers class:

```
On Error GoTo UpdateErr

    'Call for batch Updates
    ICollection_BatchUpdate = _
    m_Manager.Update(m_Recordset, m_BankID)

UpdateExit:
    Exit Function

UpdateErr:
    ICollection_BatchUpdate = False
    Debug.Print Err.Description
    App.StartLogging App.Path & "\error.log", vbLogToFile
    App.LogEvent Err.Description, vbLogEventTypeError
    Resume UpdateExit
```

Step 5

In the Project Explorer, locate the project named CustomerApp. This project contains several forms that are used to display data contained in the collections found in the CustomerModel project. Essentially, the GUI can instruct any collection to populate itself with data. The collection is then bound to display elements through the Microsoft Data Binding Collection.

This project requires that you set a reference to several components. Open the References dialog for this project and set a reference to Microsoft ActiveX Data Objects 2.0 Library, CustomerUserInterfaces, CustomerModel, Microsoft Data Binding Collection, and CustomerCommon.

COMPLETING AND RUNNING THE APPLICATION

After you have added all the code to the application, you are ready to finish the project. You must now compile the application and place components in MTS. In this section you will finish the application and get it working.

Step 1

When compiling this project, carefully compile each project in the group in the order listed following. You should be careful to ensure that the compilation paths you specify for each project are valid. Because this project is a template created on a different machine than yours, you may see invalid compilation paths suggested. This is a simple issue to fix; just specify a valid path when prompted during compilation.

Compilation Order:

- CustomerCommon
- CustomerDataInterfaces
- CustomerBusinessInterfaces
- CustomerUserInterfaces
- CustomerDataServices
- CustomerBusinessServices
- CustomerModel
- CustomerApp

Step 2

When you have successfully compiled the application, you will need to create a new Windows/NT account to run your Data Services components. To create the new account, run the User Manager for Domains applet found under **Start, Programs, Administrative Tools** on the **Start** menu. In this applet, create a new Windows/NT account named MTSUSER and enter a password of **mtspassword**. Figure 15.13 shows the User Manager applet with the correct settings.

Step 3

After you have created the new Windows/NT account, start the Microsoft Transaction Server Explorer. Open the tree view until you see the Packages Installed folder. Create a new package for your MTS components and call it ATM Customers. Be sure to set the identity for this package to the new Windows/NT account you created earlier.

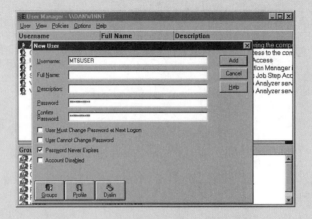

FIGURE 15.13

Create a new account to run the Data Services components.

After you create the package, you will need to install components in the package. You should install only the Data Services components and Business Services components in your new package. These are all contained in `CustomerBusinessServices` and `CustomerDataServices`. Figure 15.14 shows the MTS Explorer with the components installed.

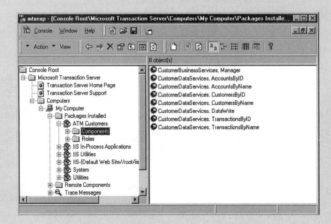

FIGURE 15.14

Add the business and data components to your new package.

Step 4

After the components are added, you may run the application by locating and starting CUSTOMERAPP.EXE. This will present a login screen. Enter the username and password for the database that you created earlier. When you're in the application, you can open a new window by selecting **Window, New Window**.

When a new window opens, you will be prompted to search for an existing customer. However, the database will be blank when you first open the application. Therefore, just click the OK button to return an empty data set. This will display a blank window. Figure 15.15 shows the window.

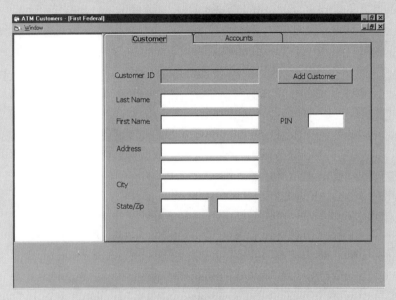

FIGURE 15.15
Open a blank window to add a new customer.

Now you can add a new customer by clicking the Add Customer button. Enter your information in the window. Be sure to enter a PIN number because it is required. Then move to the Accounts tab and add a new checking and savings account. Close the window by clicking the X in the upper-right corner, and the application will automatically update the database for you. Now go back and try opening a new window and searching for the new entry you just made.

THE USER SERVICES LAYER PROJECT

In Chapter 15, we created the ATM Customers module. After this module is created, you can use it to add new customers and accounts to the bank databases. In this chapter, you will build the ATM module. This module will simulate an automated teller machine.

PREREQUISITES

Before you begin this module, you must have properly set up a test environment. This chapter also assumes that you have set up SQL Server accounts and Windows/NT accounts. All these prerequisites will be met if you have completed the ATM Customers module in Chapter 15. However, if you want to start with the ATM module because it is simpler, you should return to Chapter 15 and perform the steps at the beginning of the exercise to meet the prerequisites for this chapter.

THE DATA SERVICES LAYER

The Data Services layer in the ATM module uses two classes in a single ActiveX DLL. These classes perform read and write operations on the database. These classes are simplified because they do not implement any interfaces. In this section, you will create the Data Services components.

PREPARING THE PROJECT TEMPLATE

Just like all the projects in this book, the ATM module utilizes a project template found on the CD-ROM. In this section you will prepare the template on your machine.

Step 1

Before you can begin assembling this project, you must locate the project template on the CD-ROM and copy it to your machine. Using the Windows File Explorer, create a new directory on your machine named MTS\EXERCISE16. On the CD-ROM, locate the directory named EXERCISE16 and copy the contents of this directory and all subdirectories into the directory you just created on your machine.

As with all the project templates you use from the CD-ROM, the files will be flagged as read-only. Use the properties dialog for the files to remove the read-only flag. Leaving any project file marked read-only will prevent you from making changes to the template.

Step 2

After you have copied the template to your computer, locate the Visual Basic project group named ATM.VBG. Open this file in Visual Basic. When the project opens, you should see several ActiveX DLL projects and a Standard EXE project.

CREATING THE DATA SERVICES COMPONENTS

The Data Services components use ADO technology to access the SQL Server database. In this section you will write the ADO code for these components.

Step 1

In the Project Explorer, locate the project named `CommonFeatures`. This project contains a single class named `Enumerations`. The enumerations in this class are used to create standard constants that are used at each level of the application. Open the `Enumerations` class and examine the definitions contained within.

Step 2

In the Project Explorer, locate the project named `DataManager`. This project contains two classes for the Data Services layer. Before coding these classes, you will need to set three references. Open the references dialog and set references to Microsoft ActiveX Data Objects 2.0 Library, Microsoft Transaction Server Type Library, and `CommonFeatures`.

In the `DataManager` project, locate the class named `Reader`. This class is responsible for reading several different pieces of data from the database. Open the code window for this class in Visual Basic.

The User Services Layer Project

CHAPTER 16

455

16

THE USER
SERVICES LAYER
PROJECT

The Reader class contains methods called GetCustomerID, GetAccountID, and GetBalance. Each of these methods is similar and simply queries the database to return information. The information is then sent to the Business Services layer as a return value of the method. In this step, we will code the GetCustomerID method to see generally how the data access is performed. Add the code in Listing 16.1 to the GetCustomerID method:

LISTING 16.1   CODE TO ADD TO THE GetCustomerID METHOD FOR THE Reader CLASS

```
On Error GoTo GetCustomerIDErr

    GetCustomerID = 0

    'Assertions
    Debug.Assert lngBank = BankEnum.atmFirstFederal _
        Or lngBank = BankEnum.atmFirstNational

    'Variables
    Dim strConnect As String
    Dim m_Recordset As ADODB.Recordset

    'Get Object Context
    Dim objContext As MTxAS.ObjectContext
    Set objContext = GetObjectContext

    'Connect to appropriate data source
    strConnect = atmDatabaseConnect
    Select Case lngBank
        Case atmFirstFederal
            strConnect = strConnect _
            & atmFederalConnect$ & atmDatabaseConnect$
        Case atmFirstNational
            strConnect = strConnect _
            & atmNationalConnect$ & atmDatabaseConnect$
    End Select

    'Run Query
    Set m_Recordset = New ADODB.Recordset
    m_Recordset.CursorLocation = adUseServer
    m_Recordset.CacheSize = 1
    m_Recordset.Open _
        "EXECUTE atm_GetCustomerID '" & strPIN & "'", _
        strConnect, adOpenForwardOnly, adLockReadOnly

    If Not (m_Recordset.BOF And m_Recordset.EOF) Then
        GetCustomerID = m_Recordset!CustomerID
    End If
```

continues

LISTING 16.1   CONTINUED

```
    'TellMTS we are successful
    objContext.SetComplete

GetCustomerIDExit:
    Set m_Recordset = Nothing
    Exit Function

GetCustomerIDErr:

    'Tell MTS we failed
    objContext.SetAbort

    GetCustomerID = ""

    'Log Error
    App.LogEvent "ERROR: " & Err.Number & " " & Err.Description & _
        "; SOURCE: " & Err.Source, vbLogEventTypeError
    Debug.Print "ERROR: " & Err.Number & " " & Err.Description & _
        "; SOURCE: " & Err.Source

    Resume GetCustomerIDExit
```

Step 3

In the `DataManager` project, locate the class named `Transactor`. Open the `Transactor`
class code window in Visual Basic. This class is responsible for writing data to the database. Its `MTSTransactionMode` property is set to `2 - RequiresTransaction`. It is called
by the Business Services layer when data must be written to the database.

In the ATM module, the only writes to the database are to adjust the balance of an
account during a transaction. The `AdjustBalance` method performs all the data writing.
This adjustment may be a single operation such as for a deposit or withdrawal. It may
also be multiple operations such as for a transfer. In any case, the transaction will encom-
pass all the calls to the `AdjustBalance` method. If any adjustment fails during a transaction, all account adjustments will roll back. Add the code in Listing 16.2 to the
`AdjustBalance` method of the `Transactor` class:

LISTING 16.2   CODE TO ADD TO THE `AdjustBalance` METHOD OF THE `Transactor`
CLASS

```
On Error GoTo AdjustBalanceErr

    'Assertions
    Debug.Assert lngBank = BankEnum.atmFirstFederal _
        Or lngBank = BankEnum.atmFirstNational
    Debug.Assert strAccountID <> ""
```

```
AdjustBalance = True

'Get Object Context
Dim objContext As MTxAS.ObjectContext
Set objContext = GetObjectContext

'Connect to appropriate data source
Dim m_Connection As ADODB.Connection
Set m_Connection = New ADODB.Connection

Select Case lngBank
    Case atmFirstFederal
        m_Connection.ConnectionString = _
        atmFederalConnect$ & atmDatabaseConnect$
    Case atmFirstNational
        m_Connection.ConnectionString = _
        atmNationalConnect$ & atmDatabaseConnect$
End Select
m_Connection.Open

'Create Command
Dim m_Command As ADODB.Command
Set m_Command = New ADODB.Command

'Adjust Account Balance
m_Command.CommandType = adCmdStoredProc
m_Command.CommandText = "atm_AdjustAccount"
Set m_Command.ActiveConnection = m_Connection

m_Command.Parameters.Append _
    m_Command.CreateParameter(Name:="@AccountID", _
    Type:=adVarChar, Size:=50, Value:=strAccountID)
m_Command.Parameters.Append _
    m_Command.CreateParameter(Name:="@Amount", _
    Type:=adCurrency, Value:=curAmount)
m_Command.Execute

'Record Transaction
m_Command.CommandText = "atm_RecordTransaction"

'Here we just add the two new parameters
'since the other two are already added
m_Command.Parameters.Append _
    m_Command.CreateParameter(Name:="@Date", _
    Type:=adDBDate, Value:=Now)
m_Command.Parameters.Append _
    m_Command.CreateParameter(Name:="@Operation", _
    Type:=adVarChar, Size:=50, Value:=strOperation)
m_Command.Execute
```

continues

LISTING 16.2   CONTINUED

```
    'Tell MTS we are successful
    objContext.SetComplete

AdjustBalanceExit:
    Exit Function

AdjustBalanceErr:
    AdjustBalance = False

    'Tell MTS we failed
    objContext.SetAbort

    'Log Error
    App.LogEvent "ERROR: " & Err.Number & " " & Err.Description & _
        "; SOURCE: " & Err.Source, vbLogEventTypeError
    Debug.Print "ERROR: " & Err.Number & " " & Err.Description & _
        "; SOURCE: " & Err.Source

    Resume AdjustBalanceExit
```

THE BUSINESS SERVICES LAYER

The Business Services layer consists of a single ActiveX DLL project. This project is the starting point for every transaction performed by the module. Therefore, you will see methods for depositing, withdrawing, and transferring funds. These methods form a single point of contact for the User Services layer.

CREATING THE BUSINESS SERVICES COMPONENT

In the Project Explorer, locate the project named ATM. This project contains a single class named Manager. The Manager class is responsible for initiating and handling all ATM transactions. In this section, you will create the Manager class.

Step 1
In the Project Explorer, select the project named ATM. This project requires you to set several references. Open the references dialog and set a reference to Microsoft Transaction Server Type Library, DataManager, and CommonFeatures.

Step 2
In the ATM project, locate the Manager class. Open the code window for this class module. This class module contains methods designed to initiate transactions for the ATM

module. Most of these methods are already coded for you; however, we will code one method to see how it is done.

In the Manager class, locate the method ExecuteInterBankTransfer. This method initiates and manages transfers between banks. This type of transaction is the most difficult for a system to manage, and if you have a Type D configuration, it will be a true distributed transaction. MTS, however, makes coding these transactions much easier.

In this method, the Manager class enlists the Data Services components in a transaction that adjusts the balances of accounts in different banks. If either the debit or the credit operation fails, the transaction is rolled back. Add the code in Listing 16.3 to the ExecuteInterBankTransfer method to code the operation:

LISTING 16.3 CODE TO ADD TO THE ExecuteInterBankTransfer METHOD IN THE Manager CLASS

```
On Error GoTo ExecInterBankTransferErr

    ExecInterBankTransfer = True

    'Assertions
    Debug.Assert strCreditCustomerID <> ""
    Debug.Assert strDebitCustomerID > ""
    Debug.Assert lngBank = BankEnum.atmFirstFederal _
    Or lngBank = BankEnum.atmFirstNational
    Debug.Assert lngDebitAccountType = AccountTypeEnum.atmChecking _
    Or lngDebitAccountType = AccountTypeEnum.atmSavings
    Debug.Assert lngCreditAccountType = AccountTypeEnum.atmChecking _
    Or lngCreditAccountType = AccountTypeEnum.atmSavings
    Debug.Assert curAmount > 0

    'Variables
    Dim blnResults As Boolean
    Dim strDebitAccountID As String
    Dim strCreditAccountID As String
    Dim intCreditBank As Long
    Dim objTransactor As DataManager.Transactor
    Dim objReader As DataManager.Reader

    'Get Object Context
    Dim objContext As MTxAS.ObjectContext
    Set objContext = GetObjectContext

    'Identify the Credit Bank
    If lngBank = atmFirstFederal Then
        intCreditBank = atmFirstNational
    Else
```

continues

LISTING 16.3   CONTINUED

```
        intCreditBank = atmFirstFederal
    End If

    'Create Objects
    Set objTransactor = _
    objContext.CreateInstance("DataManager.Transactor")
    Set objReader = _
    objContext.CreateInstance("DataManager.Reader")

    'Process Transaction
    strDebitAccountID = objReader.GetAccountID _
    (lngBank, strDebitCustomerID, lngDebitAccountType)
    strCreditAccountID = objReader.GetAccountID _
    (intCreditBank, strCreditCustomerID, lngCreditAccountType)
    blnResults = objTransactor.AdjustBalance _
    (lngBank, strDebitAccountID, -1 * curAmount, "Bank Funds Transfer")
    blnResults = objTransactor.AdjustBalance _
    (intCreditBank, strCreditAccountID, curAmount, "Bank Funds Transfer")

    'TellMTS we are successful
    objContext.SetComplete

ExecInterBankTransferExit:
    Exit Function

ExecInterBankTransferErr:
    'Tell MTS we failed
    #If MTS Then
        objContext.SetAbort
    #End If

    'Log Error
    App.LogEvent "ERROR: " & Err.Number & " " & Err.Description & _
        "; SOURCE: " & Err.Source, vbLogEventTypeError
    Debug.Print "ERROR: " & Err.Number & " " & Err.Description & _
        "; SOURCE: " & Err.Source

    ExecInterBankTransfer = False
    Resume ExecInterBankTransferExit
```

THE USER SERVICES LAYER

The User Services layer consists of an ActiveX DLL project and a Standard EXE project.
The ActiveX DLL project is used as a stateful component to maintain the workflow of
the application. The Standard EXE project is simply a display mechanism for the ATM.

CREATING THE TERMINAL MANAGER

In the Project Explorer, locate the project named `TerminalManager`. This project contains a single class named `Controller`. The `Controller` class is responsible for maintaining the session state and workflow. In this section, you will create the `Controller` class.

Step 1

In the Project Explorer, select the project named `TerminalManager`. This project requires you to set two references. Open the references dialog and set a reference to ATM and `CommonFeatures`.

Step 2

In the `TerminalManager` project, open the code window for the `Controller` class. This class contains many properties that are used to maintain state and handle workflow. The `Controller` maintains a property called `TerminalMode`, which indicates the mode of the ATM screen. These modes may indicate activities such as waiting for a PIN entry or displaying an account balance. In any case, the `TerminalMode` is used to decide what operation to perform next.

Deciding what operation to perform next is done in the `Process` method. The `Process` method examines the `TerminalMode` and sets the next `TerminalMode` in the workflow. Locate the `Process` method in the `Controller` class and add the code in Listing 16.4:

LISTING 16.4 CODE TO ADD TO THE `Process` METHOD IN THE `Controller` CLASS

```
On Error GoTo ProcessErr

    Select Case TerminalMode
        Case atmBankSelect
            TerminalMode = SelectBank
        Case atmFederalLogin
            FederalPIN = TerminalInput
            TerminalMode = LoginFederal
        Case atmNationalLogin
            NationalPIN = TerminalInput
            TerminalMode = LoginNational
        Case atmTransactionRequest
            TerminalMode = RequestTransaction
        Case atmAccountSelect
            TerminalMode = SelectAccount
        Case atmDebitAccountSelect
            TerminalMode = SelectDebitAccount
        Case atmCreditAccountSelect
            TerminalMode = SelectCreditAccount
```

continues

LISTING 16.4   CONTINUED

```
        Case atmAmountRequest
            TerminalMode = RequestAmount
        Case atmTransactionResults
            TerminalMode = atmTransactionComplete
        Case atmTransactionComplete
            TerminalMode = CompleteTransaction
        Case atmTransactionFailed
            TerminalMode = atmBankSelect
    End Select

ProcessExit:
    Exit Sub

ProcessErr:
    Message = Err.Description
    TerminalMode = atmTransactionFailed
    Resume ProcessExit
```

CREATING THE TERMINAL

In the Project Explorer, locate the project named `Terminal`. This project contains a single form named `frmTerminal`. This form simulates the visual interface of an automated teller.

Step 1

In the Project Explorer, select the project named `Terminal`. This project requires you to set two references. Open the references dialog and set a reference to `TerminalManager` and `CommonFeatures`.

Step 2

In the `frmTerminal` form, the information displayed on the ATM screen is determined by the `TerminalMode`. The `TerminalMode` is examined in a procedure named `UpdateDisplay`. Based on the `TerminalMode`, the form reads a set of strings from a resource file named ATM.RES, which you can find in the `Terminal` project. The strings read from the ATM.RES file are used to update the button captions on the form and the message that appears. Open the form in Visual Basic and add the code in Listing 16.5 to the `UpdateDisplay` procedure:

LISTING 16.5   CODE TO ADD TO THE `UpdateDisplay` PROCEDURE

```
On Error GoTo UpdateDisplayErr

    'Get Current Mode
```

```vb
Dim intMode As TerminalModeEnum
intMode = m_Controller.TerminalMode

'Read Strings from Resource File
lblMessage.Caption = _
    Trim$(LoadResString(intMode * 9 + 1))
lblAction(0).Caption = _
    Trim$(LoadResString(intMode * 9 + 2))
lblAction(1).Caption = _
    Trim$(LoadResString(intMode * 9 + 3))
lblAction(2).Caption = _
    Trim$(LoadResString(intMode * 9 + 4))
lblAction(3).Caption = _
    Trim$(LoadResString(intMode * 9 + 5))
lblAction(4).Caption = _
    Trim$(LoadResString(intMode * 9 + 6))
lblAction(5).Caption = _
    Trim$(LoadResString(intMode * 9 + 7))
lblAction(6).Caption = _
    Trim$(LoadResString(intMode * 9 + 8))
lblAction(7).Caption = _
    Trim$(LoadResString(intMode * 9 + 9))


'Show any custom messages
If intMode = atmTransactionResults _
    Or intMode = atmTransactionFailed Then
    lblMessage.Caption = lblMessage.Caption _
        & " " & m_Controller.Message
End If

'Update Input TextBox
txtInput.Text = ""
If intMode = atmFederalLogin _
    Or intMode = atmNationalLogin Then
    txtInput.PasswordChar = "*"
    txtInput.Visible = True
    txtInput.SetFocus
ElseIf intMode = atmAmountRequest Then
    txtInput.PasswordChar = ""
    txtInput.Visible = True
    txtInput.SetFocus
Else
    txtInput.PasswordChar = ""
    txtInput.Visible = False
End If

'Enable/Disable Buttons
Dim i As Integer
For i = 0 To 7
    If lblAction(i).Caption = "*" Then
        cmdAction(i).Enabled = False
```

continues

LISTING 16.5   CONTINUED

```
        Else
            cmdAction(i).Enabled = True
        End If
    Next

UpdateDisplayExit:
    Exit Sub

UpdateDisplayErr:
    MsgBox Err.Description
    Resume UpdateDisplayExit
```

COMPLETING AND RUNNING THE APPLICATION

After you have added all the code to the application, you are ready to finish the project. You must now compile the application and place components in MTS. In this section you will finish the application and get it working.

Step 1

Compile each of the projects in the application in the order shown following. Correct any mistakes as you go. You should also carefully check that the compilation paths are valid for each component. Because this template was originally created on a different machine, some suggested paths may be invalid.

Compilation Order

- CommonFeatures
- DataManager
- ATM
- TerminalManager
- Terminal

Step 2

Start the Microsoft Transaction Server Explorer. Open the tree view until you see the Packages Installed folder. Create a new package for your MTS components and call it ATM. Be sure to set the identity for this package to the new Windows/NT account you created in Chapter 15.

After you create the package, you will need to install components in the package. You should only install the Data Services components and Business Services components in your new package. These are all contained in DataManager and ATM. Figure 16.1 shows the MTS Explorer with the components installed.

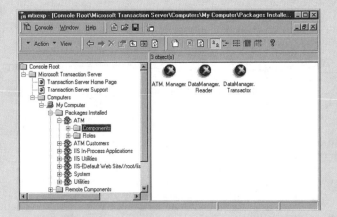

FIGURE 16.1
Add the business and data components to your new package.

Step 3

Now that you have the components installed, run the application by starting the
TERMINAL.EXE application. You should see the ATM terminal described in the functional specification. If you have established an account for yourself using the ATM
Customers module, you should be able to use the terminal. If you have not yet built the
ATM Customers module, you will have to manually place an account in the database
before you can use the terminal.

CREATING A BROWSER FRONT END

To show how a properly designed distributed application ports to the Internet, we will
create a Web front end for this project. The Web front end we create here requires Visual
InterDev. If you have Visual InterDev, you may complete this section.

CREATING THE NEW PROJECT

Before you build the Web front end to the terminal, you must create a new Web project.
This is done through the Web project Wizard in Visual InterDev. In this section, you will
create a new Web project.

Step 1

Start Visual InterDev. When Visual InterDev starts, you should immediately see the New Project dialog. In this dialog, select to start a New Web Project. Name your new project WebATM and click the Open button. Figure 16.2 shows the New Project dialog.

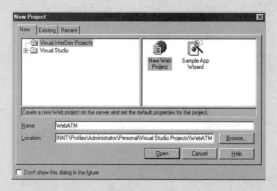

FIGURE 16.2

Use the New Project dialog to start your new Web project.

Step 2

When you start the new project, the Web Project Wizard runs. The first step of the wizard asks you to specify a server where you want to build the new project. Users with a Type A Configuration should simply enter **localhost** in the dialog. Users with a different configuration will need to specify the exact name of the server where IIS is installed. Click Next when you are done. Figure 16.3 shows step 1 of the wizard.

FIGURE 16.3

Specify the server where IIS is running.

Step 3

In the subsequent steps of the wizard, you will be asked to specify a project name, project layout, and theme. If you are an experienced user of Visual InterDev, you may edit these values. However, the default values of the wizard are acceptable for this exercise. When you have finished with the wizard, your new project will be created.

Building the Web Page

Now that the project is built, you can proceed to create a Web page for the terminal. The files that you need were all copied off the CD-ROM earlier and should exist on your hard drive under the \WEB directory.

Step 1

In Visual InterDev, add the required files to your project by selecting **Project, Add Item** from the menu. This will open the Add Item dialog. In this dialog, click the Existing tab. Navigate to the \WEB directory and select to add the files DEFAULT.HTM and RESOURCE.VBS to your project. Figure 16.4 shows the dialog with the required files.

FIGURE 16.4

Add required files to your project.

Step 2

In the Project Explorer, locate the DEFAULT.HTM Web page. Double-click this page to open it in Visual InterDev. In the editor, click the Source tab to view the HTML for this page. Scroll the page to the bottom, and you will see a comment indicating that you should place the Terminal Manager component in the Web page. In the next step, you will insert an instance of the `Controller` object at this location. Figure 16.5 shows the location in the DEFAULT.HTM file.

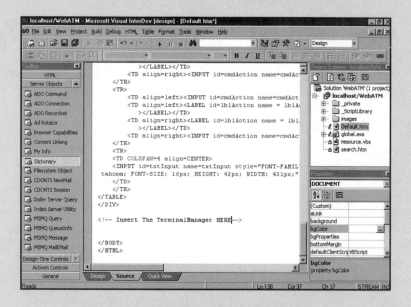

FIGURE 16.5

Here we will insert an instance of the Controller *object for the Web page.*

Step 3

To insert the Controller object in the Web page, you must place the TerminalManager component into the toolbox in Visual InterDev. To place a component in the toolbox, first click the Server Objects bar in the Visual InterDev toolbox.

With the Server Objects bar selected, start the Windows File Explorer and locate the file TERMINALMANAGER.DLL. When you find the file, drag it from the Windows File Explorer into the Server Objects area of the Visual InterDev toolbox. Visual InterDev will respond by listing the Controller object as available in the toolbox. Figure 16.6 shows the Controller object in the toolbox.

Step 4

When the Controller is available in the toolbox, drag it from the toolbox into your Web page below the HTML comment. This will make the Controller available to the Web page, which will allow the Web page to simulate the terminal.

When the object loads, you may get a message that the object has failed to load and will be viewed as text. This is expected and is not a problem. When the object is inserted in the page, you will see an HTML <OBJECT> tag. This tag contains the CLSID and the ID for the object. The ID will be set to Controller1. In order for the Web page to work, you must change the ID to m_Controller.

The User Services Layer Project

CHAPTER 16

469

16

THE USER
SERVICES LAYER
PROJECT

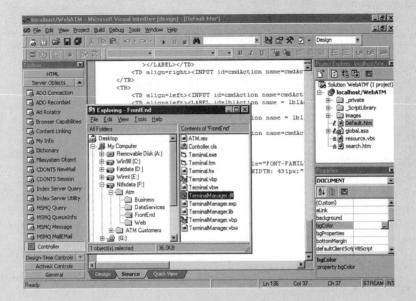

FIGURE 16.6

Drag the `TerminalManager` *component into the toolbox to make the* `Controller` *object available.*

Step 5

The last thing you have to do to get the Web page running is to mark the `Controller` as safe. Marking an ActiveX DLL as safe will allow it to be run in a Web page. Unfortunately, marking components as safe is not simple and requires two registry entries. However, we have prepared a registry macro file that you can edit. This file is called SAFE.REG and is contained in the \WEB directory on your hard drive. Locate the file SAFE.REG and open it in Notepad.

Step 6

In order to use SAFE.REG, you must change the CLSID that is in the file to the one that maps to your `Controller` component. You can find the CLSID for your `Controller` component by copying it directly out of the Web page in the `<OBJECT>` tag you just inserted. Edit SAFE.REG to replace each of the CLSID entries in the file with your CLSID. After you edit the file, run it by double-clicking the file in the Windows File Explorer. The following shows a typical SAFE.REG listing:

```
REGEDIT4
[HKEY_LOCAL_MACHINE\SOFTWARE\Classes\CLSID\
{3F763B60-6950-11D2-B5A7-0060088D02A3}\Implemented Categories]
[HKEY_LOCAL_MACHINE\SOFTWARE\Classes\CLSID\
```

```
{3F763B60-6950-11D2-B5A7-0060088D02A3}\
Implemented Categories\{7DD95801-9882-11CF-9FA9-00AA006C42C4}]

[HKEY_LOCAL_MACHINE\SOFTWARE\Classes\CLSID\
{3F763B60-6950-11D2-B5A7-0060088D02A3}\
Implemented Categories\{7DD95802-9882-11CF-9FA9-00AA006C42C4}]
```

Step 7

When the page is complete, and the `Controller` marked as safe, save your work. Then you can run the page by right-clicking DEFAULT.HTM in the Project Explorer and selecting **View in Browser** from the pop-up menu.

INDEX

Other Related Titles

The Waite Group's
Visual Basic 6
Client/Server How-To
Noel Jerke
1-571-69154-5
$49.99 USA /
$71.95 CAN

The Waite Group's Visual Basic 6 Database How-To
Eric Winemiller
1-571-69152-9
$39.99 USA /
$56.95 CAN

Sams Teach Yourself Database Programming with Visual Basic 6 in 21 Days
Curtis Smith and Michael Amundsen
0-672-31308-1
$45.00 USA /
$64.95 CAN

Roger Jennings' Database Developer's Guide with Visual Basic 6
Roger Jennings
0-672-31063-5
$59.99 USA /
$85.95 CAN

Database Access with Visual Basic
Jeffrey McManus
1-562-76567-1
$39.99 USA /
$56.95 CAN

Building Enterprise Solutions with Visual Studio 6
G.A. Sullivan
0-672-31489-4
$49.99 USA /
$71.95 CAN

Visual Basic 6 Unleashed
Rob Thayer
0-672-31309-X
$39.99 USA / $57.95 CAN

Windows NT Server 4 Unleashed
Jason Garms
0-672-31249-2
$49.99 USA /
$70.95 CAN

Active Server Pages Unleashed
Stephen Walther
0-672-31613-7
$39.99 USA /
$57.95 CAN

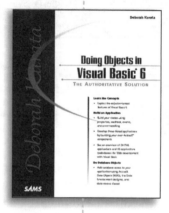

Doing Objects in Visual Basic 6
Deborah Kurata
1-56276-577-9
$49.99 USA /
$71.95 CAN

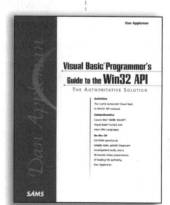

Dan Appleman's Visual Basic Programmer's Guide to the Win32 API
Dan Appleman
0-672-31590-4
$59.99 USA /
$85.95 CAN

SAMS
www.samspublishing.com

All prices are subject to change.

NEW TECHNOLOGY SOLUTIONS INC.

432 Washington Avenue, North Haven CT 06473

`http://www.vb-bootcamp.com`

Focused Training & Tools for the ActiveX Developer

 About New Technology Solutions

A prominent classroom educator of software developers since 1993, New Technology Solutions (`http://www.vb-bootcamp.com`) has trained over 25,000 developers in the art of Visual Basic programming. Headquartered in North Haven, CT with training centers in Waltham, MA, the company is well known nationally for the trademark VB BOOTCAMP ® training program. The company sponsors Microsoft Developer Days in Boston, MA and Hartford, CT. This is a regional Microsoft event especially for hard-core software developers. New Tech also sponsors the New Technology Forum, a free developer community forum dedicated to Microsoft development tools and techniques.

 About the VB BOOTCAMP ® Instructors

The instructors at NewTech have authored five VB-related books and dozens of published articles on software development with Microsoft tools. The company actively engages technical training and consulting throughout New England. The founders of the firm, Dan Mezick and Scot Hillier, are headline speakers at key industry events such as The Visual Basic Insider's Technical Summit (VBITS), COMDEX, Database World, and Internet World. In addition, the company has published over 23 articles on VB development in publications such _INFOWORLD_, _Computerworld_, _VB Programmers Journal_, and _VB Advisor_ magazines. The company's engineers and trainers are widely quoted by the trade press on Visual Basic software development issues and industry trends. New Technology Solutions is actively engaged in Visual Basic training, development, and consulting throughout the USA.

 NewTech Training Services

We have been training developers since 1993 and since that time we have trained over 25,000 in Visual Basic, Visual InterDev, SQL Server and Microsoft Transaction Server. We can get your team up to speed in the absolute minimum time possible with our accelerated, full-immersion training programs such as the VB BOOTCAMP ®.

 NewTech Consulting Services

We engage in consulting in the states of Connecticut, Massachusetts, and the surrounding region of the Eastern USA. Our consultants can help you in all areas of software development. Please call to discuss your systems analysis, design, and development requirements.

 Our Newsletter, the NEW TECHNICIAN

We publish a monthly email newsletter of interest to serious developers on the Microsoft platform. The newsletter is crammed with timely technical content and important company news. If you are a serious reader of this book, you'll want to subscribe immediately. Subscribing is simple and free.

You can subscribe to this newsletter by sending the message 'SUBSCRIBE' to `info@vb-bootcamp.com`. You can unsubscribe by simply sending 'UNSUBSCRIBE' to this same email name.

 Summary

Please call if you have training and/or consulting needs in Visual Basic, COM+, Transaction Server, and enterprise development. Please contact us or visit our web site `http://www.vb-bootcamp.com` for course outlines, schedules, and pricing. You may direct your email inquiries to `info@vb-bootcamp.com`.

New Technology Solutions Inc.
432 Washington Avenue
North Haven, CT 06473
Phone: (203) 239-6874
Fax : (203) 239-7997

What's on the Disc

The companion CD-ROM contains many useful third party software, plus all the source code from the book.

Windows 95/98 Installation Instructions

1. Insert the CD-ROM disc into your CD-ROM drive.
2. From the Windows 95 desktop, double-click the My Computer icon.
3. Double-click the icon representing your CD-ROM drive.
4. Double-click the icon titled START.EXE to run the program.

> **NOTE**
>
> If Windows 95 is installed on your computer, and you have the AutoPlay feature enabled, the START.EXE program starts automatically whenever you insert the disc into your CD-ROM drive.

Windows NT Installation Instructions

1. Insert the CD-ROM disc into your CD-ROM drive.
2. From File Manager or Program Manager, choose Run from the File menu.
3. Type `<drive>\START.EXE` and press Enter, where `<drive>` corresponds to the drive letter of your CD-ROM. For example, if your CD-ROM is drive D:, type `D:\START.EXE` and press Enter.

Read This Before Opening the Software

By opening this package, you are agreeing to be bound by the following agreement:

Some of the software included with this product may be copyrighted, in which case all rights are reserved by the respective copyright holder. You are licensed to use software copyrighted by the publisher and its licensors on a single computer. You may copy and/or modify the software as needed to facilitate your use of it on a single computer. Making copies of the software for any other purpose is a violation of the United States copyright laws.

This software is sold as is without warranty of any kind, either expressed or implied, including but not limited to the implied warranties of merchantability and fitness for a particular purpose. Neither the publisher nor its dealers or distributors assumes any liability for any alleged or actual damages arising from the use of this program. (Some states do not allow for the exclusion of implied warranties, so the exclusion may not apply to you.)